Golden Rule Days

History and Recollections

of 109 Closed Kansas High Schools

James Kenyon

Also by James Kenyon

The Art of Listening to the Heart
Ooly Booly Press, Chicago, IL — April 2017

A Cow for College and Other Stories of 1950s Farm Life
Meadowlark Books, Emporia, KS — October 2017
Winner of the 2018 Martin Kansas History Book Award

Golden Rule Days

History and Recollections

of 109 Closed Kansas High Schools

James Kenyon

A MEADOWLARK BOOK

Meadowlark (an imprint of Chasing Tigers Press)
meadowlark-books.com
PO BOX 333
Emporia, KS 66801

Cover art by Barbara Steward Kenyon

State maps attribution: David Benbennick [Public Domain]

ISBN: 978-1-7322410-4-6

Library of Congress Control Number: 2019902182

For the tens of thousands of teachers, staff, and board members
who dedicated their lives to nurture hundreds of thousands of school children.

For Mr. Ward, history teacher and coach -
You gave me such a love for history and all sports, I still would run into a brick wall for you.

For Mr. Hooper, English and literature teacher and coach -
Every writing project is still needing just a little more 'spit and polish.' You ingrained in me a lifetime
of completing each essay "just a touch better" and an enjoyment of literature and reading.

For Mrs. Fischels, science and math teacher –
You taught me the precision of the theorems, math functions, and congruent triangles,
and an immense passion for the periodic table which still lives with me.

For Mr. Eck, commerce and typing teacher –
I recall your immaculate bow ties and pushing of the drills in typing toward
a perfect paper with accuracy and speed.

For Mr. Kruse, mechanical drawing and drivers ed instructor -
The drawing skills were often used; and driving before
turn signals, seat belts, and texting was quite a sport.

For Mr. Schnautz, principal, band director, and psychology teacher –
You taught the art of being an administrator and leader. The jazz band and playing
three different instruments fostered in me a love of music.

For Mr. Stephen, janitor-custodian -
The fresh paint, intoxicating smell of waxed floors, and the expansion
and contraction noise of the steel radiators in each classroom still resonates.

For Olive Rome and Lorene Darnell, school cooks -
Oh, the aroma of fresh rolls and the wonderful meals,
always served with smiling faces and wit. The meals for 25 cents were awesome.

For Harold Irby, bus driver, elementary custodian, and electrician –
I remember all of those bus trips for athletic events and
your tolerance for rowdy kids with never a cross word.

And for my wife, Cynthia, the big city girl who married the farm boy
and encouraged this book of high schools to commemorate 20th century Kansas history.

School days, school days!
Dear old Golden Rule days!
Reading and 'riting and 'rithmetic
Taught to the tune of the hick'ry stick
You were my queen in calico
I was your bashful, barefoot beau
And you wrote on my slate, "I love you, Joe"
When we were a couple o' kids.

Lyrics by Gustave Edwards (18 August 1878-7 November 1945)
American songwriter and vaudevillian. Published 1907.

Contents

Introduction

When you lose your school, you lose your town!

It was the biggest screw job in the state of Kansas!

Stop the dam foolishness! We gave up our town and everything for a lakeshore of weeds, brush, mudflats, and muddy water too thick to swim in, but too thin to plant.

Haven't been to that town for fifty years, since they forced our school to close!

This collection of stories of the former high schools of Kansas developed as I traveled through western Kansas fifty years after graduating—Class of 1966—with a class of six from Bogue Rural High School, Graham County. I started counting the towns where I played ball as a youth. All but one of the thirty-two had lost their high school in the intervening years. This collection of high school stories was compiled in effort to preserve a small part of these schools for history. The stories are varied. There is no intent to slight any community or former high school that was omitted. By writing about just one high school in each of the 105 Kansas counties, I provide a statewide perspective of Kansas. Four counties were given a second high school story as there were such great resources available I felt they needed to be included.

Living over three-hundred miles from the nearest corner of Kansas, I made twelve trips back to visit every county in the state in fifteen months. I have met so many new friends. These interviews have enhanced this collection of remembrances, filled with joy and sorrow, with a great appreciation for our heritage and the past commitment of those who formed the educational backbone of rural Kansas. An unbelievable number of contacts I spoke to for these stories are now in alumni positions. Libraries and historical societies helped tell these stories. Telephone friendships and smiles exchanged over the digital expanse have led to a phrase most widely used, "When you lose your school, you lose your town!"

Just when were the good old days? A state's history and a century of incredible change in the landscape of the small towns and countryside covers many scenes including immigrants, homesteaders, coal miners, emancipated slaves, oil booms, and wars across the globe. Analysis of the past is complex and more difficult than dreaming of and predicting the future.

Describing the high schools across Kansas in all 105 counties, from east to west, from north to south, is a challenge. These are stories of anthropological and philosophical microcosms of society in the middle of America.

Kansas—its birth and statehood origin—came with the onset of the Civil War. It could be reasoned that conflict had been brewing, or at least kindling, since the Missouri Compromise of 1820. Slavery was the smoldering ember that not only kept people in bondage but decayed and blinded the souls and minds of those who promoted it.

The Kansas-Nebraska Act of 1854 repudiated the Missouri Compromise, which enabled territories or land masses north of 36' 50" to choose if they would be organized as slave or free states. Bleeding Kansas ensued. The Border Ruffians from the slave state of Missouri infiltrated west into Kansas Territory to spread their philosophy. Southern sympathizers were outnumbered by the pioneers and settlers seeking land as they came from the free northern states of Ohio, Illinois, Indiana, Pennsylvania, and Exodusters—emancipated slaves—from Kentucky. Several votes for statehood at the Territorial Capital in Lecompton spurred and complicated this free-state/slave-state option. The weak presidencies of Franklin Pierce and James Buchanan spawned the birth of Republicanism.

Kansas became a state on January 29, 1861, just one month after the succession of South Carolina from the United States. Every school child in Kansas learns their first Latin phrase in the first grade, *Ad Astra per Aspera*, To the Stars Through Difficulty. This motto is imprinted on the state flag. This new land was definitely dissimilar to some of the lands in the northern states. Drought, blizzards, grass hopper infestations, jack rabbit overpopulation, buffalos, Indians, dust storms, the Dirty 30s, and financial difficulties were among the few things that greeted immigrants to Kansas.

Thirty-six counties were settled in eastern Kansas from 1855-1857. Once a plated region reached a population of 2,000 people, it could become a county. As settlements and railroads spread, the counties fanned out from east to west with the last to organize in 1888, bringing the total number of counties to 105. Nearly one-third (33) were named for civil war soldiers. Others were named for Indians (14), senators from other states (8), presidents (5), rivers (3), Indian rivers (3), forts (2), Revolutionary War generals (2), War of 1812 generals (2), women (2), free state heroes (2), state politicians (2), and statesmen (2). The names of the counties corresponded with the times and locations that the counties were settled.

Education was valued in every settlement. The establishment of a school or gathering place was as important as laying the cornerstone of a church.

The need for a meeting place, a teacher, materials, and the organization of a school board or leaders to provide organization was essential to every one-room school. Schools were established nearly every two miles. The large farm families gave rise to these neighborhood one-room schoolhouses. One teacher was employed to teach all eight grades. The county seats were usually the largest towns in the county and the first to offer high school curriculum from the onset. The outlying communities started offering first a ninth grade, and soon many offered a two-year high school opportunity. Those families and children seeking further education often had to send their children away, usually to the county seat towns to board with families where there was an established four-year high school. Eventually, many small towns grew by adding a four-year high school education.

Railroads were built by entrepreneurs and crisscrossed the state like cow paths. Some benefited from generous government gifts of free land on one side or the other side of the track as an incentive to build. In order for these steel horses and parallel rails to survive, they required goods and people. The need for water to fuel the steam engines spurred the establishment of water stations every eight to ten miles. These were the spots where towns, merchants, and communities developed. The railroads sold land to pioneer settlers who farmed these areas. From 1865-1890 this practice brought the greatest expansion and influx of people to Kansas. Schools, churches, merchants, depots, livestock, and grain elevators all grew exponentially. The rural population in Kansas peaked before World War I in 1910.

The revolution from the one horse or mule farm to the "iron horse" in the early teens became a major factor the need for less manpower on the farms. Education, transportation, communication, and enlightenment led to new opportunities for jobs away from the agrarian life. A high school education led to another life. The determination to achieve and learn was the impetus for further challenges and gave way to a ticket to a job in the cities.

High schools taught math, sciences, domestic arts, Latin, band, orchestra, literature, and dramatics. Every pupil experienced this education and participated in these areas. Athletic rivalries between towns flourished.

A diploma was awarded to all who persevered through shaking knees while standing to recite a speech, or queasy stomach after a grueling sweaty race around the dirt oval track. The diploma recalled the formaldehyde smelling frog in biology, and the nurturing coach who inspired all to run into the wall together as a team. The accomplishment rekindles memories of marching in band while holding the cold trombone with the music on a precarious staff, the English teacher who diagramed sentences and conjugated verbs, and theorems and functions in math class. Experiences included sewing a straight line and the free throw that won the game. Graduates remembered laughing with friends, stealing a kiss, or not getting caught after a prank. These times were more than just a time to remember about growing up, it encompassed friendships, developed aspirations for the future, and led to marriages. This building where so much happened is gone forever. Those years which were taken for granted came to a close for a senior in May, and again when the school doors were closed for good.

Alumni reunions for so many closed Kansas high schools will continue until the last remaining person dies. With them will be buried a special century when towns on every corner and in between sprung up along the streams, railroad lines, and wagon trails.

There were five counties in Kansas that never had a high school close: Lane, Wichita, Greeley, Cheyenne, and Stevens. In those counties, I chose to tell the story of the last one-room schoolhouse or a rural grade school. The flood of 1951 destroyed three towns—Quenemo, Neosho Falls, and Florence—leading to their eventual decline and high schools closing. Three more towns—Randolph, Milford, and Webster—were moved because the Corp of Engineers was trying to dam the flooding rivers, and the result ended the town as well as their high schools. Many counties had complete athletic leagues from the high schools within the borders of the county. They have now all closed and/or consolidated to the county seat city. Two county seat towns lost enough population to close their high schools too: Logan and Gove Counties.

The first legislation to make sure that Kansans would take advantage of the opportunity for education was passed in 1874. This was for compulsory school attendance for children ages 8 to 14. By 1885, the state wanted to provide more than an elementary education to a greater percentage of children. County high schools were authorized and supported in the state.

The Barnes Law passed in 1905 to give county officials the authority to levy property taxes to establish rural high schools. (J.S. Barnes was a freshman legislator from Pratt.) The county commissioners were directed to levy a tax each year of not less than one-fourth of a mill nor more than three mills on the dollar of the assessed valuation of taxable property within such counties for the purpose of creating a general high school. Wording from the bill included the following:

At least two courses of instruction shall be provided, each requiring four years work, namely: A college preparatory course, which shall fully prepare those who complete it to enter the freshman class of the college of liberal arts and sciences of the University of Kansas, and a general course, designed for those who do not intend to continue work beyond high school.

It would be ten more years before legislation passed in 1915 titled, "Establishment of rural high schools." This law directed the following:

. . . legal electors in territory containing not less that sixteen square miles and comprising one or more townships or parts thereof have the authority to form a rural high school district and to establish, locate, and maintain therein after provided.

In 1958, Kansas had 2,794 public school districts (including grades school districts). After House Bill 377 enacted the unification law in 1963, that number shrank to 311 by 1969. By the closing of B&B Rural High School in 2004 (Washington County), there were 293 school districts in Kansas.

The goal of this legislation was to produce school districts that had at least 400 students in grades K-12, had at least 200 square miles, and at least $2 million of taxable valuation. A district had to meet a minimum of two of these three requirements. Some of the intent of the legislation in 1963 was the "general improvement of the public schools," equalization of the benefits and burdens of education, and to use state funds more wisely. (Memo from Kansas Legislature Research Department dated November 2, 2009.)

For it isn't by money you measure a school,
Or the miles that its borders extend.
For the best things you gather, whatever the school,
Are contentment, enjoyment and friends.
If you live and you work and develop your school,
In spite of the fact it is small
You may find that your school-your own little school
Is the very best school after all.
                              ~Author Unknown

Looking back on the years, I believe the greatest benefit of my high school and myriad of others like it was that we got to know one another. And, knowing each other enabled us to know others in a wider world we were about to enter.

                    James Kenyon
                    December 2018

Golden Rule Days

History and Recollections

of 109 Closed Kansas High Schools

#1

Lecompton High School

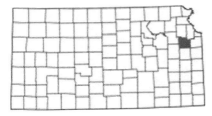

Mascot: Owls

Colors: Gold and Black

Year Closed: 1970

Location: town of Lecompton, northern Douglas County, bank of the Kansas River

Territorial Capital of Kansas — Following the passage of the Kansas Nebraska Act of 1854, Lecompton became the capital of Kansas Territory. The population peaked at 4,000 as officials from President Pierce's and Buchannan's administrations flocked to the area for political and commercial purposes. Many were Southern sympathizers and sided with the pro-slavery position. Border Ruffians flooded across from Missouri and Arkansas to vote for the proposed state to come into the Union as a slave state. The Lecompton Constitution passed and was sent to be ratified in Washington in 1858. It passed in the US Senate by a vote of 20-13 and was then voted down in the House of Representatives by eight votes. Senator Stephen Douglas debated at length on the Senate floor that the invasion of the Border Ruffians should invalidate any vote that had happened in the Territory. This debate of slavery ultimately split the party with Douglas, the northern Democrat; John C. Breckinridge, the southern Democrat; John Bell, the Union Party; and Abraham Lincoln, the Republican, running for President in 1860. Lincoln won the presidency with 39% of the vote.

Statehood — Kansas was admitted to the Union on January 29, 1861, as a free state, and Topeka was selected as the state capital. Lecompton became the site for Lane University following the Civil War in 1865. Senator James Lane promised the Church of the United Brethren the money to establish the university with the naming right. He was a Free State Jayhawker and Civil War General before being elected the Senator from Kansas. He committed suicide before donating the promised money.

Lane University started in the Rowena Hotel and remained there until the former Territorial Capital building, which had been abandoned mid-construction, was purchased from the state of Kansas. The building opened for classes in 1885 after remodeling and the addition of a second floor. That fall on September 23, 1885, David J. Eisenhower and Ida Stover, students at Lane University, were married in the building. They would become the parents of the thirty-fourth President of the United States, Dwight D. Eisenhower.

High School in Lecompton—Some United Brethren officials did not believe Lecompton was large enough or wealthy enough to support a college which was consistently in debt. The enrollment by 1900 was 175 students. An offer of $100,000 from the town of Holton, only forty miles to the northwest, lured the university to relocate in 1902.

Lane offered a preparatory course which included all the subjects a student needed to enter any Kansas college without having to take lengthy examinations. This preparatory course, which was also taught at the college site, served the students at a high school level. When the university relocated, Lecompton students were left with no organized high school, and therefore no way to meet the requirements to enroll in college.

In June 1903, a school meeting was held to discuss the possibility of organizing a local high school. The Kansas Legislature passed a special law allowing the district to increase the tax levy to an amount sufficient to cover the cost of a high school as well as a grade school. At this meeting the group almost unanimously decided to make the new high school a permanent part of the then-present school system. For students living within District 36, there was no tuition; for those outside of the district, a fee of $6.00 a year was charged.

The next obstacle was classroom location. The Lecompton grade school was located just south across the street from the Lane University. It was decided to use a room in the second story of the present grade school as the high school and to lease rooms from Lane University Church which was the sole occupant of the Lane building. The students could go from one building to the other as they were just across the street from each other.

When the trustees moved Lane University from Lecompton, they gave the local school district a large library, a piano, various musical instruments, a $700 telescope, two large professional microscopes, electrical apparatus, chemicals, a skeleton with chart manikins, maps, and globes. They also gave the high school a large cabinet of geographical, astrological, and mineral specimens. No high school program in the state had resources that surpassed Lecompton's.

Education through the ninth-grade education was offered the first year. In 1905 there were five graduates from the high school.

On October 23, 1919, a fire destroyed the grade school and homeroom used as part of the high school. The smoke was so thick and the fire moved so fast that the only things saved from the building were the Victrola, six boxes of chalk, and a few attendance records. The building was in use from 1899 to fall of 1919. The loss was estimated at $15,000 with only $4,500 insurance coverage. The next Monday, the Lane United Brethren church agreed to rent the school four more rooms for the rest of the school year for $160. The board went to Topeka and bought equipment: stoves, books, maps, globes, and desks. They also rented rooms in Constitution Hall, Hotel Windsor, the stone warehouse, and the former Presbyterian Church.

After Christmas vacation the students came back to find electric lights in the study hall and light switches in each room. Since as many as ten to twelve students were driving or riding horses to school, a shed was located near the well so the horses could be easily watered.

A bond election was held July 1, 1920, to vote $12,000 in bonds to build a school house to replace the one that had burned. This was a grade school project for

District 36. It carried 62-1. Work on the building started immediately and it was dedicated on February 25, 1921. It was remarkable because it had four classrooms, an office, electric lights, a large meeting room, running water, two bathrooms, and a furnace.

A Replacement High School

On August 4, 1927, work on a new high school building began. Once the plan was approved, a contract for the chosen blueprint was let for $30,000. Heating, plumbing, and wiring were on separate contracts for just over $6,000. The school, which stood south of the old rock church, was built of brick with a tile roof. It was two stories high, had a basement, and was fireproof. The auditorium seated 320 people.

At the dedication on February 3, 1928, the auditorium was filled with people standing in the aisles, in the halls, and in the yard. The halls and stairs were lovely terrazzo. There were seven well-lighted classrooms, a large study hall, an office, library, a splendid gymnasium, two dressing rooms, two bathrooms, a fine heating system, and plumbing. It was so impressive that it was referred to as "Lecompton's Pride" and remained so until it was no longer used.

Athletics

The high school enrollment by 1922 was forty-seven students. Nineteen were not residents. The football team was very active. A girls basketball team was organized. They played Berryton and won 34-7. The boys played the same evening and won 64-10. The school organized a baseball team for the spring term. The school also started other extracurricular activities with boys and girls glee clubs.

In 1955 the gymnasium did not meet specifications for basketball games, so a large addition was made on the north side of the building.

Boys and girls athletic teams were successful. One game played for fun was basketball, the girls team against the boys team. The boys wore rubber boots, sunbonnets, and dresses. The large crowd enjoyed the game immensely, and the spirit of levity animated both players and referees.

Chet Gibbens ('35) became a college player who drop kicked the winning field goal for the University of Kansas in a win over the Texas Longhorns. His brother Denzel Gibbens ('38) got the game ball.

The 1944 football team played eleven-man football in the East Central League. The biggest rivals were Dover and Perry. They played Washburn Rural that year. Bill Leslie ('44) said, "We played The Olathe Deaf and Dumb School and we got thumped."

Memories from Students

There was only a one-lane bridge across the Kansas River to reach the town of Perry on the north side. The bridge sloped to the north, and halfway across, one had to get out of the car to make sure there was no one coming. If two cars met on the bridge, one had to back up.

Elsie Bahnmaier ('56) remembered, "The driver's education teacher would take us down to the bridge, have us drive half way across, and have us practice backing up."

Football and basketball were part of the school day as the country kids had to ride the bus home. As late as the early 1940s, Bill Leslie ('44), Betty Webber ('44), and Opal Lasswell ('41) reported that students still rode horses to school. They also had to bring feed and would take a break to feed their rides during the day. Busing started in 1945.

Miss Daisy Bair came to Lecompton as an English and music teacher in the late 1930s. The boys were hard on her and would even make her cry. She eventually married and became Mrs. Wingfield. She was the class sponsor for the class of 1941. They took their senior trip to Branson. She took the opportunity to make the whole class return early as she caught the boys drinking beer.

Parties seemed to gravitate to the Kansas River. One night some boys turned the light on the railroad signal from green to red. The oncoming train burned and melted the rail trying to stop. Big trouble resulted for the mischievous teens.

There was a marching band. The boys had to march and play at football game halftimes in their football uniforms. "I played the trombone and didn't like having to play in my uniform, but I never complained," said Bill Leslie ('44).

Perry was located just two miles north across the Kansas River. Bill Leslie recalled, "Their gymnasium had a very low ceiling. One night, Bob Fleming ('42) made a basket at the wrong end and the crowd came unglued."

There were several other notable graduates. David Clark ('67) was the janitor's son; he became a professor at Yale University. Claire Coleman ('40) received several patents and became very successful. Charles Plumb spent five years in the Hanoi Hilton. He was a dynamic speaker and wrote the book, *I'm No Hero*, about his time as a prisoner of war. Though he only went his first eight years to Lecompton, he was known and loved by all the town.

Mr. H.L. Pasley was a renowned principal, a student favorite, and he taught algebra. One thing he said that was remembered by his students was, "Are you working here, or are you riding a bicycle?" The students were not allowed to dance while he was the principal.

An outstanding coach was Bill Nelson. He also taught history and was the driver's education instructor. He al-ways seemed to go the extra mile for his students in the classroom and in extracurricular activities such as sports, plays, and "sneak trips."

Final Year — The 1969-70 school year was the last year for Lecompton High School. The football team that year played Mayetta, Dover, Meriden, Paxico, Linwood, Harveyville, Quenemo, and Greeley, winning all games with a combined score of 483-72. The team went to the playoffs at Russell but lost to Lucas due to the "penetration rule" (a short-lived method of playing off tied games where each team would be given the ball to see how far they could penetrate into the opposition's defense). One of the stars on the team was Marvin "Buddy" Kellum ('70) who went on to play at Wichita State University and won two Super Bowl rings with the Pittsburg Steelers in 1976 and 1977.

In 1964 the State Department of Education notified the school district that they had to meet two of three qualifications to remain a high school: 400 students enrolled in K-12, a $2 million valuation, or 200 square miles of land. The valuation was not a problem, but the enrollment was too small, and the physical size of the district was not enough. Attempts to include Kansas Power and Light for valuation were unsuccessful. Several people on one side of the district then withdrew their land. In the fall of 1969, Lecompton chose to unite with Perry, their long rival across the Kansas River.

The first graduation from the second high school building at Lecompton occurred on May 19, 1928, with thirteen graduates. Noted Kansas author, Margaret Hill McCarter, delivered the address.

Lecompton High School was closed following graduation in May 1970 with twenty-one graduates in the final class. After sixty-six years, 1905 through 1970, 794 individuals had graduated from LHS. The last graduate (alphabetically) was Joe Yost.

The highest numbers of graduates by surname were Smith-18, Glenn-14, Norwood-13, Stanford-11, Hildenbrand-10, Bahnmaier-8, Dark-8, McClanahan-8, Gibbens-7, McCall-7, Anderson-6, and Leslie-6.

#2
Weir High School

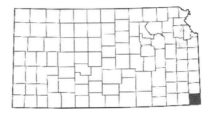

Mascot: Willie Wildcat

Colors: Blue and Gold

Year Closed: 1961

Location: town of Weir, north-central Cherokee County, near the Missouri and Oklahoma state borders

Kansas Coal Community — This southeast corner county of the state was the coal and mining region of Kansas, at its height in coal production from the 1880s until the 1930s. The Weir community was settled in 1875 by Irish, Welsh, Italians, Germans, Balkans, and Scandinavians who came to the area to work in the mines.

The first grade school in Weir was a three-room frame structure built where the present baseball park is located, called Central. It was the only school until the East School was organized and built for all grades, including the first Weir High School, in 1890. It was a three-year high school over which Mr. George B. Deem was the superintendent and only teacher. The West building was erected in 1895, and the high school was transferred into it. Central School later became the school for colored children until it closed at the end of the 1943-44 school year. The first graduating class of Weir was 1893 with six graduates. Each graduate was required to make a speech on the topic of their choice. The class motto was *Festina Lente* (make haste slowly) and Anna Veach was the valedictorian.

Anna Anderson taught in the grade school in 1893 with over ninety students, and she received a monthly salary of $25. There were 618 students in the school system. The first school was a multi-storied building which housed the high school on the upper levels and the grade school on the lower levels.

Student Stories — On November 15, 1915, this school burned to the ground. Ralph O'Malley was a fourth grader and a son of an Irish farmer. He shared his memories with his daughter, Lois O'Malley Carlson ('60). "He remembered seeing the flames in the heating vents and was upset because the teacher wouldn't let him go back to get his books. He then had to attend the Coal Valley School where he graduated from the eighth grade before returning to Weir to attend high school. Upon graduating from Coal Valley, he was awarded a $100 scholarship from Pittsburg Business College to be used then or upon completion of high school. He graduated from Weir High School and then attended Business College where he was an honor student. He would take the street car to and from Pittsburg." Lois recalled.

Lois beamed as she recalled her father and his achievements. The scholarship was a significant dollar amount in 1919 when he initially received it. She saw it as a testament of the commitment to young people and education.

Kansas School of Mines — The (Kansas) School of Mines consisted of eight rooms and occupied the basement and the fourth floor of the building. The fire hit the School of Mines hard as they lost all of their new equipment which was valued at around $18,000. There were sixteen rooms in the building. The city schools occupied the first and second stories. The space occupied by the School of Mines was "loaned" to the state by the city. The school's stock of platinum ware and chemical balances were carried out, but that was all that was saved. D.D. Wolfe, president of the School of Mines said, "The State's loss will reach $20,000. This consists of supplies for the chemicals and physics laboratories, the surveying instruments, office fixtures and supplies and desks."

President Wolfe lost his library which was valued at $400. Work of saving the supplies of the state was hampered considerably because of the gasoline and other explosives which were on hand. There were a number of explosions.

Plans for a new School of Mines never materialized though land had been donated east of town. Kansas University (as it was known at the time, now named University of Kansas or KU) extended their regrets and offered help and assistance to President Wolfe. A telegram from the engineering department and from Kansas University President Strong expressed their concern. The school never reopened, and the engineering classes for mining were then taught at Kansas University.

School opened on the Monday after the fire with the following arrangement of the grades, which seemed to be the best that could be made under the existing circumstances. Beginners, first and second grades went to the Latter-day Saints Church. The eighth grade and high school went to the Calvary Baptist Church, and all other grades went to the McKinley building.

West Weir City School — Construction for the new West Weir City School was started in 1916. The cornerstone was laid by the masons of Black Diamond Lodge in Weir. The school opened in 1917, nearly a year and a half after the tragic fire. With a great foundation and careful maintenance throughout the years, this three-story school still is used today (2018) as part of the grade school. A new grade school was built and attached to the high school building. Following the closing of the high school in 1961, the upper grade school classrooms were moved into the space vacated by the high school students. Laughter, children's voices, and the buzz of learning still fill the halls of this proud structure.

A Tragedy — Not that tragedy has to be recorded, but an event at the high school in 1934 had an impact on everyone in the school and town. Mary Mae Cowans stepped out of her classroom at the top of the deep stair well, backed up, and fell over the low banister to her death. Her mother was a teacher in the school. This loss is remembered in Weir to this day (2018).

School Trivia — The first yearbook was in 1935, called *Weirsana*. It was dedicated to Superintendent and Professor George Deem from 1890-1904:

His sterling qualities and excellent methods will always be remembered by those who had the privilege of knowing him. He was a real pioneer.

With the depth of the depression looming, a new auditorium and gymnasium were built in 1936 to the north of the high school. The financing was part of the Federal Emergency Administration of Public Works and built by the WPA.

Student Demographics at Weir — The pictures in the yearbook show twenty-three black students at the Central Negro School with Miss Helen Fleming their teacher. There were eight black students in the high school at this time. One senior was Lillian Anna Mae Jackson. Under her picture is her name and nickname, "Stonewall," with the words, "Booker T. Washington is my hero. I think he is adorable."

African-Americans came to the area in 1895 from Alabama to help break a mining strike. A stockade and barrier had to be built to protect them from the striking miners. Central School (in the center of town) was established for the colored children and closed at the end of the school year in May 1944 when the students were integrated into the Weir school on the west edge of town. There were several years when black children were not allowed to attend high school in Weir. They attended high school in Columbus and Cherokee. This policy changed when the black families filed a lawsuit against the school board in the early 1900s and won. The school was integrated long before the famous Kansas Brown vs. the Board of Education case in 1954.

During World War II, the class of 1943, the black students were to walk behind the white students at graduation because of the very biased fill-in superintendent. The black students, supported by their parents, refused to do so and boycotted the Baccalaureate and graduation. They did receive their diplomas later. One member of the class, Clarence Tice, went to Kansas State Teachers College in Pittsburg and was the first person of color admitted to the college marching band.

Birth Place of the Fly Swatter — Weir City claims to be the birth place of the fly swatter. In 1911, the Boy Scouts were looking for a public service project. Their leader, Mr. Frank Rose, who was also a school teacher, wrote to Dr. Samuel J. Crumbine, the director of the Kansas State Board of Health for assistance. He suggested that the Scouts could clean up the town by collecting garbage. The Scouts appeared before the city council to ask for an anti-fly ordinance and that the city haul away any garbage they collected. The whole town got involved in what the Scouts were doing, and many major newspapers picked up the story. Mr. Rose picked up some rulers for handles at the WJ Allen Drug Store. The boys fastened squares of screen wire to them, thus creating the first fly swatters. The Scouts distributed two to each household in the city. These facts were documented in Dr. Crumbine's autobiography, *Frontier Doctor*.

Lunches Served — In 1939, a group of parents approached the school board expressing a desire to give all students a hot lunch. The board agreed but needed a cook. Beulah Stark became the first cook, and the lunchroom remains today with the long tables and the scene of the cooks and noisy chattering children still echoing in the hallways. School lunches in 1939 were three cents a day and fifteen cents a week.

Henry Strickland ('58) remembered, "The aroma from the fresh baked rolls and yeast bread would permeate the three-story high school each morning, welcoming us."

Superintendent Herring — The following year, Mary E. O'Malley ('41) approached Mr. John Herring, the superintendent, and suggested a change in policy for the formal dress for the Junior-Senior Banquet and Prom. She recommended church attire because many of the students, especially from the Coal Valley area, could not afford a fancy dress. The dress policy was changed in accordance with this request and reasoning.

Mr. Herring was the superintendent at the outbreak of World War II. He went into the service immediately and after the war came back and taught algebra, geometry, and music until 1953. Nancy Carr Forbes remembered, "He was an extremely caring and dedicated teacher. Every day in music, we sang the 'Bells of St. Mary's.' because he said we were such poor singers. I knew that song by heart."

The school purchased its first bus in 1942. For one school year , 1948-49, Emma Herring, mother of then superintendent John Herring, picked up students in the southwest part of the district in her personal car to avoid the long bus ride.

When Coal Valley School closed about 1954, there had to be two bus routes with one bus. In the morning they would run the south route first because it was so long. In the afternoon they would run the Coal Valley route while those on the south route waited at school, about 45 minutes.

Stories from Students — Helen Fleming ('59) came down with polio in grade school in the early 1950s. The entire school had to line up in the office to get their vaccinations. Sandra Shaw Strickland's big brother, John Shaw, seemed concerned about his little sister having to get her shot before his. He asked her several times if she was going to be alright and hoped that she would not be afraid. Then he and the high school students were next in line for their shots, and John is said to have passed out when he received his shot.

One student recalled the 1960 senior class putting on a Minstrel show as the class play due to many males and few females in the class. All of the students had their faces and exposed skin darkened. The colored student also wore the makeup so that everyone was the same. Lois O'Malley Carlson ('60) remembered, "This was the most fun musical and play we ever did in my high school years." The entire class was included.

High School Band — The band was a large contingent of the student body. Complete with majorettes and twirlers, it marched at nearly every town parade for miles around. It played at the Baxter Springs Christmas festivities. While marching in a Joplin, Missouri, parade, the players nearly froze in their wool band uniforms. The bass drum split from the cold. Bob Schenherr was the very demanding band director. His pursuit of perfection inspired all the young musicians to strive to perform their best.

Sandra Shaw Strickland ('59) said, "I played the clarinet until my senior year when I was the majorette. My now husband, Henry Strickland ('58), played the tenor sax. Mr. Schenherr also had a Glenn Miller type dance band, and we all swung to that type of music, too. We played a lot of swing music. Oh, he had a temper and we thought he hollered more than some teachers. His wife was the school secretary, and she would bring water out onto the streets for us as we practiced. We could do the 'spoke wheel' at the corners as we turned better that any band we ever competed against. Talk about precision, we had it. I am so proud and appreciative for that exceptional learning experience."

Traditions — The 1952 senior trip was to a swimming hole east of Baxter Springs called Five Mile. The 1956 senior trip was to Claremore, Oklahoma. It is remembered most for the car load of sophomore boys who decided to follow the bus to Oklahoma. With Hank Strickland ('56) at the wheel, they pulled into town and one of his compatriots in the back seat just happened to use his "naughty finger" to salute a traffic cop. They were all hauled into the sheriff's office and had to be rescued by the sponsor from the senior trip. Senior trips in 1957-60 were all taken to Rockaway Beach at the Lake of the Ozarks.

Notable Graduates — A basketball star, Bob Hodgson ('52), went on to play at Wichita University (later Wichita State) and was inducted into their Basketball Hall of Fame. In the spring of 1952, with a chance to go the state tournament, Frontenac brought that dream to a halt by edging out Weir in the Regional Finals They intentionally fouled Hodgson to keep him from scoring from the field.

Ed McTavish graduated from Weir High School and took a train to California. He had no job when he arrived, but eventually worked at McDonnel Douglas in the aerospace industry. In 1969, he was one of the nine individuals in the command center to put the first man on the moon.

The six Simone brothers made up a school and town basketball team from 1924-27. They were pictured in their jerseys with Simone on the front. Their father ran Simone's Grocery store for many years. The closed store still stands on Main Street with the big lettering above— Simone's IGA. One of the brothers was not on the team as he had been gassed in World War I. The 1957 yearbook shows a very handsome Jack Simone ('57) (one of the Simone brothers' sons) as the yearbook king. Sandra Shaw Strickland was the yearbook queen that same year.

The End of Weir High School — The sports league was the Mineral Belt League which included Colgan, West Mineral, Chicopee, Cherokee, Mulberry, St. Paul, St. Mary's, and Weir. The Weir High School closed after graduation in May 1961. One record will stand forever. For its last seven years, the football team had an unblemished record. They lost fifty-six straight games.

In the fall of 1961, Weir unified with Cherokee and West Mineral to form Southeast High School, which is located about seven miles west and just outside the city limits of Cherokee.

Weir High School
Cherokee County, KS

#3
Manter Rural High School

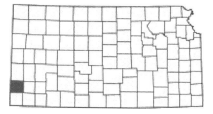

Mascot: Wildcats

Colors: Blue and White

Year Closed: 1966

Location: town of Manter, Stanton County, ten miles from Colorado border

Education in Manter — District 27 was created in 1922. Two frame buildings were built to house the grade school, and one remains to this day (2018). The first high school classes were held in the old bank building. The first high school teachers were Miss Ferguson and Professor Hume. Four students attended that first year with one senior graduating in 1922.

A brick building was built in 1924 with the high school on the upper floor and the grade school on the lower. The State Board of Education accredited the school in 1924. Eleven students were enrolled that year and thirty-three students the next year.

In 1935, a new brick building named Manter Rural High School was erected under the direction of the Federal Emergency Administration of Public Works, or the Works Project Administration (WPA). The labor was funded by the WPA, and the school district paid for the materials. It housed the high school and an auditorium for the community. The board of education members were Lester Stanton, director; J.E. Collins, clerk; and E.L. Delany, treasurer. These three gentlemen carried the big burden of supervising the building program. Glen Thomas, architect, performed all of the blueprint work. Joe Paul, builder, took the blueprint specifications and constructed what is now the beautiful high school building. The cost of the building was a little over $71,000. The Peabody Furniture Co. of Topeka supplied most of the furniture specifications for the building. D.G. Zimmerman and son from Hays, Kansas, furnished and completed the plumbing and heating. Mr. A.R. Lentfer was the principal of the high school during the time the building was being constructed. He continued tenure of service for a period of eleven years after the building was completed.

Athletics – The principal, Mr. Andy Galloway from 1950-1962, did not believe in booing. The basketball team of 1957 had the school's all-time best record by going sixteen wins with only four losses. In 1952, the basketball team played the large county seat town of Johnson and beat them. It is said that Johnson would never play them again because of that. The boys played baseball in both the spring and fall. There was no football team. County wide track meets were another springtime event.

Traditions – The music teacher, Mrs. Jefferies, was a notable teacher. She had great participation in mixed choir and took seventeen girls in glee club to Dodge City for a music contest.

Danny Jones ('58) recalled with a twinkle in his eye, "I had a permanent chair in the principal's office with my name on it, though I am sure I never did anything wrong."

The school had many teachers from Northwestern College in Alva, Oklahoma, because at the time, Kansas schools paid more.

The "senior sneak" of 1962 was a notable event. They all went to the World's Fair in Seattle. Mr. Fields, who was the shop and math teacher, organized the trip and was the class sponsor. With only three graduates in the class, it made for a great and memorable time as they trekked across the mountains to the Pacific Northwest.

Closing the School – In 1966, school consolidation forced the closing of Manter High School, and the students moved to the county's remaining high school in Johnson City, seven miles to the east. The photos of Manter High School graduates were moved to the Stanton County Historical Society. The town retained a grade school with grades K through 8 moving into the vacated high school. The empty Manter grade school burned down in 1974. Bricks from the school were scattered throughout the county and a garden area at the Stanton County Museum has some of these bricks.

The biggest class was 1957 with fifteen graduates. There were only three graduates in 1962 and 1966.

The high school was sold at auction to Robert Figgins for $10,000, and a popped wheat business occupied the building for several years.

Manter Rural High School
Stanton County, KS

#4

Jennings Rural High School

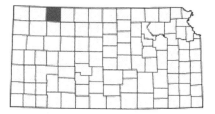

Mascot: Coyotes

Colors: Black and Gold

Year Closed: 2006

Location: town of Jennings, southeast Decatur County

Early Town History — Jennings was one of seven towns that were established along the railroad that ran diagonally southwest from Norton to Colby. This railroad was adjacent to Prairie Dog Creek.

The first school district was formed on the north side of Prairie Dog Creek. When the railroad laid its bed on the south side, the school was moved and renamed Jennings after a first settler in the area, Warren Jennings.

The terrain of this valley is quite different than the rolling prairie land beyond. When the first sod school building burned down in Slab City, the next school was built on a hill on the east side of Jennings. It was later moved closer to the main buildings of town and enlarged to include grades 1-10. The whole school had an enrollment of 100 students in 1910. Two-year high school began about that same time. High school students would have to go to the county four-year high school in Oberlin, twenty-five miles to the northwest, to complete their high school education.

In 1922, construction of a brick school building began. The two-story building was located along the west street in Jennings. Construction cost was $75,000. It was finished in 1924. The four-year high school was first accredited by the state during the term of 1923-24, with sixty-five high school students and 117 in the grade school. It operated as Jennings Grade School District No. 18.

Modern High School & Unification — In September of 1951, a new rural high school district was formed, Jennings Rural High School Dist. No. 7. A new addition was approved by the voters that would house the gymnasium, music department, and vocational agriculture department. The gym playing court was forty-eight feet by eighty-four feet and seated 1,200 persons. The high school bond issue was for $200,000 and the grade school district bond issue was for $80,000 for remodeling.

School unification plans created Jennings-Clayton USD 295 in 1964. Dresden also came into the district at this time. Allison had joined the district earlier. The unified district began operating in 1966 as Prairie Heights School. Throughout the years from 1878 to 1963, the school districts in Decatur County were repeatedly reor-

ganized and consolidated. By June 1964 only two of the original 110 school districts remained.

Enrollment in the district for the 1973-74 term was 198 for the high school and grade school. Eighteen full or part-time teachers were employed by the district, and the high school offered classes in math, social studies, language arts, business education, home economics, vocational agriculture, music, and sciences (biology, physics, chemistry, and general science).

Athletics — Published in the *State Journal* paper in 1924:

Claiming of high school football championships is a dangerous business, it seems. A short time ago the State Journal used a photo of the Goodland team explaining that that team and the Smith Center team had played for the sectional championship of the northern and western half of Kansas.

The ink had hardly become cold on the forms until along came a letter from Jennings Consolidated high school claiming just as good or a better right to the northwest Kansas title as Goodland. Goodland and Smith Center tied for the sectional title so called.

This story is about Jennings. The Jennings team claims that Goodland refused to play them. And furthermore the Jennings team claims the better record. With 171 points scored as opposed to 6 by the opponents, the Jennings team claims a better record than Goodland, which scored 173 points, but the opponents scored 22. Colby scored on Goodland and did not on Jennings, which caused the citizens of Jennings to rise up and claim more distinction than Goodland. At least Jennings thinks its team is entitled to just as much consideration as Goodland, if not more. To make this more forceful the Jennings authorities offer to put their team against any in that section of the country.

The Jennings letter states that the Kansas State High School Athletic Association does not award championships, and since it does not and since the Jennings team has made just as good a record, and in some instances better than Goodland, the school authorities and the townspeople of that western Kansas hamlet are laying in such claim to the northwest Kansas title as any other.

Only one touchdown was scored against the Jennings team during the season. Earl Reed, protégé of Hays Teachers College and an athlete of prominence himself, has trained his high school boys in the way of football and feels that his eleven could trim some of the teams now laying claims the championship.

Jennings is not a large place, but it seems that good football teams are just as likely to come from the small towns as from the large ones out in the wide open spaces. Jennings is situated between the two towns and is one of the most loyal towns in the state when the honor of its football team is at stake.

So the gate is open now, for a free-for-all claim to the championship honors, which may never be decided for post season games are rare. But it is interesting to note how well the towns in that section of Kansas rally to support of their teams. It makes the boys feel that the towns are behind them whatever happens. Some of the eastern towns in Kansas could take a lesson from this little hamlet out in western Kansas.

In the 1940s, Oberlin's football team came to Jennings to play the team as a "scrub team" for practice purposes. Jennings beat Oberlin 6-0 and the two never played each other again. "They couldn't stand being embarrassed twice," Neoma Tacha said. All the football games were played in the afternoon because there were no lights.

By the 1970s, athletics included boys basketball, football, baseball and track, and girls basketball and volleyball. Jennings was always a very musical community with as many as forty students in the band. Jennings rated very high at district festivals and contests.

School rivals were Leoville, Rexford, Selden, Long Island, Almena, Lenora, and Norcatur.

Traditions — The school song was written by Juanita Barkharst in 1924.

We firmly stand for you Jennings High School
Our hearts and hands for you Jennings High School
We do not raise a sigh for our dear Jennings High School
Cause you stand for the best that's in the land
We sing our praise to you we love the best,
Cause you're the best high school in the West:
And our hearts will all be true
When we wave farewell to you
For we'll always cheer you, JHS!

Lila Harris Jennings ('50) was in school when there were no athletics for girls. Jennings laughed at the reason given for eliminating female sports was because "it was too hard on those weak little girls." She found it humorous that it was considered embarrassing for a woman's trousers to be visible, even on a hanger hook. Like other girls, Jennings wore pants under her dress during the winter to keep her legs warm. However, they had to be removed and hidden as soon as the girls got to school. "We'd get to school, the first thing we'd do was go to the bathroom and take those slacks off . . . along the hall, they had pegs to hang the coats. The girls had to hang their slacks under those coats, not on top. Oh, it would be embarrassing to show our trousers in the hall."

The boys in school faced bigger problems than visible trousers. Larry Mizer ('45) said World War II began to take its toll on the school, and many of his classmates left school to enlist rather than be drafted before graduation. "I barely got through," he said. "I graduated on the 18th, and on the 25th I was inducted."

Lila Harris Jennings ('50) still recalls that during the graduation ceremony that year there were empty chairs with American flags on them where the war-bound seniors were supposed to be sitting.

Jennings Teachers — Neoma Tacha ('43) still remembers when she attempted to enroll in high school for the first time in 1939. She was scared off by Latin and English teacher, Alma Carlton, with her "foofed hair" and glasses worn down on her nose. "She scared me to death, I did not enroll that day," Tacha said. "But she was the best teacher I ever had." Six days later she did enroll.

Larry Mizer ('45) remembered that the students were clever enough to know that all anyone had to do was mention Carlton's trip to France and she would forget about the lesson . . . Despite their apparent ornery behavior, the Jennings kids excelled in academics. Tacha attributed that to having what she called top-notch teachers every year.

The seniors in 1950 ventured west to southern Colorado. Lila Harris Jennings ('50) shared her memories of the senior trip and Jennings High School:

> We headed out in cars with our sponsors for a trip of our young lifetime. It was off to Colorado Springs and the Garden of the Gods, Seven Falls, and Royal Gorge before heading out over the mountains to Du-

rango and the four corners of Colorado, N. Mexico, Arizona, and Utah. As we were well over 750 miles from home, we trekked back through Denver and finally home to good old Jennings. It was a thrill of our young lives and what an experience. I started teaching that fall at the age of eighteen. My first three years were in Jennings, then to Colorado and Montana. I returned to Jennings to teach thirteen more years before retiring after forty-five years of teaching. I substituted and served on the school board for five years and was on the board when we had to close the school in 2006. We had just run out of students. Very sad as the district was divided into the students going to Hoxie, Selden-Rexford, Oberlin, and Norton depending where they lived. Oh, we had wonderful students and our education was exceptional with so many opportunities for leadership and development for everyone. Our school had all classes and special education. Less than .05% dropouts and only two went to jail in the last fifty years.

School Closing — The *Hays Daily News* reported on May 21, 2006, about the closing of the Jennings Rural High School:

> From sliding down bannisters to flipping school bells over, former Jennings school students still remember the antics they pulled during their time in school. They remember teachers' names, class outings and football scores, but no more memories will be created at Jennings USD 295 schools. Because of declining enrollment the district will dissolve July 20 after 126 years of educating local youth.

There were 1,180 graduates from Jennings Rural High School in the eighty-three years from 1924-2006. The largest graduating class was twenty-seven in 1971. The last graduate was Elsie Kinzer (alphabetically) in 2006 from a class of three.

The most common surnames of all of the graduates were Wahlmeier-37, Tacha-29, Hickert-20, Petracek-17, Carter-16, Ritter-16, Vacura-16, Stephens-13, Votapaka-11, Krizek-10, Smith-10, and Spressor-8

Jennings High School
Decatur County, KS

#5

White Cloud High School

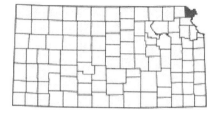

Mascot: Indians

Colors: Red and White

Year Closed: 1958

Location: town of White Cloud, Doniphan County

White Cloud Origins — Located on the banks of the Missouri River and just two miles south of the Nebraska state line, White Cloud began two years after the Kansas-Nebraska Act of 1854. Doniphan County was established by the Territorial government in Lecompton.

The town was named after Chief White Cloud of the Ioway Indians who was killed in a battle on the Nemaha River. The chief was married to Mary Many Days, the daughter of Joseph Robidoux, the French founder of St. Joseph, Missouri, which is twenty-five miles downstream to the south. The Indian reservation is just northwest of the town and was the home of White Cloud's son, Chief James White Cloud. Chief James lived to be 100 years old and made two trips to Washington DC. The last visit was with President Franklin Roosevelt. James had been a scout for the 14th Kansas cavalry and helped chase Quantrill out of Lawrence in 1862.

White Cloud once claimed it was "the Queen of Kansas river towns." When the railroad was built and crossed the Missouri River south about thirty miles at St. Joseph, White Cloud's future was doomed. There became no need for a shipping and ferrying center across the Missouri at White Cloud and its growth and prosperity dwindled.

One of the thirty members of the town company who were stockholders in the organization of White Cloud was Dr. Richard J. Gatling. He was to later patent the famed Gatling gun.

First Schools — In the summer of 1859, a small frame structure for a school was built in White Cloud in the northwest part of the town. After less than two years, the building was struck by lightning and so badly damaged as to necessitate its abandonment.

On June 21, 1871, the community held a special election for a bond of $15,000 bearing an interest rate of 10% for the construction of a new school. This vote was testimony to the liberality of the early settlers of White Cloud. History reports that the construction began in May 1871, and the school was completed in February the following year. A contract was set for the cost of $11,000. Bonds were issued to cover all expenses up to $15,000.

Wakefield and Company built the building, but the bill came to $13,500. After a compromise, contractors paid a portion of the excess cost. The district portion came to $12,000 which came in below the original amount allowed on the bonds.

The materials for the structure were mainly taken from near the town. The stone was quarried near the river and the brick made within a "stone's throw" of the school. The school had four rooms besides the usual closets and cloak rooms. This school had its first class in 1875. The top story became the high school with the first class graduating in 1914. This remained the high school until it closed in 1958. This incredible structure stands today and is the location for the historical society and school memorabilia. The stately red brick school stands overlooking the town and the nearby Missouri River.

A separate school for African-American students was maintained from 1872-1886. In 1887 these students were integrated into the new school building. The larger towns in the county, such as Elwood and Troy, had separate schools into the 1950s.

A notable youth from White Cloud was Wilbur Chapman. In 1913 he answered the call of an evangelist who came to White Cloud. The evangelist preached about leprosy and the lepers who lived destitute and in shacks in a mission. The evangelist asked that the people give $25 for each leper. He vividly described the conditions and challenged the community to help ten lepers. Wilbur decided to give his pig named Pete to the cause. That fall when the pig was sold, his money was placed in a metal bank shaped like a pig. As the origin of the term may date back to the middle ages, local lore is that this story inspired the piggy bank and word spread around the world.

Wilbur would have gone to the White Cloud schools at this time.

Tragedy — School athletics and physical education took place in a gymnasium in the bottom of the Community Church. A tragic fire on October 5, 1955, in this gymnasium took the lives of two boys and severely burned two more. The superintendent, Kenneth Poppe, and the boys were working on the gymnasium floor using gasoline to help clean the floor. An explosion occurred, the cause unknown. One of the boys, Claude Collins, was in critical condition with burns over most of his body. He was hospitalized in Kansas City for six months while he recovered. He later married Sharon Watts who was a year behind him in school. She graduated from Hiawatha after the White Cloud school closed.

Closing the School — A total of 385 students graduated from White Cloud from 1914 through 1958. In forty-five years, the most common surnames of the graduates were Taylor-23, Nuzum-14, Tracey-6, and Keller-5. These four surnames represented 13% of the total to graduate from White Cloud. The last class in 1958 had two graduates. Those graduates were Claude Collins who went on to a great and respected life working as a county maintenance boss, and Larry Waggoner who flew helicopters and the Mohawk fixed wing in the Viet Nam War before retiring from the military. The boys who died in the fire would have been in this class.

White Cloud High School
Doniphan County, KS

#6
Mulberry High School

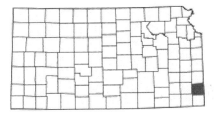

Mascot: Tigers

Colors: Black and Orange

Year Closed: 1966

Location: town of Mulberry (first called Mulberry Grove), northeast Crawford County

Area History — One of the problems of the early settlers whose farms bordered on the Military Road was the Indians traveling from Ft. Scott, Kansas, to Ft. Gibson, Oklahoma. They camped in the nearest available barn or pasture at night, and although they harmed no one, the settlers feared them. They developed the habit of appropriating the farmers' livestock at night, leaving very early the next morning with an increased inventory of meat.

When the Cherryvale division of the Gulf railroad was built, a town was laid out and named Mulberry. On the north side of the ridge, which was partly in Lincoln and Washington townships near the state line, stood a beautiful grove of wild mulberry trees.

In 1869, Nicholas and Julia Taylor moved into the area and purchased 160 acres of land one mile west of what would become the town of Mulberry. Nicholas gradually accumulated more land until his total was 560 acres. The first 160 acres had been purchased from the government after the Department of Interior purchased it from the Cherokee Indian Nation. The government was given the right to sell the land through an amendment to Article 17 of the Cherokee Indian Neutral Lands agreement. Taylor, a preacher as well as a farmer, opened the first grocery and general merchandising store in Mulberry. In 1871, coal mines were opened near the town, and the volume of business grew extensively. Mulberry became a huge shipping point.

Education in Mulberry — The first school was in a little log cabin about two miles west of town. In Mulberry proper, school was taught in small buildings until a small frame building was built near the Frisco Depot. It was replaced by a larger frame building.

In 1886, the *Mulberry Grove Gazette* described "the common practice of carrying articles enticing workers to come to their location . . . the land is a beautiful valley situated in Crawford County Kansas. Everything in the way of grain and vegetables can be grown in our soil. We have a number of railroads making transportation easy. Our wagon roads compare to country roads in general. The county is divided into 113 school districts each about two miles square and each containing a school house. We need more men to develop the coal interest. Our professional men include . . . you will find agricultural implement business, wagon and carriages for sale . . ."

Mining Town Growth — In 1904 Mulberry grew more rapidly than any other town in the county due to the expanding of coal mining. Mulberry's future was bright. Mining coal was the chief industry plus the city was situated in the middle of a splendid agriculture district.

Mulberry was an ethnic melting pot as mine workers streamed to the area from Italy, France, Germany, and the Balkans. Kenny Cattaneo's ('64) grandfather came from Northern Italy to America to work in the Mulberry coal mines. This grandfather lived at the mining camp for seven years before he brought his girlfriend to America to become his wife. She only spoke Italian but soon picked up some English though she was never very fluent.

Robert Massa's ('54) grandfather came from Italy to France to Ironwood, Michigan, in 1890. His grandmother spoke three languages—English, Italian, and French. She would often quip, "I can go anywhere with my tongue." When Robert's grandfather was three years old, the Massa family resettled in Kansas to work in the coal mines.

Lee King Massa's ('62) grandfather was killed in the mines in 1927, leaving a wife with seven children ages six months to sixteen years. Their only support from the Kelly-Carr mine was that they were given the company house.

In the *Mulberry News* dated 1905, "The Report of the Grammar grade has a total of 44 children enrolled and an Intermediate room of 50 students enrolled."

From a 1906 article about the East Mulberry School in the *Mulberry News*:

. . . one of the students reports of a much loved school custodian from her childhood was Frank Tracy. This Lincoln school was an eight room brick building with modern heating appliances. Such a building costing $10-12,000 made it necessary to issue bonds. When it opened the other little schools closed and the Lincoln School housed both the grade and high school.

In 1908 a $55,000, two-story brick building was built to serve as the primary and high school grades. An elementary school across the border in Burgess, Missouri, sent their students to high school in Mulberry where they paid tuition.

In 1919 a huge three-story brick high school called Highland was built in a beautiful grove of trees on a hill in the west part of town. The Class of 1919 was the first graduating class from this building. The school year started using both the Lincoln and newly built Highland building. The $35,000 new school building had seven classrooms, a study hall, library, and superintendent's office, an auditorium with seating for 400 people, a stage suitable for high school plays, and a large gymnasium. The high school enrollment that year was 133 students. The largest enrollment in the 1920s was 800 grade school children and 161 in high school.

Depression Era — A football field was built just east of town, and on October 3, 1930, the Mulberry Tigers played their first game in the Mineral Belt League. After the 1933 season, the next football field was constructed by WPA workers near Highland school. The WPA workers dozed down trees, cut down the hill, and hauled in rock to build a retaining wall.

The Great Depression took its toll on Mulberry as the public did not have money to spend with the coal mines closing. The Mulberry Bank failed in 1928. Years of prosperity were gone. Mulberry's financial problems seemed insurmountable. Teachers worked without pay. The high school enrollment was at its peak during these difficult years with the 41 seniors in the Class of 1933. The state became concerned with the school's financial woes. In 1936, the school board completed negotiations for the sale of Lincoln School building which was dismantled. The school was purchased by a group of 175 people and businesses for the price of $1,000. This money was used to help pay the teachers' salaries until new tax money was available.

These were also poor years for farmers; therefore, the businesses in town were hurt. No one had money to spend, and the lack trickled down to the school. Though children still needed an education, it looked as if the school might have to close. The teachers continued to work without pay, hoping there would be money to catch up on their back pay in the near future.

On August 2, 1936, between 2,500 and 3,000 people attended a political street dance and three-minute political talks sponsored by the Mulberry High School alumni. The event netted thirty-five dollars for the association.

Extracurriculars and Academics — Driver's education training classes were offered in the fall of 1951. The district received a new Chevrolet through the program. The school was remodeled in 1954, including a new coal hopper, reroofing, a furnace room, repaired showers, rewired show rooms, and new plumbing.

Both boys and girls basketball were offered from the beginning. Girls basketball was played only in the early years. The 1953-54 boys team won twenty-six straight games, losing only their first game of the year and their last in the regional finals to Cambridge by six points. Bob Palmer ('54) was the league's most valuable player.

The football teams played eleven-man until 1959 when they changed to eight-man. In 1953, there were sixteen boys on the team. The spring brought out the track team. The biggest rivals were Arma (seven miles away), Frontenac, Erie, Cherokee, and Colgan (St. Marys). There was only one bus to take the students to the away ball games. The girls would sit in the back and the boys in the front of the bus.

Kathleen Stewart Henegar ('60) told of the Halloween "when a cow was put on the top floor of the fire escape at night. This was during the war years. The next morning announcement [we] heard a gruff voice from the Superintendent, 'Would the Stewart and Parson boys report to the office!' Busted. How could anyone have known the culprits? They were told to get that cow off of the fire escape, now! The only problem was that the night before the cow could not see through the grated steps. Going down was not nearly as easy for her as she balked at every step fearing the near death fall that she might incur. All five of these boys (brothers and cousins) would later serve in World War II."

There was no indoor plumbing in the school until 1950. The boys outhouse was to the north, and the girls outhouse was to the south. The teachers and staff all used the same outbuildings.

People and Traditions — A plaque at the historical museum and community center commemorates Ernest Cattaneo ('30) who was the editor of the Mulberry newspaper. He died of a brain tumor at the age of 37 while he

was the school board president. Warren Jones ('38) took a load of men to Kansas City to donate blood for their friend and newspaper editor. Ernest Cattaneo's widow, Josephine, a young mother with two small sons, continued to publish the *Mulberry News* for many years after. These are stories of brave people who did what they could for their friends in Mulberry.

Frank Tracy was a beloved janitor. He not only started the furnace each morning, but he drove the bus and cleaned the school every day.

There were six Mulberry boys killed in World War-II—Raymond Stewart (Kathleen Stewart Henegar's ('60) brother), Darrell "Happy" Neil ('40), Walter Hamilton ('40), Kyle and Harold Sayre (brothers, the only sons of David and Myrtle Sayre), and Robert Hall (drafted before he graduated from Mulberry High School).

Two other Mulberry boys became prisoners of war—Billy Glasgow ('47) was a POW in the Korean War and Warren Jones ('38) was held in the infamous Stalag 17 in Germany for two years. Warren came home to become the postmaster in Mulberry for many years.

Miss Dorothy Rasmuson ('27) Johnson was the superintendent during the war years. She started teaching at the age of seventeen. She taught in Wichita before she came back to marry her high school sweetheart who was working in the mines in Mulberry. They were married in Wichita on a weekend, and he drove back to Mulberry to work on the following Monday. Dorothy stayed in Wichita to complete her contract that year before coming back to teach commerce in Mulberry. She was the principal from 1938-1943 and the superintendent from 1943-1947. She was called "Miss J."

Robert "Nook" Massa ('54) remembers, "If you were in her class, you would get a job anywhere. And she could keep discipline too!"

The column heading the *Pittsburg Headlight Sun* on May 6, 1942 stated, "The City (Mulberry) is unusually proud of their school system, which in recent years has overcome its depression problems."

Sharon Haynes Jennings ('62) was known to back the miles off the family car, thus reversing the odometer before returning it to her father's garage for him to see how far she had driven the night before.

The forbidden coal pits were also the greatest swimming holes. All the kids were warned that there were undercurrents and old mine shafts that could suck them in. Needless to say, everyone learned to swim in these old pits.

The senior trips were usually to Rockaway Beach where the students would stay overnight. They would travel by cars.

Hot lunch started by Mr. Howard Curry ('39) when he was the superintendent in 1960.

Tragedy struck in 1965 when Bob Manahan and Kathy Buche were killed in a car accident after junior play practice. Bob's mother was the school cook at the time. As the district did not have the money to pay for a replacement cook, Pat Billard, Paula Reihnart, and Margie McCleod volunteered their services and love to help the grieving mother so she could have a month off from work with pay.

School Unification—The forced unification with nearby Arma in 1966 was met with lobbying and trips of protest to the State Department of Education in Topeka. Dr. Throckmorton, the State Superintendent of Schools, was not bending on the decision to close the school. He reported to the protestors that the decision was already made as Arma said that they had enough room. The Mulberry High School students would go to Arma. The Mulberry townspeople had purchased their own bus, so the protesters said to the superintendent that their kids were going to Girard. Throckmorton said, "We (the state) are not paying for that." The Mulberry supporters said, "No problem, we've got it covered, we have our own bus." So the next year, 1967, nearly 100 students were transported past Arma to Girard.

Closing — Mulberry High School closed after graduation in 1966. The elementary school closed in 1972. A total of 1,029 graduated from Mulberry High School from 1914-1966. The largest graduating class was in 1933 with 41 graduates. The last class had twelve graduates with John F. Yenic III (alphabetically) the last to receive a diploma from Mulberry High School.

The most common surnames of graduates were Stewart-10, McCoullough-9, Hamilton-8, Radford-8 Johnson-7, Massa-7, Maxwell-7, Thompson-7, Hendrickson-6, Smith-6, Williams-6, Jones-6, Humphreys-5, and Long-5.

Mulberry High School
Crawford County, KS

#7

Santa Fe High School

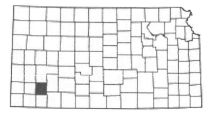

Year Closed: 1920

Location: central Haskell County, intersection of today's US Highways 83 and 160

Area History — Haskell County Kansas was named for Dudley C. Haskell, a member of Congress from Lawrence who died in office in 1883. The first settlers to the county came in 1887. In a research paper about the county, John M. Barry, a Distinguished Visiting Scholar at the Center for Bioenvironmental Research of Tulane and Xavier Universities, concluded that Haskell County was the location of the first outbreak of the Spanish Flu in 1918, which killed between 21 million and 100 million people worldwide. This is of particular interest as the following history of Santa Fe High School coincided with this time of the world-wide deadly epidemic.

The following is from a collection of stories by Lawrence Stude and Helen (Miller) Wells, printed in an Old Santa Fe article that appears in the centennial book on Haskell County.

Perhaps a sod school house was erected at the very first settlement of Santa Fe as there is a reference to one during the hard times of the 1880s and 1890s. In 1890 there were 102 students in the Santa Fe School.

Just when the large, two-story, four-room school house was built is not known, although it is still remembered by everyone who has ever lived at Santa Fe. It had even the luxuries of a bell and flagpole above it. Probably not all four rooms were used until the high school began sometime after 1900. One year of high school work was offered as early as 1920 in Santa Fe, but ten years elapsed before a four-year high school was established. A county high school was opened in Santa Fe about 1913 but the rivalry for the county seat interfered with its support. Jim Patrick was on the school board for a number of years, and he thought there were 30 to 40 students in each classroom of the big school house. In 1912, eleven students graduated from this Haskell County school.

The Santa Fe Monitor had a column entitled "Santa Fe School News" for 1918. Excerpts follow:

January 24. Physiology takes the place of Civics and Commercial Geography the place of Business Arithmetic for the remainder of the year . . . The Girls Music Club met with Mary Unsell Tuesday night . . . Last Thursday on account of the storm there was no school in the grade room and only a few pupils in the high school.

January 24. Military drill has taken the place of basketball practice this cold weather.

February 28. We wish to invite all the schools of Haskell County to a field and track meet to be held at Santa Fe Thursday March 23. Class A will include all grade students over 15, Class B all between 10 and 15 years and Class C all between 5 and 10. (The events offered were the same in modern track meets.)

March 14. The entertainment to be given Saturday night, March 23, consists of a play, 'Convalescence of Robbie,' and a sketch, 'Their First Quarrel,' and some music....The Ladies Aid will serve dinner at the school the day of the track meet, so you can come and stay all day; play baseball, or tennis in the forenoon and see the track meet in the afternoon . . . Teacher's meeting in Santa Fe, March 16, in the schoolhouse, 1:30 mountain time.

May 20, 1920, from the "Santa Fe School news" column in the *Santa Fe Monitor*, "The Baccalaureate services at Santa Fe last Sunday were largely attended."

In the next year's paper there were no references to Santa Fe schools. The high school closed around 1920 after Sublette established a high school. The grade school remained in session for a number of years, closing in 1938.

A Student Remembers — From Helen Miller Wells ('17)—"In 1917 when I graduated from Haskell County High School in Santa Fe, it had sixteen students. Leon Bethel and I were seniors. We wrote to Governor Arthur Capper and he came and gave our graduation address. Our motto was 'Quality Not Quantity.' We had a crowd. Folks didn't think the governor would come for just two kids."

Ghost Town — There is no remnant of the town site of Santa Fe today. The highway intersection is the only reminder that once there was a thriving community of settlers who worked to provide an education for their children.

#8

Herndon Rural High School

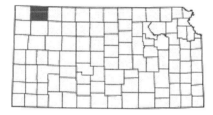

Mascot: Beavers

Colors: Blue and Gold

Year Closed: 2004

Location: town of Herndon, Rawlins County

Herndon History — Herndon Rural High School was located just six miles from the Nebraska state line. Nestled in the valley of Beaver Creek, it is natural that the school mascot was the Beavers.

The community was settled by many German Catholic immigrants who homesteaded in the 1870s. There was a long-established parochial grade school taught by the Catholic Sisters. All of these grade school graduates attended Herndon High School. The grade school closed in 1970, and students then went to the Herndon public school. Any animosity between the public and parochial school students quickly dissipated with school activities and sports involvement. As in any unification or merger, it is often the parents that have the most problems with change.

Much of the following information was provided by Marita Portschy about the school's history:

> Herndon was the eighth district in the county in 1881 as a subscription school. The following year it became a public school. The first high school was organized in 1915. It started as a one-year high school and the second year more subjects were offered. A new building was constructed in 1917 because of the growing population. In 1923, Herndon Rural High School became District #2.

That same year, the Catholics in the area organized their own high school, St. Mary's High School, which ran through 1939 before closing.

The gymnasium was built with a WPA (Work Progress Administration) grant from the government and completed Christmas 1937. Many area farmers helped build the facility. This modern building even had showers. The 1938 graduates were the first to walk across the stage as they graduated.

Some controversy accompanied this new building. The "Swedes" from south of town wanted the money to be used to build a new high school six miles south along US

Highway 36 because of the condition of the high school. Another rumor was that one board member wanted to shut down the school altogether and send the students to Atwood. The decision to build the gymnasium upset the "Swedes" enough to pull their school children from the Herndon school system. This school was condemned in 1949 because of a two-inch crack in the upper level and had to be torn down. Rebuilding began. School was held at St. Mary's, the Evangelical Reformed Church, and various places around town. The new school was constructed on the site of the old school. The class of 1951 moved into the facility by the spring of that year. In the fall of 1966, Herndon Rural High School became USD #317. It remained until the fall of 2003 when the decision was made to consolidate with Atwood.

Notable Graduate—Herndon was the birthplace of Rudolph Wendelin ('28). This Herndon High School graduate studied architecture at the University of Kansas and art at several art schools. He was the creator of the Smokey Bear campaign in 1944 while working at the United States Forest Service. He designed several US postage stamps.

Athletics & Activities—Basketball was long a dominant sport in Herndon. One year after a successful season in boys basketball, there were not enough boys in school to have a team. Therefore, in the fall of 1990, two girls, Debbie Green and Andrea Franke, stepped forward and played with the boys so the school could field a team.

The rivals in athletics were Jennings, Brewster, Selden, and Rexford. Some believed that another German community of Leoville may have been the dirtiest with their rough play.

There was a band and an active glee club. During the war years, music teachers were difficult to find, and the music program was dropped.

The Beaver mascot was on the 1937 school yearbook. James Trotter ('37) was the artist and a member of the 1937 yearbook staff.

The school song was to the tune of the Notre Dame Fight Song. (Yearbook 1963)

> *Hail, Hail, to our Herndon High.*
> *With blue and gold boys our goal is high.*
> *On you Beavers keep that glow*
> *Fight for old Herndon, don't let it go.*
> *Forward for Herndon, put on the steam.*
> *We've got the spirit, we've got the team.*
> *On to vic-tor-y, we'll fly*
> *Fight! Fight! Fight!*

This song replaced the first school song that referred to the boys as the fleetest and the girls as sweetest.

About the Herndon/Atwood rivalry, Paul Versch ('42) wrote the following:

> There was no love between Herndon and Atwood. I transferred from St. Mary's High School to HRHS in 1939. I drove a horse and buggy from the Versch farm to Herndon in the mid-1930s along with three siblings, then tied old Barney to a post in the alley at granddad Adam's home and ran off to St. Mary's via a quick stop at Slocum's store to trade a dozen eggs for a tablet or some candy. The Class of '41 was very concerned about their future—no jobs, no opportunities. When the Class of '42 graduated, we knew what was going to happen. Everything changed on December 7, 1941.

A bronze plaque was molded and mounted at the high school which was testament of what one individual's leadership can mean to a school and community regardless of the size.

DAVID J. CHITTENDEN
Superintendent of
Herndon Public Schools
1928-1959
His dedication to his Church
His Unselfish Loyalty
To His community and the
Dedication of his life
To the education of youth
Will long be an inspiration
To future citizens.

Modern Academics — In the year 2000, the finals for an international science competition, known as the d2k Destination ImagiNation, took place at Iowa State University in Ames, Iowa. The Destination ImagiNation Team from Herndon High School competed with students from thirty-one states, five foreign countries, and two Canadian provinces. Over 15,000 attended the finals competition. The Herndon team of six students and three coaches not only competed but won the second place trophy. Team members competed in three tasks, including how well they solved a hands–on engineering problem in four minutes, the strength of a pasta structure, and creativity of a skit. Using dried manicotti and linguine, the Herndon team built a structure that supported 724 pounds of direct weight, equal to the weight of five men supported by a structure that weighted 83 grams (less than three ounces.) This was representative of the education and scholarship talents of even the smallest of high schools and the teachers. With only twenty-seven students in high

school in a town with a population of 179, it proved that athletics were not the only cornerstone of these schools. The team took second place out of thirty-nine teams that made the finals competition. The team members included senior Jeff Leitner ('00); sophomores Adam Ketterl ('02), David Sattler ('02), Kenzie Michel ('02) and Andrea Brown ('02); and freshman Nik Martin ('03). The coaches were Judy Ketterl, team manager; Liane Martin, assistant team manager; and Jacque Leitner, program coordinator. Just six students represented all students, but their education led them to be extremely significant educated professionals in their careers as follows:

Adam - auto repairman in Atwood, employs three full time, married with one child
Andrea - RN psychiatric nurse, married to serviceman in Alaska
Kenzie - financial advisor in Great Bend, married
David - engineer at manufacturing company in Norton, married, three children
Jeff – manager, cellular telephone company in Colorado, married, two children
Nick - engineer in Kansas City, married, two boys

Educated to be lifelong learners and citizens, small-town values and dedicated teachers helped make these seven Kansan's dreams come true.

Closing the School — A number of Nebraska students came across the state line to attend Herndon High School. At the closing of the high school in 2004, the remaining students went to neighboring districts in Atwood and Oberlin, Kansas, and Culbertson and Trenton, Nebraska.

When the high school closed, exactly 1,000 students had graduated in eighty-seven years. Family names of graduates show the significant German influence of the area. The most numerous surnames were Leitner-50, Solko-36, Grafel-28, Marintzer-25, Green-25, Franke-16, Lippold-14, Poatschy-14, and Bobinmeyer-11.

Only six months after having won the state runner-up on the six-man state football title, the last graduate, Daniel Riener ('04) walked across the stage to accept the last diploma from Herndon Rural High School.

Herndon High School
Rawlins County, KS

9

Robinson High School

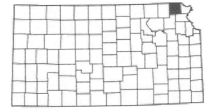

Mascot: Cardinals

Colors: Red and White

Year Closed: 1966

Location: town of Robinson, east-central Brown County

Free State Origins – Dr. Charles Robinson was the first Free State Governor of Kansas. He was a doctor in Massachusetts who came to the state on July 28, 1854. He possibly did more to make Kansas a free state than any other man. He made several trips to the east and brought companies of hundreds of anti-slavery settlers to Kansas. The town of Robinson was named after him and incorporated on February 9, 1859, by the Robinson Town Company. The streets of the town were all named and numbered. The town soon became a thriving settlement, but never had the phenomenal growth that was expected by the promoters and founders. During the Civil War years, the town growth was slow; however several homes, a hotel, a blacksmith shop, and two general stores were added. One building built in 1854 is still standing. It is an old stone barn, today owned by the Tietjen family, that is sometimes opened for tours and weddings. (source: Mrs. Myrtle Martindale)

A sawmill was started and located on Wolf River. This helped the settlers in building their homes as previously lumber had to be hauled from St. Louis or Iowa Point. Rumors of a railroad running from Elwood to Marysville became a certainty on March 20, 1860, when the first railroad iron was laid on Kansas soil. The railroad became known as the St. Joseph and Denver Company and passed through Robinson. In the beginning, a station was to be built a mile or two east of Robinson, to be called St. Francis. The depot was built there, ignoring the requests of a delegation from Robinson to locate it in their town. One Sunday, a group of determined men took wagons and oxen and went to the St. Francis station and brought the small depot back to Robinson on wagons. Nothing was done about this action and the depot remained in Robinson.

Education — The first school in Brown County was formed in nearby Claytonville in 1857. A log cabin school house was built in Old Robinson soon afterward. In 1867, a barn was remodeled into a schoolhouse in the town of Robinson. In 1874 and 1878, two school buildings were erected: a two-room building on the hill where the now-vacant grade school is located, and a one-room building downtown on Main Street, which housed the lower grades.

By 1896, the schools needed a new building, which was erected and divided into primary, intermediate, and grammar divisions. In 1909, an addition was added on the north and the building remodeled to its present grade school size.

When the community voted a nine-month school term instead of the usual eight-month term in 1913, the school qualified for credit as a high school by the State of Kansas and the four-year high school curriculum was added. All the teachers possessed state certificates and, as a result, Robinson became an accredited high school with a football team. The first football game was against the larger county seat town of Hiawatha with Robinson the winner, 27 to 0.

On May 21, 1914, Robinson High School graduated its first four-year class of four girls and three boys. Alta Byers was the first graduate (alphabetically).

Robinson Rural High School became District No. 3 but had never built a building. Rooms were used in the grade school building which crowded both schools. On April 19, 1923, a petition to build a new high school building was presented to the school board. The petition was signed by a sufficient number. A $100,000 bond issue for a building had been voted down in 1920, but this bond issue of $60,000 carried by 115 votes after a bitter fight. The new high school building was first used in 1925. Some new courses were added to the curriculum. A library and music rooms were added to the school.

Two late improvements were added with an extensive remodeling in 1948. In 1954 a new gymnasium-auditorium was built and more remodeling done for $165,000.

Though there were three teachers at the start, the school grew to seven teachers by 1957. By the time the school closed in 1966, there were eight teachers with a curriculum of band, mixed chorus, boys and girls chorus, typing, bookkeeping, office practice, speech, English, French, home economics, history, mathematics, auto mechanics, drivers education, shop, science, and psychology.

Athletics — The boys played basketball and football. The boys played eleven-man football with only thirteen players in 1961. The coach at the time was Chris Schwang. Jim Koelliker ('62) recalled that his pep talk to his team was always the same: "We're not very good, but when they finish with us they're gonna to be tired of us because of our conditioning!"

Koelliker continued, "We were getting spanked one night, and I was about as big of a player as we had. I made a tackle and sort of blacked out for a second and staggered to the sideline. I told Coach that I was seeing double, and he said back, "We don't have time for you to see double. Get back in there and tackle two of them!"

The sports league was the Brown County League with the teams from Everest, Hamilin, Powhattan, Reserve, Morrill, Willis, and Fairview. The biggest rivals were Powhattan and Everest in the league and Troy and Highland outside of the league. Robinson had its share of winners. The league first place trophies were won in basketball in 1921, '26, '32, '33, '45, '47, '48, '49, '50; in baseball in 1930, '34, '37, '38; in track in 1953; in football in 1927 and 1957; and in tennis in 1928, '29, '30.

Modernization — The first school buses were purchased in 1949. The town barber, Don T. BeDunnah, and another businessman, Byrom Truex, were the first drivers. BeDunnah drove the north route (going almost to the Nebraska line) and Truex drove the south route. Just ten years later at the age of 16 years and 4 months, Jim Koelliker ('62) started driving the twenty-four passenger bus on the north route. He made 80 cents each way ($1.60 each day or $32.00 each month) as he started from his home northeast of Robinson (only four miles from White Cloud) and picked up students. He then drove the activity bus home with the students who stayed for sports after school. The big forty-eight passenger bus drove on the hard surfaces for the rest of the routes. Quite a responsibility to be given to high school junior!

The Robinson School system started a cafeteria program in the fall of 1950. It was held in the Home Economics room. Remodeling was done to bring students in and out by assembly line. The cafeteria was such a great addition, and all the students were grateful to have a good lunch instead of sandwiches. There was an hour allowed for lunch. Prior to the cafeteria, the town kids went home for lunch and the country kids brought sack lunches.

Student Stories — Dorothy M. Gibbons BeDunnah ('51) recalled her time as a student:

> My tenure at Robinson High School was from September 1947 through May of 1951. We didn't have football during those years but had good basketball. In the school year 1948-49, the Robinson Cardinals made school history. We won the Brown County Tournament. The coach was Lester Holman and the Principal was M.D. Koontz. We also won the District Class B Tournament in 1950.

There were five teachers and the principal at these times: math and home economics teacher, business teacher, English and yearbook teacher, the music teacher who taught band and all chorus groups, history, and shop.

Coach Holman was the history teacher. He had been a marine during WWII and we loved to get him started on his "adventures." One day, in the middle of his dissertation on being a marine, he stopped, smiled, and looked out over the class and said, "I know what you are doing, but you'll need to know what you missed today. It will be on the test tomorrow."

Miss Illola Jaukins was fresh out of college when she came to Robinson. She was very pretty and the boys all liked her classes. She taught all choir, vocal, and band. She made us proud when marching in the band. She wore a uniform and marched beside us. She was so elegant!

Miss Browning, our business teacher was fun. My mother also had her for a teacher some twenty years before. She taught bookkeeping, shorthand, and typing. She was an easy teacher to tease and always took it well. She allowed absolutely no mistakes, erasures, or strike-overs in typing. She could always find them and the guilty one would be given an F for the day.

Mr. Koontz was a strict principal, but well-liked by most. As usual, those who didn't like him were the ones who disliked the rules. What he said, he meant. He had played minor league baseball in earlier years and was a great help to me, a pitcher for our girls team. He also helped us make free-throws in girls basketball. He would tell us to, "keep your eye on the rim and it will go in." How true!

The last day of school trip for all four classes in the late 1940s and early 1950s was always by bus to Lake Contrary in St. Joseph. There was a large amusement park there that we would spend the day and ate from the many concession stands. What a way to end the school year!

The senior trip for the ten seniors in 1962 was to Lake Ten Killer. The Class of 1963, nineteen students and their sponsors, journeyed to southern Colorado by cars.

Judi Bruning ('63) shared memories of the trip:

> We hit all of the big tourist things in and around Colorado Springs—the Garden of the Gods, Seven Falls, Royal Gorge, and we even ice skated at the Broadmoor Hotel. We traveled over the mountains to Durango and went to the Four Corners of Colorado, New Mexico, Utah, and Arizona, eventually coming back by Denver and going to the Lakeside amusement park. Still over 700 hundred miles from home, we headed back east with a lifetime of great stories, experiences, and memories. We had raised the money for this trip through concession stand sales, school plays, suppers, and donations.

Closing Robinson—The District valuation was $1,728,020 and covered an area of seventy-four square miles. With the School Consolidation Act of 1963 by the Kansas Board of Education and the State Legislature, this fell far short of the requirement to maintain a high school and receive state aid for education. The legislation required, in order to continue as a high school, a district must as a minimum meet two of the three criteria: 1) At least 200 square miles, 2) At least $2 million valuation, and 3) Have an enrollment of 400 students.

The last year of Robinson High School, the enrollment was sixty-seven students. There were numerous organizations, including National Honor Society, Fellowship for Christian Athletes, Y-Teens, Red Bird Majesty (school newspaper), The Cardinal Year Book, and a band of sixty-one members and seven twirlers.

A total of 817 graduated from Robinson in its fifty-three years from 1914-1966. The largest class was 1935 with thirty-nine graduates. The most numerous surnames of the graduates were Oltjen-10, McCauley-8, Idol-7, Koelliker 7, and Lange-5. The Idol and McCauley graduates were from the families of two of the earliest settlers of the town and banking businesses.

Robinson High School
Brown County, KS

#10

LaHarpe Rural High School

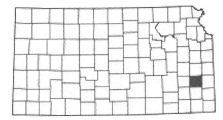

Mascot: Panther

Colors: Red and White

Year Closed: 1966

Location: town of LaHarpe, central Allen County

History of LaHarpe—It is doubtful if there is a city in the United States, either large or small, that has experienced more ups and downs than this pleasant little village of slightly less than 700 people. Its ups, while they lasted, were sufficient to revive the smashed ego of a disappointed Alaskan gold hunter, and its downs when they fell upon the town at last, would have broken the spirit of a Captain Merriweather Lewis, Thomas Jefferson's friend who was the first man to penetrate our western wilderness.

There were several school buildings in the 1880s and into the new century. Charlene Limes ('39) Bowman remembered an account of the town and school:

> As a child my mother and I stood on the front porch and watched the east building burn. This red brick building was the only school house I remember. It was located on the property where the City Hall is now located. There were three levels. The high school, an auditorium, and the superintendent office were on the upper story. Grade school was on the first level. Each room with one teacher held two grades: first-second, third-fourth, fifth-sixth, and seventh-eighth. The basement contained a small gym, science lab, and rest rooms. The main gymnasium was located on Main Street a block east of the school. The football field was north of Highway 54.

Since Charlene graduated in 1939, her account would place the school burning in the mid-1920s.

In 1897, when Lanyon Zinc Company of Pittsburg began the construction of its first ore (zinc and lead) smelters here, the town had a population of less than 500. After the completion of the first smelters in 1898, the population increased rapidly, and two years later it was incorporated as a city of the third class.

At the turn of the century, the citizens of LaHarpe had good reason to believe their town would someday become one of the largest cities in Kansas. Miss Lucy Jury, who was born on a farm between Salem and Allen Center, moved to LaHarpe in 1903 with her parents and her eleven brothers and sisters. Miss Jury, whose memory would reflect upon a person fifty years her junior, recalls that when she first saw LaHarpe, it had two large smelters humming at full blast, three brick plants that were making stockholders rich, and the largest zinc rolling mill in all the world. The town had two railroads furnishing transportation to distant points, two sound banks, a thriving business district, a hotel, and a number of fine eating houses. The town had a population of 2,000 and soon reached 3,500.

The reason for such sudden and rapid growth was that LaHarpe was sitting on a supply of natural gas that was believed to be inexhaustible. The problem was, however, that it was exhaustible. This reality was realized about twenty years after natural gas was first discovered in Allen County.

The first commencement at the LaHarpe High School was recorded in the *LaHarpe Journal* on May 6, 1904. "This is commencement week and LaHarpe is finding out for the first time what it means. Until the last few years no such thing as a high school existed here and never before has the school sent forth a graduating class The class that will receive the first diplomas awarded by the high school is a small one, but the two young ladies and one young gentleman who compose it are the sort that are to be found only in Kansas and make up in quality what they lack in number."

A second account of this graduation was in the *Iola Daily Register* on May 7, 1904:

> The commencement exercises were given last night at the Presbyterian church as was planned and a great deal of interest was taken in it as this was the first class that had graduated in LaHarpe. The church was prettily decorated with bunting of the class colors which are orange and black, and with flowers, and

looking fine. The church was well filled, but not so crowded as to make it uncomfortable. The Invocation was given by Rev. W.L. French. The class was composed of Virgil McCarty, Bertha Sickly and Hattie Ferris. The two young ladies dressed in white and looked very nice and all wore carnations which are the class flower. Each read a paper; Miss Sickly, 'The Aristocracy of Brains,' Miss Ferris, 'Women in History,' and Virgil McCarty, 'The Modern Nazareth.' The papers were all good and were a credit to the school. Prof. Lough, of Baker University, delivered the class address, which was more than good and as one hearer remarked he had 'heard a good many class addresses but that was the best that I have ever heard.' The address was to tell the graduates more what the world expected of them, than to give them advice. It was an address that the class as well as the audience will not forget for a long time and will have an influence on their future. When Prof. Patton delivered the diplomas he gave the class a little talk. The music was furnished by Prof. Lieurance (refer to the Prof. Lieurance in the Buffalo and Neosho Falls stories-and a major musical genius of the times) and was extra good.

Athletics—In the early days LaHarpe became known nationally in baseball circles. At one time there was scarcely a baseball fan in the nation who did not know that LaHarpe was the home of Ad Brennan, pitcher of the Philadelphia team in the National League. For many years, Brennan, a left-hander, competed with Hall of Famer Walter Johnson for first honors as Allen County's baseball immortal.

Willis Ross ('39), 97 years old in 2018, recalled, "We had basketball, football, and track in the spring. I went to country school for grade school. I drove to town to high school and picked up kids along the way. I did not go on a senior trip after graduation because I was needed at home and because of the cost."

The boys played in the Marmaton Valley League against Elsmore, Moran, Fulton, Uniontown, and Bronson. All of the games were played in an offsite gymnasium one block to the east of the high school on Main Street. It was the focal point of community events, social gatherings, and all basketball activities.

Student Stories—The first bus driver was Mrs. Brown, and she owned the bus in the 1940s. There were later more busses in the district. Linda Hennegar Sweany ('54) said, "Mrs. Brown one morning slid off the road at Bird Hill. We had to wait there until we were towed. I had to milk cows before and after school. My next bus driver was my later to be father-in-law, Emerson Sweany ('50). He often had to wait at the end of the driveway while I changed out of my chore clothes and cleaned up."

The bus drivers held a big spring picnic for their kids on both the north and south routes. The beloved driver on the south route was Frank Stevenson ('47).

N.L. Lancaster was a teacher and superintendent. Mary Manbeck Clay ('55) remembers him fondly. "He was a science and social science teacher, class sponsor, and a significant mentor to all. He was very strict. His wife, Mrs. Lancaster taught home economics, English, and math and was like a mother to us!"

Mr. Lancaster would post on the study hall black board at the top with the note for the following names to report to the principal's office first hour. "Skipping school always found Mr. Lancaster there to catch us," said Wayne Chandler ('53).

Betty Crogan Daniels ('51) with her beautiful eyes dancing as she sat in her wheel chair recalled, "I had polio in the seventh grade and remained in a wheel chair throughout school. My dad would come to school two to three times each day to carry me in the wheelchair up and down the stairs in the high school to my classes."

Traditions—Senior trips were annual events dating back to at least 1939. During the war years they were called off. By the 1950s, Rockaway Beach and Branson, Missouri, became the favorite trip. "The boys went fishing every night," according to Wayne Chandler ('53). One particularly scary night in 1954, Darrel Sayles ('54) nearly drowned and was taken by ambulance to a nearby hospital. "Mr. Lancaster was really upset and again provided leadership and advised us about the responsibility and taking caution for our safety in life. The money for the trips was raised in many small activities but primarily from the school carnivals."

Halloweening was an annual event in which most of the teenagers participated after dark. The bell at the school seemed to always ring just after the one-armed town constable, John Barns, turned his back. He was a notable city marshal who was responsible later in his career for cracking a Kansas City gang. Gun shots ensued. John Barns was kidnapped and taken to the country and given the option to run or else! Needless to say, he ran back to LaHarpe.

Sugar was rationed during the War. After the war rationing, Mrs. Mitchell would get candy into the store and save one piece of candy for each kid. Linda Hennegar Sweany ('54) remembered, "Only the big high school girls were allowed to read off the shelf the 'True Stories'

magazine. For the younger elementary girls, it was off limits."

School Closing—The school closed after the 1966 graduation and was unified with Iola some six miles west. There had been 831 graduates in the sixty-three years of the school from 1904-1966. The class of 1966 had twenty graduates with Steve Utley (alphabetically) being the last to receive a diploma from LaHarpe Rural High School.

The most frequent surnames of the graduates were Morrison-13, Smith-11, Green-9, Manbeck-7, Johnson-6, Pennington-6, Smart-6, and Stewart-6.

LaHarpe High School
Allen County, KS

#11

Plains Rural High School

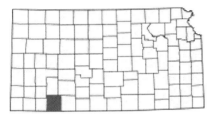

Mascot: Plainsman

Colors: Red and White

Year Closed: 1965

Location: town of Plains, west-central Meade County

Area History & School Timeline — The busy Rock Island Railroad came in 1888 when it was constructed running southwest from Pratt to Liberal. US Highway 54, built in 1926, runs through Plains.

The farmland surrounding Plains was settled by pioneers in the 1880s. The railroad and the road from Dodge City to Santa Fe provided passenger trains and transportation for commodities for the area farmers. As the people came west, having no schools, they often volunteered their homes. As time permitted, they built a high school. One of the earlier schools in Plains in 1885 was a store building rented and transformed into a school house. Don T. Edwards, starting at eight years old, was one of the dozen school children who attended. The first class was taught by Lizzie McClung.

Two years later, material was hauled from Cimarron for a two-room school building which was completed in 1887. Among the teachers were Tom Dillinger (1887), Miss Clara Ellis, Mrs. R. R. Singley (who taught for an eight-month term in 1891-92), and Mr. A.L. Vaught (1903).

After the railroad was built in 1888, the schoolhouse in Plains was moved to the present site.

In 1893, in early West Plains, school was held in the Ebenezer Taylor home, which had two large rooms with six to eight students attending. It was also used as a place for public meetings, dances, and church affairs. Jack Evans, a Liberal businessman and county treasurer, was the first teacher. In 1894, the school was moved to a big one-room home that belonged to one of the early settlers. It was three and one-half miles west and one mile south of the original West Plains. Five to six years later, not enough students attended to hire a teacher, so each student was allowed ten dollars a month tuition to go to another school. The Eli Keller, one-half dugout home thirteen miles southeast of Plains, was also used at one time as a school.

In 1901-02, Albert Hempel and Don T. Edwards (from the first school in 1885) surveyed and laid out the main street of Plains. Asked why they made it so wide, they answered, "There was plenty of no-good ground, so it just as well be a street."

Grand Avenue is nearly a half block wide. It is the widest main street in the United States, so stated Bob Ripley in his column, "Believe It or Not." It was paved in 1929 with red bricks. Noticing that the street was twice as wide as most city main streets, Simon Elliott, the mayor of the town, added a raised brick sidewalk down the center of the street. The walk, stretching three blocks through the center of town, is known as "Simon's Monument." (Information from *Plains Kansas-100 years,* by Joyce Knott.)

During hard times in 1903-07, the two-room school dwindled to a one-room school, and a Miss Ruth Bennett, who was also county superintendent, consented to be the teacher. The teacher elected from Missouri had stayed only one month before resigning.

By 1914, a two-year high school was formed in the grade school building. It was on the second floor, and ten students started that first year. It was expanded into a four-year high school with three in the first graduating class in 1919. Enrollment that year was thirty-seven students.

With the consolidation of the rural country schools and the formation of the Rural High School, the building became too small for the anticipated enrollment. A bond election was carried by a large majority in 1922. The existing building became the grade school, and a new $46,000 high school was built. The building contained twelve rooms, a full basement, and a small gymnasium. As enrollment increased rapidly, three more teachers were added at the high school and four more teachers were added at the grade school.

Transportation was essential to bring the country students into town. An old picture that shows eight buses parked near the school was indicative of this transportation effort. During a time when some high schools in other parts of the state existed without ever having had a bus, these eight large trucks and a Ford touring car stood out. A garage was maintained for the care of the busses. The average daily trip for a bus was 398 miles, and in total they carried an average of 184 children per day. Mr. Hiatt was a most efficient mechanic and a long-time district employee. Local lore is that the Plains school bus service excelled over any other in the state of Kansas.

From the 1925 yearbook, *The Plainsman*:

Superintendent N.R. Nyquist reported to the state superintendent's office: "During the month of September the buses operated a total of twenty days and traveled a total of 7,426 miles carrying an average of 327 pupils a day. Eight school buses operated at a cost of $573.48, for maintenance at a daily cost of .47 cents per child."

By 1928, the enrollment had risen to 110 in the high school and the departments of industrial arts and music were added to the curriculum.

The period from 1930-40 was very difficult for the school. The depression lowered the fiscal evaluation which lowered the number of teachers employed and the salaries paid to teachers. Superintendent W.E. Woodward's salary was $311 per month in 1930 and in 1936 it was $175 per month.

The 1930 *Plainsman* printed the story of the girls basketball team: "Superintendent H.C. VanVoorhis first brought fame to the Plains High School girls' basketball team by taking them through two undefeated seasons . . . the first year taking first honors in the Panhandle Tri State Tournament at Goodwell, Oklahoma, defeating Dalhart, Texas, in the finals-a team that had not been defeated in three seasons."

In 1941, the school entered the Little Six League with Kismet, Copeland, Montezuma, Kingsdown, and Englewood. League activities consisted of six-man football, basketball, baseball, track, music, speech, and drama. As enrollment grew, the school switched to eleven-man football and changed to the Hi Plains League and finally the Iroquois League.

Modernization — The patrons of the district voted in 1947 for an extensive remodeling and building program. Plans were initiated for the building of a vocational agriculture and a lunch room, along with a new gymnasium and extensive remodeling of the grade school. Plains then had the best gym in the area and was awarded the opportunity to be the host of many district and regional tournaments.

On September 23, 1950, the first night high school game was held in Plains thanks to the addition of lights for the football field. The American Legion dedicated the field in memory of the men who had given their lives during World War II. Those honored were Jack Staples, Joe Fleming, John Hatcher, Donald Knott, Bob Elliott ('37), and Charles Woltje. A crowd of 1,200 were in attendance and Plains defeated Fowler 12-0.

Drivers Education became part of the curriculum in 1951-52. This was approximately ten years before most of schools in the state started this program. The first new Chevrolet dual-control car was furnished by Holmes Motor Company.

The Special Education program was implemented in 1952. This was, once more, a very early program compared to most school districts in the state.

The school song was "The Plainsman" sung to the tune of "The Caisson Song."

Over hill, over dale, we have hit the dusty trail,
as those Plainsman go rolling along.
Up and down, in and out, we are marching all about,
as those Plainsmen go marching along.
For it's Hi! Hi! Hee! On the field, we'll always be,
shout out your numbers loud and strong . . . 1, 2, 3
For where e're we go, we will always know
that those Plainsmen go rolling along!
That those Plainsmen go rolling along!

Closing Plains High School — The high school closed after graduation in May of 1965. Plains joined Kismet in Seward County in building a new high school to the west called Southwestern Heights. It opened in the fall of 1965. There were 842 graduates from Plains High School from 1919-1965. Like Kismet, which would join Plains at Southwestern Heights High School, the final graduating class would also be the largest in school history with twenty-six graduates. The last to receive a diploma from Plains High School was Joyce Winfrey Brackey ('65) (alphabetically). The most numerous surnames of all the graduates were Angel-11, Wallace-11, Elliott-10, Fox-10, Vail-10, Armentrant-8, Utz-8, Langhofer-7, Brown-5, and Gollitter-5.

#12

Bogue Rural High School

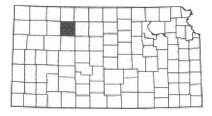

Mascot: Bluejays

Colors: Blue and Gold

Year Closed: 1978

Location: town of Bogue, eastern Graham County

Town History — The town of Bogue was named after an administrator working on the railroad when the tracks reached Bogue in 1888. The railroad ran from Salina west to Colby and was referred to as the Lincoln Branch. The passenger train came from the east in the morning, carrying mail and passengers. It turned around in Colby and headed back east in the afternoon. Not known for its speed, it was called the "Jitney."

School Timeline — Early education in Bogue led to the construction of a three-story, red brick building in 1918, which housed both the grade school and high school. Those wanting to get a four-year diploma traveled to the county seat to attend Hill City High School.

J.R. Gibbins became the superintendent in the fall of 1919. He had on his faculty his sister, Emma Gibbins, and daughter, Ivanoel Gibbins. The third year of high school started in the fall of 1921. Along with a farmer and businessman, B.C. Kenyon, Professor Gibbins headed an effort to form a rural high school under the provisions of the Barnes Legislation of 1915. A vote of all of the people from the area, rural one-room school districts was needed to enable the start of the rural high school. B.C. Kenyon's own brother, Charles, brought wagonloads of rural voters to Bogue to vote against a high school because it would raise taxes to support the school. It was brother against brother, neighbor against neighbor, but the high school vote passed in 1920. The first graduation class, 1923, included seven graduates with both Professor Gibbins's and B.C. Kenyon's children—Anita Gibbins Kenyon and Everett Kenyon—in this first class. (Anita and Everett are the parents of this author.)

The new high school opened in the fall of 1926. The three-story, red brick building dominated the west side south of Main Street. It was the pride of the community. During the fall of that year dedication services were held with W.L. Lewis, a former president of Fort Hays Kansas State College, as the main speaker. The new school had a gymnasium with a balcony around three sides and a stage on the east side. Basketball, proms, dances, school carnivals, volleyball, lyceums, baccalaureates, and commencements would fill this gymnasium.

A Diverse Student Population — Few schools in Kansas, of any size or in any city, compared to the diversity of students in Bogue. Nicodemus, just four miles northeast, was the oldest all-African-American town west of the Mississippi. Students from its grade school, District No. 1, came to Bogue after the rural high school was formed. Another town just seven miles to the southeast was Damar. It was a French Acadian community that did not have a high school prior to sending students to Bogue. Hubert Newell ('35) was once quoted as saying, "we were one third white, one third black, and one third French."

The Six-Man Football Legacy — In 1936, W.H. Gray organized a six-man football team. The football teams of 1948 and 1949, featuring Veryl "Joe" Switzer ('50), were undefeated with opponents scoring only nine touchdowns in sixteen games against the Bluejays. Fourteen of the sixteen games were 45-point, mandatory-called games. (Bogue was 45 points ahead.) Eleven games were shutouts. This was before state football playoffs or rankings, but this was an elite class of six-man football in the state of Kansas.

The "Big Nine" team members were Veryl Switzer ('50), 185 lb. halfback; Jack Conn, center; Leon Stephen ('51), end; Clyde Cooksey ('50), halfback; Francis Jones ('51), end; Waymon Williams, end; Eugene Jones ('51), 180 lb. halfback; Francis Truesdell, center, and Delmar Metheny ('50), quarterback.

Bogue's principal, Cecil Smith, was the football coach. There were thirty-two students in the school at the beginning of 1949. Mr. Smith also had a requirement that every student in school had to play in the band. Switzer played the tuba. When walking into the district band contest in Hays, a boy from nearby Codell recognized Switzer and said with exasperation, "You mean you play in the band too!"

Switzer attended Kansas State and became an all-American half back and kick returner. He was drafted by the Green Bay Packers and became the first African American player for the team in 1954.

Football had its ups and downs after those great teams. The rest of the 1950s were mostly downs. Interest and talent for the six-man game waned to the point that football was discontinued after the 1958 season. It was resurrected in the fall of 1962 with a switch to eight-man. That year there were nine boys out for football, and four of them were freshman. Techniques, training, and coaching kept the young gridders enthused. Coach Larry Ward, a former lineman for the Texas Christian Horn Frogs, was patient and encouraging. The first game of the season was against Codell on a hot September afternoon. A last-second lob to Gary Alexander ('65) gave Bogue a score to finish with a 76-6 loss.

Memories from Bogue Students — In scenes that were likely reminiscent across rural Kansas, Tom Thompson ('55) told the following stories:

> Growing up in Bogue, I remember the summers as being much longer than they are now. The warm weather was perfect for roaming the railroad tracks and river which, of course, was much wider and deeper than it is today.
>
> My first recollection of Bogue was arriving in the back of Everett Kenyon's truck with my folk's furniture. They had sold their store in Edmond, Kansas, and were moving back after being away from Bogue for several years.

We arrived in Bogue shortly before World War II, and once the war began, Claudie Kenyon, my brother Jamie, and I spent most of our free time defending Bogue from attack by the enemy. Very few people realized the heroic effort that went into defending the western edge of town. Many missions were flown in Everett's combines and tractors, many forts built and defended. The battles were fought daily, and the outcome was often in doubt, but each day as the sun set in all its Kansas glory, three tired boys would return home victorious and Bogue was once again safe.

Also from Tom Thompson ('55):

My sophomore year in football, we were not having a good year. I had not been in a game yet that year. We were playing Codell at home under the lights. They were beating us pretty badly and were down on the end zone again ready to score. For some reason the coach looked down to the end of the bench. He waved to me and told me to go in and play end. I put on my helmet and headed onto the field, not knowing quite what to expect. I was going up against an older and experienced end. He was covered with dirt and sweat from the game and there I was in my shiny clean uniform. I was tall and skinny, and he was big and strong. In their huddle they must have looked over and saw me and figured that a green lineman would be easy pickings, so they called for a fake into the line with the quarterback keeping and then passing to the end on my side of the line—an easy six points. The big end lined up across from me with a smile on his face, likely thinking, "It doesn't get any easier than this." For some reason, known only to God, I did not take the fake into the line, nor

did I rush the quarterback as I probably should have, but stayed with my man. The quarterback, not paying much attention to a small, green sophomore, lobbed a pass out to the end who was waiting with open arms in the end zone. I looked up at that moment and saw the ball coming high above my head. It was on a line to fall into the waiting arms of the end. I jumped as high as I could and, much to my amazement, tipped the ball up into the air and it dropped back down into my arms . . . The only thing I could think to do was to get out of there as fast as I could, so I started down the field from about mid-point in their end zone. Slowly I made my way straight down the side of the field, right in front of the cheering hometown fans who were urging me on. History was in the making. It was a moment in time to remember. With great blocking by my teammates and a great deal of luck, I did make it all the way down the full length of the field and scored what was to be our only touchdown of the game. Upon crossing the goal line, I fell on my back in total amazement and exhaustion from the excitement. My teammates were jumping and screaming around me. The home fans went wild and knew that another great football player was beginning his career in Bogue. There was hope for the future.

I don't remember scoring once after that in the remainder of my three-year career.

Thompson, the master story teller, concluded with the following story:

In addition to all my other accomplishments, I did have the distinction of being the only Thompson ever to be expelled from school. It began with the girls in Home Economics class putting up a bulletin board with jokes on it in the hallway. Richard Van Loenen and I were walking by when we realized that there was an opportunity to improve on the jokes, so we proceeded to rearrange the wording to make what we thought were terribly funny captions below each cartoon. The teacher, on discovering our creative endeavor, promptly asked us to change it back to its original condition. Richard and I realized that the freedom of speech and press were at stake. For some reason we refused to make the requested changes, standing on the grounds that our changes were an improvement. We were promptly sent to the principal's office. The principal, whom we liked very much, explained the need for control in the school and the error of our ways. Then with a smile in his soul, I remember him saying, "You are therefore suspended from this institution for a period of one week; bring your parents at the end of that time and we will see about getting you re-instated." Richard and I left school and went home. We found my mom in the dining room ironing. On telling her we had been expelled, she said, "You got out, you get back in!" Richard and I enjoyed a week's vacation and, thanks to it being a small town, got back in without any problem.

Norma Jean Switzer ('65) wrote after a request for her memories of attending school at Bogue High School:

My dear friend, I will take you back to when I first came to meet everyone on the night of eighth grade graduation. I was the last student to graduate from Nicodemus grade school, District No. 1. I came to Bogue to participate in graduation with the Bogue eighth graders. I walked into the grade school gym and saw nothing but strange faces. Some of the other graduates were smiling but some were not. They looked me over and I looked them over. Some spoke, some didn't. I had to wait off stage while all of the other eighth grade graduates marched out in single file. I was not allowed to walk in with them at this time. I was the only one graduating from Nicodemus grade school. It made me feel so unwanted and I stood out as being the outcast at their graduation. I believe that this was a decision made by the teachers or the principal of the school. I had time to get over being an outsider during the summer. By fall of 1961, we all came to start high school, and it was a little different. We were all in uncharted territory with new teachers and a new principal. It gave the freshmen more of an even footing. I believe what we experienced at that high school was to learn to make wise decisions. Those high school years went like lightning. I enjoyed it and got to make friends. There were eleven in my class with only three boys. The girls were all great and became my good friends.

I believe I made choices because I stood at the "candy store window" on the outside and peering to the inside. When I graduated, I knew exactly what I wanted and what I was going to do. I knew that I had to work to get it. I didn't care for high school that much, but my parents said get the education so I would not be stuck in western Kansas without a choice to make a better living. That thought kept me going. I used that for years as a learning tree. When I went to the big cities, it paid off. I took classes at Washburn University to further my ability to get jobs that I knew I needed and to raise a family and to have the ability to retire. As I reach an age to reflect, I know that there was nothing negative that I could not turn into a positive. That's what I learned in high school. I would not let anything pull me down in this world and the background of my hometown of Nicodemus gave me the strength to continue to be the person I am today. On a serious note, the love we have for one another could not come because of the color of our skin. Some of us probably would've married each other if it wasn't for that.

Richard Van Loenen ('56) broke the ice and confessed to incidents involving teachers and students at a reunion in 2016:

> A snake was wrapped around the steering wheel in one female teacher's car. The snake fell in her lap while she was driving. I never knew what happened to that woman!
>
> We put two baby possums in the drawers of Miss Brungardt's desk. We were only a few minutes into class when she opened one of the drawers and discovered the varmint. She screamed, and the boys were instructed to dispose of the animal. They took it by the tail and carried it out. It was only a few minutes later when she opened the other drawer and we went through the drill again!

The more Richard shared, the more another classmate in attendance at the reunion, Steve Cooksey ('56), denied having anything to do with any of it.

The father of Debbie Gustafson Wilson ('75), Eric Gustafson, was the principal when she was in high school. It was an era of short and then shorter skirts and long hair and Afros. She and classmate Gil Alexander ('75) each tested the school policies and rules. Her recollections at the 2016 school reunion were recorded by Marlyss Gustafson Yelton ('58):

> Some classes said their high school years revolved around the dress code. I was fortunate enough to live with the principal and had double scrutiny. We pushed the borders on the length of skirts. I had to "scrunch" down when I saw Connie Worcester, an upperclassman coming, as she carried a ruler with her to come up behind other girls to measure the distance between their knees and their hems!
>
> My love for teaching today came especially from Mr. Bob Hooper (English) and Mrs. Mary Lou Pennington (elementary teacher).

Gil Alexander would not be outdone—he said they were so caught up on the length of hair, it had to be so many inches above the collar. He never had any problem with the length, but it was a lot of work to keep his Afro up and out. He was called in to Mr. Gustafson's office, but he was ready with his handbook in hand with the hair requirements underlined. He showed Mr. Gustafson the handbook, which said nothing about the width of hair, only the length. Mr. Gustafson finally said, "Get out of here!" He also relayed his one claim to a "civil rights sit-in protest" on the football field bleachers for the school not celebrating Martin Luther King Day by dismissing school. It was mighty uncomfortable sitting out on those bleachers in January! But Gil guessed he got his point across since sometime after, they started celebrating the holiday with the day off.

Kim Stephen Nutting ('74) said that the school only celebrated the holiday every other year as the off-year was for President's Day, which brought the remark from Gil that he guessed he would just have to have another protest!

Gil also said that their class of twelve—which consisted of three black boys, three white boys, three black girls, three white girls—should have made the national TV and news because it was the "perfect" class. Someone then reminded him that there were also three Irby's in the class and he said he knew there was some reason it wasn't considered the perfect class.

Robert Thompson ('67), the youngest brother of Tom Thompson ('55) of the long touchdown fame, graduated from the eighth grade in the spring of 1963. Rob remembers the following:

. . . attending our graduation was the high school coach, Larry Ward. Immediately after the ceremony he cornered all of the boys and asked how many of us would come out for football in the fall. Being ignorant of what really did lie ahead of us, enough of the class said yes. Mr. Ward needed to know so he could schedule games with other schools. That fall we started school and football with I believe ten players to play eight-man football. Needless to say, we didn't win any games. The following year we beat Woodston a team that was as young and about as inexperienced as we were. By our Junior and Senior years, we were a pretty good team. We even helped Alton to a Kansas record for wins in our class. That may have been our only loss those two years. Many of us can say we played every minute of every game, offense and defense, for four years. I played center and middle linebacker all four years. Getting knocked around as a freshman center by a bully named Butch from Morland made me wish I was an end. Putting on some weight and learning some techniques made us all feel like stars and we so depended on each other.

What I remember and think about still today is the feeling that I was attending school, not with other classmates, but with a feeling that I went to school with my brothers and sisters. In a school with maybe thirty students total, you participated in everything. You went to the Junior-Senior Prom for four years; you lettered in every sport for four years; you were in choir for four years; and you were in the Junior-Senior play for four years. Our class even had a

classmate's mother graduate with us. Iva Lee Switzer ('67) attended several classes with us our senior year to get her diploma. This was a lady that had five children: Norma Jean ('65), two years ahead of us; Louis ('67), in our class; Tom ('69), a freshman at that time; and Earlice ('72) and Philip were in grade school. She had the courage and desire to finish what she had started years before.

Dianna Stephen Hart ('71) recalled the following:

My cousin, Jolene Kenyon Alexander ('69) and I had taken piano lessons so were able to play for the girls' glee club and mixed choir. We went to regional and state music contests and came home with top ratings. I played the tenor saxophone all four years. The band marched at the Kansas State Fair, but I got to carry the bass drum since I had rhythm and could beat loudly.

A Pep bus was always provided for out-of-town ball games. We studied on the way to the games and sang on the way home.

I loved learning to type on manual typewriters. Typing and office practice were my favorite classes. These classes put me on the track of becoming summer secretary at a law office, at a bank, and the business department at Fort Hays State. It led me to career as a business teacher for thirty-nine and a half years. Teachers were the best at Bogue High School. I was always motivated and my transition to Fort Hays State went smoothly.

Our favorite pastimes were dragging Main in my friend's 1955 Chevy (granted, Main was only four blocks long), going camping at the sand pit, playing cards, and going to movies in Hill City on the weekends.

Finally, a Trip to State—The State Tournament in basketball eluded Bogue High in both 1966 and 1967 with regional's final losses to Luray in 1966 and Jewell in 1967. A win was the ultimate pinnacle for any small school. The chance did come in 1976 as the Bogue Bluejays were crowned state champions in eight-man football. Members of that championship team were Greg Stephen ('77), Mike Davignon ('77), Tim Thompson ('77), Brice Hooper ('77), David Gustafson ('77), Arnold Carter ('77), Bryan Van Loenen ('77), David Towns ('78), Dan Irby, and Phil Switzer. Just one year later, in 1977, with so few boys on the team, two girls—Tammy Thompson and Tina Irby—suited up for the team so that there were enough players for the eight-man team. They were the first high school girl football players in the state of Kansas. When two very serious injuries occurred midway into the season, the final six games were forfeited.

Another All Big Eight player to come from Bogue was Marvin Switzer ('73) who played for the Kansas State Wildcats. He later played professionally for the Buffalo Bills.

Closing Bogue High School—After graduation in May 1978, a vote of the community passed by eight to close the high school. A total of 499 graduated from Bogue Rural High School from 1923-1978. The last to receive a diploma was David Towns ('78) (alphabetically) in a graduating class of three. In the school's fifty-six years, the most numerous surnames were Irby-22, Kenyon-18, Alexander-18, Jones-16, Desbien-15, Gosselin-13, Van Loenen-12, Stephen-10, Davignon-8, Switzer-7, Johnson-7, Beecher-7, Elliott-6, Conyac-5, Napue-5, Williams-4, Radcliff-4, and Young-4.

The final yearbook, published in 1978, was titled *Seasons in the Sun* with Tammy Thompson as the editor-in-chief. The worldwide musical hit from that time with the same name gave a close to this great school with the words:

> *We had joy, we had fun,*
> *We had seasons in the sun.*
> *But the joy and the fun,*
> *Like the seasons, have all gone.*

Bogue Rural High School
Graham County, KS

#13

B&B High School

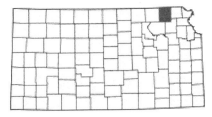

Mascot: Falcons

Colors: Blue and White

Year Closed: 2014

Location: town of Baileyville, Nemaha County

Unification of Two High Schools — This became a unified high school in 1964 when the high schools of St. Benedicts and Baileyville joined in one of the most harmonious mergers in Kansas. Due to declining enrollment and the State Consolidation Law of 1963, St. Benedicts and Baileyville began discussions. The school boards of both schools recommended unification and it was approved in a September 1964 election. The consolidation took place in July 1966.

A five-dollar prize was awarded to the pupil whose suggestion was chosen for the name of the new district. The school board reviewed all entries and voted by secret ballot. Students Bonnie Rogers and Steve Bergman of St. Benedicts, and Mary Beth Mache of Baileyville shared the prize money as their suggestion, B and B, won the vote. St. Benedicts and Baileyville schools would become a legend known as "B&B."

The unification of these two schools brought together two predominantly German and Catholic towns. Excerpts from the school board minutes provide a unique perspective of some of the interesting decisions, budgeting, and finer details of governing in a school district.

1966
July 5 - Board approved budget of $230,000
Aug 1 - Discussion on purchase of a portable class room for St. Benedicts at the grade school at cost of $11,000
Sept 20 - Coach granted permission to purchase lumber to build seats for the football field
Nov 29 - Decided to paint the new shop building blue trimmed with white
1967
Feb 21 - Revised salary schedule to $5,200 base salary for beginning teachers
Apr 3 - In an effort to prevent the delinquency of students in the district, the Board unanimously adopted a policy that any pupil who went downtown or to the filling station before or after school without the written permission of his parents would be subject to a three day suspension from school.
Aug 7 - Decided that buses should pick up all children so they can arrive at school by 8:30. Mass should be held after school is dismissed in the afternoon and during daylight saving time.

Sep 18 - Agreed to pay four cents per mile from school district funds of actual miles traveled by football students driving to and from practice through the use of carpools.

1968

Jan 30 - Meeting with priests to discuss the request of the teaching nuns to be paid on a 100% basis of the salary schedule. Father suggested the Board meet with Mother Superior and attempt a compromise between the current 80% and 100%

June 27 - Decided the wives of the Board of Education would be in charge of purchasing and rental of the textbooks

Oct 17 - Decided the next pay check of a teacher who is not paying their lunch be held until payment is received in full

1969

Jul 17 - "Do we want kindergarten" ballots were cast with 135 patrons in attendance voting 45 in favor and 85 opposed. The Board recessed and returned voting unanimously in favor of Kindergarten, but due to the mandate of the patrons by a 2 to 1 vote against kindergarten, the Board Decided not to implement kindergarten for next school term.

1970

Feb 23 - Negotiated agreement to set the base salary at $6300. The maximum salary for a master's degree plus 15 hours and 14 years of experience was $9300. Teaching nuns' salaries were set at 95% of the salary schedule

Jun 19 - Approved obtaining a driver's education car

Jun 29 - Voted by secret ballot to purchase a calculator was approved with 3 in favor, 2 opposed, and 1 abstaining

1971

May 1 - Field trip policies were established: only one field trip per student or Instructor per year; not to exceed 100 miles one way; adequately sponsored with 2 faculty per class and two adult couples; proof of educational value must be submitted for prior approval; trip schedule must be submitted one week prior and no shopping centers allowed

1973

Mar 21 - Agreed to tell both parishes to prepare the Kindergarten classrooms, agreed the District would pay for the cost of student physicals

Academic Highlights — Scholarship was a hallmark of B&B. Dr. August Bergman donated the first $25,000 to start the fund for the creation of the B&B challenge, later named the B&B Legacy Scholarship. This went to B&B graduates.

The Scholars Bowl teams started in 1985 under the direction of Mrs. Barbara Vitt. B&B originally called these "Quiz Bowl" teams and held contests with neighboring schools. The team also traveled to Topeka to participate in High Q contests sponsored by Washburn University and WIBW each year. Those contests were held from 1985-2005. The program was renamed "Quest" in 2005 and B&B placed 2nd in 1-A in 2011. In 1987, the competitions became a KSHSAA sponsored activity. B&B hosted the regional competition and qualified for and attended their first state meet taking 4th place. That was the first of eight trips to state Scholars Bowl meets for the Falcons. They finished 6th in 2012.

B&B was always very competitive in Scholars Bowl league competition and had a three-peat (three years in a row) in league in the early 2000s. In the last year as a high school, B&B tied for first out of 313 high schools in Kansas for the State Assessment Tests.

Clubs and Organizations—In fifty years, some of the B&B Clubs were Kayettes, Latin Club, Drama Club, Ecology Club, Photography Club, Drill Team, Future Homemakers of America, Family Career and Community Leaders of America, Scholars Bowl, Forensics, Future Business Leaders of America, and SADD. Not only was there student participation, but a dedicated teacher led each of these clubs.

Music and band, under the leadership of Mr. Gene Barrett, got the students involved in parades and performances. They won awards for best band at the St. Joseph Apple Blossom Parade. The band won an award for excellence at the American Royal three times. There were Band Days at KSU and KU. "The band was known far and wide for its great marching and pep band performances, especially in the late 80s and 90s," said Mr. Barrett. He said the greatest performance was in Seneca in 1996 when seventy-seven B&B students, grades 7-12, performed in festivities for Ed Broxterman ('92).

Broxterman, a B&B graduate and KSU track squad member, competed in the 1996 Summer Olympics in Atlanta, bringing the community alive with excitement. The sign at the bridge reads, "Home of Olympian Ed B." Broxterman qualified for the Olympic competition in high jump with a qualifying jump of 7' 6.5".

Athletics—Regarding state championships, Coach Lary Anerson said in 1978, "[State,] A place I've always wanted to go to . . . something I've always waited to experience . . . a world I've waited to become a part of, a big coliseum to play round ball in, a dream that became a

reality for our guys." And state would be the goal for every sports team thereafter. No state tournament in boys and girls basketball, girls volleyball or boys football would be complete without the B&B Falcons as a participant and frequently the state champions of the sport. The "three peat" in volleyball and the final year to win state in football were some of the crowning glories. Bus trips for regionals, sub-state, and state were annual events.

This B&B Athletic Legacy was shared by Mrs. Barbara Vitt (counselor and Scholar Bowl leader): "A legacy is not born but is built upon hard work and determination."

Declining Enrollment—From the first year as a district in 1966 through 2011, the budget went from $230,000 to $1,609,506 and the enrollment in grades 1-12 from 460 to 171.

From 1966 to 2014 a total of 1236 received diplomas as B&B Falcon graduates. The top twenty surnames made up nearly 56% of all the graduates. They were Schmidt-83, Deter-63, Stallbaumer-55, Holthaus-55, Sudbeck-47, Bergman-47, Haug-42, Buessing-34, Rottinhaus-34, Broxterman-29, Havercamp-27, Strathman-25, Dallinghaus-22, Hummingbake-19, Mache-18, Huling-16, Meyer-14, Reiniche-14, and Fangman-12. The last graduate (alphabetically) from B&B was Nichole Sudeck in 2014.

The students from this district now attend the Nemeha Valley School in Seneca.

B&B High School
Nemaha County, KS

#14

Geuda Springs High School

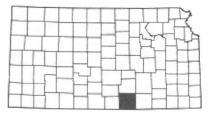

Mascot: Warriors

Colors: Purple and Gold, 1957 changed to Red and White

Year Closed: 1962

Location: town of Gueda Springs, Sumner County at county line of Cowley County

An Early Kansas Summer Health Resort — The Arkansas River runs near to the east of Gueda Springs. The village of Salt City was adjacent, and its chief attractions were the salt and mineral springs. There were two railroads that passed through the town, the Kansas Southwestern and the Midland Valley.

From an article in *Sumner Press*, dated January 1, 1880:

> During the past season over 300 invalids sought relief from these healing waters and mans wonderful cures are well attested. A stone hotel and bath house are being erected and before another decade rolls by Salt City will be a famous summer resort.

And from *Sumner Press*, dated May 25, 1882:

> At the springs, Illinois seems to furnish the largest number of visitors after Kansas, and there were at least a dozen persons from the Sucker State who were either boarding or keeping house and in almost every instance they claimed to be benefited. There are people here from Kansas City, St. Louis, Philadelphia, and in fact from every part of the country . . . the baths are as good as any in the country, and I can see no reason why Geuda will not be a good town as nature has done more for the spot than any other place in the world. The salt works are using 100 vats and will add another 100 this summer.

The springs at Geuda changed hands several times from 1873 into the 1930s. Clinton R. Mitchell became the sole owner in 1881. New hotels and bath houses were built and the springs were becoming very popular. Mitchell later served in the Kansas House of Representatives. He became the chairman of the first Board of Regents in Kansas. He not only helped establish the major universities in Kansas, but also helped organize the school district in Sumner County.

The Oklahoma Land Rush of 1893 took businesses and people away from the area. A fire in 1908 destroyed many buildings in town.

A side note: gun slinger Luke Short died in one of Geuda's hotels. He was staying at the Gilbert Hotel taking treatments for dropsy. Short was a friend of Wyatt Earp and Bat Masterson. He had shot several men and sold whisky to Sioux Indians.

School Timeline — The Geuda Springs School District was organized in 1876 and classes took place in various town buildings. In 1883, a brick building was constructed on South Second Street. In 1913, finding the building unsafe, this old building was torn down and a new more modern school was erected. The school board found that the condition of the old school building was so unsafe that they decided to have a new building erected. Work commenced about the middle of April. The plan was to have the building ready for fall 1913. The new school was built of vitrified brick and cost $11,000. It was two stories, with three classrooms each on the first and second floors. The basement contained the auditorium with a seating capacity of 250, and also a library. The new school had an enrollment of 147 pupils in the first year. A gymnasium was added in 1927. Some reports were that Dr. James H. Stallard donated the money for the building. The school became a four-year school in 1926-27. The first class had two graduates.

Athletics — Boys sports included basketball, baseball, and track, while girls sports consisted of only of basketball. Oxford was the arch rival. There was no football except for a short time starting in 1952-53. When a player broke his arm in 1955, the mothers of the students rallied to have the sport discontinued. Some of the towns played were Oxford, Bluff City, Cambridge, Latham, Atlanta,

Grenola, Dexter, Argonia, Milan, South Haven, and May-field, all in Kansas, and Kaw City, Oklahoma.

School Trivia—The senior trip in 1950 was to Colorado with six seniors. The principal and his wife, Mr. and Mrs. Falls, were the sponsors for the trip. The 1955 and 1958 classes would go to Lake Takoma in Missouri.

There was no music department in the high school.

The buses were driven by the senior boys who also provided bus maintenance.

An outstanding athlete, Francis "Tuffy" Swanson ('55) ran the mile at the state track meet. He would run to school on the railroad track bridge because the bridge over the Arkansas River was washed out. He was still running with his grandchildren well into his sixties.

Ronald "Dick Tracy" Smith recalled the following:

Larry Payne and I would let the air out of tires and drive on the railroad tracks to Oxford and South Haven some twenty miles away. We got off the tracks, cruised around town, and would either come back by the rail or drive the country roads.

School Closing—The school was closed after the 1962 graduation and became unified with their arch rival, Oxford. The students were bused to Oxford. The last class had nine graduates. Robert Webb ('62) (alphabetically) was the last to receive a diploma from Geuda Springs High School.

There were 303 graduates from Geuda Springs High School in the thirty-six years from 1927-1962. The most numerous surnames of the graduates were Rutter-13, Swaim-8, Nugren-6, Paton-6, Randall-6, and Smith-6.

Gueda Springs High School
Sumner County, KS

#15

Protection High School

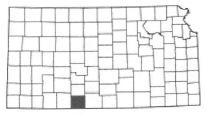

Mascot: Blue Panther

Colors: Blue and White

Year closed: 1999

Location: town of Protection, far western edge of Comanche County, fourteen miles from the Oklahoma border

Subscription School Beginnings — As was common in the settlement of prairie towns, the first schools were held in community buildings until a school could be built. The town newspaper, the *Protection Echo,* beginning June 1, 1885, reported the names of nineteen students and one teacher that comprised the first school. The names were quite interesting and representative of the times. The teacher was Mr. E.C. Clayton and students were Isaac Climer, Johnie Connaughton, Albert and Bertha Hager, Maudie Hutson, Dora Kidd, Stella and Rufus Manning, Wilke and Alberty Myers, Willie Pearson, Belle Emma, Johnnie, George and Allie Square, Susie and Eddie Tomlin, and Willie Vance.

Much of the following information was compiled by David West, Marge Sangster, and Evelyn Hoch for a book published in 1981 by the Comanche County Historical Society.

Classes were held on the first floor of the new two-story town hall. The newspaper was printed upstairs. Mr. Clayton's school was by subscription, as was common in other schools in the county. Since the school closed for hot weather the newspaper reminded patrons in August to be prompt in making payments to the teacher. A second subscription school opened in September 1885, by Miss Minnie Curl.

Public High School — The first public school opened in 1887 with enrollment of 22 boys and 29 girls. Protection High School was started in 1909. The boys in that freshman class were interested in only one sport, the all-American game of baseball. Boys basketball was introduced in 1911.

In the fall of 1912, the high school and first four grades were housed in a frame building, and other classes were held in a new frame house built by Rocky Bayless. In 1913 a two-story brick building was built to house the high school and some of the elementary grades. That year was eventful as a third teacher, Miss Evelyn Cox, was added to the faculty, joining Professor Davis and Mrs. Clark.

Blue and white were chosen for the school colors. (The mascot became the Panther in the 1940s.) The school became accredited by the State University and passed under the Barnes Law which allowed for rural high school formation and to receive county tax aid. The first graduating class of three graduates was in 1913. Basketball and baseball were of great interest for the boys in all classes. The cup was won in the Triangle league between Protection, Greensburg, and Bucklin.

In 1914 the track team coached by Mr. Dale Davis took the first-place cup in another Triangle league formed by Dodge City, Protection, and Bucklin. Football was introduced in 1916.

Early graduates were also talented in other fields. Charles Sibbitt ('15) went from Protection High School, with an enrollment of forty-five students, to Kansas University. He graduated Phi Beta Kappa. Margaret Hind Cox ('17) became a member of the American Grand Opera Company and was a soloist at St. Patrick's Cathedral in New York City.

By 1919 there were eighty-four students in high school. The next year the freshman class had seventy-four students, which was the largest in the school's history. This was indicative of the growth in the town and surrounding farms in the second decade of the 20th century.

A new high school was built in 1930. This spectacular architectural building was designed by architects Routledge and Hertz from Hutchinson in Late Gothic Revival style. A new addition to the high school in 1959 housed the gymnasium, shop, and music room. The building was placed on the National Register of Historic Places in 2005.

The 1939 class, with thirty-five graduates, was the largest to graduate from the new high school and the first to enjoy a senior trip. They traveled to Carlsbad Caverns in New Mexico in the back of Charlie Leeper's truck. Old car seats were put in to accommodate the passengers and a tarp protected them from the elements. There was motor trouble while on this ten-day trip. A student mechanic, Edwin Rainbolt, was able to get it going again. Money was scarce, so the group fixed most of their own food. Superintendent Kirkhart, Lucy Landon, and Lewis Stoelzing sponsored the trip.

Athletics & Activities — Annual football games were played with Ashland on the afternoon of Armistice Day and Coldwater on the afternoon of Thanksgiving. Other primary opponents were schools along the railroad that stretched from Wichita to Englewood. Two passenger trains ran daily, and in the early years, fans would travel by train to the away games in Spivey, Norwich, Coats, Wilmore, Coldwater, Ashland, and Englewood.

Train travel to games had ended in the early 1940s when many boys were called into service before they could finish high school. Football players traveled to games in cars driven by their fathers because there were no activity buses due to gas rationing. Boys were released from school to help their dads on the farm. Teachers were hard to find. One year there were as many as seven different teachers for one subject.

Perhaps the best all-around athlete to attend Protection High School was Melvin "Mutt" Thornhill ('25). He excelled in all sports, especially baseball. He went on to Kansas University where he starred on the track team. Thornhill was invited to take part in the 1928 Summer Olympics, but wasn't able to afford to travel to Amsterdam. He was a close friend of legendary KU basketball coach Forrest "Phog" Allen. Other notable athletes from

Protection High School included Delane "Skip" Wool-folk ('52), who was outstanding in track and set records in the javelin and shot-put events. Gary Girk ('61) was named All-American High School in Football in 1961.

As well as football, organizations included Kay and Kayette Clubs. In years before World War II, the band and music department, under the direction of Robert Helman, earned high ratings at state contests. In addition to maintaining high academic standards many extracurricular activities were offered.

The 1960 football team was the first undefeated Protection team in 30 years. The 1978 football squad took the state title in Class A. The football team repeated with a state championship in eight-man division in 1983. The girls basketball team won the state championships in 1975, 1978, and 1979.

Notable Alumni

Harold Shields Herd ('36) was a Washburn Law school graduate who became a Kansas Supreme Court Justice.

John "Big Jack" Ashcraft ('16) and his younger brother Francis Ashcraft ('24) were well-known pilots during the days of "barnstorming." Both perished in airplane crashes during the 1920s.

Stan Herd ('68) left his family's three generation farmstead to become a renowned earthworks artist.

Nathan Leeper ('96) (grandnephew of Charlie Leeper, the owner of the 1939 senior sneak truck) went on to be a world class and Olympic high jumper. He starred at Dodge City Junior College and Kansas State University. After winning the US indoor and outdoor titles in 2001 and 2002, he appeared on the *Late Show with David Letterman*.

Closing Protection High School

USD 300 was the only school district in Kansas that covered all of one county (Comanche) and parts of two others (Clark, Kiowa). The high school closed following graduation in May 1999. In the eighty-seven years from 1913-1999, a total of 1,424 graduated from Protection Rural High School. The most common surnames of the graduates were Herd-33, Jellison-29, Riner-25, Edmonston-24, Leeper-24, Moore-24, Smith-24, Petty-21, Sanders-21, Maris-19, Selzer-18, Eubank-17, Hazen-17, Hopkins-16, Lindsay-16, Sangster-16, Webster-16, Young-16, Baker-15, Morton-15, Miller-14, Williams-14, Brown-13, Park-13, Rowland-13, Webb-13, Zimmerman-13, Dale-12, Woolfolk-12, Dowling-11, Filson-11, Martin-11, McGee-11, McLaughlin-11, Norton-11, Rich-11, Schultz-11, Shrauner-11, Thomas-11, Wymer-11, Thornhill-11.

The last class had fourteen graduates with Tyler Woolfolk (alphabetically) being the last to receive a diploma. The next year students would attend the reorganized district of South Central High School in Coldwater and Ashland High School.

Protection High School (image 1999—courtesy of Dave Webb) Comanche County, KS

#16

Kanarado High School

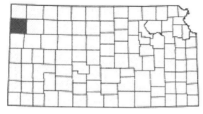

Mascot: Bears

Colors: Green and White

Year Closed: 1969

Location: Sherman County, one mile from the Colorado border

From the *Goodland News Republic* on July 7, 1905:

Educated interests of Kanarado have been well fostered as a two story brick school building, having two large rooms, in each of which a teacher is employed every year is proof that this district has been maintaining one of the greatest things possible in any community-a good school . . . The course of study includes work from the primary up to and including the ninth grade, which gives a graduate of that school a year's advanced standing going into the Sherman County high school.

The Sherman County High School was in Goodland, sixteen miles east. Students who continued for additional high school education had to travel to Goodland by horse or buggy. Some boarded in Goodland with people who took students into their homes to live during the school term.

US Highway 24 at one time ran down the main street of the town but was replaced in the 1960s by Interstate 70 which skirts the city on the south.

Kanarado's School History—The first school in Kanarado was called the Glen Himes School and may have been built on land that was donated by Mr. Himes. A picture of this school house taken in 1915 was captioned "the old and new school" with a new school house in the foreground. The new school burned down in 1919. It was replaced in 1921 to become the third school in Kanarado.

In 1949 a one-story high school was built. Classes were held in this building until the high school was closed in 1969. An account in the *Sherman County Herald* on September 1, 1949, detailed the new $155,000 consolidated school:

One of the finest consolidated school buildings is under construction in Kanarado, Kansas. The new school is a one-story T-shaped brick and concrete structure. Directly opposite the main entrance is the auditorium -gymnasium, which is 88' x 68' court for basketball. It has a seating capacity for 500 persons. There is also a large stage with a music storage room on one side and an athletic storage room on the other. There were seven new classrooms on the eastern division of the wing with two restrooms. On the west wide side of the main entrance are located the superintendent's office, teachers, office, reception room, class room, science room, and boiler room. Back of the gym and stage are the vocational agriculture shop and a classroom. West of the gym are located the cafeteria and kitchen. The kitchen will also be used for the home economics classes. Enrollment in the new school will be approximately sixty in the high school and a hundred forty in the grade school. Several of the eastern Colorado rural schools and one rural school in Wallace County are also planning to send their students to the new consolidated school.

Sports Teams — Football began in 1922 with William L. Law as the coach. There was an eleven-man team until the early 1950s when, due to smaller enrollment, a six-man football team was started. Track was initiated to replace baseball in the spring months. Just before closing of the high school, golf became a sport to replace track.

One former student shared that during his high school days (1954-1958) the schools their teams played against included Arapahoe and Cheyenne Wells in Colorado, and Weskan, Sharon Springs, Winona, Gem, Rexford, Bird City, McDonald, Edson, and Brewster in Kansas.

The girls program consisted of basketball only with the first team in 1929. During a few years, the only schools played were Edson and Brewster. The program was then discontinued until the advent of Title 9 when basketball was again initiated. The 1966 girls team played a full schedule and was undefeated.

The school mascot was the Kubs until 1949-50 when the mascot was changed to the Bears. The junior high team had been the Midgets, but it assumed the Kubs mascot at this time. The school colors were black and orange until 1953 when they were changed to green and white.

A school song sang to the tune of "Put on our old gray bonnet" was:

> *Put on your old black sweater*
> *With the big orange letter*
> *And we'll help Kanarado win the game*
> *Down the floor they will take it*
> *And a goal they'll make it*
> *As we cheer them on their way.*

A later school song was to the tune of "On Wisconsin":

> *On Kanarado, On Kanarado*
> *Fight to win this game*
> *Put the ball right through the goalpost*
> *Touchdown sure this time, rah, rah, rah*
> *K A N A R A D O*
> *Is how we spell our name*
> *Fight fellows fight, fight, fight*
> *And win this game.*

Early Consolidation Efforts — Western Star was a county school located fifteen miles south of Kanarado in northern Wallace County. It was consolidated and closed in 1949, and the rural students were bused to school in Kanarado.

Hazel Estes ('54) shared a typical school day experience:

There were three bus routes bringing students to Kanarado. The bus our family rode picked us up at 7:40 in the morning. Getting on the bus at that time meant getting up around 5:00 to milk a bunch of cows, do the milk separating, feeding the hogs before breakfast, jostling in line with four siblings and one bathroom to get to the bus on time! We got home from school about 4:30, grabbed a bit of a snack, milked the cows again, separated milk, fed the hogs again—all before supper. Then it was homework time and to bed by 8:00! The country kids did not have time to do school pranks, but two of my favorites I remember were outdoor toilets upset or put in Main Street intersections or the brave one, climbing the water tower to write their name.

1920s and 1930s Teaching Conditions — The following list is of teachers and teacher salaries for the Western Star School (District #45):

Mildred Simpson 1923
Arthur McKinley 1924
Vivian Utterback 1925 ($90/month)
Melrose Barton 1926 ($100/month)
Helen Motsinger 1927 ($90/month)
Helen Motsinger 1928 ($100/month)
Harriet Esson 1929 ($100/month)
Luella Gorsuck 1930 ($100/month)
Luella Gorsuck 1931 ($110/month)
Florence Hays 1932 ($70/month)
Fern Lowe 1933 ($40/month)
Wm. Stewart 1934 ($45/month)
Albert Beckley 1935 ($45/month)

Often these teachers lived with a family in the rural area and paid room and board. In addition to teaching, other duties included building the fire, taking out the ashes, cleaning the building, and sometimes hauling kids to and from school. Some teachers would have to teach five or six different grade levels.

Beginning to End — The first graduate from Kanarado High School was Reed Bogart in a class of five in 1922. The last graduate was Nancy Wright in a class of eight in 1969. There were 539 graduates from Kanarado High School in the 48 years from 1922 until the school closed in 1969. The most numerous surnames of the Kanarado graduates were Jones-15, Wright-11, Pettibone-11, Middleton-10, and Burd-10.

Earlier students attending Kanarado and graduating from Goodland High School before the upper three grades were added were Lula Germann ('09), Walter Germann ('10), Walter Wright ('18), and Creston Cramer ('19). LuLa Germann would come back to teach in Kanarado and is pictured in a 1915 school photo. These names are included in the total Kanarado graduate numbers.

1949 Illustration of the New Kanarado High School
Sherman County, KS

#17

Delia Rural High School

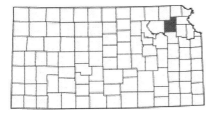

Mascot: Bulldogs

Colors: Green and White

Year Closed: 1966

Location: town of Delia, extreme southwest corner of Jackson County

What Came Before—The town of Delia came into being later than many in the region when it was established in 1905. Delia is located on the then-branch of the Topeka Northwestern railroad which ran from Topeka to Marysville. The town was originally named David on one side of the track, after David Cunningham, and Delia on the other side of the track, after David's mother.

In September 1874, the county superintendent came from Holton and organized District 54. The first board members were David Cunningham, Mike Murray, and Thomas Hanrahan. The district was the first public school in the southwest corner of Jackson County.

Laverne Zlantik ('47) recalled the following:

> The first school was a log cabin. About 1880 the school was built on the Michael Murry farm, and it became known as the Murry School. As students were mostly Irish and Czech with a few others thrown in, the great experiment was started to see if people could learn a common language. They did learn to live together, each respecting the ancestry of the other. There were hurdles to cross, and to this day, there are still some animosities between certain parties. As a community and like the entire country, they became another melting pot in the world.

New Town, New School—With the construction of the new towns of Delia and David in 1905, there was much politicking as to whether the school should be moved to Delia. Newspaper articles and advertisements of the time indicate that there were those who felt that the school should not be removed from a rural environment and that the students should not be exposed to the "sins" of the new city. After a close bond election, the electors voted to move the school to town. There was a faction that thought the town should be named Murry, and when the new school was built, it retained the name, Murry School, through 1911. School was held for a term of three months as decided by the voters. Mike Devine was hired as the first teacher for $35.00 a month.

In 1908, a two-room school building was built on the present school grounds. It served District 54 until 1928 when the present grade school was built. The old building would not accommodate the enrollment of over 100 pupils. Today (2018) it is a private residence.

The new grade school building cost $11,000, and Mrs. Roy Murry was the first principal in the new building. This continued to be the grade school for the next thirty-eight years. In the spring of 1913 a township meeting was held in Delia to discuss the organization of a high school. The result was the voting of $8,000 in bonds for the high school. The 1928 grade school was in use until the high school came to an end in 1966, closed due to unification and state mandates. The high school classrooms were then altered to fit grade school standards.

Washington Township High School — On September 14, 1914, Washington Township organized a high school with E. Curran McCormick, Jr. of Chicago as the first principal and Miss Maude L. Darby as assistant. Mr. McCormick also served as the janitor. The first high school board was made of J.H. McClain, Dr. Frisbey, and W.T. Dowling. The first classes were held upstairs over Bryan's store. They had neither desks nor books, but after a few days, the desks arrived and regular work began. They moved into the new building in January 1915. The true pioneer spirit was so successful that the results of the term included publishing the first annual, *The Shamrock*. A coat of arms was chosen as well as the school colors and songs, literary and science organizations. A domestic department was established, as well as the founding of a loyal school spirit.

Twenty-four students attended that first year. On April 13, 1915, the citizens planted twenty-three trees along the school property. The trees on the north side of the west yard entrance were dedicated to Mr. McCormick (the janitor). The tree south of the entrance was dedicated to Miss Darby (assistant principal). On May 28, 1915, Louis Cowan became the first graduate.

The second school year opened on September 4, 1915, with the same teachers and thirty-four students. The term closed on May 26, 1916, with four graduates.

Ties to a Renowned Kansas Citizen — Helen Frisbey Tollefson ('22), whose father was on the school board and the doctor in town, wrote an account of a Kansas renowned citizen:

> Dr. James Naismith substituted in many churches in eastern Kansas. I remember him especially because he had been coaching basketball at KU when Dad (Dr. WR Frisbery) was at Washburn about 1900. Naismith went up to Topeka to teach the Washburn coach and the Topeka YMCA how to play basketball. A team was formed at each place. Dad was on the first team to play at Washburn and got to know Dr. Naismith. When he came to Delia to preach, they renewed acquaintance and he often spent Sundays with us. Naismith was a great man in many ways besides athletics. He supplied Delia and Rossville churches, something they should be proud of. Not every church has had such a world-known man as a pastor.

Mrs. Tollefson reminisced that because KU had no dorms in 1923, her folks were reluctant to let her transfer from Washburn, so Dr. Naismith found a room for her at the Presbyterian Youth Center in Lawrence.

The years of World War I found the affairs of Washington Township High School directed by women: Sarah Porter Risser, Ruth Whitaker, and Rachel McCoy. The high school at this time boasted a football team coached by the grade school principal, Mr. Neece.

A new auditorium and gymnasium were completed in 1927. This gymnasium, with its high ceiling, was the nicest in the area, and many tournaments were held there because surrounding schools had very low ceilings and the out of bounds line was right at the walls.

By 1928 there were fifty-two students enrolled. Special Manual Arts Training, Domestic Science, and Commerce were parts of the curriculum. Glee clubs and high school orchestra allowed all to enjoy musical training.

During the early years of the high school, there were Jackson County Literary and Athletic contests held separately between the schools. The whole county was involved in the competition from 1913 to 1925. The towns involved in the competition were Circleville, Delia, Denison, Holton, Hoyt, Mayetta, Netawaka, Soldier, and Whiting. Of all of these schools, Delia had the lowest enrollment. The following are a few excerpts taken from a report that involved Delia students:

1913-Delia, the smallest school, excelled in yells and school spirit with 31 persons attending.

1918- Vincent Problislo and Steven Simecka won the "loving Cup" for their Literary Abilities.

1919-Delia had the largest proportion of students from the prior year. It was noted that George DeBacker has the making of an excellent athlete. George won the Broad jump with 20 feet 5 inches. Delia won the double quartet singing completion.

1920-Delia won 16 points [at the track meet] but had poor attendance due to the poor roads. None of the roads were graveled and due to two days of rain were just two deep ruts going down the middle of the road. George DeBacker placed first in the 50 yard dash.

Cecile Thompson Zlantick ('23) reminisced, "A high school education in the early 1920s was a privilege, an opportunity which usually demanded sacrifice and dedication on the part of parents and students. For scholars from rural areas, it frequently meant renting a room in town and "batching" from Sunday evening until Friday afternoon. As in other small towns boasting a high school, many Delia families rented spare bedrooms as sleeping rooms for students. We'd bring food from home—bread, cured meat, and canned fruits—and it lasted all week."

Cecile attended the High Prairie Grade School where as many as forty students crowded into the one room school. She remembered, "It had a good library for a country school, so you could always read and not get into mischief."

Cecile took the Normal Training Course and earned a teacher's certificate. She became the heart and soul of every organization in Delia from her church, the E.H.U., and school, serving on the school board for many years and on the Kaw Valley Unified school board following unification and the closure of the high school in 1966.

Some School Trivia by Year—In 1936 the school installed a radio in the study hall for the students to listen to the World Series. Some of the last magazines on the racks were *Pathfinder*, *Gygeria*, and *National Geographic*. The public speaking class presented a three-act play, "Berties' Cave Women." The grand prize at the carnival for the year was a dog and a $10.00 dog house.

The year 1936-37 was a good year for bargains. Mr. Paige advertised baseballs for five cents each. At the Cozy Café in downtown Delia, one could buy a hamburger for five cents or a complete meal for thirty-five cents.

The new green and white corduroy basketball suits arrived, but they did not seem to help much as the team lost to Silver Lake in basketball by a score of 74-10. The public speaking class debated the question, "Resolved, that it was better to live in the country than in the city."

In 1941-42, the Bulldogs started a track team. The Girls Glee Club was organized and they were busy practicing "Home Town," "Glow Worm, "and "Alice's Blue Gown." The whole school took a hike to the hay meadow and played "Spin the Bottle." The Student Council was organized and a constitution adopted.

In 1942-43, the "growling Bulldogs" beat Emmet by a score of 20-17, although half of Delia's team couldn't get to the game due to bad roads. The freshmen and sophomores debated the question, "Should the Japs be exterminated." Another debate question was the need for a phone in the school was discussed. One of the main reasons was the need to conserve gas due to rationing, and the students believed they could cut out many trips by car if only a phone was installed in the school.

Two new teachers came to the high school in the fall of 1942. The life of a freshman boy, Laverne Zlatnik, was greatly affected by one of these new teachers. The new English teacher was Dorothy Dooly. One day in English class, Laverne astonished her when he sang a number. "Where have you been, I didn't know you could sing too?" she announced. Not only did she teach, she also started a trio with Laverne Zlatnik singing, his cousin, Wanda Park, playing the clarinet, and Benjamin Simecka playing the saxophone. They played many places for community events and school recitals. Laverne sang two solos for the end of year operetta.

Laverne Zlantik '47 recalled, "There never was another teacher that inspired me like Miss Dooley. My final three years of high school were not memorable as Miss Dooley left after just that one year. I had the mumps at Christmas that year and was out of school for three weeks. Miss Dooley came to our farm and held my hand for 30 minutes while I was in bed and it really made a difference for me."

Now 92 years old, Laverne said, "I remember it like it was yesterday; she made a difference in my life."

In 1944-45, the school bought a magazine rack to relieve the congestion of too many magazines. The senior class held a successful sneak until the seniors missed their bus and had to spend Saturday night at the bus depot in Kansas City.

In 1953-54, it took five tries to find sufficient water for a new well on the high school property. Delia won its first Jackson County Baseball League Championship since 1928.

A New School for Delia — April 14, 1954, the high school burned, leaving only charred bricks. Classes continued at the grade school, city hall, vacant buildings in town, and at private homes. On September 7, 1956, the new school was dedicated. Nearly two years after the school burned, Delia High School again had a building of its own. This year saw the revival of six-man football.

The 1957-58 school year started with a football field addition on the south side of the school. The first home football game was played. Delia ended the season with no wins. The following season, Delia decided to go to eight-man football with the Jackpot League. (Jackson-Pottawatomi). In 1958-89, the school again lost all of its football games. News about a missile base, a $33 million project near Delia, was announced.

The End—In 1964-65 Delia had the highest enrollment in twenty-two years with forty-five students. In the school's last year, 1965-66, the senior class presented "We Dude It." With fourteen seniors, it was the largest graduating class in years. Delia Rural High School closed after graduation in May 1966.

The most common surnames of the graduates were Thompson-20, Simecka-20, Keller-12, and Hanrahan-10. There were 413 graduates in the 52 years from 1915-1966. The last graduate from Delia Rural High School was Shirley Thompson (alphabetically).

As the end of the high school came, a feeling of sadness was evident as the community thought of losing its school once again. Yet the citizens looked forward with the hope that unification would offer all the advantages which the educators felt it would, to give the children a better education.

18

Kincaid Rural High School

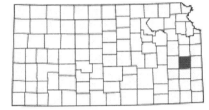

Mascot: Blue Devil

Colors: Royal Blue and White

Year Closed: 1967

Location: town of Kincaid, southeast corner of Anderson County

Town History—Since this was the second county in from Missouri, the county did not see the same bloodshed during the "Bleeding Kansas" days as did Linn County to the east. The years before and during the Civil War brought skirmishes between the proslavery groups from Missouri and the "Free-soil" abolitionists in the Kansas Territory.

In a Kincaid history collection titled *The First 100 Years*, the writer Albert Irwin writes that there were Indians still living in the area when the white settlers arrived. These were primarily the Kansas and Osage tribes. Indians would come to the settlers to do trading. Several Indians came to the Sam Irwin house in the 1871. One time they had an exceptionally large hindquarter of venison hanging on the saddle and back of a sweaty pony. They offered to trade the meat for the baby girl. Some remember that the baby was Emma Shields. No trade!

Railroads were expanding across the state with the new network of tracks. Villages would soon be platted, and settlers would come to places marked on maps with an "X". The term "grassroots" could have easily been used for these settlements. In 1885 Robert Kincaid was promoting plans for a railroad through Linn and Anderson Counties to be known as the St. Louis-Emporia railroad. Two years later the KATY (Missouri, Kansas, and Texas) was built on tracks from Parsons to Paola.

Early Education in Kincaid — The first school in Kincaid was private with thirty to forty students taught by Miss Molly Hardy. In 1889, School District #89 erected a two-story, four-room brick building. The brick in this building was fired from clay dug within the city limits of Kincaid. Over the course of the next twenty-five years this building became too small and was condemned because of material and construction deterioration.

In 1914, a new building was constructed on the same site. The first floor had the high school study hall, a large hallway, and two grade school classrooms. The second floor consisted of two classrooms on the west side and one on the east for high school classes and one classroom on the east for the grade school. That year the high school published its first school paper named *The Tattler*. It carried an editorial page, community news, and advertise-

ments. It was self-supporting and had money in its account for school needs.

From 1914-1916, special trains were run on the Missouri Pacific to Westphalia, Greeley, and Welda for county track meets. Banners and streamers decorated the two coaches, and even the locomotive was well adorned with a large red tin rooster that stood on the top of the steam dome.

In 1919, both grade and high schools had an unscheduled smallpox vacation. There was a smallpox case in town, and it was stopped as rapidly as it had started. Some had a small reaction to the vaccine that formed "the smallpox scar" and others became very ill from the vaccination.

The first recorded graduating class was in 1890 from a less than four-year school. In 1922, the first class of the newly formed, reorganized Kincaid Rural High School graduated.

Modern School — The high school moved to the new Kincaid Rural High School building in 1937 and left the old building for the grade school. The new building was made possible by a federal grant as well as some district funds. The cost was approximately $55,000. The federal aid grant was for $22,500 to be used for the construction of a $50,000 high school building. It had been necessary, however, to call another election to vote on the $27,000 in bonds that the district needed to apply on the building. Owing to the insistence by the federal authorities that federal aid be used quickly, it was thought best to call for bids before the date of the second bond election. The majority for the bonds was so overwhelming in the former election that no doubt was entertained as to the outcome of the second election. However, should the bonds be defeated, the federal aid would have been lost.

School Transportation — Tom Herynk ('42) said, "I rode a horse to the Lone Elm School just west of Kincaid which closed in the 1930s. I had gone my first two years of school there. We had sixteen kids and three teachers."

There was only one bus which ran the north route. The school paid students to pick up three kids in the southwest corner of the district. The student driver was paid $2 per week per student.

This same 1937 bus would take the senior class to New York City, Niagara Falls, and Washington D.C. for their renowned senior trip following graduation in May 1941. They were all decked out in their hats and dress clothes and had their picture taken with the congressman on the steps of the capitol. There were seven seniors who were unable to make the trip because of lack of money. The bus driver was Bill Brown, who bravely maneuvered the two-lane highways, down Fifth Avenue in New York, and down Pennsylvania Avenue in Washington D.C. On the way home, money became short, so the boys slept on the bus and the girls at the YWCA in St. Louis.

Academic Programs — Sam Harris was a distinguished Vocational Agriculture teacher from 1949 until the school closed in 1967. In eighteen years, he coached judging teams, helped with livestock projects, and guided the FFA boys in leadership and understanding of agriculture. A photo wall with over 600 boys and their projects remains in the high school to this day.

Driver's education was started in 1950.

Glenda Thompson was a wheelchair bound student because of polio. She was an artistic student and had her wheelchair carried up and down the stairs daily for her classes. She became a renowned Indian artist.

Kincaid had a great marching band. Ann Herynk Donaldson ('64) played the trombone. "We always marched in the Pittsburg State homecoming parade and at the football game. We played at the annual Farm Expo, later called the Kincaid Free Fair, each fall. As many as twelve bands would proudly march down our main street and around our town."

Tom Herynk ('42) vividly remembers, "They played "76 trombones," and "Baby Elephant Walk." The parade would be the feature of the three-day fair."

Athletics — Football was started in the 1920s, and eleven-man football was played until 1959 when the eight-man game was started.

Jack Donaldson ('58) competed at the state track meet from 1957-58 in the high jump. He had been to Manhattan for the FFA judging and received pointers from a K-State track athlete in the high jump. Several weeks later he was unable to use these training tips and missed out on the first-place jump. Jack, with a twinkle in his eye, recalled a prank that brought a wet fanny to anyone who may have been in the sitting position at the time. "A yet to be named individual, flushed a lighted cherry bomb which exploded in the plumbing pipes. It caused a back pressure on all the toilets to get all the innocent bottoms wet as they were relieving themselves." Some sixty years later the culprit has not stepped forward.

The athletic teams played in the Lucky 7 and Linn County Leagues. Other teams in the leagues included Moran, Pleasanton, La Cygne, and Mound City. Gary Louk ('60) said, "We had lights as the Oil Lease had provided the steel poles for the lights for the football field."

Kincaid had one of the best gymnasiums, built in 1937 by the WPA. The janitor, Jack Holding, would not let anyone wear street shoes on his floor as he meticulously cared for its beautiful surface. Eighty years later (2018), the same gym floor shows well, and the loving care that Mr. Holding provided can still be appreciated.

The basketball coach had team rules and players were to be in bed by 10:00 PM the night before the game. A fire siren at midnight awakened the whole town and everyone answered the alarm. The coach and numerous basketball players were at the scene of the fire. The next day Coach Howard Gray summoned the boys to the front and asked anyone who was out after 10:00 PM to step forward. Most of the boys stepped forward with guilt. This coach, who also taught history and driver's education, made the boys put their hands behind their backs and crawl on their bellies the length of the gym. Coach Gray had gone to nearby Ottawa College and played basketball. He had never been involved with football. At Kincaid he was required to coach football too, though his knowledge of the game was not quite up to the rules. During one game, Jack Donaldson remembers an unusual turn of events that had Coach Gray asking one of his players on the sideline, "Can they do that?"

The biggest rivals were Blue Mound and Moran. But in 1942, the fiercest rival was Colony. A game in 1963 pitted the undefeated Kincaid football team against the undefeated Colony team. A storm came up during the game, and it had to be called off, leaving the game a tie and thus, both teams, undefeated.

Assorted Stories from Kincaid—The principal was not at school on the day that cabbage sticks were served for the school lunch. They made perfect missiles for some of the high school boys in a food fight. That night these same boys happened upon a six pack of beer and shared it between the ten to twelve boys. The next day the principal called all the culprits to his office for an interrogation session. Richard Sence ('58) was reported to have said, "I just threw a little piece of cabbage and only took just a little sip of the beer." The principal said that "a little" was enough. All the players were suspended from that night's basketball game. By 4 o'clock that afternoon, they were reinstated with the stipulation that they all meet with the school board right after the game.

Charlotte Southerland ('58) became a famous fiction author under the pen name Charlotte Hinger. As a student with a handicap, she had to be carried up and down the stairs in her wheelchair during her high school years.

The senior trip in 1958 was a five-day adventure to Bagnall Dam in Missouri at the Lake of the Ozarks. Each senior was given $2 each day for spending money.

The 1959 seniors went to Rock Away Beach near Branson. Irene Pinneo ('59) Louk smiles as she recalls this trip. "It was quite a fun time considering my mother was one of the sponsors on the trip. I think fondly of that experience nearly 60 years ago."

The seniors in 1960 repeated the same destination trip to Bagnall Dam. This was the year before the establishment of Silver Dollar City and the explosion of tourism to the Branson area. Gary Louk ('60) said, "We almost did not get to go on the senior trip because some mischievous boys had shot out some of the city street lights with BB guns."

Tom Herynk ('42) chuckles about a teacher, Nora May Craig, "Who was a pretty good- sized old gal. She did not put up with any foolishness. One day a boy had leaned back in his chair and put his feet up on the back of another chair. She flipped the boy over on his rear. She was here many years and married Coach Frankhauser."

Herynk also remembers, "For my senior day and sneak, the seniors went by cars to Ottawa to see *Gone with The Wind*. The juniors thought they would just follow the bus in their cars. The sophomores, not to be outdone, decided it was a good idea and followed the juniors in their cars. The only ones left in school that day were the freshmen."

Final Days — The school closed after graduation in May 1967. There were 811 graduates from 1890-1967. The first graduate in 1890 happened to be Zula Kincaid. The last graduate in a class of fifteen in 1967 was Jeanette Schnider (alphabetically).

The most frequent surnames of the graduates were Smethers-13, Adams-10, Thompson-10, Church-9, Henderson-9, Marsch-9, McCollam-9, Osborn-8, Shepherd-7, Wren-7, Reynolds-6, and Woods-6.

19

Mullinville High School

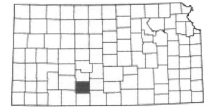

Mascot: Tiger

Colors: Maroon and White (Previously Purple-Gold & Scarlet-Pearl Gray)

Year Closed: 1990

Location: town of Mullinville, west central Kiowa County

Early Education in Mullinville — It was the spring of 1884 before a town site was established in "Buffalo Land." Alfred A. Mullin, a twenty-five-year-old Chicagoan, established a store and named his town Mullinville.

Some of the following information is paraphrased from articles compiled by former superintendent Randall

Gallion, teacher Keith Chadd, and graduate Mildred McFadden Douglass.

Early education in the area was first recorded to have been subscription schools. Individuals paid to have their children taught by teachers in a formal setting. The first school in Mullinville was a subscription school conducted by Mr. Carpenter in 1885. This was only one year after the naming of the town site. The school term lasted until all the available money was exhausted, which was the usual practice in these schools. The following year, in 1886, Miss Belle Wells opened a subscription school in Union Hall, which stood just west of the bank on Wall Street. The school closed the next year after a three-month term.

An organizational meeting for a new public school was held on October 7, 1886. School District #36 was formed. The first term in the new district opened three weeks later on November 1, 1886, with fifty students attending for a three-month term. The teachers were Miss Belle Wells and J.B. Hunt from Kentucky. Their salaries were $30 and $35 per month. That same year, there were fifteen rural schools formed on the boundaries of the Mullinville district. A petition requesting a bond election for a new school house was circulated by June of 1887, and $2,500 was approved for the construction of a two-room, white frame building. With $300 worth of furniture, the building was ready in three months for class in the fall of 1887.

In 1911, patrons again voted to build a brick building on Washington Street, the second block east of Main Street. The building was completed that fall and school opened with Mr. C.C. Perry as the superintendent. Mr. Perry started the first high school freshman class in 1912 with nine students. The following year a two-year high school was adopted. In 1915, two more rooms were added to the building, and the final two years of high school were conducted. This four-year course of study was adopted under the direction of Professor Frank J. Cline. The first graduating class was in 1917 with two graduates, sisters Mary and Ottie Graham.

A Shaky Start — Growing pains again overtook the Mullinville School, and the community became interested in forming a rural high school district. A meeting was organized by the county commissioners after a petition was circulated on the question. Three judges were appointed, and two clerks were named to record the meeting. After this meeting, Kiowa County was reorganized under the rural high school law. Mullinville Rural High School District #3 was formed. The district constituted a nine-mile-wide area bounded on the north, west, and south by Kiowa county lines and consisted of 216 sections. A meeting was conducted by the county superintendent of schools for an election of a board of education. Mr. Benjamin O. Weaver was elected president of the board, a position he held continuously for the next forty-five years until stepping down in 1965.

On November 8, 1924, the Board of Education for Rural District #2 met to review a petition signed by 368 patrons of the district, calling for a bond election for $50,000 to erect a new high school building. A census showed that there were 454 children in the district under the age of twenty-one, 309 women, and 353 men. In the election which followed, there were 213 voters out of the 662 eligible. One hundred and eighty-three voted for the school bonds and thirty against. Controversy soon arose on where to build this new high school with the "south site" winning in an election over the "north site." Three days later construction was in progress.

In an extensive history by the former school superintendent, Randall Gallion, titled *From Past to Present*, the following story appears:

> . . . as work progressed, the board was accosted again by a number of societies, clubs, lodges, bureaus, and associations for the privilege of laying the cornerstone. Finally, the board chose the Ku Klux Klan, which was the most active organization, and whose members were also among those who had entered a request.
>
> The Exulted Cyclops was notified that May 23, 1925, had been selected as the date. He, in turn, notified the Imperial Wizard, who was the Emperor of the Invisible Empire of the Knights of the Ku Klux Klan. Plans went forward for a gala day. Soon wild rumors were afloat, the worst being that 1,000 robed knights would parade the streets of Mullinville from 10:00 AM until noon, followed by a grand barbecue. At 1:00 PM, the Imperial Kludd was to open the ceremony followed by a speech by the Imperial Klaff. The cornerstone was to be laid by the Imperial Klighapp, the Imperial Klobee, and the Imperial Klexter, closing with the benediction by the Imperial Klorard, while in the center of the street the Klan would burn the biggest fiery cross ever seen in Kansas.
>
> Soon the sheriff came to town with a pocket filled with writs and warrants to enjoin the school board from holding the ceremony. The dedication ceremony was never held, but one evening the board discovered the cornerstone was in its place. A quiet investigation began as to how it got there. While this was under-way, the stone disappeared and was gone for over a year. Who laid it in the first place, who re-

moved it, and where it spent so many months is still shrouded in uncertainty.

Additions to the High School — In 1952, a petition was circulated to request the board of education of R.H.S. #2 to hold a bond election for the construction of a new gymnasium. The first bond was for $170,000 and was not adequate for the project. Another bond election was held six months later for the $65,000 needed to complete the project. The first basketball game was played against Montezuma on February 9, 1954, with the Mullinville Tigers scoring an upset victory of 65-54.

The first school colors were purple and gold, followed by scarlet and gray in the early 1930s. By the late 1960s, the well-known maroon and white was adopted. The emblem of Mullinville High School was always the Tiger, a symbol recognizing the strength and spirit of the school, the parents, and the community patrons supporting it.

Many special-interest youth organizations helped MSH students become well-educated and able to participate in different activities in many walks of life.

Examples of these organizations were in a review by Jeanne Caywood Carson ('61) of the yearbook annuals:

1926 - *The Progress*—first known MRHS yearbook printed
  Stock and Grain Judging
  Public Speaking
  Senior and Junior Class Plays

1936 - *Tiger Eye* (Yearbook)
  First Class Will
  First Junior Class History
  Debate
  Girl Reserve—a girls organization started in 1927 became a standard club

Girls Athletic Assoc—every girl has opportunity to engage in P.E.
Annual Staff (second annual published)
Orchestra
Boys and Girls Glee Club

1938 - First Senior Class History
First Senior Trip - their hope was that by departing from the custom of a one-day sneak, their senior sneak would establish a precedent for the senior classes to come. They spent five days in Colorado Springs. Senior trips continued annually until the school closed in 1990.
Orchestra
News Staff - supplied the junior class this year
Gym - gave girls the opportunity to participate in basketball, baseball, volleyball, clogging, sitting-up exercises, track, and hiking during the year
A typewriting tournament was held 4/15/1938
Classisi Caesaris
Agriculture-Boys
Dramatics-Hi-Y, Junior and Senior plays
Manual Training-Fire department training

1949 - Boys Football Team started
Y-Teens-Girls organization
1950 Hi-Y & Y-Team Carnival
First junior senior class banquet. Hosted by juniors

1951 - *Tiger Tales* the yearbook published by the journalism class
Pep Band
Senior Melvin Coates set state record for scoring the most individual points at the state track meet. He took first in the low hurdles, first in the high hurdles, and second in the 220 dash. He holds the record to this day.

1954 - Forensics competition
Marching Band

1956 - Swing Band - Mr. Jerry Hind (a blind music teacher)
1956-65 - Girls & Boys Tennis
Camera Club
Girls Golf added as a sport
Pep O Mints Band

1964 - Kansas State High School Boys Basketball Champions Class BB
Foreign Language added to the curriculum

1967 - Girls Track-first year
Tri-Hi-Y Organization
Model Legislature

1968 - Symphonic Band
Gymnastics
Student Exchange Program with Chattanooga, TN

1971-89 - Aeronautics Class
Spirit Band
Future Homemakers of America
Driver's education was offered to freshmen starting in the early 1960s.

Transportation & Travel

Transportation & Travel—When the school first got buses, sixteen-year-old farm boys were allowed to drive them. They took them home at night and returned the next day with the students along their route to deliver them to school. Boys who lived in town would return the buses to the bus barn after running their route. Adult drivers drove to athletic events out of town.

Senior trips, started in 1938, took the students to some amazing places: 1962 - New Orleans & St. Augustine; 1966 - California, Las Vegas, Grand Canyon, and the Glass bottom boat at Catalina Island; 1967 - Hawaii; 1987 – a Caribbean Cruise.

Special Occasions—Halloween was a big deal in Mullinville. There were bonfires in the middle of the street, the typical upsetting of outhouses, cars on top of the school, a merry-go-round in the middle of the street, and painting of windows. The next day, the school boys would be hired by the city to clean up all of the damage from the antics of the night before, and they got paid for their efforts!

Senior Night was held near the end of the school year with the seniors performing a skit, reading the class history, and choosing a senior song. The Senior Prom and Banquet were planned and decorated by the juniors. The juniors' mothers prepared the meal, and the sophomores were the servers.

Closing of Mullinville High School—The high school closed in May of 1990 with the secondary students from Mullinville attending the USD 422 district in Greensburg.

A total of 987 graduated from Mullinville High School from 1917-1990. Twenty percent of the graduates were made up from thirteen surnames. The most numerous surnames of the graduates were Ralstin-23, Zimmerman-22, Headrick-19, Copeland-16, Sherer-16, Douglass-13, Miller-13, Brensing-12, McFadden-12, and 11 each of Schmidt, Brown, Kilgore, and Sloan.

Mullinville High School
Kiowa County, KS

#20

Prairie View Rural High School

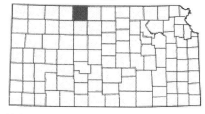

Mascot: Pirates

Colors: Blue and Gold

Year closed: 1966

Location: town of Prairie View, Phillips County, eleven miles south of the Nebraska border

An Unusual Move-in Day — This area was settled and homesteaded by many Dutch immigrants in the 1870s. These tall genes carried forward for the next 100 years and influenced the area's success in basketball.

In January 1923, the president of the school board, Dr. G.A. Van Diest, came to the first Prairie View School with a truck to move the teachers and their equipment. Two high school teachers sat in the front and two grade school teachers sat in the back holding the portraits of Washington and Lincoln. Crowded in the truck were the desks, a reed organ, library books, and other supplies. The beautiful new high school was ready to welcome the first students. This was an unusual moving day as the town residents pitched in to make this a ceremonial event. The day was highlighted by a dedication program with a speech by the President of the Hays College (later Ft. Hays State University). The four teachers and the school board sat on the stage behind the speaker.

At noon there was a dinner in the gymnasium to which the patrons of the seven surrounding school districts were invited. All of these districts were later consolidated with Prairie View.

The school mascot was the Pirates, and the colors were blue and gold. The mascot could have been called the "giants" because the students always were much taller than their athletic opponents.

Basketball Was the Main Game — With the small gymnasium and the wall being the out of bounds line, many a nervous opponent would spend an unsuccessful night on the home court of the Prairie View Pirates.

The 1962-63 boys team touted the tallest starting lineup of any high school in Kansas. They went to the state tournament that year and were defeated by the eventual champion, Durham, 57-50. Early in the season Prairie View averaged well over 90 points in each game. They visited the much smaller and very young Bogue team, which averaged ten inches shorter than the Pirates. Bogue's gymnasium was newer and regulation size. This epic game of the time ended with a Prairie View win, 9-7, in overtime. Bogue only had nine boys in school and started two freshman, two sophomores, and a junior against Prairie View, the number one team in the state.

The Bogue coach, Larry Ward, was frustrated at a referee call and kicked at the air, only to have his slip-on loafer sail to mid court. (The author for this story was one of the freshman starters from Bogue playing in this game. To this day, it is a vivid memory, missing a free throw that could have won the game for Bogue and upsetting the number one team in the state of Kansas.)

To prepare for big games and tournament games thereafter, the team would practice at the Phillipsburg gymnasium twelve miles to the east. Prairie View belonged to the Little Six league made up of Edmond, Densmore, Damar, Bogue, and Webster. They considered Bogue and Damar their greatest rivals, but they really disliked the larger neighboring Almena team in Norton County.

Other boys sports included baseball and track. On days of a track meet, students were allowed out of class to scoop out the water from the puddles on the track following overnight rains.

The girls played 3-on-3 basketball which had a rover that could cross over the half court. The players' size in that small gymnasium was always intimidating for any visiting opponents to Prairie View.

Stories from Prairie View — Dennis DeWitt ('66)
recalled a buggy mysteriously disassembled and put back together on top of the high school. Another prank and unsolved "mooving" experience found Mr. Kroese's cow also on top of the high school roof.

Donna Smith ('53) had a class ring go missing. It was considered lost for good until the day in 2016 when the school building was being demolished. John Prinson ('53) admitted putting the ring in the railing going down into the boys' locker room. Sure enough, the crew disassembling the structure was led to the exact railing, and the ring was found in mint condition.

Alumni Stats — The first senior class of seven graduated in 1924. The Dutch names were very prominent in those first ten years. Names such as Spoestra, Kats, Pakkebier, Vander Beek, Schemper, Vandervelda, Van Diest, Van Grueningen, De Young, Schakelaar, Capstick, Englesman, Heersink, Jaenicke, Creutzberg, Erickson, Reusink, VanDyke, VanKooten, and VanDerWege were among the graduates from 1924-1933.

The largest graduating class was sixteen students in 1943. There were thirty-two enrolled in high school when the school closed in 1966. All the remaining students traveled the next year to Logan High School, twelve miles to the south. A total of 320 graduates in forty-two years received diplomas from Prairie View High School. The most numerous surnames of the graduates from 1934-66 were De Boer-16, Stutterheim-16, Jansonius-14, De Young-9, Heersink-7, Schra-7, Schemper-6, Van De Wege-6, Van Diest-6, and Van Loenen-5. These surnames are just a representation of the many Dutch names that lived in the area. Other surnames—not as numerous—but tell the rich history of the school and area: Spoelstra, De Witt, Van Der Veen, Verhoef, VanDerplas, Van Kooten, Breathhouwer, Creutsberg, Pakkebier, Schakebar, and Soodsma.

#21

Paxico Rural High School

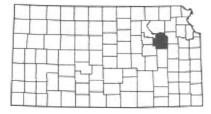

Mascot: Pirates

Colors: Orange and White

Year Closed: 1974

Location: along Mill Creek in north central Wabaunsee County, Flint Hills

History of Paxico Education — There were many German settlers in the surrounding countryside. The city of Paxico was founded in 1886.

The community of Newberry was a large catholic town with a convent one mile north. The parochial school in Newberry attracted many students from Paxico. The public school buses would pick up some of the Paxico children at the general store and transport them to the Newberry to attend school.

An early Paxico grade school later burned down and was replaced on the same site as the current Paxico grade school. In 1907 and 1908, a movement was started in the Paxico community to organize a high school. In order for an application to be approved by the State of Kansas, the community needed to prove an enrollment of twelve to fourteen students. By canvassing the community for all who would finish eighth grade by 1909 and want to continue into high school, the requirements were met, and the application for a Paxico High School was approved.

The school opened in September 1909 with three teachers and sixteen students. Classes were held in the north room of the grade school building. It was a wooden structure which had been built in 1888. Of the sixteen students who began the school in 1909, six graduated four years later in 1913.

No school was held in 1913-14 because there were not enough students. During that year, the principal, R.C. Warder, along with N.G. Schumaker went door to door in the district and found enough students to have school again in the fall of 1914. The next class to graduate was in 1918, five years after the first graduating class of 1913.

Building a High School — By 1921, Paxico High School outgrew the space in the grade school building. Ground work for a new, separate high school was started in the spring of 1922. Commencement was held that year in the new Paxico Rural High School. This rural high school was built with a deep red brick which was identical to the red brick in the very large Sacred Heart Catholic church one mile north on the hill at Newberry.

The building contained six classrooms and a gymnasium. It was a unique design as the building had three entrances. Above the west entrance was an inlaid stone marked "GIRLS." Above the east entrance was designated "BOYS" in the same inlaid white stone. The main entrance to the school faced south toward the community. The construction cost was $40,000 which was raised by bonding. The first year of the new high school in 1922, there were forty-eight students enrolled. The enrollment grew to 102 in 1939, dropping to twenty-five in 1952. New residents moving into the community in the 1960s slowly increased the enrollment again.

The building would remain the same until a new gymnasium was added to the north side of the building in 1956-57. The old gym was remodeled into classrooms, a library, office, stage, and dressing rooms. This addition cost $45,000 and was covered by bonding.

1967 Consolidation — The Paxico High School district consolidated into USD 329 in 1967 under the State mandate which required a district to meet two of three criteria. The district did have a large enough enrollment, but not enough square miles and was under the valuation of $2,00,000. The new unified district included the high schools at Paxico, Maple Hill, and Alma. Maple Hill High School was closed in 1969.

Closing Paxico High School — In 1973, the USD 329 Board of Education commissioned a study of the district by Emporia State Teachers College to suggest improvements in the educational program. After a short study, it was recommended that the Paxico High School be closed and the students be sent to the county seat town of Alma. The high school building would be used for grades 6-8 and the grade school would house grades K-5.

The closing of the high school was opposed by an overwhelming majority of the Paxico community, but their protests were in vain. The majority of the students for the high school, including the entering freshman class, chose to leave the district. Most of these students would attend Wamego and St. Mary's.

Several teachers were honored in the last yearbook in 1974. Special recognition went to two teachers who were at Paxico High School the longest. Mrs. Suzanna Salyer taught for twenty-two years in music, choir, and band. Her students earned many "ones" at area contests. She was raised in Lawrence and a graduate of Kansas University in music. She taught for four years in Winchester before coming to Paxico. Mr. Paul Wurtz taught English and math at the school for thirty-five years until the school closed in 1974. A testament to his dedication and devotion to education and students, he was the senior class sponsor for most of the years he taught there.

A school song was written by Marilee Berry ('69). It rings with sentiment and meaning for those who attended Paxico Rural High School.

In the Valley of the Flint Hills,
Where ole Mill Creek flows,
Stands our noble Alma Mater.
Sing her praises High.
We always bring her honor,
As the years go by,
While we always love and honor,
Dear ole Paxico High.

The school closed with graduation ceremonies in May of 1974. The last graduate was Michael Zeller (alphabetically). In sixty-six years, the most numerous surnames of the graduates were Glotzbach-36, Muckenthaler-28, Zeller-27, Hund-25, Michaelis-20, Meinhart-17, Hesse-16, Moch-13, Wurtz-11, and Flauch-9. These ten German sounding surnames made up 30% of the 678 graduates from Paxico High School.

Many of these names are noted in an early school annual as business sponsors in the back of the yearbook. Businesses who donated to help the students in printing the yearbook were:

- State Bank of Paxico (Officers-AB Hesse, JH Michalis, Jos. W. Hund) est. 1906
- C.J. Glotzbach garage—Honest prices built in 1870s
- Paxico Lumber Company—Frank X. Muckenthaler, Manager
- Intall an Acetylene Plant—J. Kaul
- Paxico Livery Barn-Wilt Brothers, Proprietors—Horses and Buggys to rent
- C. Thomson & Sons-General Merchandise—est. 1887 our motto: "Quick Sales & Small Profits"
- The Paxico Restaurant-JC Phipps: Proprietor—Confections, Cold Drinks, Cigars 1901

Who would believe that their advertisements in the yearbook would still be receiving recognition over 100 years later?

#22

Cambridge Rural High School

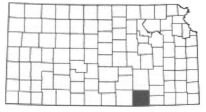

Mascot: Bulldogs

Colors: Orange and Black

Year Closed: 1963

Location: east central Cowley County, eleven miles south of the Butler County line and seven miles west of the Chautauqua County line

Early History and Education—The area was inhabited by Osage Indians when the first settlers came to homestead at Grouse Creek and Walnut Creek following the Civil War. John Tull filed a claim on land two miles north of where Cambridge is now located. It was common to pay the Indian Chief Chetopah five dollars each year for protection from the Indians. The early histories state that John Tull built the first house. He also taught in the first school. It is very evident that education received high priority with the early settlers.

Bonds were voted in the summer of 1880 to erect a stone schoolhouse in Cambridge. The native stone building was completed in the summer of 1881, and school started the following October. The Kansas City, Lawrence and Southern Kansas Railroad came to Cambridge in 1880 and, as a result, many businesses from the nearby town of Lazette relocated. The Lazette School District No. 15 was moved to Cambridge in 1881.

The Modern High School — By 1916, the citizens of the area saw the need for establishing higher education for the area. Bruce Tull, the son of that first settler and teacher John Tull, spearheaded the petition drive. On April 9, 1917, Windsor Township voted to organize a rural high school. The early native stone building was torn down, and a red brick grade and high school building was erected in its place. Though the school was not quite completed, the building was dedicated on Thanksgiving Day 1917. The program was performed in pantomime by all of the rural, one-room country school students around Cambridge. The flat roof of the furnace room was used as the stage for this dedication ceremony. The first five students at the high school made the big rock "C" on the hill south of town and painted it white so it could be seen from Main Street.

The second year, two more teachers were added and courses taught were home economics, woodworking, agriculture, geometry, and English. In the spring of 1922, five graduates received their diplomas.

School enrollment increased steadily and necessitated more space. In 1927, a two-story brick grade school was built directly across from the high school. By 1933, the grade school enrollment was fifty-six pupils. At this time, there were 138 school districts in Cowley County. With this many rural, one-room country schools, the Cambridge Grade School remained relatively small.

Prior to 1936, Horner's Hall was rented for school activities. The auditorium-gymnasium was built that year in seventy-five days. The graduating class of 1936 was the first to use the gymnasium for graduation ceremonies even though the building was not completed.

Transportation & School Lunches — The school bus service was started in 1943. The school began serving lunches when the one room country school named Box school house was purchased and moved north of the high school building. It was remodeled and made into a modern school lunch room. Jewel Bolack was the cook the first year. Mabel Ensley became the cook in 1955 and remained until the school was consolidated in 1963.

Athletics — The high school was crowned the 1925 State of Kansas baseball champions. From 1956-58 the baseball team was 63-7. Baseball was played in the spring, summer, and fall. Cambridge lost in the state baseball tournament to Odin in 1958. The school had no football program. In the 1950s basketball had a great run. In 1958, with a record of 24-0, Cambridge was defeated in the first round of the state tournament by Rolla.

Armand Hillier ('58) was on those teams. He would later play four years of basketball at Southwestern College. He then coached and was in administration for thirty-seven years at Oxford and Augusta.

Stories from Students—Hubert Gailey ('22) was spraying plants in the agriculture room. Leona Atkins Gailey ('22) told this story: "It was just after World War I, and the grade school classes were not aware that Hubert was spraying plants. When the spray fumes penetrated the grade school rooms, the students ran from the school screaming that they were being bombed."

Armand Hillier ('58) recalled, "All the boys from Cambridge hunted, fished, and played ball. We would hunt ducks on Saturday and Sunday and clean the ducks in my dad's garage. When we opened the doors, it was like a snow storm. You could shoot a shot gun off at midnight in town and no one would think a thing of it. Though I still claim innocence, three ducks were taken from my pens at home and put in a classroom at school. It made quite a mess!" Armand's eyes sparkled while giving this recollection.

A note from the school yearbook, the *Cambria*: "The ten seniors from the class of 1958 took their senior trip to New Orleans. They went in private cars with several parents and the class sponsor, Ms. Anna Wakefield, a 4'10" teacher who would take no lip from anyone."

School Closing—During the winter of 1963, the county superintendent of schools held meetings with both the Cambridge and Burden district's board of education separately. The vote to consolidate was overwhelming in both school districts. The new high school would be called Central of Burden and include Burden, Cambridge, Grenola, and Atlanta.

Thus, after forty-six years, Cambridge High School was closed. There was a total of 336 graduates. The last class of four received their diplomas in May 1963. There were only fifteen students in the high school that last year. The last graduate was Sandra Lundy (alphabetically).

The most common surnames of the graduates were: Brunton-10, Hendrickson-9, Brown-9, Hawley-8, Booth-7, and Allison-6.

Cambridge Rural High School
Cowley County, KS

#23

Englewood High School

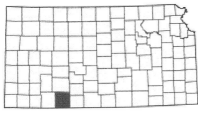

Mascot: Bulldogs

Colors: Maroon and White

Year closed: 1966

Location: on north-south highway US 283 just two miles from Oklahoma in the town of Englewood, Clark County

First High School—Englewood is an elm tree lined town in cattle country. Clark County is the sixth smallest populated county in Kansas.

As in many Kansas prairie towns, the first schools did not include high school. Classes started in the first high school building on October 3, 1910. The building was two and a half stories made of white brick. The school started late that year as the building was not completed in September. The school was accredited in 1912. Both lower grade and high school was held in this building. Due to lack of space, and also to add home economics and industrial arts to the curriculum, another school building was built to house the high school and the fifth through the eighth grades. The graduating class of 1923 had the privilege of being the first graduates from this building.

The town's opera house was available for all extracurricular activities. It was replaced by a new auditorium in the latter 1930s. Enrollment peaked in 1933 with 118 students in high school. The graduation class of 1940 was the first to have commencement in the new auditorium. Graduations were held there every year until the high school closed in 1966.

School Trivia and Notables—Early highlights included the girls basketball team playing in the state meets at Lawrence in 1913 and 1917. The first eleven-man football team was organized in 1917 by Mr. Bachman.

- The school paper was edited by the English department and given the name *The Sand-bur Special*.
- The 1926 class had the distinction of being the first to wear caps and gowns.
- Wanda Goodnight scored 116 points in a single game in 1929.
- Myrl Walker ('21) taught geology at Ft. Hays State College and directed the Sternberg Natural History Museum.
- The debate team, under the direction of Miss Edith Harp, did not take a back seat to any performances.

- The first annual was published by the journalism class in 1946.

The decade from 1933-1942 was a time of big things, both good and bad, from rolling blinding dust storms, the building of the new auditorium, and the bombing of Pearl Harbor. The school superintendent, R.S. Turner, was called into service two months after the US entered the war. Football was discontinued, and teachers became difficult to attain and retain. Many teachers came to the school from Northwestern State in Alva, Oklahoma, because Kansas paid more than Oklahoma.

The 1950s team played six-man football. Many of the students who once came from Oklahoma returned to attending school in the "red-dirt" state. In 1951 the *Clark County Clipper* headlined "Englewood Wins First Football Game in Thirty Years," but neglected to say that for many of those years it did not have a football team.

Under the tutelage of Dean George, the school excelled at district and state music contests. Instructor Jim Hood presented a very concentrated science program. School plays, carnivals, glee clubs, and girls physical education were some of the groups and activities. Band was started in 1946.

Dale Walker ('58) set the state javelin record at 199 feet, 1 ½ inches in 1958. The 1959 football team was undefeated at 7-0, outscoring its opponents 280-57. The school became part of the Santa Fe League in 1961. The 1961 basketball team became the only team to ever play in the state tournament in Dodge City.

Closing the Schools — As enrollment continued to decline, extracurricular activities were reduced. A bold move in 1965 to build a new grade school was made in an attempt to draw more families to Englewood. The high school, after fifty-four years and 522 graduates, closed its doors for the final time in 1966 with six graduates in the final class. Gary Taylor ('66) was the last graduate (alphabetically) to receive an Englewood diploma. Unification with Ashland that year meant that most of the remaining high school students were bused to the county seat town of Ashland. The attempt to attract more families to Englewood did not prove successful, and the grade school closed in 1969.

Englewood High School
Clark County, KS

#24

Densmore Rural High School

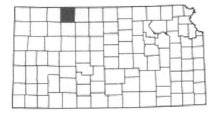

Mascot: Warriors

Colors: Red and White

Year Closed: 1965

Location: town of Densmore, southeastern corner of Norton County

History of Densmore Rural High School — The town of Densmore was laid out along the north fork of the Solomon River by Thomas J. Densmore who came to the area to homestead in 1874. Railroad tracks came from the east and extended west to Lenora (20 miles) in 1881.

Much of the following history of Densmore Rural High School was taken from the school paper "The Optimist" and school annuals compiled by Rose French Gulik, a 1939 graduate of Densmore.

A high school education prior to 1922 for the children of Densmore and vicinity was only available from neighboring schools in the towns of Logan and Edmond. A great many of these children did not get to attend a high school because of the distance to travel. For this reason, the people in Densmore decided that they needed their own high school.

A petition was circulated for the purpose of forming a district, and an election was called. The election was a success and the district organized, but there was considerable opposition, and some people brought suit because of a flaw in the petition.

District boundaries were rearranged, and another election was called. The people voted for the high school, but the bond issue was defeated. So in 1922, with a vote for a high school but no bond to pay for it, the school board of Fred Spatz, Carl Mullen, and Denver Archer raised funds to build the school by issuing warrants. To be official, they found that they had to have school at least a part of the year's term. They rented a vacant house, hired two teachers, Mr. A.W. Jones and Miss Hindman, and they taught a semester of school. Nineteen students were enrolled but there were no graduates that first year.

A new building was completed in time for school the next year. The teachers were T.I. Gifford, principal, and Miss Brawley, assistant. Thirty-eight students were enrolled. Averill Loughry was the first and only graduate in the class of 1924.

The surname of Archer was becoming very important in the community. Cyrus Archer was an original settler in 1878. Professor Glenn L. Archer submitted names to the students for a school paper. *The Optimist* was chosen, and Mrs. Nora Mullen was the editor. Additional issues of the paper were distributed on the occasion of a Christmas program. The name was chosen because all the students were looking forward optimistically to the day when they could have a gym, modern plumbing, and commercial and vocational subjects.

The boys played basketball outdoors on a dirt court. They bathed in a community tub in the furnace room. Those who hit the water first looked fairly presentable when they emerged from the tub. The boys who brought up the rear came out looking as though they had been through the muddy Jordan River.

Many articles written by the students appeared in their school paper with pleas for a gym. The boys and girls of the high school were using the opera house at Edmond six miles to the west to practice basketball. Articles continued asking, "Do We Need a Gym at D.R.H.S.?" and "Why We Need A New Gymnasium?" Professor Archer recalls that the school did get that new gymnasium in 1932. With the gym also came a stage, but no funds were available for a curtain. Board member A.K. Thompson canvassed the businesses in Densmore and surrounding towns and was almost entirely responsible for the stage scenery and equipment. He individually sold $1000 worth of ads with which the stage scenery, canvas drop, and curtains were purchased. This new gymnasium and the stage furnishings were built and paid for in the height of the Great Depression.

The 1932 and 1933 football teams were the greatest that the Solomon Valley had ever known. Mr. Ed Mullen was a tower of strength in sponsoring athletics. The school adopted the mascot of the Bulldog and red and white as the school colors. The official cheer was adopted in 1927.

Razzle, Dazzle, never a Frazzle, Not a thread of wool.

All together, All together, That's the way we pull. Densmore! Densmore!

School Firsts—The first P.T.A meeting was held in 1929. Again, the Mullen name appears as Nora Mullen was the first president. Very active through the years, the P.T.A. held a reception the last year of high school in Densmore. Leland Archer was the master of ceremonies.

The first annual *Densmoreland* was published in 1947. All the pictures were taken and developed by the students. The mascot was changed from the Bulldog to the Warriors.

The first school song "Hail Densmore" was written by Maxine Klagg, a teacher from 1930-32. In later years the pep song was "Hep, Hep, Hep."

The "Little Six League" was organized in 1948 for athletics and activities competitions between Webster, Bogue, Clayton, Edmond, Prairie View, and Densmore. Harold Sutley and Alvin Gulik ('37) (a Densmore graduate/later teacher-coach) were responsible for organizing competition in music, one act plays, and sports among the schools.

The hot lunch program was started in the 1940s. The first cooks were Norma and Eleanor Methany and Averill Loughry Smith (the first graduate from 1924).

Student Memories—The school was always very active in athletics and, considering the size of the student body, did very well. Students took part in debate and music contests, and no school year passed without at least one or two plays.

The fiercest rival was Edmond. There were a number of families from each school that were cousins. The Riemann surname was found at both schools, and the competition was keen.

In 1950, a classroom incident led to Doyle Archer ('51) being expelled. His friend had just sharpened a pencil and walked behind Doyle and jabbed him with the sharp end. He mumbled "go to hell" under his breath, but just loud enough that the English teacher, Iva Lee Hunsinger, heard the words. She was aghast and sent Doyle to the principal's office. He was promptly expelled from school. His requirement to reenter school was that he had to apologize and get the permission of the three school board members. He received permission from Wendell Morgan and Roy Walters. The third board member just happened to be his father, Leland Archer. After three days of trepidation, he confessed and told his father and was allowed back in school.

The end of Densmore High — The largest graduating class was fourteen students in 1932. Three surnames of Archer, Riemann, and Glennemeier made up nearly ten percent of all of the graduates for the high school throughout the years. The high school closed in May 1965 when the last graduate, Edward Wilcox (alphabetically) walked across the stage to receive his diploma. In forty-two years of Densmore Rural High School, there were a total of 274 graduates.

In the fall of 1965, the remaining students were bused to the town of Logan to the newly formed Unified District 326 comprised of students from Logan, Prairie View, and Densmore.

#25
Winchester Rural High School

Mascot: Eagles

Colors: Purple and White

Year Closed: 1968

Location: northeastern corner of Jefferson County. The early road — called The Fort Road — from Ft. Leavenworth to Ft. Riley ran directly through this area

Early Life on The Fort Road — Winchester was known to have an ample supply of good quality water and became a gathering point along this road, which was also used to move many livestock. A narrow-gauge railroad was built on this route in 1882. The well in Winchester attracted settlers. In the 1890s, this railroad was converted to the wider, standard gauge track and was a vibrant freight and passenger line into the 1930s.

Education thrived with many rural one-room schools in the surrounding countryside. One such school, No. 61 for Jefferson County, is remembered as Possum Trot. Possum Trot was built in the timber and near the center of the district. It was just three miles southeast of Winchester on the bank of the Walnut Creek. As many as seventy pupils were enrolled during its early days. But by 1943 the school was closed because there were no children left in the area to attend.

A subscription high school preceded the public grade school for up to six years from 1875-1881.

A Public High School — In 1891, a county high school was proposed for Jefferson County. Great controversy came between Valley Falls and Oskaloosa as petitions for signatures were circulated encouraging the county commissioners to call for a special election for a high school. *The Winchester Herald* reported on May 8, 1891, "Winchester is the best place in the county for a high school, and our people should take some action on this matter at once."

One week later, May 15, 1891 the *Herald* reported:

> If Winchester cannot get the county high school, we are in favor of Valley Falls as the next best place to locate it, provided they offer as good as the inducement as Oskaloosa. The [competition for a] County High School has now commenced between Oskaloosa and Valley Falls. Winchester will take no part in the fight, preferring to take chances as the 'dark horse.' We think that Winchester should take no part in the county high school fight, but keep quiet and let the belligerents go ahead and have a special election

called then our time will come to act. Votes count. If Oskaloosa and Valley Falls are both defeated we believe the latter place will throw her support to us, in preference to any other place.

The next week's copy on May 22, 1891 read, "We have got a double dose to take, a county seat and high school war. Good Lord, protect us! Valley Falls offers $50,000 in cash for the county court house and high school building."

A fall election resulted in a defeat of the proposition. *The Winchester Herald* showed that of the 252 votes cast in Winchester, only three were for the county high school in Oskaloosa. The proposition was snowed under in the rest of the county by about 2,000 votes.

The crowded conditions of the Winchester schools by 1919 led to discussions for a new larger and separate building for the grade and high schools. Notice of an election was posted, proposing a sum of $100,000 for the construction of a high school building upon the described site. The election, held in September 1920, passed with 410 voting yes and 169 voting no. An election in Oskaloosa on that same day for building a new high school passed by four votes.

The dedication of the new high school building was on March 31, 1922. The music was presented by the W.H.S. orchestra. The invocation given by the county superintendent, Miss May Nincehelser, was very appropriate for the occasion. The address given by a Jefferson County native and ex-state superintendent of schools, W.D. Ross, stressed the value of education, not from an educational point of view but in money value. He congratulated the community for making possible such a complete and up-to-date building, lauding its architectural beauty and fitness for school needs. The new school had three floors and 250 lockers for the students. The building had lights, water, and steam heat. The ozone machine furnished a ventilating system that was to be a safeguard to the health of the boys and girls. The system could empty the building of impure air and would fill the whole building with fresh exchanged air every thirty minutes. The structure was built to meet the needs of this community, not only for educational purposes, but for social and recreational as well. It was a credit to the town.

A Personal Account — *Bertha Lillie Curry ('13) wrote in her papers in 1972, the following account for her early education in Winchester.*

> Old Number 91 was where the Old Park once was, it faced West on Walnut Street between Grasshopper on the South and Delaware on the North. The long building was erected in 1860 and used until a frame building called District 7 was built. . . . The Academy was in the process of being built when a cyclone hit it and demolished it sometime in the 1880's; it was never completed . . . Next the Winchester Grade and High School, 1898-1911—I attended second grade and my brother was in first grade. Maude Varner was our teacher in 1904, she died that winter. I had my first two years of High School here in this old white frame two story building. I think it offered a 3 year High School course. The last class to graduate from there was 1911, the first was 1898. This building was torn down and the lumber used by Lewis Stoeffler to build his house. The new brick grade and high school was built at the north east corner facing east on the same school plot now known as City Park named for John Steuart Curry. The building was used from 1912 to 1921. Dr. Lewis A. Curry, Rev. Alvin Smith and Eva White were the first graduating class in 1912. (Lewis

Curry was later married to Bertha and became the doctor she described). I graduated in the class of 1913-with 10 in my class only 3 living . . . Winchester High School had the first girls basketball team in the County. In fact there were only three teams we could compete against; Campbell College, Lansing, and Eaton. But we had two good girls teams and played in competition between our own teams . . .

Banning Books — With the first graduation class from the two-year high school in 1898, the idea of a county high school was put aside. An account of the library was in the county superintendent's, W.H Rice, notes written in the *Winchester Star* newspaper on December 25, 1908 issue:

> In a certain library of 120 volumes in this county we noticed the following titles and recommended that the books be destroyed: *Family Pride, Hidden Hand, Wife in Name Only, Dora Dean, Not Like Other Girls, Shadow of a Sin, Won by Waiting, Mona's Choice, Edith Lyle's Secret, Tried For Her Life, Cruel as the Grave, East Lynn, Tempest and Sunrise, English Orphans, Thelma, Dora Thorne, Madcap Violet, The Duke's Secret, A Terrific Temptation.* Is there a parent living who would knowingly put such poison in the hands of their children to read? Yes. One of the most "blistering" letters we have ever received came from a mother who had children in a school in which there was a list of just such books in the library and which were removed, brought home and burned. The letter was accompanied by the demand that we pay for the books. We accordingly paid the teacher of the school twice the price of the books destroyed on the condition that good books be purchased in their place. In referring to one of the books named above a certain teacher defended the purchase of it by saying "Why,

that is one of Holmes works," evidently under the impression that Oliver Wendell Holmes and Mary Jane are one and the same. We want to repeat that the following authors, never wrote a proper book for a school library: Mary Janes Holmes, Bertha M. Clay, Rosa N. Carey, Edna Lydall, Mrs. Alexander, William Black, Mrs. Southworth, Charlotte. We believe a Reading Circle Board should be provided for a statute and no books placed in rural schools libraries except those which have been approved by this board.

Athletics — The school had a football team as early as 1910. As reported in *The Winchester Star*: "The football game went to the High School by the score 20-0. The Thanksgiving game came off at Magers' pasture, Wednesday evening. It was a very good game for about the first 10 or fifteen minutes, the High School made their first touchdown and the town boys went up the air."

Mr. John Morando came to Winchester High school in the fall of 1948 when athletics were at an all-time low. On April 27, 1952, the *Winchester Star* wrote, "From the cellar positions which our teams had held for a few years both in football and basketball he developed them into teams that have been a real threat in the County League the last two years, bringing home 7 championships. When we consider the loss and win columns Coach Morando has done an excellent job. But there is something else about Mr. Morando that was a far greater value, and that was his ability to get along with the students, and the effort he put into his work. He has not missed or been tardy a single day during his three years at Winchester High. That in itself is very commendable. It shows that he felt his responsibility to the school . . ."

Dr. Forrest C. "Phog" Allen, the head coach at the University of Kansas, was the commencement speaker for the class of ('51). Allen had been voted basketball's "Man of the Year for 1950" in a poll of the National Basketball Coaches Association. He was considered by many to be the nation's No. 1 basketball personality. In forty-one years of coaching, thirty-three of them at KU, he led twenty-eight teams to championships. "Phog" was famous also as a speaker, teller of sports stories, as an athletic trainer, and treater of injuries. He was credited with curing the ailing shoulder of Johnny Mize, the slugging first baseman of the New York Yankees, making it possible for Mize's home run socking bat to push the Yankees into the 1950 World Series.

Raymond Riley ('51) became a volunteer coach of the boys summer Pony League baseball program during the 1950s and 60s. He was blessed with many great ball players. Among them was Al Reynolds, who continued at Tarkio College in Missouri and played professionally for the Dallas Texans and the Kansas City Chiefs. Jerry Robertson ('61) excelled in baseball and played professionally for the Montreal Expos. Jerry O'Neill became one of three high school basketball players in Kansas to score over 60 points in a game. Coincidentally, all three of these players were from Jefferson County. Jerry would go on to become the President of the Reformed Seminary in Pennsylvania.

Academics — The three-year high school curriculum was started in the fall of 1907, thus there was no graduating class in the spring of 1908. The same happened in the school year of 1909-10 when the four-year high school began, so there was also no graduating class in 1910.

The curriculum for the school year in the fall of 1912 read as follows:

First year
English I
Latin (beginners) or German
Algebra
Ancient History

Second Year
English II
Latin II or German II
Algebra (advanced)
Botany

Third Year
Modern History
English III
Geometry (solid)
Latin III or German III

Fourth Year
Latin III or German II
American History
English IV or Psychology (elective)
Zoology or Physics (elective)

The enrollment for the year 1912-13 was fifty-two students. The Athletic Association turned down Mr. Jewel's proposition regarding the rent of his hall for basketball games. They would have accepted it if a deed to the hall had been granted.

Winchester Star, October 8, 1915, reported, "Frances Willard's birthday was observed in the school last Tuesday afternoon. This was in accordance with a measure, adopted during the last session of the State Legislature which set aside one fourth of a day on September twenty eighth as a tribute of honor to the founder of the "Women's Christian Temperance Union."

The program printed also listed the agenda. It began with devotionals and followed with music and talks from Rev. Elliott. It closed with the Kansas W.C.T.U. Song.

Bible class in the high school was reported in the *Winchester Star* August 29, 1924: "At a meeting of a number of representative citizens and school board at the High School building last Tuesday evening it was decided to put a class of Bible study in the course of the local High School. Editor Roberts, who teaches a class of Bible in the McLouth School, and Rev. Almon, who teaches in the Oskaloosa school, explained the course and it met with very favorable comment. At the conference Rev. Patton, pastor of the Reformed Church, and Rev. Knouse, pastor of the Christian church were selected as teachers of the course. It will be an elective credit class, meeting once each week, on Wednesday mornings and will be open to all students. It will be a non-sectarian course and will be taught in such a way as to be acceptable to everybody, regardless of church or creed."

One of Winchester's Best Known Students —
The first yearbook was published in 1916. John Steuart Curry was a junior that year and drew some of the sketches in this yearbook. Being in trouble at home, he was sent back east to family in Maryland for his last year of high school. This artist scholar became a renowned artist and muralist during the 1920s through the 1940s. His painting of John Brown's fury in the Kansas State Capitol is one of his best known paintings. Other murals were painted in the Farrell Library and Kansas State University. Known as a painter of the Regionalism Movement—along with Thomas Hart Benton and Grant Wood Curry finished his career as the artist for the University of Wisconsin.

Extracurriculars—The Homecoming Queen at Winchester High in 1949 was an attractive brunette, Barbara Moon ('51), a junior. She was selected by the W Club, the boys letterman organization. Barbara Moon reigned at the football game between McClouth and Winchester. Elaborate ceremonies were carried out at halftime intermission at which the queen was crowned by the football captain, Raymond Riley. This was the last game of the year, and it drew a large crowd. McClouth was undefeated and in first place in the Jefferson County League.

Barbara Moon was also a champion at debate. In 1950, Winchester won the State Championship Debate Crown. The team of Barbara Moon, Nina Noll, Betty Trower, and Melvin Cox won the state contest in Lawrence by defeating all of the other state district champions, University High, Ford, and Bucklin, by a total of 14 to 4. *The Winchester Star* wrote, "The accomplishment in the fields of debate for those four students was outstanding. Good debate means lots of study and hard work; therefore, these four debaters deserve much commendation for the efforts they put into this activity and the success they made out of it."

With the help of the Lions Club and individual people, new band uniforms were purchased in 1960. These much-needed uniforms came from Craddock Uniform Company in Kansas City. The dedication ceremony of the suits was at a Friday night football game on October 14, 1960.

The Winchester Star wrote three months later on February 3, 1961: "The Winchester Lions Club has had a number of fund raising events to help pay for the new band uniforms. It is appropriate at this time to let the community know how the uniforms fund is progressing. The original cost of the uniforms was $2,147. Donations and the fund raising events have brought in approximately $500. The members of the band have turned in $146.50 from the sale of community calendars. The Lions Club and band members express their appreciation for the fine support which the community has given to the campaign for the band uniforms. However, the community support is still needed to push the total over the top."

Transportation—By 1950 there were still separate grade school and high school districts. There were separate school boards and separate budgets. There were meetings between the boards to buy a bus for the high school. With the rural high school buying the new bus and operating it in cooperation with the grade school, it made it possible for all students to ride the bus. This eventually allowed for two grade school buses and one for the high school to accommodate all scholars. A new bus barn was purchased in 1952 for $1800 with both districts paying one half.

School Closing—The school closed after graduation in 1968 when the last of twenty-three seniors received their diplomas. The last graduate was Marcia Vaughn (alphabetically). A total of 1,118 graduated from Winchester High School from 1889 through 1968. The most frequent graduate surnames were Curry-36, Dormann-27, Davis-24, Noll-22, O'Neill-20, Reynold-20, Robertson-20, Dill-18, Edmond-15, Miller-15, and Smith-15.

With the Winchester school closing in 1968, the high school was moved to Nortonville and named North Jefferson High School. In the ensuing years, and a nine-vote win by the constituents, the high school was moved back to Winchester in January 1981 and named Jefferson County North High School.

#26

Fulton

High School

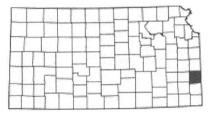

Mascot: Bearcats

Colors: Red, White, and Blue

Year Closed: 1966

Location: northeastern Bourbon County near the old fort military road running from Ft. Leavenworth to Ft. Scott

Town History — The town site was founded in 1857 and was first named Bugnolia and then Osaga (after the Osage Indians). In 1876 the name changed to Fulton, after Dr. Fulton, a physician from nearby Uniontown. From the *Ft. Scott Tribune*, November 12, 1912: "J.H. Green, the present postmaster who has served continuously in that capacity for the past 25 years, is one of the oldest settlers of Fulton and he recalls very well the old days prior to and during the Civil War. Fulton was at the head of the border troubles and as the Jayhawkers and the Missourians had many a clash within earshot of here. The name John Brown was a household name in Fulton in those days and General Price (confederate general) made himself cordially disliked by the residents of the little city."

The town flourished in 1878 when the Kansas City, Ft. Scott & Gulf railroad came through Fulton. A large depot was built to ship goods on the railroad. By 1887, there were seventy-five businesses complete with brick structures, three churches, a bank, and a large-scale rolling mill along with the school. The town population had reached 1,000 residents.

Early School Buildings — In 1870, the first school was a frame building and the teacher was E.T. Schaffer. This name of Schaffer would become very significant fifty years later in education and in the construction of a new high school in Fulton.

The *Ft. Scott Tribune* reported on November 5, 1912, in the Fulton news section:

> The Fulton Schools will also compare favorably with any school in the County. The building is a large handsome one of stone, surrounded by up to date concrete walks. Both the high school and grammar school courses are taught at the Fulton school. The enrollment is very large with 140 pupils attending this year. There is a marked increase every year.

This four-room structure had been built of native stone in 1882. This school building would be the center point in a community dispute over its structural soundness and the need to build a new high school. From the *Ft. Scott. Tribune*, April 7, 1916:

> $11,000 was voted Saturday for the erection of a more suitable school building. The town of Fulton is to have a new school building. Much to the delight of the School patrons in that thriving little town. The vote was 95 to 85, a close vote, considering that it was all one way. The contest against the bonds did not develop until the day of the election, when it became known that (C.T. Shaffer) there was some opposition . . . Those who favor the bonds claim that Fulton is greatly in need of a new school building, as the one now in use is antiquated and not fit for school purposes. It is the intention to build a strictly up to date school building. One of which the patrons in that district could well be proud.

In the *Fulton Kansas Weekly Globe*, March 17, 1916:

> C.T. Schaffer attended a town meeting and moved that the (1882) building not be disposed of . . . that he considered the old building good, that it had been good enough for his children, and many others. He threatened a lawsuit if the school board moved forward with the demolishing of the old school.

From the *Fulton Kansas Weekly Globe*, May 19, 1916:

> The special school meeting held . . . Mr. C.T Schaffer after a long diatribe . . . who is a dealer in general merchandise carrying on a prosperous business . . . largest land owner in town . . . claims the fire marshal could not condemn the stone school building . . . the opposition to the new school centered on higher taxation. And because the plan for a new school called for tearing down the 1882 school.

A New High School — The contract for the erection of the new high school was let to the Clicker Construction Company from Hutchinson. The contract price was $10,700 for the building only (no fixtures and no heating). It called for seven rooms, and the building was to be completed in 100 days. The published dispute between the editor of the *Fulton Kansas Weekly* and C.T. Schaffer's faction was further reported:

> A better building than can now be got for the money could have been built a year ago for probably $4,000 less only on account of the advance price of materials, but it seemed to be necessary to spend a year fighting over the proposition after the bonds had been legally voted. There was really no necessity for a town row over a public necessity like this, but it seemed we must have it . . . community can not get together and be united proudly . . . the rising generation will be able to look back to Fulton and its school with pride and satisfaction.

A fourth year of high school was offered in the fall of 1915. The first graduation from this four-year high school was held in May 1916 with three graduates.

From the *Fulton Weekly Globe*, August 1915:

> Application to have Fulton High School made an accredited High School was made to the State Board of Education. Thus, a graduate may enter the higher institutions of the state, the University, the Agricultural College.

During the depths of the Great Depression, the town voted bonds of $7,500 to go toward building a new gymnasium. The District WPA approved the federal government to help construct it in 1936. The WPA project was done by twenty-two laborers and two carpenters. The special gymnasium stone came from the 1882 condemned building which had been the center of the controversy in 1916 when the opponents of the new high school had tried to defeat the new building construction. The 1882 school building was closed and had sometimes been used as a wood shop. It became quite a sensation, to not only see a vacant building taken down, but also the stone re-used in the new gymnasium.

A Basketball Town—Fulton was a basketball town. The new gymnasium was the site of many winning seasons and community enjoyment. Three busses provided transportation to away games—a boys' bus, a girls' bus, and a community bus for all the eager, supportive fans.

High school football did not begin until the later years when eight-man was played. The school played in the Marmaton Valley League against Mulberry, Arcadia, Bronson, Elsmore, Kincaid, Greeley, and Fontana. In 1965, the last year of the school, the record was 3-3-1 with wins over Bronson, Mulberry, Fontana, losses to Elsmore, Kincaid, Greeley, and a tie game with Bronson. That same class of boys advanced to the school's only state basketball appearance, finishing in third place. They defeated Luray 72-60, were beaten by Gove, and won in the consolation third place game over Paxico 78-62.

A notable coach and teacher was Art Frisbie. From the 1966 school year book:

> Because of his outstanding success in coaching basketball and his great interest in the game, Mr. Frisbie has been called "Mr. Basketball" by the press. In his career previous to coming to Fulton he has produced winning teams for Mound City, Kansas, Alberton, Montana, Gallup, New Mexico, Pleasanton, and Fort Scott, Kansas. He has directed teams to more than 500 victories. During his fourteen years at Fulton, he has had winning teams every year but one. His Fulton teams have won 242 games to 61 lost. In the last four years, Fulton has not lost a game in regular season play. In the 1966 season, Fulton won third place in the Class BB State Tournament in Dodge City. But even more important, he has won the admiration and devotion from the community as well as from the many boys and girls he has taught. He will be long remembered as "Coach Frisbie."

Mrs. Letha Frisbie (Art's wife) also taught in Fulton for fourteen years. She taught home economics and social sciences. She was a very interesting teacher and only pretended to be unaware that the students would try to get her off-subject to talk about life's issues. There were a total of five teachers in the school at this time.

Preserving Memories—The first school annual was printed in 1920, *The Osaga*. From the inside cover: "The purpose of the annual is twofold, first as a book of memories which grows more valuable with age and second as a banner of the schools ideals, serving as an inspiration and an incentive to those who get to attend High School."

"Retrospection" by Vesta Dexter, showed that the high school was started in 1900 and it was an accredited high school course of four years with seventy-two members. Twenty were in the senior class.

The Osaga yearbook was a very remarkable, quality publication. The 1955 yearbook shows that the boys basketball team lost in the regional tournament finals to Arma. There were seventeen girls on the basketball team that year, and Mr. Frisbie was their coach. There were great numbers in the boys and girls glee clubs, speech, and dramatics. The 1964 yearbook was dedicated to the late President Kennedy.

Notable Students—Kathy Talbot recalled a story from a biology class. Clifford Roach had brought Indian turnips (jack in the pulpit) to class. He offered a taste of the root of the Indian turnips to the other students. Mr. Frisbie was the teacher and knew all about the effects of this seemingly harmless root. When tasting even a small bite of Indian turnip, it would send a pins and needles feeling to the tongue, mouth, and throat. Mr. Frisbie laughed long and hard as the students ran to the bathroom to try to wash out to this stinging irritant.

A renowned graduate, Tommie Ray VanSickle ('55) attended Baker University and the University of Kansas. Elected to the Kansas House of Representatives at the age of twenty-two, he would graduate from Washburn Law School while in the legislature. He later became a state senator and state treasurer. He led the way for the Highway 69 widening project and was instrumental in keeping it part of the Kansas freeway system and preventing it from becoming a turnpike. He traveled to Washington D.C. to meet with Joe Skubitz (from West Mineral) who was the administrative assistant to Senator Andy Schoeppel. Together they worked on getting a National Historical Site designation for the remains of the Old Ft. Scott. He later practice law in Ft. Scott and Arizona and was a community leader.

School Closing—The school closed after graduation in May 1966 with seventeen graduates in the class. There were 793 graduates in the fifty-one years from 1916-1966. The last to receive a diploma from Fulton High School was John Wunderly (alphabetically).

The most frequent surnames of the graduates were White-17, Clayton-13, Keating-12, Wimmers-9, Van Sickle-8 Brown-7, Hill-7, and 5 each for Clark, Grubb, Gump, Hennessy, Lyons, and Smith.

Fulton High School
Bourbon County, KS

#27

Pierceville High School

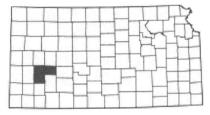

Mascot: Indians

Colors: Gray and Red

Year Closed: 1965

Location: town of Pierceville, extreme eastern edge of Finney County

High School History—Originally Finney County was named Buffalo County and Sequoyah County. The county is shaped like an inverted boot because in 1893 the current northeast region (then known as Garfield County) was annexed and the merged counties renamed Finney County after the then Lieutenant Governor of Kansas David Finney.

The Pierceville Rural High School was built in 1919 for $17,000 by J.J. Gigot. The two-story school building had the distinction of being built with a flat roof which would cause problems for the next sixty-five years.

The grade school building in Pierceville burned to the ground in 1920. It served as the meeting place for Sunday school and church services. Following the fire, the grade school and Sunday church services were held in the new high school until the new brick grade school building was finished in 1923. This was the meeting place for the church until a new church was built in 1949. The high school class of 1949, due to a rainy Sunday evening in May, held their baccalaureate in the first newly built church in Pierceville. The class of 1949 was the last to graduate in the original gymnasium in the high school building and the first class to wear caps and gowns for graduation.

Sports and Yearbook—In 1950, the new gymnasium, or the remodeled gym, was completed. It was referred to as the "Little Theater." It was the site of some fantastic basketball games. Tennis was also a big sport at PRHS though records do not show any out-of-town competition.

The first yearbook, *The Indian*, was published in 1955. It continued each year until the school closed.

Closing the School—Due to the state legislation requiring school districts to have at least 400 students, 200 square miles of land, and a $2 million valuation, the school was closed following graduation in 1965. Bill Cronin ('32) was a long-time school board member, and his son Louis Cronin ('65) was in the last graduating class. There were no options other than to close the school and disband the district. The students were bused to Garden City for high school the following year.

A total of 247 graduated from Pierceville Rural High School from 1923 through 1965. The largest class was 1938 with twelve graduates. Twenty couples married within the Pierceville graduation pool. One couple Bill Cronin ('32) and Thelma Runnell Cronin ('31), both being PRHS graduates, has seven children and a daughter-in-law graduate from Pierceville: Floyd ('56), Mada ('59), Loren ('60), Marsha ('61), Jon ('62), Louis ('65), and Moleta ('60). The most numerous surnames of the 247 graduates were Rundell-11, Cronin-8, Stephens-7, Horton-5 and Snodgrass-5. There were seven graduates in the last class of 1965 with Barbara Rodrock (alphabetically) being the last to receive a diploma from Pierceville Rural High School.

#28

Webster High School

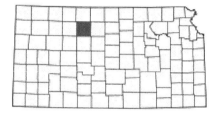

Mascot: Eagles

Colors: Black and Orange

Year Closed: 1963

Location: town of Webster, Rooks County, just west of north-central Kansas

A Personal Account of Webster — Webster High School and the quaint little community of Webster are colorfully described in a historical collection by Jean Grover Lindsey ('53). In this story is a delightful recollection by Jean's cousin, Carol Grover Devlin, from her personal memoir of life in rural Kansas in the 1940s titled *What Do You Do with the Yolks?*:

Eight miles west of Stockton on US Highway 24, one of the primary coast to coast east-west highways, a dirt road intersecting dipped into a valley a few miles to the south. Nestled under a canopy of trees, a rarity in western Kansas, which was practically treeless, sat the town of Webster. My life long quest for tranquility stems from the too-few years of my youth spent there with our relatives. Snatches of conversation and memories of that town are forever imprinted in my mind.

Thick trees made the sound and feel of the air in the grove remarkable: everything so quiet, calm, soft, and cool. Birds . . . mourning doves . . . a car passing in front of my grandparents' house created interest.

Webster's streets were lovely . . . silky dust, so soft to walk on barefoot. We rarely wore shoes in the summer . . . floury dust puff . . . rain barely penetrated the fine, dense dust . . . drying fusing . . . smooth quarter-inch crust . . . broke into an odd shaped puzzle . . . curled up around the edges. We loved to step on them . . . crinkly crust dissolve . . . without leaving a trace of the puddle.

A lone gas pump, with its hose hanging on the side. The store, groceries, hardware, parts for cars . . . ice cream . . . light meals and coffee. The ice in the pop chest . . . Chocolate Soldier, Grape or Orange Nehi.

This description is so personal of the little community that was eventually demolished for the reservoir that would cover the valley and the town of Webster.

Town History — In 1876, a trading post was established along this section of the Solomon River. With the abundance of underground water, a settlement grew. Ten years later, by 1886, there were thirty-six new buildings in the town and 300 residents. There were two doctors, two churches, and a school. When the railroad construction stopped at Stockton, it was a death sentence for this growing community. Another possible north-south railroad ended in 1907 with a money panic, and the rails were never laid.

Education — Webster School District #23 was organized in 1879 in an old log cabin with a dirt floor. Twenty-one grade school students were taught by a teacher earning $12 per month. In 1886, a two-story, frame grade school building was built for $1,200. This village school consolidated in 1911 with two other township schools totaling twenty-seven sections, or twenty-seven square miles of land. Consolidation was an experiment, and Webster became only the second such district in the state to try it.

A new building was dedicated on January 1, 1914, with the grade school on the lower floor and the high school on the upper level. The students in outlying areas stayed with residents in Webster during the week. Before long, horse-drawn buses, and later motorized buses, transported the rural children.

The school was fully accredited with courses in vocational agriculture, home economics, normal training, and music. The first graduating class in 1918 had three graduates. From 1918-1954, 341 graduates received their diplomas at Webster. 1954 was the last class that graduated from this school before the demolition of the whole town for the creation of the Webster reservoir.

A new high school was built high on a bluff two miles to the southeast of the original town site. Some houses were also built at this site, and a few businesses tried to relocate to this windswept "new" Webster. Controversy about whether to build the new school splintered the community. Many parents enrolled their children at neighboring schools of Stockton, Plainville, and Palco rather than at the new school on the hill. Another thirty-three graduated from this new high school in the next nine years.

A Memorable Teacher — An excellent music teacher, Mr. Paul Darnell, who suffered from seizures, landed at this small school. As remembered by Wayne Grover ('58):

> Mr. Darnell was an excellent teacher and his classes were full, from band to all of the choirs and ensembles. He had been hired by the school district possibly because other larger districts shied away because of his handicap. He drove daily from Plainville and could make music from his students that was exceptional and gave lasting life time memories. The district bought band uniforms and even instruments like the piccolo that helped him educate and teach music. The band marched at the state fair in Hutchinson and at parades in Ft. Hays. Possibly out of step, and not with the largest complement of musicians, the Webster Band played with spirit and pride of their abilities for their school and student body. It is a testament to a brilliant teacher who shared his passion for music with his students and the community.

Clubs & Athletics — Y- Teens was a club that had as many as twelve girls involved. They met with the YWCA. Webster did not field a football team, but competed in baseball, basketball, and track.

The rivals were all of the Little Six League teams: Densmore, Clayton, Edmond, Prairie View, Damar, and Bogue. The team that posed the biggest challenge and frustration was Prairie View because those Dutchmen were always four inches taller. Damar may have been the dirtiest foe, and Bogue was the most fun to defeat.

School Closing — Due to lack of enrollment, the relocated Webster school closed in May 1963. A total of 374 graduated from Webster High School in the 46 years from 1918-1963. The largest graduating class was 1941 with twenty-three graduates. The most numerous surnames of the graduates were Lowery-13, Grover-9, Blauer-7, Brown-7, Burton-7, Lindsey-6, McCormick-6, Ricardson-6, and Sammons-6. The last to receive a diploma in 1963 was Shannon Veverka (alphabetically).

#29

Potter Rural High School

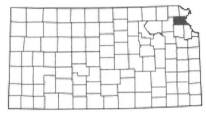

Mascot: Bulldog

Colors: Royal Blue and White

Year closed: 1957

Location: town of Potter, southeast corner of Atchison County, one mile from the Leavenworth County line

The Father of Potter, Kansas — Joseph Potter was the original owner of and the first settler on the land which became the town site of Potter. This occurred after passage of the Kansas-Nebraska Act which opened Kansas Territory for settlement in 1854.

Joseph Potter was born in Lincoln County, Kentucky, on April 4, 1819. In 1841 he moved to Buchanan County, Missouri, and settled about half way between Weston and St. Joseph. In 1846 he enlisted in Company B of the Missouri Battalion and served in the Mexican War, making the great overland march to Santa Fe. During the border troubles in Kansas, he was one of the leaders in the Free State cause. In Civil War times, he was a recruiting officer for the federal government and served as an officer in the state militia. He served in the state legislature in the 1880s and was one of the one-hundred who voted in favor of the prohibitory law. He was the first man to introduce John J. Ingalls (who would become governor) to a Kansas audience.

Kansas Legislature Paves Way—The Fairview School House was built in 1868. It was larger than the average district school of that period and had a belfry and a good bell. Fairview was all that the name implied and more. It afforded not only a fair view, but a fine view of the surrounding country. Religious services were held in the schoolhouse for many years. The Fairview School was consolidated with Potter schools, and the old schoolhouse was torn down in 1910. On April 2, 1908, the community voted to build a new school east of the old building. The three-story Potter school was built in 1911. The Fairview cemetery marks the site of the first school in the area.

Potter Rural High School District was established in August 1915 in accordance with the Rural High School Statute passed by the legislature in the spring of 1915. The school was the first rural high school in the state organized under this act. The Board of Education leased the top story of the Potter grade school and the high school opened on September 6, 1915, with eighteen students. Classes were held in this building until January 1941 when the new WPA building was completed.

The Potter Kansan reported on July 28, 1932:

The town of Potter reached its 45th birthday on July 21st, 1932. It was platted July 23, 1887 as Bennet Springs and the plat was filed in the office of the register of deeds of Atchison County. Bennet Springs was dedicated by Fred W. Poos and Joseph Potter on April 1, 1890. The town was never platted under the name of Potter, and there is no record in the Register of Deeds office that the name was ever changed from Bennett Springs to Potter. They had conceived the idea of establishing a health resort at the place on account of the mineral springs near there and thinking to interest eastern capital in the venture it was named Bennett Springs in the honor of James Gordon Bennet the noted eastern journalist of that period . . . The Santa Fe railroad had previously established a station there and named it Potter for Joseph Potter who owned the land comprising the town site. The post office was originally established as Potter. Tom Potter was born in 1856 and was the first postmaster. He served there for 38 years.

As reported in *The Potter Kansan* on January 24, 1929:

The Faculty-Board Luncheon. Five girls from the class in Home Economics and their supervisor Miss Stoops attracted considerable credit to themselves last week by preparing the first Faculty-Board luncheon at the High school. The meal was complete in every detail, even to the tiny marshmallow snow men who stood by each plate to extend greeting and best wishes for the Happy New Year . . . The meal included Veal loaf, scallop potatoes, tomatoes, apple salad, jelly, Carmel dessert and coffee.

Student Memories—The new school built by the WPA was completed at Christmas time 1940 on a hill east of town. This was a combination grade and high school with the first indoor gymnasium for Potter. Ed Theis ('52) recalled the day that the new school was finally occupied: "We had been instructed to bring a sack or box to school to help move our books and desk contents. I was in the first grade and this move was quite an experience. That year I rode to school every day on the back of a neighbor's bicycle from out in the country from our farm house."

George Highfill ('42) gave a colorful remembrance of his years at Potter Rural High School:

I started high school in 1938. We did not have a gym for the first two years, but our coach, W.B. Elliot, marked off a court in the dirt, got some logs for a goal post, and bolted two hoops on the backboard and we had an outdoor gymnasium. We practiced outside until the new high school and gym was finished in the winter of 1940.

On February 9, 1940, the seven basketball players from Potter High School piled into one car and traveled fifteen miles to Atchison to play the Lincoln School Kittens. The Atchison school was integrated but would not allow the colored players to play on the high school team. The district did allow them to have their own colored team. The night is as vivid to me as that night my favorite boxer, Joe Louis, was fighting the Chilean boxer, Arturo Godoy, in Madison Square Garden.

I had followed Joe Louis for a long time. I read about him in the newspapers and listened to his fights on the radio. We lived on a farm and didn't have electricity, but whenever Joe Louis was scheduled to fight, I would quit work in the fields early and walk to town to sit outside the mechanic's garage. The mechanic would play his radio loud so that people outside could listen.

That night in Atchison we suited up to play in the brand new gym at Lincoln School. We played a junior varsity game, but the varsity game was held up. At first I didn't know why. Then I noticed some of the Kittens' fans had radios, and they were listening to the Louis-Godoy fight. My team went back to the locker room, but I went up into the stands and sat with the families and listened to the match. It lasted fifteen rounds with Louis winning by decision. After this long delay we played the first team from Lincoln. I am pretty sure we lost.

What happened that night has stayed with me for a lifetime. At the time, I didn't know much about the history of racial injustice in the United States. I think I understood something of what Joe Louis and his successes in the ring meant to African-Americans in those days.

That same year we drove down to Piper in Wyandotte County for a game. They had a concrete gym floor. The game was rough and a fight broke out on the court. Don "Dutch" Binkley ('42) was a fighter. He picked one of the Piper players up and dropped him on the court. After a time out the game was called off and we retreated to a classroom to change our clothes. Looking out the window we saw an angry crowd gathered to meet us in the parking lot. Luckily, the Piper superintendent was still in the building and called the police. We were escorted out of town.

The players on that team were Melvin Stewart ('41), Nelson Pohl ('42), Donald Binkley ('42), Charles Piper ('42), George Highfill ('42), and Lester Lohman ('43).

George Highfill ('42) went immediately into the service after graduation in May 1942. He recalled, "There were four Potter graduates killed in World War II: Russel Cline ('38), Donald "Dutch" Binkley ('42), Robert Ode ('43), and Melvin Roach ('38). Binkley was killed on the Biak Island. On that night there were three others from Potter within fifteen miles of that site. I was on an LCI (landing craft infantry). My cousin, Norman "Nooks" Highfill ('43) was in a ship nearby. Charlie Piper ('42) was in Dutch's same unit. Such a small high school, such a high percentage killed in the war, and so many of us around this small Island in the far-off Pacific was quite a deal."

The 1954 senior trip was to Kansas City. Cheril Adams Hefner ('54) recalled, "There were eleven in our class, four girls and seven boys. We had the evening all planned to go to the Ice Capades. The boys outnumbered us and so outvoted us and we had to go to a John Wayne movie. I have not forgiven them to this day (2018). We girls only had one room at the hotel to share. Three slept in the bed and one of us slept in the bathtub.

"My mother, Marsha Mildred Adams, was a teacher here for nearly fifty years, retiring at the age of seventy. She had bought a Model T Ford and drove to Potter from Minden, Nebraska, freshly out of Cotner College. She would marry one of her students, Jack Adams ('27). During the war she was principal for two years."

Pranks in Potter were not much different than most other small towns with the shenanigans of Halloween being most remembered. One rather comical scene was Norman "Nooks" Highfill ('43) staying in the school one time after a fire drill was called. He later would jump out of a first story window to much laughter from the students, but Principal Floyd Talley looked upon the incident differently.

Notable Student/Teacher—Eugene Lee ('20) became an extra special man to the community of Potter, Atchison County, and the state of Kansas. He taught at the high school in the 1920s and 30s. He stepped down from teaching to become an Atchison County Commissioner, serving for twenty-four years. He served on the Potter school board until the year the school closed in 1957. He also served on the state tax appeals board. Lee returned as a volunteer coach of the basketball and eight-man football teams in the 1950s. He coached town team basketball for years. The 1956 Potter yearbook was dedicated to him. This Potter graduate gave so much back to his fellow man.

Closing Potter High School—There were 245 graduates of Potter High School from 1916-1957 when the school closed. The largest class to graduate was thirteen in 1942. The last class, 1957, had two graduates-- Claudia Frey and Donna Theis. The most numerous surnames of the graduates in forty-two years of Potter High were Highfill-9, Cline-8, Lohman-8, Kruse-6, Piper-6, Theis-6, Bell-5 Meinhart-5, and Ode-5. There were four African Americans among the graduates. Their last names were Johnson and Lovejoy.

The high school closed following graduation in 1957. The district unified with Effingham. For years there were ill feelings toward Effingham for having sent buses right into Potter to take students away to school. Many believed this caused the declining enrollment in Potter which led to the school's closing. The disagreement was so deep that when the school was closed, a vast majority of families sent their students west into Jefferson County to Nortonville.

Potter Rural High School
Atchison County, KS

#30

Peru High School

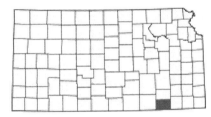

Mascot: Trojan

Colors: Orange and black

Year Closed: 1966

Location: town of Peru, southeast Chautauqua County

History of Peru — While the town was just a cluster of cabins in 1870, the first school was started in the home of J. Milton for two months in the fall term. School District #47 was organized in the fall of 1871 and two more months were taught as part of a subscription school.

The town grew with the development of a stagecoach line. Two railroads came to town with the Missouri Pacific line on the north side, and the Santa Fe on the south side. The county seat was moved to Peru and remained there for two years. It was moved to Sedan in 1873. A newspaper called the *Wide Awake* was started in 1872, and it had big news to report as a tornado destroyed the school that summer. A new, two-room structure was raised on the site of the old school. The rooms were called the "big" room and the "little" room.

The oil boom of 1902-1906 brought jobs to the area and the population of Peru swelled to 1,500. A large brick plant was established on the east edge of town. This plant and a glass plant flourished for many years.

School History — The Peru High School was started in the "Big" room of the school. W.A. Tanksley, a much beloved teacher for fourteen years, started teaching advanced classes.

A new, eight-room high school was built at the cost of $10,000 just south of the two-room school. It was completed in 1904. This school was organized as a three-year high school with the first graduating class in 1907. Two years later it would expand to a four-year high school.

The next superintendent, Bell, began a three-year administration in 1922. He started planning the new school building which was built on a ten-acre plot donated by the Prairie Oil Company. It was erected for $75,000. The building was completed in 1924. It was a classic red brick building with the building material coming from the local brick company. It was beautifully designed with the front facing the west. PHS was a grade A school with home economics, typing, bookkeeping, dramatics, and music courses offered. Each class presented a play, and an all high school play was given. The glee clubs gave the first operetta, "The Gypsy Rover."

When the new school opened, the stage roll curtain and parts of the stage properties were trimmed in the school colors of purple and gold. The alumni later donated the heavy velvet pull curtains. The colors were changed to orange and black when PHS joined a league with Cherryvale, which also used purple and gold.

The Peru schools underwent consolidation efforts and became the R-3 District in 1946. It was not until the school closed twenty years later that the final unification would occur with Sedan.

Athletics — Basketball was introduced for both boys and girls in 1910. They played on an outdoor court in a vacant lot. The next court would be in the opera house. Many parents objected to basketball, and it was not until 1914 when the boys team began to play other schools that the sport became popular in the community. The first teams were made of seventh and eighth grade boys, as well as high school students. This practice continued until 1925 when the junior high league was organized in the county.

The girls did not play much until Superintendent W. Rankin Young succeeded in convincing the parents that it was a proper sport for girls. Great girls teams existed from 1919-1925.

The boys started playing football in 1939. The 1959 team was undefeated and played eight-man football. The biggest rival was Sedan for both baseball and basketball. The girls played six-on-six half-court with a rover.

A new basketball coach, Eldon Mrstic, came in 1955. One of his players, John Uhls ('56), starred on the team that year. Uhls is featured in the book, *Club 50*, written by Steven Michael Farney, as one of the few Kansas players to score over fifty points in a game. He never scored fewer than twenty-seven points in a game that

year with forty points four times and fifty-six against Elk Falls.

Travels beyond Peru — Senior trips entertained students for many years. In 1959, all four members of the class went to New Orleans and Biloxi, Mississippi. Evelyn Palmer, a grocery store owner, escorted the group as she drove a new, beautiful gray and white Ford. The faculty sponsor who also accompanied the group was Willene Richardson.

The 1961 class also journeyed to New Orleans. The sponsors were Mr. Oxford, Barney Mecom, and Barney's wife Melba. In Baton Rouge an incredible story unfolded. They all stayed at the La Fontaine Blue Motel which had a restaurant called the Stork Club. They dressed up for this quite formal dining experience and soon found out that it was a night club. They sat right there on the front row. Following a very lewd comic act, the striptease act began. They went about as far as they could go. At first the sponsors acted dumbfounded, but they later indicated that they may have had an inkling of the acts. The school bus would later drive right down Bourbon Street. The students ate at the Two Sisters, swam in Lake Pontchartrain, and stopped in Natchez on the way home. It was quite an education for the new graduates.

The 1963 class headed for Rockaway Beach in Missouri. The sponsors were Miss Bertha Cain (born in 1900) and Harry Daniels.

Student Organizations — The first yearbook was printed in 1935. It was titled *The Echo*. Possibly left to the discretion of the annual staff or their sponsor, the names of succeeding yearbooks varied. 1938 was called the *Pro-Memoria*. 1940 *Trojan*. 1947-50 *the Peruvian,* and again in the 1950s called the *Trojan*. No year books were published during the war years.

One of the most outstanding organizations at PHS was the Pencrafters Club. It was organized with thirteen members in the fall of 1957. Nancy McMullen ('63) says "Mrs. Jesse Mae Coker was the most influential teacher I ever had. She taught English, journalism, and history. She had published eighty-five articles in magazines and won more than 150 literary prizes." The club sponsored the County Teenage Writing Contest for five years. Peru High school would win more than eighty-four prizes in journalism during that time span. McMullen said that they stayed after school every day to write "Confessions" for the Ft. Lauderdale, Florida newspaper. Mrs. Coker drove her home every night after school. Mrs. Coker was a renowned Kansas author.

Speechville, a unique project in the English department, was started in 1958 and continued for four years. PHS students began entering a four-state Press Day competition at the University of Tulsa in 1958. Mrs. Coker would judge and was quite instrumental in the organization of this event for the students. Peru won several honors and prizes each year.

Participating in the world-wide observance of the 400th anniversary of Shakespeare in 1964, PHS students had a Shakespeare festival. Again, honors were received for their work.

Memories — Jim Rinck ('43) graduated at sixteen years old. He was too young for the service but said he begged his father who would not sign the papers to let him enlist. He said of the school bus, "which was even old when I rode on it. If I missed the bus, which happened quite often, I would just wait about fifteen minutes and the Jun-gle Bread Truck from Coffeyville would always stop and give me a ride. There were four boys in our family and the family across the field had six girls. I had my pick and I chose the tomboy. We are still together today [2018]."

In 1943 there was a gas shortage because of the war. Jim Rinck ('43) remembers, "a semi-truck trailer had turned over in the ditch. Everybody and his half-brother was out there dipping up the spilled gas!"

Under the leadership of Superintendent John Hedges, a homecoming queen tradition was started in 1959 with Pat Hull being the first queen. Lights were installed and the first night football games were played that same year. Undefeated, Queen, and lights, all in the same year: the student body must have believed that things could not be any better.

A talented and inspiring drafting teacher, Harry Daniels, came in the 1950s. He started pupils in the fifth and sixth grade with drafting, mechanical drawing, and construction projects. By starting this early with the addition of four years of high school classes, many students were able to go directly into engineering and mechanical construction businesses.

A beloved janitor was Charlie Young. He always smoked a pipe. On one occasion, some mischievous boys sneaked in and put gun powder in his pipe and tamped it down. The explosion is remembered in story to this day.

The End of Peru High School — There were 625 graduates from Peru High School from 1907 through 1966. The most common surnames of the graduates were Jones-11, Reed-11, Palmer-10, Smith-9, Ferrel-9, Henderson-7, Rayl-7, and Endicott-7.

The last graduating class was in May of 1966 with nine graduates. The last one to receive a Peru High School diploma was Linda Smith (alphabetically).

The school district was consolidated with Sedan in 1966. "Now the Peru High school is no more!" were the words for the final year book. "We are part of USD #286, and future Peru students will be sent to a building in Sedan. No human mind can estimate the influence of the school that has served for 60 years."

Peru High School
Chatauqua County, KS

#31

Windthorst High School

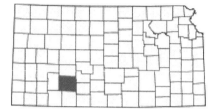

Mascot: Bluejays

Colors: Blue and White

Year Closed: 1970

Location: town of Windthorst, extreme east-central Ford County

Windthorst in Germany — Though the high school was built nearly forty years after the town was founded, the story of the town's beginning is relevant to the community and the education of their families.

Ludwig Von Windthorst was born in 1812 at Keldendorf, near the city of Osnabruck in the Kingdom of Hanover. Windthorst became a lawyer and was known as an outstanding Catholic leader in Germany. He sought civil justice for his church with the slogan *"Fur Wahrheit, Freiheit, und Recht"*—"For Truth, Liberty, and Right."

Under his leadership, the Catholics formed a political party called the *Centre Verein* (Central Party) to protect the church from state domination. In the 1860s and 70s, Otto von Bismarck and his followers began their fight against the German Catholic people. This controversy continued for twenty years, and in the end, Bismarck acknowledged defeat.

By unity of purpose and action, its unflinching devotion to Catholic principles, and strictly lawful methods, per the author Thomas P. Neill, the party won the admiration of right-thinking people all over the world. An Irish author writing in the *Catholic World* said of Windthorst, "Never . . . has there arisen a more valiant and successful advocate of Catholic rights than Ludwig Windthorst. It may be said that he found a way to protect the things of God from the encroachment of Caesar." (from *They Lived With Faith*, by Thomas P. Neill)

Windthorst in Kansas—A nephew of Ludwig Windthorst, Msgr. Ernest M. Windthorst (1864-1923), came to the United States in 1869. He was ordained to the priesthood on June 2, 1871, in Cincinnati. He served in many parishes of Cincinnati and baptized a few of the early pioneers of the Windthorst, Kansas, parish.

In a pamphlet titled *Centennial*, it is defined as lasting 100 years, is also the definition of the faith on which Windthorst parish was founded and the faith on which it has continued. These words written in 1977 were of the strong faith, brought to this area 100 years ago, and still is its future today.

In 1876, a number of men from various trades met at the Arbeiter Hall in Cincinnati, Ohio. Cobblers, tailors, carpenters, foundry workers, guilders, tanners, blacksmiths, and common laborers met with a desire to better their conditions as times and wages were not at their best. Several meetings were held by these German men and the German Catholic Aurora Homestead Association.

They instigated correspondence with D.C. Schmidt, the Topeka General Land Agent of the Santa Fe Railroad, who showed great interest in the proposed aims of the Aurora Homestead Association. Mr. Schmidt went to Cincinnati to meet with the Society. There, he wholeheartedly recommended a tract of land in Ford County, Kansas, for their settlement, ten miles south of Offerle, extending to Osage Indian Territory. Thus, the town of Windthorst was created.

A School is Built—The *Spearville News* reported in the April 7, 1970 issue: "By 1915 it became apparent that the two-room school with its adjoining building could no longer accommodate the children satisfactorily. Plans were undertaken to erect a school that would be the pride of the community as well as a place to educate grade and high school students."

In 1919, the high school was fully accredited by the State Department of Education.

On April 18, 1926, a contract was awarded to Alex Helwig, Hoisington, Kansas, for the sum of $27,723.59. The cornerstone of the new Catholic school building was laid on June 8, 1927. The building was completed December 1, 1927. Approximately $30,000 worth of equipment was purchased for the school.

From 1921 to 1939, the grade school teaching staff was increased to three sisters, one each for the primary, intermediate, and upper grade pupils. At first the high school had one instructor for all subjects offered, but as enrollment increased and the need arose, the staff was increased to eight teachers to instruct the students on the secondary level.

A Music Program — Although music had been taught to some extent, there was no music teacher until 1939. Several attempts were made to organize a band and an orchestra, but none proved successful until October 1947 when Sister Praxedes organized an all-school band. The high school choir had by then been under the direction of a music teacher for over twenty years. Glee clubs for both boys and girls, mixed chorus groups, quartets, sextets, and octets added to the enjoyment and education of the Windthorst students.

Private Catholic School Becomes Public — From *The School Booster*, September 12, 1940, "Arrangements have been made through District 12 to maintain the Immaculate Heart of Mary High school as a public school. This does away with the tuition charge and enables a larger number of pupils to attend. In 1940, the enrollment had increased to 40 pupils. Prior to this time, a fee of $40 per year was assessed each student enrolled in the high school."

First Consolidation in Ford County — Windthorst Booster information from the April 9, 1970 issue of the *Spearville News*:

> At a special meeting of the voters of District 11 on May 17, 1945, it was decided to consolidate with District 12. The voters of that District unanimously agreed to make the consolidation possible. It was decided to call the union Consolidated District I since this was the first consolidation in Ford County. A few

years later, the legal title of the Windthorst schools was changed to District 77.

In the summer of 1948, the patrons of District 77 voted bonds to build a $65,000 gymnasium-auditorium on the ground across the road from the school. The vote carried 55 to 37. The project was begun in the fall of 1948, but due to a cement shortage, it was not completed until the spring of 1949. The structure was 130 feet long and 70 feet wide.

In the spring of 1952, the district patrons voted to build a modern industrial shop that would compare favorably with those of other schools and give the boys more opportunity and better equipment. Not all of the improvements were for the boys, however. Included in the upgrade was a model kitchen, fully equipped for preparing food, as well as sewing machines for sewing.

The *Spearville News* May 7, 1970:

> We have decided to end the history in this issue. We shall tell you of the happenings during the last year at Windthorst High.
>
> Windthorst High School opened its doors for the 45th consecutive year to an enrollment of 59 students. Early in the year, we were confronted with the prospect of closing W.H.S. As the year progressed, it was announced that the Windthorst High School would be closed. A new mascot, the Royal Lancer, was chosen for the coming 1970-71 school term for Spearville High School. Grades 8-11 from both the Spearville and Windthorst schools voted on names submitted to them.
>
> On December 7, the senior class presented "Butter on the Bacon," as the annual senior play.
>
> Sports wise, the Bluejays football record showed 4 wins and 5 losses. The record for basketball stands 13

wins, and 11 loses. This year the Bluejays advanced to the Regional Tournament to win third place.

At present, two senior girls have received scholarships to continue their education. Aleta Tasset received a music scholarship from St. Mary of the Plains College. Diane Ackerman received a scholarship from KLEO to attend Professional Beauty College in Wichita.

The staff of the Booster hopes that you have enjoyed reading these articles. Through these articles, we have tried to pay a final tribute to our great school. Always remember though, that the memories of your days at Windthorst High will remain forever.

School Closing—The Windthorst High School closed

following graduation in May 1970. There were 431 graduates in forty-five years, from 1926-1970. There were eighteen in the final graduating class. The last graduate from Windthorst High School was Janet Wetzel (alphabetically).

The most frequent surnames of the graduates were Hornung-38, Ackerman-29, Tasset-27, Troline-21, Stein-16, Peintner-12, Burkhart-11, and Issinghoff-10. These eight family names made up over 38% of the total graduates.

Windthorst
Ford County, KS

32

Collyer High School

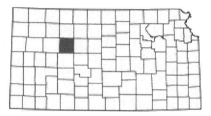

Mascot: Wildcats

Colors: Black and Gold

Year Closed: 1966

Location: town of Collyer, northwest corner of Trego County

From Coyote to Collyer — The growth of the Kansas Pacific Railway attracted homesteaders to western Kansas. In January 1878, a colony of soldiers, sailors, and citizens was formed in Chicago. The Rev. Robert Collyer, D.D., a Unitarian minister, was the president and an honorary member of the colony. The first location of the town was three-quarters of a mile southwest of the eventual town site, and these homesteaders called it Coyote because it was the terminus of the railroad and a pumping station. A year later, the colony was moved east because of better water. The new location was called Collyer.

Irish Catholic immigrants arrived with the Chicago colony on March 17, 1878. It is not known of the significance or the happenstance that they arrived on St. Patrick's Day. These immigrants became the nucleus of the Catholics in the settlement.

In 1880, eight more Irish families arrived. A large colony of Bohemians arrived in 1889. The first German immigrants from Odessa, Russia, came in 1901. They had fled the Kaiser and farmed in Russia in the 1700s. Now they left because of the Czar in Russia and for inexpensive land in America. Another group of these Russians came the next year, including Theodore Ziegler, Christian Ziegler, J. Malsom, and J.B. Walt.

First Schools — The first notice to form a school district, No. 2, was dated August 13, 1879. The first school south of the railroad track was constructed of stone and served as a community center for many years.

In 1907, a new school was built directly south of the old one. It was a two-story, frame building and served from 1907-1936.

When Father Michael P. Dreiling came to St. Michaels Parish in Collyer in 1913, there were forty-five families listed on the parish census. Father did not feel that there was enough religious education. He initiated plans for a parochial school building. The parishioners and the bishop responded favorably, and contributions were solicited. The wheat harvest project on eighty acres of rented land netted $787.82. (These eighty acres may have been deeded to the church.) Construction of the school building began in the fall of 1916. The school was dedicated on September 29, 1919.

A public high school was organized in 1919 by Mr. Sam (S.S.) Long. He served on the faculty for nine years with eight of those years being the principal too. In an article published in the town newspaper headlined, "The New Principal," it was written as follows:

> One of the strong men of the Farmers Union was, at the same time is accounted to be one of the foremost educators in Western Kansas. Samuel S. Long has been engaged as the new principal of the Collyer school for the upcoming term. Mr. Long holds a State Certificate on permit to teach in any high school within Kansas. The report is also that his teaching record ranks way above average, especially in Gove County. And he has constantly kept himself in touch with things educational we can confidently expect that he will give us a most satisfactory service. The Advance (newspaper) begs to congratulate our school board for their good judgement and fortune in securing for Collyer the services of such an excellent educator.

From the WaKeeney paper, August 25, 1919:

Notice to Collyer High School students
Commercial Arithmetic by Von Tuly
Commercial Geography by Brigham   Price $1.50

The first and second year's high school work will be offered requiring the following texts:
First year
English I-Elements of Composition by Canby and Updyke
                                        Price 85 cents
Algebra by Hawks and Luby   Price 97 cents
General Sciences - First Year Science by Hessler
                                        Price $1.07
Ancient History - Outlines of European History Part 1
by Robinson   Price $1.32
New Physical Geography by Tarr   Price 88 cents
Second Year
English II - Elements of Composition by Canby and Updyke
                                        Price 85 cents
Plane and Solid Geometry by Ford and Ammermon
                                        Price 70 cents
Outlines of European History (Medieval and Modern)
Part II by Robinson   Price $1.32

Bonds in the amount of $23,000 were issued against the district on October 15, 1935. This amount was matched with government aid, and a new brick school was finished in the summer of 1936. This would be the first high-school-only building in Collyer, independent of the grade school in the same building.

Notable Graduates—Gerald Tomanek ('38) went into education with his expertise in the field of botany. He served as the President of Fort Hays State University from 1976-1987. Education was instilled in him by many. It could have started with his mother, Hazel Tomanek, who taught in Collyer from 1924-1966, taking fourteen years off, presumably to raise children.

Other graduates of Collyer High School have been successful in all walks of life. Because it was primarily an agricultural community, many became farmers and took on inherited family farms.

Sports in Collyer—Baseball and basketball were the sports at which the boys of Collyer most excelled. During the decade of the 1950s, the basketball team reached regionals four years but never did reach the state tournament. The baseball team finished second in the state in 1959, 1960, and 1962. Gale Scanlon ('61) was an outstanding pitcher during those years. He was very talented in music, served in the air force, received his MBA, and became a prominent businessman in Wakeeney, Kansas.

Collyer's End—The first and only graduate of Collyer High School in 1920 was Marie Miller Walsh. There were no graduates in 1921, 1922, and 1925. A total of 364 graduated from 1920 through 1966. There were 225 teachers that taught school in Collyer grade and high schools. The last year there were thirty-eight students enrolled at the school (five Zieglers). There were ten graduates in the last class, 1966. Mary Ziegler was the last to receive a diploma from Collyer High School.

The name Ziegler was a significant surname in the school's history. A total of fifty-five Zieglers graduated from Collyer which is over 15% of all of the graduates in the forty-seven years of the high school. Many of those were descendants of the group of German-Russians that came to the area in 1902.

#33

Jarbalo Rural High School

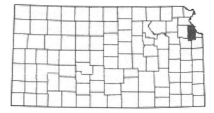

Mascot: Panthers

Colors: Purple and Gold

Year Closed: 1966

Location: village of Jarbalo, south-central Leavenworth County

The Origins of Jarbalo—The name Jarbalo came from the area's first German immigrants in the 1850s. Among these early settlers were the John Zoeller family who came from Heidelberg, Germany. These settlers heard the name for this hilly region called "Diablo Hills," but corrupted it with their pronunciation and it came to be called Jarbalo.

According to the archives of the *Leavenworth Times*, the original name of Diablo came about when Col. Alexander W. Doniphan and his men were in route to take part in the Mexican War. Doniphan led his men through very strenuous drills, up and down over the steep and rugged hills, hardening them for the long and tedious journey ahead. One of the recruits remarked, "This is a devil of a place." From that incident the locality was named Diablo Hills. Diablo is the Spanish name for devil.

The Santa Fe Railroad crossed this area in 1875, causing the town site to be relocated about a mile in order to be next to the railroad. In the new town site, Zoeller started a mercantile. The business was sold several times. Sam Oplinger bought the property and built his store on the site in 1912. For the next sixty-two years, this store would provide goods to the community. It was leveled by one of the rash of fifteen tornadoes that hit northeast Kansas on June 8, 1966. Rebuilt from the ground up, it remained a viable business until it closed in 1974.

At one time there were two passenger trains and one freight train running daily through Jarbalo. There were two grocery stores, a lumberyard, garage, blacksmith, post office, a creamery, and the Stranger Valley Grange Hall.

Education in Jarbalo — The high school was dedicated on October 26, 1917. It had the distinction of being the first rural high school in the county. Following selections played by the Yeoman Orchestra, Governor Arthur H. Capper gave the address.

The first principal was Sam Smith, a graduate of Emporia State Teachers College. He taught math and physics and coached athletics. There were two graduates that first year in 1918.

Mrs. Lena Jent was the next principal in 1918-1819. She taught normal schooling (a teacher training class). Some of those who completed her course became among the finest teachers in the rural schools of Leavenworth County. She was succeeded the next year by her husband, Henry Clay Jent, as the principal.

Mr. and Mrs. Jerry Loveall were the first caretakers for the building. There were approximately forty students the first year in the new high school.

Reported in the *Leavenworth Post* on February 4, 1923:

> Old man "Jinx" still camped on the trail of the Jarbalo high boys' basketball team last Friday night when they lost the game . . . to Tonganoxie high school boys . . . The Tonganoxie players were brawny and very rangy although not any faster that the Jarbolites . . . Although the boys lost their game, the girls evened up things when they played the Tongie girls . . . The girls game was exciting. Interest ran high. It was predicted that without the help of the senior girls, some of whom had played in every game for four years, Jarbalo would lose. But it would take more than six girls of the basketball caliber that Tonga offered to overcome the offensive taken by Jarbalo.

In 1926, Mr. Loren O. Gaddis became the principal. He stayed for the next sixteen years.

On the fateful night of December 31, 1933, a fire completely destroyed the high school. After the first shock had passed, board members Edward Wager, William Somers, W.B. Kiester, and principal Gaddis began plans for the continuation of the school. The trustees of the Methodist Episcopal Church offered the use of the church building. Stranger Valley Grange No. 11 offered their hall. And the Rev. and Mrs. Carl French offered a part of their parsonage. Immediately after Christmas vacation, school was resumed.

A teacher, Miss Julia Farrar, wrote, "After the school burned, the old church building became a study hall with small classes recitation sometimes in odd corners, the parsonage was used by the school, the upper floor of the Grange Hall, and after grade school was out for the summer, the grade school building was used. During the 1934-35 school year, the same buildings were used with the addition of the old pool hall.

Bonds of $5,000 were voted on in the winter of 1934. Insurance from the old building amounted to $15,000 and a WPA grant for $8,847 was received from the government covering the total cost of $26,610. Construction for the new high school began on February 11, 1935, and was completed in 133 days on June 21, 1935, by Green Brothers Construction Company of Lawrence.

Coincidently, two bricklayers, George Bacon and Antone Slapezynski, worked on both of the high schools. Mr. Bacon who laid the first brick and last bricks in 1917 left the honor of laying the first and last bricks on the second building to Mr. Slapezynski.

From the *Mayflower*, 1938 school yearbook opening page:

> We leave this Mayflower of the old English origins, with you in remembrance of the class of 1938 so you may spend many happy hours reminiscing of the days spent in old J.H.S. We, the senior class of 1938 dedicate the Mayflower Annual to Miss Pearl Branson for her sincere interest and eight years of loyal service. Without ostentation, she implanted the seeds of love, honor, loyalty, truthfulness, ambitions, unselfishness, cleanliness, and righteousness. It is sincerely to be hoped that these seeds will grow as she intended them.

Class Day Programs — A traditional end-of-school potluck dinner was held on the last day of school. The event included awards, letters, and recognition of students. The May 19, 1939, "Class Day Program" was highlighted with the mixed chorus singing "Water Boy" and the "Volga Boatman's Song" and the presentation of awards by Mr. Gaddis. A speech was given by Mr. Gaddis titled, "I don't want to die."

The next year's "Class Day Program" at the community dinner on May 17, 1940, listed the boys glee club singing "Yo Ho! For the Rolling Sea and Bells of the Sea." The President's address was given by George New, titled "Worthy Successors." Both years' programs ended with the singing of "God Bless America."

A Beloved Teacher — One of the most distinguished and beloved teachers, Mrs. Mae Henry, was honored in the yearbook. Mrs. Henry began her teaching career when she was fifteen in Leavenworth County, District 67, five miles east of Tonganoxie. She had twenty-three pupils in grades 1-8. She attended the Kansas State Normal High School at Emporia, Kansas. Her freshman and sophomore college years were completed at Emporia State Teachers College. She transferred her credits to the University of Kansas at Lawrence where she continued for the next three years, earning B.A. and M.A. degrees. Mrs. Henry taught three years at Tonganoxie High, did an interval of substitute teaching in Douglas and Jefferson counties, taught at Longford Rural High School in Clay County for six years, then transferred to Jarbalo High School where she taught for eighteen years.

One of her students, Joyce Wager Terry ('54) stated, "Mrs. Henry was a fabulous art teacher. She also taught English, math, and even home economics. When a project would be a disaster, she could always find something good about it."

School Activities and Events — The junior and senior prom was an annual event in the spring of each year. Virginia Seymour ('41) remembered, "It was my first ever date. What did I do but become violently ill!"

A bus service owned privately by Ernest Trackwell transported students for both the grade and high schools. There were four bus drivers, two males and two females.

Numerous senior trips were enjoyed.

- The 1941 class of thirteen students drove to Kansas City in just two cars. Principal Gaddis and James Seymour ('34) were the drivers. They toured the Swift Packing Plant and the sight of the Judas goat leading the cattle to slaughter made a lifelong memory. They picnicked at Swope Park before returning home the same day.
- The 1950 class of two girls and one boy went all the way to the Lake of the Ozarks.
- The 1954 class took a train from Kansas City to Chicago. They slept on the train going, spent the whole day in Chicago touring many sights, including the science and history museum, got back on the train and slept all the way home.
- In 1955, seventeen seniors made a trip to Kansas City. They ate at the famous Forum Cafeteria. They were accompanied by their principal, Mr. R.V. Shinkle.

Athletics — There was no football until 1956 when six-man team was introduced with a limited schedule. Principal Shinkle would lead calisthenics before the games. In the fall of 1957, an early game against Easton, Missouri, caused the state athletics association to force Jarbalo to forfeit the rest of the year's games. They had started the season too early. By the fall of 1965, the team would defeat Harveyville 33-20, Easton 21-13, Lecompton 40-20, and Auburn 27-14.

A dilemma was addressed in the late 1950s with a basketball game against Potter High School. Because Potter had so few boys out for basketball that year, one girl played on the starting team. It was considered traumatic to be the one chosen to guard the girl. Finally, Larry Vestal was given the dubious honor.

Closing the High School — The high school closed following graduation in May 1966. There were sixty-four students enrolled that last year. A total of 410 graduated from Jarabalo High School in forty-seven years. The most common surnames of the graduates were Mason-11, Somers-10, Wagers-9, Gasts-9, Schultz-7, Vestal-7, Brune-6, and Murphy-6, and News-6. The largest class was twenty-four graduates in 1937. The last graduate was Judy White (alphabetically).

The school song, with two verses and a chorus, is sung at each alumni banquet, led by Virginia Seymour ('41). The chorus rings with the pride of the graduates at this event.

Yes! We're from Jarbalo. Colors purple and gold,
We stand for Jarbalo,
and to its colors we'll ever be true.
We'll carry then up to that envious round

#34

McCune High School

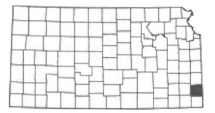

Mascot: Eagles

Colors: Black and Gold

Year Closed: 1979

Location: town of McCune, southwest corner of Crawford County

History of McCune — The county population reached over 20,000 in 1910, which was also the peak for the mining industry in southeast Kansas. This area was Osage Indian land until the Cherokee Nation was moved by force from Florida via the Trail of Tears in 1838. The Confederate States of America purchased a portion of this territory for the Cherokees, planning to make Kansas a slave state. Kansas became a free state on January 29, 1861, and this region was admitted along with the rest of Kansas as a state.

McCune had no mining and the town was primarily merchants and farmers. The railroads owned much of the land. This town was the crossroad of several railroads that came through the area: The Memphis Kansas & Colorado Railway Co., the Kansas City Ft. Scott & Gulf Railroad, the St. Louis & Santa Fe Railroad (later called the Frisco), and finally, the Burlington Northern Railroad.

Early Education — The first school was a combination grade and high school. The first full high school graduating class was in 1908 with nineteen graduates.

In 1924, a new high school was built with the Masons laying the cornerstone, leaving their insignia. This school building still stands today (2018), ninety-four years later. The bell from the first high school was moved from the bell tower to the front lawn. The clapper was wired down so no one could ring it, but in 1950 the wire was cut, and it rang when the basketball team beat Arma High School. This emblem of education in McCune was then moved to the front of the McCune Historical Museum and Library when the grade school was closed in 2014. The clock from the high school had been manufactured in 1924 in Springfield, Massachusetts. The 1924 high school was on the second floor and the grade school on the first floor. In 1958, the grade school was moved into a new school to the north of the high school.

Spooky Tales — This town and high school were renowned for their Halloween escapades. The FFA boys would decorate Main Street with outhouses and hedge apples. The next morning, Mr. Ralph Utermoehlon, the Ag teacher, loaded the boys up in his pickup truck and they went on a cleanup trip. The outhouses were all delivered back to their respective locations and placed on their foundations.

The FBI was called to town following one ghoulish Halloween as Hap Green's (Benjamin Franklin Green) buggy mysteriously ended up on top of the post office. Since this was a federal building, it became an unsolved crime. To this day, though the statute of limitations has probably passed, the culprits have not been identified.

And Other Memories — Miss Eva Turkington was an "old maid" who taught math. She was often the senior class sponsor. The senior trip in 1960 was to New Orleans. The seniors, Miss Turkington, and the superintendent, Mr. Barker, boarded the train in Pittsburg early on a Saturday morning. They slept on the train and pulled into the "Crescent City" the next morning at dawn. They spent the day touring and experiencing Bourbon Street and boarded the train to sleep overnight on the way home to Kansas. Miss Turkington believed it was scandalous for the girls and boys to sit together. One of these seniors was a pert little Sharon Huff Leonard ('60). Sharon recalled, "Miss Eva had an eye out for me. She would often catch me in the act and usually made me shake. It was typical for her to catch me smirking or giggling in class and would call attention to it by saying, 'Sharon, what do you think is so funny? Why don't you tell the whole class so we can all laugh?' Busted, I would be an angel for a few weeks."

The yearbook in 1920 was called *The Alpha*. The name of the yearbook rotated. In 1922, it was called the *Black and Gold*; from 1936-38, the *MuRuhiscan*; 1941, the *Black and Gold*; and 1942-79, *The Eagle*.

Athletics—The football team always played eleven-man football. They played in the CNC League (Cherokee, Neosho, Crawford Counties) against Girard, Arma, College High-Pittsburg, Colgan (St. Mary's), Oswego, Erie, Arcadia, Cherokee, Weir, and West Mineral. The biggest rival in the 1950s was Arma. Roy Parsons ('64) remarked, "Those guys were always so big!"

Brothers Dean Kelly ('49) and Allen Kelly ('50) both played on the 1952 University of Kansas National Championship Basketball Team. Dean Kelly won a gold medal at the 1952 Helsinki Olympics in basketball, and Allen Kelly would do the same in the 1960 Rome Olympics. Both are in the Kansas Basketball Hall of Fame.

The 1949 boys basketball team went to the state tournament, class B finals. This was the middle of a four-year run of winning the league basketball championship.

Two McCune boys, Conrad Morrison and Leslie Hobson, were killed in World War II. Both young men, along with several others, were drafted before they could finish high school.

The Fall Festival in McCune is a three-day town celebration that continues to this day (2018). The high school band was always a part of the parade and celebration.

The End—The high school was closed in 1979. The remaining students went to Girard, Oswego, and Southeast Cherokee. Though part of the Southeast Cherokee District, there were problems with the unification, and deep resentment in losing the McCune High School existed for many years. It seemed to continue as the grade school closed in 2014 and rekindled the bad feelings of a loss of yet another school in town.

The first graduating class from McCune High School was in 1896. The last graduating class in 1979 had twenty-eight graduates with Kelly York Duffin (alphabetically) the last to receive a diploma from the school. A total of 1,698 graduated in the eighty-four years from 1896-1979.

The most frequent surnames of the graduates were Stewart-23, Parsons-20, Nutt-17, Allen-16, McColm-13, Trayor-10, White-10, Kirby-9, Smith-9, Baker-8, Johnson-8, Kirk-7, and Morrison-7.

35

Dermot School

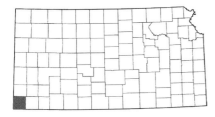

Where, oh where could this little school be? Once located in Stevens County and named Antelope school, it was moved just two miles west and rebuilt in 1953 in northeastern Morton County which is in the furthest county to the southwest in Kansas.

The Last One-Room School House — A rather inconspicuous one-room school became the last of its kind in Kansas to close its doors to elementary students on May 24, 1990. Due to foresight and leadership by the rural patrons, this school house continues to serve the neighboring community. A unique mill levy was placed to provide funds for upkeep and maintenance of this school as well as the former Richfield High School building, also in the northwestern corner of Morton County.

The Angus cattle now come running to see the visitors in the school parking lot. The teeter totters and slippery slide face the sun, waiting for kids to jump on and give them a ride like they did for two-thirds of a century.

The tables are set for the Saturday night community reunion supper. The stage—which once hosted plays, valentine box suppers, Halloween skits, and Christmas programs—is still in mint condition at Dermot School.

Memories of Dermott — Black Friday, April 14, 1935, was at the peak of the "Dirty 30s." Students hunkered down at the school as the wind blew rampantly, sweeping black clouds of dust through the countryside.

When the school was moved to the new location in 1953, there were fifteen students at Dermot for the opening. The teacher, principal, and playground supervisor was Mrs. Seola Lewis, who taught at the school for thirty-seven years. The board members were Charles Williams, Howard Drew, and Elver Milburn. When the building was new, there were no screens on the windows. The weather in the spring was warm and gnats were thick making it miserable when the windows were open. The school board soon added screens and an air conditioner for the classroom, hall, and kitchen.

Hot lunches at Dermot were brought out from the Rolla community school. The original cook had great meals and the flexibility to use government surplus foods to make leftovers into jams and cobblers.

Almost all of the boys wore cowboy boots, and the clomp, clomp, clomp was very noisy. Some days the noise seemed to bounce off the walls. It was worse when the air pressure changed. The school board once again rose to the occasion and carpeted the classroom and hall. This made the school a much quieter place to work and study (from the book, *A One Room School.*)

The graduates from Dermot School would go to Rolla High School, fifteen miles to the south. One of the great grandfathers of John Milburn had homesteaded and lived in a "soddie" just across from the school. John still owns and farms the land adjacent to the school. He recalled,

"In 1961, for President Kennedy's Inauguration Day, the band from Rolla marched down Pennsylvania Avenue in the country's largest inauguration day parade to date. The band was led by a very unique conductor on a one-year contract with the school district. His bands had played at every inauguration parade, from Woodrow Wilson to Kennedy. Albert J. Pesses—teacher, educator, and innovator—raised money for the train ride from western Kansas to Washington D.C. and return. Sandwiches and homemade lunches enabled these rural school students to witness a once in a lifetime experience and represent Kansas at the Inauguration."

Another notable local character from Morton County, Buddy Heaton, participated at this same 1961 Inauguration. Buddy and his buffalo were featured in this event as Buddy rode a buffalo named Gunner (who was only moderately broken) before President Kennedy and Jackie in an arena.

The water fountains, desks, teachers' work area, and clothes hooks are still in perfect condition where these little cowboys would hang their hats.

Sign of the Times—The Rules for Teachers, 1872, is still posted on the walls of the classroom:

1. Teachers each day will fill lamps, clean chimneys.

2. Each teacher will bring a bucket of water and a shuttle of coal for the day's session.

3. Make your pens carefully. You may whittle nibs to the individual taste of the students.

4. Men teachers may take one evening each week for courting purposes, or two evenings a week if they go to church regularly.

5. After ten hours in school, the teachers may spend the remaining time reading the Bible or other good books.

6. Women teachers who marry or engage in unseemly conduct will be dismissed.

7. Every teacher should lay aside from each pay a goodly sum of his earnings for his benefit during his declining years so that he will not become a burden on society.

8. Any teacher who smokes, uses liquor in any form, frequents pool or public halls, or gets shaved in a barber shop will give reason to suspect his worth, intention, integrity, and honesty.

9. The teacher who performs his labor faithfully and without fault for five years will be given an increase of twenty-five cents per week in his pay, providing the Board of Education approves.

These interesting rules for the times reflected the religious beliefs and the values the people of these schools applied to their teachers and practiced in their homes.

A plaque on the wall reads:

The Dermot School was the oldest one-room school house still in use in the State of Kansas until it closed on May 24, 1990. Dermot was organized June 28, 1888. The building was erected in 1919 and used until September 1954. Classes were commenced in the new brick building built on the site. Seola Lewis taught at the school 37 years.

Donated by Elver C. Milburn Family this building filled with hard times, endless winter storms, and where memories live on in the states last one-room school.

To this rural community, Dermot truly lives on.

Dermot School—September 2018
Morton County, KS

#36

Wheeler School

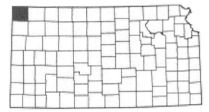

Year closed: 1968

Location: town of Wheeler, near the middle of Cheyenne County.

Early Education in Wheeler—Cheyenne County was named for the Northern Cheyenne Indians. The school opened on September 1, 1887. This was less than ten years after the last Indian conflict only fifty miles away. Wheeler was also the last one-room country school in the county when it closed at the end of April 1968. There was no kindergarten. School started after Labor Day and closed in late April. Students took their lunch every day because there was no hot lunch program. They ate at long tables in the basement. If the weather was bad, they would play games in the basement during recess.

The school was a two-story structure. Upon entry to the bi-level building through the front door, there were stairs leading up to the upper grades and stairs leading down to the lower four grades.

On the east side of the building was a swing set with a slide and merry-go-round. The younger kids played there. On the west side was a ball diamond and where the older kids played. In the southwest corner of the playground, there was a horse barn. In early years, children rode horses to school and kept them in the barn during the day. By the 1940s, a school bus picked up the rural children.

Each year there was a last day of school, county-wide track meet for all the country schools. This was held at the fairgrounds in St. Francis. Along with the ball diamond, there was a broad jump and high jump practice area. For the high jump, two fence posts with a row of nails about two inches apart was used with a bamboo fishing pole for the bar. There was a small pile of sand to land on below.

No music or art was taught. Curriculum was structured around the three R's. Every day following the noon recess, the teacher would read a chapter from a book. There was a Christmas program each year where the students would have lines to recite. This was held for the parents in the basement.

Student Memories

Gary Cooper:

I started school in 1948. The teacher was Sylvia I. Daniels. In the second through fourth grade, the teacher was Mabel Randall. From the fifth through the eighth was Mettie Gillispie. There were two rooms where each teacher taught four grades. The individual school desks each had a place for books and lunch pails in the front much like a magazine rack. The American flag was in both rooms, and the two rooms were divided by wooden folding divider

doors. I graduated from the eighth grade in April 1956. There were four in my graduating class. All of the country schools had their graduation together. It was held in the high school auditorium in St. Francis. There was a program, and each graduate would receive their diploma as they walked across the stage.

Garald Paxton:

I got a whipping the first day of school in the first grade in 1946. We had just moved into Wheeler from the sod house on the farm. We never had electricity or water until we moved to town. We never had indoor toilets until my freshman year in college in 1958 when my parents moved to St. Francis. We lived about 100 yards from the Wheeler school. I had never used indoor plumbing and thought it was really crazy to go inside to go to the toilet. So when the bell rang from noon recess, I just stepped around the corner of the building to take a leak. A teacher saw me and paddled me and warned me to never do that again.

That fall of 1946, as a first grader, I can still see the images of wave after wave of B29s and B17s flying west to probably California after the war.

Our school usually had about twenty-five to forty students. Each grade had about four pupils. We all moved on to high school and participated very well against the "city" kids. They had the upper leg on us for a time because they had been playing sports. I was a wrestler and the instincts for wresting came very easily and there was no catching up in this sport. I went on to Fort Hays State on a wrestling scholarship.

Bill Stull ('54):

We were farm people and had land about one and a half miles north of Wheeler. I rode a bus which came our direction to pick up the kids. I had the occasion to have a first-grade teacher name Sylvia Daniels, and then in the fifth grade, another Sylvia Daniels as a teacher. They were no relation. The second Miss Daniels played the harmonica and taught us music. She had all of us get harmonicas, and we played in Hays in front of the big crowd at the Kansas Teachers meeting. Miss Daniels had us memorize many of the great documents of history, and we would stand in front of the whole school to recite them. I can still remember the Gettysburg Address to this day.

When we went to high school in St. Francis, it seemed that the country school kids had more common sense and became the leaders in the high school. My education did me well as I had no problems in college at Kansas State University majoring in Economics.

Karen Jackson Keller ('56) was a nearby farm girl who came to school in her parents' car. They lived just a mile and a half east of school but did not ride the bus.

Karen's Recollection:

The Wheeler store was such a great place to meet after school for some candy and wait for my family to pick us up. I had three siblings who also all graduated from Wheeler School. Miss Daniels would also always prepare a huge pot of vegetable soup each week for all of us. Since we all took our lunches, this was such a wonderful soup to warm us up. She was the best teacher I ever had. She would read to us after lunch and I believe it has made me to love reading to this day. We played baseball and had some basketball on the dirt play grounds.

I started school right after the war. There were many kids in my first-grade class. These numbers dwindled as families moved away for jobs in the cities. By the time I graduated from the eighth grade, there were only four of us.

After grade school, we all went to St. Francis to high school. It seemed that the country kids were not as socially adept at first, but we were well accepted by the town kids. We drove ourselves to high school and would car pool with families until we got our licenses. We still own some of the land we were raised on, and wheat and cattle are still seen today among an occasional gas well.

Wheeler school was the last country school to close in Cheyenne County. There was never a high school in this little community along Highway 36. The Rock Island Railroad passed through the town site, and it paralleled Highway 36. Most of the graduates would go to either St. Francis or Bird City to high school.

37

Morrowville Rural High School

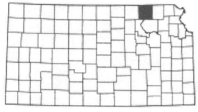

Mascot: Bulldogs

Colors: Blue and White

Year Closed: 1967

Location: unincorporated town of Morrowville, Washington County

Town History — Rufus Darby left Maryland in 1854, spending time in Ohio and Iowa to earn money in order to continue his trek west. He arrived in Kansas and founded the Morrowville area four years after his arrival. He purchased a quarter section of land just north of the town site which would remain in his family name until 1984, a total of 126 years.

The early history of the Morrowville area was often dotted with Indians and their interactions with the new white settlers. Rufus was a painter by trade and was very handy with tools, often inventing devices for catching wild turkeys and other game that became food on the Darby table. Mr. Darby never owned a gun, which may explain why his life and the lives of his family members were spared at different times by the Indians. One of those times occurred in 1864, and was recounted by W.C. Hallowell, who had heard the story so many times that it seemed that he had been there:

At that time, the Cheyenne Indians rode out of the west, emboldened by the knowledge that the state troops were away fighting during the Civil War, and could not protect the settlers as they had been doing. History says they were quarreling with the Otoes who were living northeast of here, and in their war-like manner, they were ready to fall upon the white settlements wherever they could.

Jesse Hallowell, maternal grandfather of R.V. Darby, lived on Mill Creek near Washington, and to the surprise of the family, one day a large band of Indians came riding in. In their company was Rufus Darby, paternal grandfather of R.V. Darby, whom they had captured as he returned to his homestead near Morrowville from a trip to Marysville for provisions.

The Indians demanded that the Hallowell's "swap" bedding for buffalo robes, robes which they later stole back. When the Indians asked for milk and Mrs. Hallowell brought it from the cave, one Indian, displeased or disappointed at the feast, ran his spear through the pan of milk. At that Mrs. Hallowell slapped him. He would have given here a thrust with his spear, but the other Indian's interfered saying "brave Squaw."

Leaving the Hallowell's, they camped for the night just north of the present city of Washington, keeping Rufus and another man prisoner. About 40 men from scattered farms gathered in defense and with any available firearms, at least half of which would not fire, went after the Indians. At the sight of the advancing army, the Indian's became frightened and ran, leaving their prisoners behind. They escaped unharmed.

W.C. Hallowell remembered seeing the Otoe Indians hunting in the area as late as 1872 or 1873. They were friendly, and the settlers had nothing to fear.

Morrowville was a shipping center for grain and livestock in those early days. A stockyard was built as soon as the railroad was completed. By 1896 there was an elevator to handle small grain. The stockyards were very busy, shipping as many as 1700 head of sheep in one week in 1901.

An incredible reunion of old settlers was held sometime just after the turn of the century. A news article recalled this event:

> The old settler's reunion was noted as the greatest gathering of people that has ever been in Morrowville and the largest per cent of old settlers. The day was fine. Thousands of grateful ears mingled with the old pioneer benefactors of Washington County. The sham Battle with the savage Indians presented some of the pioneer life in Kansas. Buffalo Bill and his company of guides whipped and drove the red skins back inflicting great loss of life as usual. The five mile bicycle race was a 'warmer'. First place gained a prize of $3.50. Roll call by states for the benefit of old soldiers revealed the fact that forty old soldiers from the Civil and Spanish-American Wars responded which was as follows: Illinois 13, Iowa 8, Ohio 7, Wisconsin 3, Indiana 3 and one each from Massachusetts, Minnesota, Pennsylvania, Kentucky, Missouri, and Kansas.

Teaching in the 1920s — An advertisement in the nearby *Glasco Sun* newspaper in 1923 gives insight on the teachers that were attracted to the county schools of that time titled "You've Come a Long Way Baby." The ad specified that the standard contract was eight months of school at $75.00 per month. This form was included:

Miss _____ agrees:

1. Not to get married. This contract becomes null and void immediately if the teacher marries.
2. Not to keep company with men.
3. To be home between the hours of 8:00 pm and 6:00 am unless in attendance at a school function.
4. Not to loiter down-town in ice cream stores.
5. Not to leave town at any time without the permission of the chairman of the board of trustees.
6. Not to smoke cigarettes. This contract becomes null and void immediately if the teacher is found smoking.
7. Not to drink beer, wine, or whiskey. This contract becomes null and void if the teacher is found drinking beer, wine, or whiskey.
8. Not to ride in a carriage or automobile with any other man except her brother or father.
9. Not to dress in bright colors.
10. Not to dye hair.
11. To wear at least two petticoats.
12. Not to wear dresses more than two inches above the ankles.
13. To keep the school clean.

A. To sweep the classroom floor at least once weekly.

B. To scrub the classroom floor at least once weekly with hot water and soap.

C. To clean the blackboard at least once weekly.

D. To start the fire at 7 am so the room will be warm at 8 am when the kids arrive.

14. Not to use face powder, mascara, or paint the lips.

This is in sharp contrast to today's school contracts and administrative policy which do not refer to dress codes, make up, or out of school time. Contracts and pay today are the same for both men and women, and custodial work is a separate position.

Education in Morrowville — The first grade school in Morrowville was built in 1886. This building was moved to the northwest corner of Main and Oak when a new two-room building was constructed in 1905. From 1886 to 1920, the salaries per month ranged between $40 and $80, but most were in the $40 to $50 range. In 1917, the school was remodeled into a four-room building. In the early 50s, two rural schools were purchased and moved end to end on the southeast corner of the schoolyard. A hardwood floor was laid inside the "new" building so that it could be used as a gymnasium.

From a newspaper clipping dated August 29, 1926:

The little city of Morrowville can justly be proud of the new high school, which has been completed north of town, and which will open September 6, to the high school pupils of the district or others who are residents of county districts, who wish to enter high school. They will offer four years of high school and the program as outlined, includes five courses, which pupils may choose. In the past Morrowville has had but two years of high school and the last two years of the work was taken in other schools. The teachers for this year are: W.C. McGuire, principal; Arminda Garton, home economics; Mary Rees, history; Hazel Craft, English; and P.A. Holliday, coach.

The school opens September 6, 1926. Classes will be taught in the following subjects: English I, II, III; History; D.S.; Agriculture; Phycology; Spanish; Psychology; Constitution; Biology; Typewriting; Bookkeeping; General Science; Algebra; Geometry; Manual Training; Geography; Grammar.

There were seventy students enrolled that first year. In contrast, by 1983-84, after three schools unified to form North Central High School (Morrowville, Haddam, and Mahaska), there were combined only sixty-four students enrolled.

There were no halls or stairs in the building, so the students lost little time passing to and from classes. The assembly-gymnasium had oak floors and was equipped for plays and indoor games with entrances and exits conveniently located. The study hall had unilateral lighting with individual seats and an adjacent library. The laboratory room was equipped for biology, agriculture, physiology, and general science. The recitation rooms were supplied with tablet arm chairs, a teacher's desk, and ample blackboard space. Typewriting was located next to the English room and was equipped with six machines as well as necessary charts and blackboard. The domestic science room was furnished with Coleman stoves for ten pupils, and beside these were double ovens, five double tables, and a cupboard. The manual training room was equipped with work benches and tools for sixteen boys.

In 1954, the citizens of Morrowville school district voted on a bond issue to build a new grade school in the amount of $116,850. In 1955, Pat Hutson Construction Company, general contractor, commenced building the new grade school. A new gymnasium had been added to the project, raising the total cost to approximately $200,000.

Yearbook News

1929 - A very nice yearbook had activities from the previous school year listed. They included an operetta, *Gypsy Rover*. There was a dramatics department that produced the senior play, *Paying the Fiddler*, and the junior play, *Two Days to Marry*. There was a glee club, girl reserves, and the *Blue M* staff. That year the senior trip was by bus to Wichita.

1932 - The senior trip was to Manhattan, Kansas and a visit to Sunset Zoo.

1962 - The yearbook listed clubs such as Future Homemakers of America (chartered in 1936) and Future Farmers of America (chartered 1930), which were designed to help young people become better homemakers and farmers. The senior trip was to Colorado Springs by school bus, taking in the Garden of the Gods, the Royal Gorge, Cheyenne Mountain Zoo, and a motel with a heated pool.

Most of the men in the Morrowville area were members of the FFA, and they cite the leadership abilities they gained through the organization as having strengthened the community. Both FFA and FHA continued after unification at North Central.

Athletics & Music — The biggest rivals were Haddam and Mahaska. The nine high schools in Washington County were all in one sports league.

Besides good curriculum, the music department was outstanding, and sports played a significant role in building school spirit. Football was the fall sport from 1926 until 1936. Baseball replaced football in the fall from 1936 until 1950 when football again became the fall sport. Depending on the enrollment, eleven-man, six-man, and eight-man teams played on the football field.

Morrowville Statistics — The first graduating class was in 1927 with eleven graduates. A total of 735 students graduated from Morrowville Rural High School in forty-one years. It closed in 1967. The most numerous surnames of the graduates were Durst-15, Hanschel-14, Barnes-12, Lull-11, Smith-9, Elliott-8, and Young-8. The last class to graduate had ten graduates with Fred Zimmerman ('67) (alphabetically) the last to receive a Morrowville diploma.

In the fall of 1967, old rivals Haddam, Mahaska, and Morrowville unified to form a new high school named North Central with the school located in the former Morrowville Rural High School. The new district, #221, had school until it, too, closed in 2006. The area students now attend high school at the county seat in Washington. Thus, all of the once nine high schools in Washington County now attend high school in the town of Washington, Kansas.

Morrowville Rural High School
Washington County, KS

38

La Cygne High School

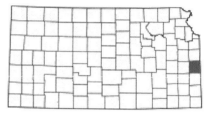

Mascot: Indians

Colors: Red and Blue

Year Closed: 1969

Location: town of La Cygne, eastern Linn County, eight miles from the Missouri border

Origins of the Name--The name was from the French influence of the pre-Louisiana Purchase days in 1803. French trappers would establish fur trading outposts along this river which also took on the French name of Marais de Cygnes, meaning marsh of the swans. The name La Cygne is French for "the swan."

Early Education — The high school yearbook was mainly called *The Swan*, though occasionally it was named *The Chief. The Swan* prevailed until 1969 when unification led to the closing of the school. A bit of history about the school from *The Swan* in 1961:

> The first hall of education in LaCygne was a log cabin. No records are available of when it was built. In 1870 there is a record that seventy school seats were ordered, ten of which were placed in the school building and 60 in the Methodist church. In 1871, a demand for an adequate school building became pressing. A meeting was called and a committee appointed to select a site and cost. The committee reported that all of block 43 could be bought for $600 and the approximately cost of the building would be $8,000. The contract to build the first school building was given to Millard and Bartholomew for $8,000-the building to be completed by November 1, 1871.

This building lasted only thirteen years when it was condemned and a campaign started for a new school building. Two bond elections of $8,000 failed to carry because of hard times. School was closed in March 1885, because of these poor facilities. In desperation, the minority carried their troubles to the state legislature who passed a bill legalizing the issuance of $10,000 in bonds by the La Cygne School Board. It was from this school that a graduation ceremony for the class of 1888 took place, indicating that this was a two-year high school. This building was destroyed by fire due to lightning on June 23, 1906.

Yet another building was constructed at the same site at the cost of $18,575. It, too, was condemned in 1924 and the final high school was built. This two-story high school would be the final high school for La Cygne. It was closed in 1969 due to unification. A consolidated high school, Prairie View, was built five miles west in the country. The unified school included Fontana, Centerville, Parker, New Lancaster, and La Cygne.

The final lines penned in the 1961 *The Swan*:

> Early history of La Cygne is clouded by legend— Evangeline and the Indian legend of the swan. As the time and dust dims the pages of history, even the Jayhawker era preceding the Civil War takes on a flavor of legend. The little village in the marsh of the swan had weathered the changes, but history did not allow the La Cygne Rural High School the same privilege.

Athletics — There was both boys and girls basketball. The girls played six-on-six. There was no baseball in the later years, though football in the fall and track in the spring were the other boys sports.

The football coach, Mr. Ventura, had the duty of teaching girls physical education class. He suspected that there were devious acts such as using wet towels to moisten the face and hair instead of showering after PE classes. The home economics teacher was enlisted to supervise the girls locker room to make sure all followed through on the showering requirement.

Nancy Feldman Heidrick recalled, "With such a lackluster PE class, I was determined that this was so important that I went to Pittsburg State and became a PE teacher. I became just one of the sixteen Feldman family members to become Pittsburg State Gorillas."

Memorable Teachers — Another teacher who had a great impact on the Feldman family was the vocational agriculture teacher, Emil Klutz. He was drafted while teaching during World War II. Louis Feldman ('41) was inspired by Mr. Klutz's commitment to education and his judging at Kansas State University for crops and livestock. Mr. Klutz encouraged Louis to attend college. However, with the inspiration he had received in the vo-ag classes, he opted to farm right out of high school. He prospered, becoming a very successful lover of the land and livestock.

A new teacher to the high school in the early 1960s was Clayton Jones. A first-year instructor, his methods and operation of a class room may have seemed naïve to a seasoned group of teenagers. Paulette Obermeier Curry ('63) smiled as she remembered and told this story.

> We thought he let the kids run rough shod and do anything in his classes. We thought he had no clue of our chicanery until the grades for the first nine weeks were posted on our report cards. There was an 'F' for conduct on everyone's cards. Our parents had to sign these report cards before they were returned to the principal. Needless to say, Mr. Jones had the nicest class the rest of the year and didn't have to yell to get our attention. Talk about carrying a 'short stick' on an 'F' on a report card to get his message across!

Nancy Feldman Heidrick ('69) recalled Miss Louise Mitchell:

> She had taught my Dad, Louis Feldman ('41), who had her for English. Here I was some twenty-six years later with the same Miss Mitchell teaching me math and geometry. She was a master with the stare and could melt you in your chair. But what a teacher!

David Long ('64) had the same Miss Mitchell for Geometry:

> She was my favorite teacher. Right out of high school, during the Viet Nam years, I attended drafting school. Talk about my education and background. I was the only one in these classes who didn't have to retake my geometry and math classes just to peruse my drafting. I made my life's living with this education and think of Miss Mitchell with such fond memories. She was such an inspiring, dedicated teacher.

Extracuricullars — This same dedicated math wizard, David Long, told stories about drag racing:

> Drag racing for the La Cygne school boys was a passion. The souped up cars we drove seemed to take on any challenge out north of town on the black top with clearly marked start and finish lines. This quarter mile of blue smoke screaming dashes were regular epics after school and at nights just after ball games.

Nancy Feldman Heidrich ('69) recalled a story by her father, Louis Feldman:

> Busing came in the late 1930s. The seats were lengthways on each side of the bus. This was the style of the buses. This all changed the day that a wandering pig happened in the road causing the bus full of kids to come to a screeching, fishtailing stop. Of course, all of the kids with no seat belts went sailing into a heap to the front of the bus. It was not long until these buses were replaced by the standard bus with the row of seats facing forward.

There was a school walkout by the Class of 1950, led by Leo McRae ('50). Ruth Ellen Stainbrook ('50) told this story:

> Superintendent, Mr. Handley, took our open lunch hour away from us because of a couple that was

"spoonin'" during our lunch time. We were all upset about our lunch hour being taken away and we had to go to study hall. Leo McRae felt this was unfair and led the senior class and some sympathetic underclassmen in a strike. We walked around until the school board informed us, on behalf of the superintendent, that we had to return to our classes. We were only absent all of about two hours in total, but we felt victorious!

This action and type of demonstration was unheard of in these times.

Equality Stories—Though pranks and acts of good humor were usually attributed to boys, this stereotype did not seem to always play out in La Cygne. A group of girls in the early 1960s seemed to break this mold. They were noted for trying to steal the football goal posts on a Halloween venture. The father of Paulette Obermeier Curry ('63) was on the school board. He was also a volunteer watchman for the town to keep the revelry under control. He had caught wind of the goal post heisting mission. He mentioned that he was off duty at 10:00 PM and suggested potential thieves avoid his time frame, if any unusual thievery were being considered. Sure enough, a horde of nearly ten girls huffed and puffed to loosen the north goal post. It gave some, but they had to get reinforcements from four or five guys to complete the caper. Propped on the back of a pickup truck, the goal post proceeded down the road. Protruding, it just happened to come in contact with the mailbox of none other than the football coach, Mr. Ventura. This clumsy goal post somehow ended up on a hillside out of town referred to as "The East Hill." There was no recollection of consequences.

This gang of girls [some later identified as Paulette Obermeir Curry ('63), Judy Long Patterson ('63), Carol Reece Creager ('63), and Linda Royer Miller ('63)] slowly drove the roadsides picking up empty beer cans. None of them touched beer themselves, but a scheme was brewing. They stowed these empty cans in the back seat until Friday and Saturday nights. Following ball games, while "dragging Main," they would nonchalantly toss the cans out the windows to lure the boys. The boys would chase them down, wanting to know where they had gotten the beer!

The junior play of 1961 brought on yet another humorous memory, but it didn't happen on the stage. Certainly not! Once again, these girls were involved in a classic. The Obermeier family was notorious for leaving their keys in the ignition of the car when parking it at school, church, or on Main Street. As luck would have it, Paulette Obermeier had play practice. The girls mischievously moved the parked car to a hidden place, anticipating panic after play practice. However, Mr. Obermeier just happened to be the one who had driven the car that night to the high school where he had a school board meeting. Snickering soon turned to panic when it was revealed that this was the unplanned moving of the car of a school board dad.

Where was the car? How could this be? These were questions being asked by a wide-eyed Paulette and her exasperated father, as well as the girls who had instigated the prank. All of the juniors and the school board went for a hunt that mysteriously led to the translocated automobile. It was later determined that perhaps LeRoy 'Joe' Turpin ('63) and Eddie Brown ('63) may have been responsible as, after some apprehensive moments, they led the posse to the innocent auto with the keys still in the ignition.

Athletics — The main sports rival was Pleasanton or "P-town" as is was called by the La Cygne Indians. The boys had such a distaste for them, but the homecoming queen in 1962, Paulette Obermeier Curry ('63), quipped, "But they had good looking guys!"

Senior Trips — The 1963 trip was by train to Chicago. In 1964 and 1967, the seniors went to Denver, Colorado Springs, the Air Force Academy, Garden of the Gods, Seven Falls, and then back home on the train, sleeping both going to Colorado and coming home. The seniors of 1969 descended on the Lake of the Ozarks for two nights at a motel by Bagnall Dam. They saw the Lee Mace Country West Show. This was the last senior trip of LRHS as the school closed following graduation that year.

La Cygne Statistics — In the eighty years from 1888-1968 there were 1,407 graduates. The last class had twenty-seven graduates with Ron Wade (alphabetically) the last to receive a diploma from La Cygne High School.

The most frequent surnames of the graduates were Miller-26, Johnson-14, Smith-13, Stainbrook-13, Plumb-12, Trinkle-11, Creager-9, Ross-9, Teagarden-9, Cox-8, McClanahan-8, White-8, Wolfe-8, Karr-7, and Patterson-7.

39

Pawnee Rock High School

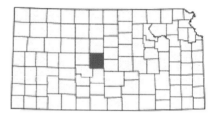

Mascot: Braves

Colors: Blue and Gold

Year Closed: 1972

Location: town of Pawnee Rock, Barton County

Town History — The town was established in 1871 along the Atchison, Topeka, and Santa Fe Railroad as it ran diagonally across Kansas from Atchison, Kansas, to Santa Fe, New Mexico. Forty years earlier the Santa Fe Trail, starting in Westport, Missouri, took this same route. Pawnee Rock was the half-way point to Santa Fe. The Arkansas River, flowing northeast to the great bend (city of Great Bend) is one mile south of Pawnee Rock.

US Highway 56 now parallels this same route and runs directly through Pawnee Rock.

The famed rock, just north of town, was detailed two hundred years ago by George Sibly in 1825, ". . . we rode nearly north about a mile to a remarkable rocky point . . . above the plain . . . charming view of the country in every direction."

The historical marker near the city limits reads, "The Santa Fe travelers referenced the Dakota Sandstone outcropping in their journals. Pawnee Rock was covered with so many names carved by the men who had passed it. 'It was so full that I could find no place for mine. The 'prairie citadel' raises some 100 feet above the prairie.' - John Birch."

Education— By the early 1900s, Pawnee Rock's population reached nearly 1,000. The high school was started in 1910 with twenty-six freshman and three others. This first high school was in the existing grade school building. The first graduating class was in 1914 with seven graduates.

A new three-story high school was constructed in 1921 for $70,000. It had a central gymnasium with a balcony around all four sides. The first girls basketball teams were in the 1920s. This gymnasium saw some great boys teams during the 1920s and 1930s.

In 1957, a new high school and grade school was constructed for $624,000. This beautiful building also featured heated floors for the kindergarten room. Enrollment in the high school that year was eighty-eight students.

Sports Teams— Pawnee Rock participated in state basketball tournaments in 1922, 1923, and 1928 when there was only one division for the entire state of Kansas.

They also went in 1934 when there were two divisions in the state. In 1957, the boys basketball team lost to Sublette in the regional finals to finish with a 22-2 record and missed going to the state class-B basketball tournament. The last trip for Pawnee Rock to the state tournament was in 1967.

Pawnee Rock played in the Barton County League with Great Bend, Hoisington, Ellinwood, and Claflin. They were the league champions in basketball in 1922, 1923, and 1926. In the 1950s, Pawnee Rock joined the South 50-56 League with Hudson, Radium, Belpre, Trousdale, Garfield, and Zook.

The 1960s were incredible years for boys basketball and football. The football records in the 1960s were sixty-five wins and twenty-two loses. There were undefeated teams in 1964, 1965, and 1968. The basketball record during that same time was 159-52. Steve Crosby ('68) starred at Ft. Hays State and played three years for the New York Giants. He coached for another thirty years in the NFL.

Stories from Students— In the 1940s there were still 115 one-room schools in Barton County. The eighth graders would go Great Bend to take the county test to qualify to get into high school. Keith Mull ('41) vividly remembers taking this test and that day in 1937. Keith's story:

> The test was a snap for me, but there was a quite pretty girl playing a baritone horn that caught my eye. Little did I know that in the fall I would see this same Marion Schmidt ('41) as I entered Pawnee Rock High School. By the time we were sophomores, we were dating, and married after the war.
>
> We had a great time on an unannounced senior sneak day on a spring day in 1941. However, when

returning to school we were all awarded the task of learning Brutus's speech.

I enrolled at Emporia State but was soon in the Army Air Corps. We headed for England on the St. Mary with over 4,000 troops plus crew aboard. We landed in Scotland and I was sent to a base west of London. On D-Day plus 8, my platoon of forty-eight men were sent to the Isle of Wight to set up radio communication equipment. It was back to the mainland on D plus 6.

After the war I returned to marry and start the family farming and cattle business. I was on the school board from 1957 until the school closed in 1972.

Senior trips became annual events in the 1940s. The class of 1964 traveled to the Ozarks. The class of 1966 went to Osage Beach. Two of the sponsors were Earl Schmidt ('46) and Janice Flick Schmidt ('47). Earl was the bus driver and drove for the district for thirty-seven years. They were beloved by the students as sponsors and also in the community.

Earl Schmidt ('46) recalls one event that stayed with him some sixty years later:

I had just let this student off the bus in the country. When I stated to back up in the driveway, I saw him in my mirror behind the bus. I got out to tell him to leave and chased him into the house. By the time I got back in the driver's seat, he was behind the bus again. Several more attempts to chase him away led me to finally call him a little shit. As is the case in most fights, the one who gets caught is the last one to say something. This little imp reported me to his parents who then called the principal. The next day I was called in the principal's office for a reprimand.

Every student remembers their bus driver, but Earl Schmidt was special. A former student told of a time when Earl had backed out of the bus barn and accidentally broke off the new radio antenna on the way out. That day there was a snow storm and drifts had blown over the road. With a head of steam, the bus plowed into one of the drifts, but did not make it through. The mile and a half walk to school was quite memorable.

Marvin Kroker ('45) was also one of the bus drivers for the district.

Few people in Pawnee Rock schools went by their real names. Nicknames were the norm. To this day, many people do not recognize others except by a nickname. The Unruhs were known as Domple, Biggie, Bugs, Gill, and Bush. The Tutaks were Tuk, Diggs, Buck, and Tub. The Hixsons were Goofy, HS, and BJ (Baby John). The Smiths were Cricket, Cotton, Shitty, and Boo.

Music Department — Music and band were a very important department at the high school. The marching band had over fifty students when there were about ninety students enrolled in the high school. Kent Tutak remembered, "Band was a big deal. We always marched at the State Fair in Hutchinson. I may not have been quite as committed to music as I was to sports, but gave it a try anyway. I had played the drums in grade school but they did not need another drummer. I was given a clarinet and told to just march."

When the school unified with Larned in 1967, senior trips and freshman initiation ended. Rick Tutak ('69) had this to say:

My class was the first class to *not* get to take a senior trip. All freshmen were given the duty of carrying the tackling dummies out onto the practice field. They were really heavy, and it seemed like initiation.

Clarinets must have been in my family as I too was given a clarinet to play in the band. One day the instructor found me trying to play without a reed in the clarinet. That was the end of my musical career.

Ed Crosby ('66) chuckled as he told of a dedicated history teacher, H.A. Smith:

Mr. Smith was a wonderful history teacher. He was passionate about maps and pointing out locations and battlefield events. He would lecture and suddenly pull down a map and immediately point to the location. I innocently will say that one day when he yanked down the map, there was a *Playboy* centerfold there to greet his yardstick pointer.

The 1963 Kansas Unification Movement—

These great times and athletic success were marred by the 1963 Kansas legislation to unify school districts. It led to the eventual closing of over a thousand high schools in the state of Kansas. None was more divisive or provoked more deep-seated resentment than the Pawnee Rock experience.

A district could unify with an adjacent district. Pawnee Rock had four districts that touched their boundaries. Great Bend said that if they were to unify with Pawnee Rock, they would close the high school. Otis, to the north, had already made a unification deal with Bison. Radium, to the south, had merged with Macksville. Only Larned, to the southwest, promised not to close the high school at Pawnee Rock. This promise lasted for five years.

In the spring of 1972, the Ft. Larned school board announced that Pawnee Rock Junior and Senior High

Schools would be closed and the students bused the nine miles to Larned schools.

A parents group filed suit in district court to stop the closing. The *Great Bend Tribune* reported on August 22, 1972:

Last week Judge Herbert Rohleder issued a finding favorable to the request for mandamus against the USD 495 Board. The suit was brought by the parents of Pawnee Rock students asking the court to stay a play by the School Board to close the Junior and Senior High facilities at Pawnee Rock.

Last May the School Board of USD 495 announced the closing of the Pawnee Rock High school for economic reasons . . .

In the courts decision on the action sought by the parents was entered that the school could not be closed without the consent of the patrons of the old Pawnee Rock district.

The announcement Monday night by the USD 495 board leaves the Pawnee Rock Students at a crossroad.

The Ft. Larned board said that the Junior and Senior high students in the Pawnee Rock area were to enroll and attend school at Larned until a decision is made on the appeal to the State Supreme Court.

Representing the Ft. Larned School District at the Supreme Court hearing was Glee Smith, who was also the president pro tem of the Kansas senate. Ft. Larned, USD 495, eventually won the case, and the Pawnee Rock School closed August 1972.

"It was the biggest screw job in the State of Kansas," said one 1964 Pawnee Rock graduate. "It essentially killed the town. Larned had won the battle, but lost the war. There would have been eighty-nine students in the high school that fall of 1972. Instead of going to Larned to high school, a vast majority would go thirty miles south to attend Macksville High School."

The high school was shuttered, and the Supreme Court of Kansas made it official. The class of 1972 would be the last graduating from Pawnee Rock. There were fifteen graduates, with the last graduate being Randy Wilson (alphabetically). There were 968 graduates in fifty-nine years from 1914 through 1972. The most numerous surnames of the graduates were Unruh-79, Schmidt-50, Smith-50, Dirks-33, Bowman-21, Miller-18, Schultz-11, Flick-10, Houdyshell-10, Moore-10, Wilson-10, Koehn-9, and Williams-8.

Pawnee Rock High School
Barton County, KS

40
McDonald High School

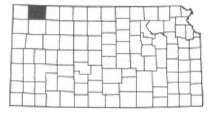

Mascot: Tigers

Colors: Black and Orange

Year Closed: 1975

Location: town of McDonald, far western edge of Rawlins County, two miles from the Cheyenne County line.

Town Origins—McDonald was a Bohemian community. The McDonald High School was organized in 1917. The families did not approve or encourage dating anyone from the next town west, Bird City. Interestingly, when the school closed in 1975, the district unified with Bird City. As was the case most often, the students did fine with the merger, but the parents needed a few years to mellow before accepting this new alignment.

School Clubs & Activities

- The school was noted for its excellent Future Farmers of America club and agriculture departments. As many as thirty-three boys participated in FFA.

- Forensics was always emphasized as the junior and senior plays were a school tradition. One senior play was *No Boys Allowed*. There were five boys in the play.

- Y Teens was a girls Christian organization. There were many participants. The National Honor Society recognized the outstanding scholars in the junior and senior classes.

- McDonald boys played eight-man football, basketball, and track. The girls played basketball. Bird City was the fieriest rival in all sports.

- The music department was extremely successful. Nearly half of the school was in band. There were nearly twenty-five students in each of boys glee club, girls glee club, and mixed chorus.

- The student body voted to honor students with titles such as most athletic and best dressed boy and girl in school.

- One student, Patty Rooney ('65), became the first lady of Kansas when she married Governor Mike Hayden.

Student Memories — Lila Howard ('66) shared this memory:

My class of 1966 had twenty graduates. I was a basketball player, played in the band, and sang in the glee club all four years. Being in the class plays both the junior and senior years gave me experience of performing on stage that I will long remember and gave me confidence in a public performance. I was the co-editor of the school newspaper.

There were 821 graduates of the McDonald High School from 1917 through 1975. The largest graduating class was twenty-seven in 1945, followed closely by twenty-three graduates in both 1935 and 1972. There were seventeen graduates in the final class of 1975.

#41

Olsburg Rural High School

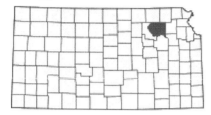

Mascot: Norseman
Colors: Blue and Gold
Year Closed: 1957
Location: town of Olsburg, northwest corner of Pottawatomie County, just east of the confluence of the Big Blue and Black Vermillion rivers

Area History—The region's settlement was predominately Swedish and Norwegian immigrants who came in the 1860s. There were so many men with the first name of "Ole" that the small village was first called "Olesburgh." Though time of this change in the spelling of the name from Olesburgh to Olsburg cannot be documented, the "e" and ending "h" had been dropped by the coming of the railroad in 1880. Some pictures as late as the turn of the century still had captions written in the margins titled "Olesburgh Main Street."

In 1880, the Kansas Central Railroad ran its line through this part of the prairie. This branch from Leavenworth was projected to run all the way to Denver, Colorado. The furthest it was built was to Miltonvale, seventy-five miles west. In 1887, a prediction in the town's newspaper, *The Olsburg Gazette*, was optimistic about the town's future:

> When the Rock Island buys the Kansas Central Railroad and the Santa Fe builds its line northwest to Olsburg we will become the most accessible city in the county. The county high school will naturally be located at this point. The present Swedish Lutheran School will increase in importance as attendance increases, the county conventions and public meetings will be held here at the most easily reached point in the county. An account of our splendid shipping facilities, the gypsum beds will be opened up and a plaster mill will operate, the creamery will flourish, the broom factory increase its force of hands, the city will spread itself and wax large.

What actually happened was that the Kansas Central went into receivership and was reorganized in 1897, ten years after this prediction. The Leavenworth, Kansas and Western was known affectionately as "The Little Kansas Wiggle," the "Leave Kansas and Walk," or the "Little Kids and Women Railroad."

A College Dream—Another dream of the Olsburg townspeople was to found a college. A newspaper clipping in *The Olsburg Gazette* of September 16, 1887, tells the story:

There are possibilities of establishing a college in Olsburg. All agree it would be a fine thing for the town. Studies could be optional—either the English or Swedish language or it would receive liberal support. As a location for a school, Olsburg is unsurpassed and would be of easy access to a large territory settled by Swedes and rapidly filling up with Americans. If the Swedish Lutheran Church could be induced to take charge, its success would be assured.

This may seem rather farfetched now, but around this same time, Lindsborg, Kansas, established a Swedish college called Bethany College in their community, which at the time was not much larger than Olsburg.

First Schools—Oscar Fagerberg was born in Sweden in 1849. He came to America with his family and lived first in Indiana. When coming to this area with so many Swedes, Oscar and his brother C.W. built a shanty. From this small structure they built the economic pillars of the community. From *The Olsburg Gazette* on October 6, 1899:

The firm of Fagerberg and Brothers is now 50 by 80 feet (compared to the school house at 25' by 36') with cellar and warehouses carried $15,000 worth of goods. [Author's note: This was no small sum when one considered a typical years salary at this time was less than $1,000 and the aggregate stock of Olsburg's stores was then $31,000.] Their implement and vehicle house disposed of two carloads a year. They handle up to 50,000 bushels of corn a season, buy and ship 50 to 60 car loads of porkers a year, and own 85 acres adjoining town and feed a hundred cattle. The Brothers own the Olsburg saw mill with a 55-horse power machine and 60-hourse power boiler . . ."

The Fagerberg Mercantile store would later become the Olsburg High School. The first school building was a log building located about a half mile west of town on what was commonly referred to as the Will Olson place. In 1880, a school was built in the village. This frame building was 24' x 36' and cost $1,200. This building was just north of the present grade school.

In 1894, a large stone building was constructed. It was heated by a coal burning stove, and there was no plumbing. Drinking water was carried from a pump outside and poured into a large stoneware drinking fountain located in the hallway. Everyone had their own drinking cup or glass. Later, gas heat and indoor bathrooms were installed. The high school was located in this building until 1939. In the late 30s, the need for more space to properly teach the required courses and to have an indoor gymnasium led the school district to hold a bond election. On April 24, 1939, an election was held for the purpose of raising $15,000 to purchase a site, a school building, and improvement of the same. The election carried by a large majority, 190 to 34. The red brick building on Main Street, formerly occupied by the Fagerberg Store was purchased for $5,000, and in the fall of 1939, the high school moved to this remodeled modern building. High school classes continued to be held there until May 1957 when the school closed due to lack of students and the inability to continue meeting the requirements set by the state of Kansas.

The first high school was described in the *The Olsburg School News* dated September 28, 1917:

Olsburg an Accredited High School. The last year of the history of the Olsburg High school has been and eventful one. During this brief period of time it has risen above the normal level of average High school and is now on the accredited list of this state. This unusual rapidity of advancement is in a large measure due to the progressive spirit of the community as a whole. This community is behind the school, the town is behind it, and in a word the people are behind it ready to back it up and boost. The needed improvements required by law for an accredited High school were made. Among these perhaps the most important and also most difficult to secure was the third teacher in the grades. Next the remodeling and modernization of the upper story is the most consequence. This floor now contains four rooms and one large hall . . . The value to the community at large of an accredited High School cannot be overestimated. On the other hand it is often underestimated. In the first place, state credit is given right here in Olsburg where the rising generation of this vicinity can enjoy the privileges without going to Lawrence, Topeka, or some other distant city.

Later that same fall, on November 23, 1917, this was reported by *The Olsburg School News*:

Travelling Library: The English class of the Olsburg High School have received their traveling library, which they received from Topeka and this will be in their possession for six months. It contains classics, historical fiction, and any number of miscellaneous books, and is a great benefit to students in their English outside reading . . .

Rural High School Law: What it means to Small Schools. Contrary to some opinion the Rural High School Law does not have any connection with grade work at all. All rural districts and graded schools remain unchanged. The law does give a district supporting a High School the right by special election to broaden out and create an entirely new High School

District . . . The advantages of the new law for a small school are many. In the first place why should anyone district support a High School for the benefit of surrounding districts when they should and in most cases would be glad to pay their share . . .

Olsburg vs. Garrison. The Olsburg high school basketball team went to Garrison during the second week of school this month and lost by a score of 21 to 22. Garrison played mostly a defensive game, keeping three men under the goal nearly all of the time and this made it impossible to get a close shot. They were forced to take long shots and their skill in doing this was the only thing that let us off like it did . . . The second game played and the first to be won was played with Stockdale. Olsburg won by a score of 52 to 7 . . .

Miss Cannon to English class: "Do not say, I don't think, because you do think."

Olsburg in the Bigger Picture — A column heading in *The Olsburg School News* on January 18, 1918 stated, "Volunteered.":

Following his sense of duty Prof. R.S. Bahret has answered Uncle Sam's call and enlisted in the army. Owing to this fact he has resigned his position as superintendent here, which position he has successfully held for the past two terms this being his third term. We the students cannot but regret his departure although we respect and honor him for the course he has taken . . . What has been accomplished by Prof. Bahret during his stay here cannot be overestimated. Among the most important results of his work it will be noticed that the standards of the school have been raised to such a point that the state authorities have seen fit to place it upon the accredited list, thereby making it a recognized first class school . . .

In a letter back to the *Olsburg School News* just three months later, Prof. Bahret reported:

> To Former pupils and Friends of the Community:
> My interest is centered on the Rural High School election at Olsburg today and I think by the time you read this Olsburg will have taken another step in increasing the possibilities of the school. I sincerely hope such is the case . . . in active service now for almost three months . . . Fort McPherson is beautifully situated among tall straight pines, only four miles from Atlanta . . . There are five hundred German prisoners brought here recently . . . our training in gas making and gas protection is very interesting. Eighty per cent of all shells shot by the Germans is gas and since such is the case . . . with best wishes to all my friends . . . sincerely, Roscoe S. Bahret B.H. No. 28

This report back to the school and community is a reminder of the war and the sacrifices that our country and its men and women gave for freedom. It was not recorded at this time, but in March of that same year, 1918, the first cases of Spanish flu were found in Haskell County, Kansas. By June of 1918, thousands of soldiers were dying at Camp Funston (Ft. Riley) just thirty miles away from Olsburg. Twenty-four of the thirty-six army forts in the United States had an epidemic and Prof. Bahret certainly was exposed, though no accounting of his fate is available.

Life in Olsburg, 1947-48 —

The school mascot was the Norseman, and the yearbook was named *The Norseman*. The graduating class sizes began shrinking during the depression and World War years and were indicative of the dwindling of the business community and population of the countryside. The 1948 yearbook showed only three seniors graduating. There were twenty-two in high school that year. The school newspaper, *Noise of the Norseman,* was edited by Darlene Samuelson.

Jewell Smith entered an essay contest on the subject of "Kansas Courthouses." She won first place in Pottawatomie County. The custodian, Ruben Gustafsean, was pictured on the first page of the yearbook, indicative of his importance to the school and the students. An all-school roller skating party was held in Leonardville. The freshman class was the guest because it had sold the most tickets to the junior play titled, *And Mary Did.*

The boys won no basketball games that year. A side note written in the column of the yearbook noted, "Brother they really stunk this year!" The Little Six League had only five teams—Cleburne, Westmorland, St. George, Fostoria, and Olsburg. The girls basketball team fared somewhat better. Their regular gym classes included tumbling, exercises, and softball, along with basketball.

The phone rang on February 20, 1948, and the whole school was invited to an afternoon party at Fostoria. Singing, playing games, and a volleyball tournament with the neighboring school "Get Together" was enjoyed by both the students and faculty.

This year of 1947-48 showed a glee club, Luther League, and Brotherhood as organizations. Music under the direction of Mrs. Willard Pierce was held twice weekly. The boys glee club had twelve members with five tenors and seven basses. There were ten voices in the girls glee club which was indicative that all of the high school students were in a glee club. Lessons included fundamentals of recognizing the different band instruments and studying lives of composers such as Bach, Handel, Beethoven, Paderewski, and Chopin. The outstanding novelty number of the term was by Linn Fagerberg and Darrell Johnson, featured in "When You Wore a Tulip."

Closing Olsburg Rural High School—By 1954, per the yearbook, the fortunes of the Norseman had somewhat improved. The boys won seven basketball games, but the girls lost all of their softball games. The boys played both baseball and softball. Almost miraculously, they won two softball games and played close in three baseball games with only seven players.

In May 1957, the last graduation was held with three graduates—Martha Samuelson, Rosalie Ingalsby, and Cleon Larson.

Olsburg Rural High School
Pottawatomie County, KS

#42
Walton High School

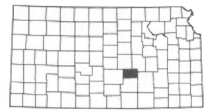

Mascot: Wildcat

Colors: Royal Blue and White

Year Closed: 1964

Location: town of Walton, northeast Harvey County

Town History & First School—The Walton community was originally settled by many Mennonite families, as were several other counties in central Kansas. The town was centered in a rich agricultural area. There were seven churches at the time that the high school was being built.

The first school house was a one-story frame building. Residents of the school district approved a $12,000 bond to construct a new school building in 1913. The total of the bond did not cover the costs for heating and a furnace. Altogether, the building cost was around $15,000, including $25 paid to Jake Richman, a nearby farmer who dug the basement. This was according to O.L.Spangler who was on the school board in 1913. The gymnasium and auditorium were built by Wiens Construction Company of Newton in 1923 for $10,000.

The newspaper in Newton interviewed O.L. Spangler in 1964: "The original plans called for a sort of concrete stave construction. After it was partially finished it was badly damaged during a storm. The insurance company that had the construction policy agreed to pay for the damages but it was decided to rebuild with tile. The original construction was a bit of an experiment."

Following the closure of the high school in May 1964, the building was demolished. In this same article, Spangler continued, "They don't make them like they did in those days." That was the verdict of O.L. Spangler, veteran Walton banker, as he watched a demolition crew tear down the 53-year-old building.

The Davis Legacy — The Davis family was a longtime presence in Walton. J.W. Davis, a farmer just outside of Walton, brought his family to the area in 1876. His son, C.M. Davis, was a barber, insurance agent, owned the first phone system, and was the mayor of Walton. His son, Max Davis, ran the Standard Oil bulk plant in the 1960s. Max was the first fire chief and was on the city council for forty-five years. His son, Dean Davis, worked for the city and has been working with the fire department for over fifty years (as of 2018). Over 142 years, four generations of the Davis family continue to leave a lasting mark on the community of Walton.

Walton Activities — The boys played eleven-man football in the 1930s. By the 50s, eight-man and six-man football were played. Glen Esau ('50) recalled, "My years we played six-man. All home games were played in the afternoons as we had no lights. Basketball was a much stronger sport. We had track in the spring but not baseball."

The sports teams played in the McPherson county league. The biggest rival was Goessel, closely followed by Windom. In 1940, Walton played teams from Leon, Sedgwick, Burns, Andale, Hillsboro, Burrton, Canton, and Galva.

There were no girls sports after the war, but basketball was played in the 1920s and 1930s. The 1958 basketball team only lost two games. The 1962 team lost in the regional finals to Durham, which went on to become the state champions in class BB.

The twelve seniors of 1958 took a trip to Colorado on a school bus. The dozen were still living and doing well today (June 2018).

The yearbook was called *Royal Blue*. There were no yearbooks during the war years.

School Closing — The school closed in May 1964, following graduation. An auction was held in July to liquidate all of the contents. There were deep feelings of disappointment with the quick dispersal of the remains of the school.

Dean Davis was a seventh grader when the high school closed in 1964. He had his eye on the lathe which had been part of the industrial arts department and was to be auctioned. His father had told him not to bid over $35 when the lathe came up for auction. When the auctioneer barked and asked for a bid for the lathe, the towhead immediately raised his hand and said, "I'll bid $35." There was a soft snickering among those at the sale, and the auctioneer paused and nudged for no one else to make a bid. This lathe is still used today in Dean's local wood-working shop in Walton. This is a remnant of the Walton High School that is being used today.

Demolition in the fall of 1964 completely erased any visible remains of Walton High School.

The first Walton graduating class was in 1915. In the fifty years from 1915-1964, there were 525 graduates. The last class of 1964 had eleven graduates. The enrollment was forty students at this time. The last graduate was Max Wiens (alphabetically).

The most numerous surnames of graduates were Schmidt-38, Voth-19, McClure-13, Janzen-12, Ames-10, Gutherie-10, Spangler-9, Esau-8, Hiebert-8, Dubois-7, and Woelk-7.

After Walton Closed — With the closure of the high school the students enrolled in Newton, Hesston, Peabody, and Berean Academy (Mennonite). There remains in Walton a very viable grade school called Walton Rural Life Center. It functions as a charter school, offering K-4 education, and is part of the Newton School District. There are over 200 children on a waiting list to attend the school.

Walton High School
Harvey County, KS

The 1st Walton High School
Harvey County, KS

#43

Kendall Rural High School

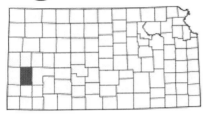

Mascot: Bobcat

Colors: Purple and Gold

Year Closed: 1976

Location: town of Kendall, extreme east-central border Hamilton County/ western Kearny County

School History — Kenny Waechter and Kim Lohman ('74) researched and printed the history of Kearny County schools. Some of the following is credited to them for their diligence in recording this story.

In 1887, the same year that the original borders of Kearny County were reestablished, the citizens of Kendall felt the need to have a school. A school district was organized and students were admitted from both Kearny and Hamilton Counties. Construction of a two-story limestone school started in 1888. The school was for students from first through eighth grades.

Kendall High School was organized in 1920, and the two-year high school took place in the upper floor of the grade school building starting in 1921. There were two elementary teachers and one high school teacher. The next year, 1922, lightning struck the school, and it burned to the ground. Arguing had already developed over the need for a high school. Some of the farmers in the area believed that boys of that age should be working on the farm.

Though a replacement was built, it was voted to close the high school in 1923, but citizens pushed for another vote. In 1929, the high school was reopened as a four-year program and became Kendall Rural High School.

In 1931, three rural school districts were created in Kearny County. Kendall was named as District No. 1. Kendall's school continued to take in students from both Kearny and Hamilton Counties. With the formation of the Kendall Rural School District came the need for a larger school with a gymnasium. A new school included a gymnasium, classrooms, and a cafeteria in the basement.

The first school bus was a pickup truck with a covered top. It had bench seats on the sides and a heater in the middle. Soon after World War II, it was replaced by a used yellow school bus.

County Seat Struggles — Early records of Hamilton County indicate that there was a struggle over the location of the county seat between Syracuse and Kendall. At that time Kendall had numerous banks and a thriving business district on Main Street. Whether the county seat was stolen is not well documented, but it was relocated to Syracuse in the center of the county. With the relocation, the fortunes of the town of Kendall began to diminish. There remains today a very large Farmers Co-op, a Methodist church built in 1915, a post office, and little-self serve vending shop.

Extracurriculars — Sports, especially basketball, became very popular. Football was never played. Athletic and debate leagues were starting to form across the state. Kendall became a member of the Western Arkansas Valley League (WAVL) along with Lakin and Deerfield.

The Western Arkansas Valley League (WAVL) expanded to included Shallow Water, Holcomb, Deerfield, Pierceville, Manter, and Coolidge. Coolidge was by far the greatest rival. If ever the teams wanted to win at least one game a year, it was against Coolidge. There were no after school sports as the practices were all held during the school day. The Bobcats participated in basketball, cross county, track, and baseball. Volleyball was added for the last two years before the school's closing in 1975.

Being a member of the WAVL allowed girls to continue competing in sports when other leagues phased out girls teams during the Dirty Thirties and World War II. When Title IX brought women's sports back at the national level in 1972, these smaller schools had a jump on the competition. Kendall's 1972-73 girls basketball team qualified for the first ever Kansas girls state basketball tournament in the class A division.

When the WAVL disbanded in 1968, Kendall went looking for another league. They joined the Western Twin Valley League for a short time before ending up in the Santa Fe Trail League.

Kendall had many fine athletic teams, athletes, and coaches. As long as there are former students alive, the school's traditions, player efforts, wins and losses, will not be forgotten

Splitting the District — With the School Reorganization Law of 1945, the forced consolidation of the smaller one-room schools began. This reorganization expanded the Kendall school district along the western edge of the county, from the northern edge of the county line to the southern edge of the county line.

A beautiful new grade school was built in 1962. It was connected to the existing high school building by a long hallway. The rooms off the hallway included two locker rooms, a music room, science room, lunchroom, and kitchen. This new school was to enhance the education in the community and to build hope that the community would grow and families would be attracted to the great schools. By this time, the district had five school buses that traversed the countryside to pick up the rural students along the county lines.

At the end of the 1975-76 school year, Kendall USD 478 was disorganized and the State Board of Education divided the district among adjoining school districts. The district was split along the Hamilton-Kearny County line. That portion in Hamilton County, with a valuation of five million, was given to Syracuse. The Kearney County land valuation of three million was given to Lakin. Students were given the option to attend either of the new school districts of Lakin or Syracuse. A hearing was held, and Syracuse officials requested a larger portion of the land from Kearny County. Their position was that the additional land would help close the assessment gap between the relatively rich Lakin district and Syracuse, where the assessed valuation was lower than most surrounding districts. The request was denied and a State Board of Education member pointed out that the Syracuse school district was getting the larger share of the valuation, as well as all school buildings, free of debt, plus other property and equipment divided between the two districts.

Teachers and Students

An all-star teacher/superintendent and his wife, Glen and Velma Allison, came to Kendall in 1949. Mr. Allison taught history and was the coach until 1958. Velma Allison taught bookkeeping and typing. Their daughter, Zena Lee Allison ('50) would graduate from Kendall. Anna Ploeger Graber ('54) recalled, "Mr. Allison made Kendall schools what they were to become. He had exceptional drive and a passion for education that lived well after he retired from Kendall. Mr. Allison and his wife were the most intelligent people that I was ever around. He also started the band where I learned to play the trombone."

Marvin "Babe" Graber ('52) gave an account of Coach Allison's first year as the coach in February 1950. He said, "We had a record of 19-0 entering the game with Deerfield. I was a sophomore on the team. One unusual memory is of this basketball game against a rival Deerfield team. Kendall entered the game undefeated with a record of 19-0. At the beginning of the third quarter, and much of the fourth quarter, the Deerfield coach had his team set the ball on the floor around midcourt. They were not to touch the ball unless Kendall players challenged the ball. The ball rested untouched for nearly the entire eight minutes of the quarter as the clock ticked off. Coach Allison instructed his players to not challenge the ball as the clock ticked away. At the last seconds, the Deerfield boys picked up the ball and made a last attempt to win the game. Kendall lost the game, 15 to 19 . . . I believe that Deerfield went on to the state tournament that year. Kendall finished the season with a record of 23-2, but were kept out of the state tournament with a loss in the regional tournament."

Traditions

Some students were able to go on two senior trips. At Kendall High School, the junior class president was usually able to go on the senior trip. So also traveling to Mississippi and Louisiana in May of 1953, was Anna Ploeger Graber ('54), the junior class president. Glen Allison and Joe and Rose Englert drove the cars. Mr. Allison loved history and took the class to see some of the Civil War battlefields. They spent a big day at Vicksburg, Mississippi, touring the battlefield and visiting museums. It was such an eye-opening experience for these seniors getting on a bus in New Orleans. They were told that they should not go to the back of the bus because that was where the blacks were supposed to sit. They had never heard of such treatment of people in their western Kansas experience.

In 1954, the seniors journeyed to Carlsbad Caverns, the Grand Canyon, and a border crossing into Neuvo Laradeo, Mexico. Herman Marquez ('54) was of Spanish ancestry and, for a time, he was held up at the border getting back into the United States. It was yet another vivid learning experience for this class of six seniors. The sponsors for this trip were Elmer and Elsie Ploeger and Mr. and Mrs. Charles Pelphrey.

Anna Ploeger Graber ('54) had this to say about the trip:

> We rode mules down into the Grand Canyon. I was told that I had to ride up front with my mule between two of the boys. When asking why I could not

be back in the line with the other three girls in the excursion, I was told that my mule was the safest mule in the pack, but it was blind and needed to be up front in the line between two other very trusted mules.

The next day Dorothy Summers ('54) was down on the floor of the car with her backside up in the air. My father asked if she was praying and she shot back, "No, but my backside hurts so much, this is just the most comfortable way to sit!"

We raised money for these trips by selling about anything from pies at the ballgames, to tee shirts and caps.

Spanish was taught as a foreign language in the 1950s. For several years in the late 50s and early 60s, Russian was offered as an elective to all of the students.

Closing Kendall — The closing of the high school in May of 1975 brought an end to fifty-three years of the Kendall Rural High School. From 1932-1975, Kendall had 260 graduates. The most numerous surnames were Wright-7, Graham-6, Lohman-6, Miller-6, and five each for Baker, Patterson, Reynold, and Trussell. The largest class was twelve graduates in 1969. The last class, 1975, had seven graduates with the last to receive a diploma being Marcia Trussell (alphabetically).

Kendall Rural High School
Kearny County, KS

#44

Wallace High School

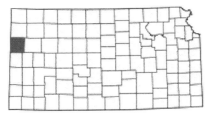

Mascot: Eagles

Colors: Blue and White

Year Closed: 1943

Location: town of Wallace, near Fort Wallace, Wallace County

Town History — The town of Wallace was established because of the building and staffing of nearby Ft. Wallace. Wallace once had a population of 3,500 people.

Following the Civil War and westward expansion of the United States, the so-called Indian Forts were spread across Kansas, Colorado, Texas, Oklahoma, and New Mexico. The army and cavalry guarded mail routes, escorted wagon trains, and provided protection from outlaws and Mexican revolutionaries. Crews building western railroads were at the mercy of the hostile Indians and outlaws.

Buffalo soldiers in the 9th and 10th Cavalry were African Americans who helped gather information about the western terrain. Scouting and exploring thousands of miles of wilderness, they located scarce water holes, mountain passes, and grazing areas. They helped build roads and put up many miles of telegraph wires. They helped build dozens of forts and outposts along the isolated frontier.

The First School — Wallace School was first held in a building rented from the Union Pacific Rail Road. In 1887, a large two-story school was built. This school burned down, and a smaller building was built to replace it. Due to overcrowding, another small building was constructed a short distance to the west to house the lower grades. This building still stands and is owned by Joe Moss (2018). In 1923-24, a new two-story brick building was built across the road to the east. A few years later, the original 1887 old school house was torn down.

Some high school subjects were taught in Wallace as early as 1912.

After the consolidation of Wallace and Sharon Springs, the students were given the choice of attending grade school in Wallace or being bused to Sharon Springs. The seventh and eighth grades were transferred to Sharon Springs in 1979. The enrollment for the 1990-91 school year was twenty-nine, with Louise Pearce as a very capable teacher.

A School Sleep Over — A memorable blizzard forced the students to stay at the school to ride out the dangerous storm. The janitor kept the furnace going. The girls slept in the auditorium and the boys slept in the gym. The men from town took soup to the school house from downtown by following the ditches along the road. The teachers cooked in the home economics room. They stayed two days and one night in the school house. In the late afternoon of the second day, the men came and took the children to homes in Wallace. As they left the school building, they were face to face with a cow that had frozen to death standing up on the sidewalk.

A First-Hand Account — Though the school had been closed for nearly seventy-five years, a member of the last graduating class of 1943, Lenetta (Nettie) David Lock, (age 93 in 2017) told this story:

> I played the clarinet and Mrs. Torkelson was the high school teacher. We had home economics where there was cooking for half of the year and sewing the other half. I know spelling had been taught throughout high school, but I was never a very good speller and I always had a problem looking up a word that I could not spell. Softball and basketball were played by the girls and I loved basketball. Our rivals would have been Weskan and Sharon Springs. The school colors were blue and white and the mascot the Eagles. Our senior sneak was a trip to Garden City where we stayed at a motel. There was so much traffic and the cars were slow.
>
> My husband, John Lock, graduated in the 1942 class. He was very ornery and was always pulling pranks. The father of a friend of his had a store, and the boys swiped some Ex-lax and slipped it into another boy's lunch pail. A very hasty exit from class was experienced.

The first graduating class was 1924. The last class in 1943 had six female graduates. The high school was closed due to a shortage of teachers during World War II. The last graduate to get her diploma from Wallace High School was Emma Yehle (alphabetically). In the twenty years of Wallace High School, there were ninety-three graduates.

#45

Berryton Rural High School

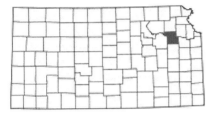

Mascot: Buffalo

Colors: Red and White

Year closed: 1962

Location: town of Berryton, southeastern corner of Shawnee County

School History — The town of Berryton had three high school buildings in its forty-five years of existence. The first was part of a three-story frame structure which included the elementary grades with the high school on the third floor. The first graduating class was in 1918

The school now referred to as the "old" high school was constructed in front of the original school in 1927. In this building, the gymnasium was on the second floor. The basketball goal was on the outside brick wall and the spectators would sit above the court with three rows of bleachers on three sides. There were chairs all around the perimeter of the basketball court. When the gymnasium was full and in use—such as for ball games, school plays, or other events—the entire floor support system would sink enough that the side walls would deviate and the doors could not be opened. To alleviate this problem, these doors would remain open when the gymnasium and stage were in use.

From an article in the *Topeka State Capital Journal* on April 3, 1952:

> The residents of Berryton school district voted unanimously Wednesday night to negotiate purchase of the old Berryton high school for the use of elementary grades. A new high school is under construction and will be occupied about September 1, S.W. Simpson principal, said Thursday. The price of $10,000 has been set for the old building.

Thus the third or the "new" high school was built and occupied for the 1953 school year.

Academics & Activities — Organizations in the 1930s included Kayettes and K Club. Vocational agriculture was taught, as well as algebra, geometry, and woodworking. By the 1950s, only a general math class was part of the math curriculum.

Mr. Tom Morris was a memorable vocational agriculture teacher. One day in trying to diagram on the board, a picture of a chicken laying an egg, Homer Wulfkuhle remarked, "It looks like the sunrise to me!" Mr. Morris was known to take a swing at him.

The Breeze was the school paper and copies can still be read at the Kansas State Historical Society.

Athletics were played with the boys competing in baseball, basketball, and football. In the 1930s, there were champion girls teams in basketball. Eleven-man football was played into the 1950s when it was changed to six-man football. By the 1950s, girls basketball was discontinued. In 1951, the boys baseball team won the Kansas state championship.

Baseball and football were played on the same field. When the field was used as a baseball diamond there was a bare spot where the shortstop was located. When used for football, this area became a quagmire when it rained. Bobby Waldon ('52) was known to always run the ball in this area, so either it was so hard and dirty or, at other times too muddy. Opposing teams disliked the conditions of the fields. Wayne Howbert ('38) remembered that Auburn had white uniforms and in no time at all, their uniforms would be caked in tarry mud from this home field advantage.

Busing started in the 40s. One bus would have to make two runs to pick up students.

Stories from Berryton—

Mrs. Lucy Skaggs was a long-time teacher and an institution. She was very strict and the students were wary and afraid of her. She seemed to be all-serious and did not condone misbehavior. This image would change as she was one of the sponsors on the 1955 senior trip. Larry Howbert ('55) drove his car for the trip. It was a "souped up" car and, when going under bridges or through tunnels, he would let up on the accelerator and the car would backfire. No one had more fun and laughed more at this antic than Mrs. Skaggs. She continued to have great fun with the class as they journeyed on to the Ozarks for their trip.

Wayne Howbert ('38) was a farm boy. He taught math and drivers education in the summers at Washburn Rural High School after two years of college. When money ran short, he left for California and worked for Consolidated Air. With the World War, he enlisted into the service and became part of the air force ground unit in Britain for twenty-six months, from July 1943 through August 1945. He finished college at Washburn University on the GI bill before returning to Washburn Rural to teach for many years. His mother is credited for writing the first verse of the Berryton school song in the early teens. The words are to the tune of "Sailing, Sailing."

Berryton, Berryton
Colors of red and black
Berryton, Berryton,
Knowledge we'll never lack.
We'll be loyal, to teachers and friends and you,
We'll join the throng and travel along
And be victorious, too.

The End—A total of 734 students graduated from Berryton High School between 1918 and 1962 when the school was closed. There were twenty-five graduates in the last class. Mildred Royer (alphabetically) was the last to receive a diploma from the school.

#46

Severy Rural High School

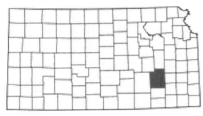

Mascot: Wildcat

Colors: Crimson and White

Year Closed: 1970

Location: town of Severy, south-central Greenwood County

Area History — The Santa Fe Railroad passed through this area in 1879 and a previously named settlement, Gould, was renamed Severy after a railroad worker.

The early education in the community consisted of eight grades. In 1882, a neat stone building with four rooms was constructed at a cost of $4,000. School exercises began on October 1, 1882, with an attendance of 150.

In 1905, community discussion was ongoing to build a new school to include high school classes. The existing school was already overcrowded and needed more room for the expanding enrollment. The closest high school was in Eureka, twenty miles north. If parents chose to send their children to high school, they would pay tuition and sometimes board them in the adjacent towns during the school year.

On May 31, 1905, an election was held to issue bonds for $2,500 to add a two-story, two-room building onto the existing frame structure to accommodate high school training. The proposition passed, 303 voting yes and 13 against.

The contract was awarded to Thomas J. Robinson. For $1,500, the stone work was done and readied for the carpenter. Simon Conaway finished the two rooms for $1,200. The local furniture store, operated by James S. Maben, furnished the seats, desks, and slate blackboards. This addition to the north of the existing school had one room upstairs for high school and one room on the first floor for lower grades. There was a wide hallway and entrance hall under the belfry. The gymnasium was in the basement with fifteen feet high ceilings. The first floor had four classrooms and the upper floor had the auditorium, stage, and two classrooms. The building was steam heated and lighted with electricity. Due to a late arrival of lumber materials, the school board rented the hall over Maben's store for use until mid-October when the addition was completed.

With increasing enrollment and the desire to offer a full four-year high school, there was a reorganization in September 1913. Normal training and a business course were added to the curriculum and another teacher was hired. By 1914, there were five high school teachers and seventy-four students. The hallways were being used for recitation, and the faculty was working at a great disadvantage.

Responding to a petition at the annual meeting on May 17, 1915, the board of education called for an election to issue $15,000 in bonds for a new high school. By a vote of 100 for and 32 against, the community passed the bond for the construction of a free-standing high school. The location was chosen, and seven lots were purchased from Thomas Robinson and Irvin Benest. The alley between them was closed, enabling the property to be large enough to accommodate the new building. It adjoined the present school property. The architect was S.S. Voight of Wichita, and the building contract was awarded to Zollars & Carson of Independence.

The establishing of the school as a rural high school would again take a vote to add the rural country schools into the Severy high school district. On April 12, 1920, the proposition was presented to the voters. This provided the community with a first-class high school for all area children. The rural children would not have to be sent away for schooling. It was promoted among the one-room schools. Should the proposition fail, it was thought that Howard, just south by ten miles into Elk county, would try to take the opportunity to form their own rural high school and take these students away from Severy. The proposition passed, though not by overwhelming numbers in the rural areas.

A special meeting of the Board of Education was held in August 1920 to transfer the high school building, with its existing $8,000 in debt, to the new Rural School District No. 7. This gave the new district a fine building, fully equipped and worth at least $50,000, for paying off the bonds.

Athletics & Activities — A basketball team was organized in December 1908. Students were required to have their lessons done before participating. Practices and games were held in the second story of the opera house. In September 1916, an orchestra was started, as well as the first football game played. Baseball was played at Hilyard's Park.

In 1922, the football team defeated Fredonia, a much larger school to the east. When a student, Jim Rue ('24), was seriously injured in a game, the school board banned football. For the next forty years, until the fall of 1967, there was no football program at Severy Rural High School.

Tennis was started in 1926-27 for both boys and girls. High school county tournaments were held in Eureka. The first school newspaper was also started in the fall of 1926 and was named *High School Life*. An article in the December issue titled "Signs of Progress in Severy High" had the following to say:

> Signs of progress in Severy High School are many. Here are a few of them: First, the issuing of our school paper; second, the publishing of our school annual; third, the purchasing of a radio; fourth, the instructing and maintaining of a school orchestra; fifth, the voice of the student council; and last, but not least, the total refrainment from smoking among the boys of S.R.H.S . . .

A Smallpox Scare — Christmas vacation in 1926 was extended an extra week due to a smallpox scare. The school board ordered the school dismissed in hope that the disease would not spread. To date, only one person in school, Loren Henderson, had contracted the malady, but a number of students were exposed. All students that had any chance of exposure were vaccinated.

Academics — Classes offered in 1926-27 were three levels of English, domestic science, domestic art, algebra, geometry, biology, typewriting, shorthand, music, grammar, physical geography, industrial geography, social civics, American history, psychology, constitution, Latin I, and agriculture. The debate team traveled for a triangular with Climax and Neal. There were five triangulars in the district and all were debating at the same time. The debate team season ended with a trip to the sand dunes of southern Kansas where they won over Kiowa.

The school band was organized in 1928, and the band room was placed in the basement of the high school. The yearbook was called *The Wildcat*. By the 1940s, there were two buses for the district, a Ford and a Chevrolet, as these were the two car dealers in town.

At least three boys, Darrell Knapp, Paul Nichols, and Harold Walter ('46) enlisted in the army during World War II before graduating. They were later awarded diplomas when they returned home safely. Harold told this story:

> We celebrated VE Day (Victory in Europe) on May 8, 1945. It was a cold day and the high school band marched in a parade in the streets of Severy. I was very happy that the war was over, but I remember that my hands became very cold playing the trumpet as we marched.

A Center for the Community — Severy was the only school in the county without a gymnasium and yet it was the wealthiest school district in the county by valuation. In 1948, the new gymnasium and auditorium were added to the school This allowed it to be used as a community building for public gatherings, banquets, county music contests, county teachers' meetings, farm project demonstrations, lyceum courses, plays, meetings, and athletic events. Prior to the new gym, the games were played above the drug store which had a very low ceiling. It had steel posts on the floor and two coal burners at the ends. This did provide for quite a home court advantage.

Athletics were played in the Greenwood County League, and teams seldom traveled outside of the county except to play Howard. The biggest rivals were Piedmont, Fall River, Climax, Reece, Tonavay, Toronto, and Hamilton. The girls played basketball and softball. In 1953, showers were added to the school for sports and physical education.

Traditions — Senior trips were an annual event. In the late 1930s, students traveled in the back of a stock truck with a tarp over the top to Texas. In 1953, they went to Nashville and New Orleans. In 1956, twelve seniors traveled to Juarez, Mexico, by school bus. The seniors of 1957 were off to Tennessee. In 1962, they traveled to New Orleans and Memphis to see Elvis. They traveled that year by a bus and a car. Great angst and (later) laughter occurred when they got separated from each other and lost in Baton Rouge. The classes of 1963-65 traveled to the Lake of the Ozarks. Money for these trips was raised selling nuts, holding car washes, and picking up corn in the fields behind the combines.

One particular trip, it was noted that the superintendent called teacher Jerry Hall to his office before the trip and warned him that this was a very ornery class and that he should beware. Mr. Hall said, "If they misbehave, we will just send them home." To which the superintendent, covering his backside said, "You better have a pretty good reason for doing that." So, Mr. Hall invited a school board member to accompany him as chaperone. The trip came off without incident, and Mr. Hall even handed back some money to each student on arriving home and advised them to keep quiet about any reimbursement of funds.

Notable Faculty — Carl Tyler, a colorful principal in the 1950s encouraged teachers with the phrase, "They are not going to kill you, and they are not going to eat you, so just stay in there!"

The new vocational agriculture teacher, Jerry Hall, came in the fall of 1960. On his interview trip the previous May, he had witnessed a rowdy bunch of boys that were running rough-shod over their teacher. He was quite concerned on his first day of class when an observer from Kansas State University, who was sitting in the back of the room, folded up his notebook and left without saying anything. The teacher observer had previously noted in his reports of a very disruptive climate at this high school, particularly in the vocational agriculture class. Classes went reasonably well for the first-year teacher until time to take a group of FFA officers to the state fair for judging and an FFA event. He informed the six students that they should come the next day in a shirt and tie and trousers. They immediately said they had no trousers or ties. Mr. Hall compromised and said that blue jeans would be fine, but that they would still need to wear ties. The next day came, and all six sat in front of him without any ties. They claimed they did not own ties. Mr. Hall reached down and pulled a tie for each one of them from a box. The ring leader spouted, "I said we ain't wearing no ties!" To which Mr. Hall grabbed the shocked, much larger student by the collar, took him into a closed office, proceeded to thump him, held him down with his knee in his chest, and tied the wrinkled tie around his neck. The other five students heard all of the noise, commotion, and knocking around of furniture from the room. When the dazed student and Mr. Hall reappeared, the other five students had miraculously all put on their ties and looked wide-eyed at this new teacher's actions. Mr. Hall had very few problems with his students in the next twelve years of teaching at Severy.

Mrs. Donna Coble from Southwestern College came in 1961 as a new home economics teacher. She made a lasting impact on all of the students that she was able to teach in her department. She was caring, interested in her students, and emphasized manners.

In a Master's research project, Mr. Hall surveyed students that had been at least ten years out of high school. Mr. Hall asked the survey question, "In your lives, which were the most influential classes taken at Severy High School?" Home economics with Mrs. Coble was No. 1, vocational agriculture was No. 2, and athletics was at the bottom of the list.

The biology teacher, Mr. Arch Wallace, brought a live chicken to school in attempt to show his class the heart and its beating motion. He used chloroform to knock out the chicken, but in opening the chest cavity he accidentally cut the aorta. End of experiment!

Curriculum — There was a heavy emphasis on farm mechanics. The students would go to the American Royal, FFA state conventions in Manhattan, the state fair, and the Mid-American Fair in Topeka. The vocational agriculture department would spend days helping to decorate for the Senior Prom and Sweetheart Balls.

The hot lunch program was always excellent. There were two cooks who prepared good meals. The kids refused to eat their beets, so the cooks found a way to disguise them and made a cake. When students passed on sauerkraut, cake recipes also disguised the sauerkraut. Waste not-want not!

There was no foreign language taught until the final few years of the school when Spanish was offered.

The band would go to Emporia State University for band day and band contests. They marched in parades in Independence and Arkansas City. Practice started in August and students were in fine form by the time of the Annual Severy Labor Day parade.

Chemistry was first offered in 1960. The very versatile Jerry Hall taught this class in addition to vocational agriculture.

Other Stories from Students

There were many stories of noteworthy pranks. The cow on the second floor upset Tom Lacey, the janitor. He was a "really good guy" according to one of the students involved in the incident as he related the story sixty years later. Mr. Lacey also drove one of the school buses and went on some of the senior trips as the bus driver.

Richard Bunyard ('70) told of a renowned Halloween stunt which he vividly remembered from the time when he was just an eighth grader:

> I had found an old feather tick mattress in an abandoned house. Two of us took the mattress to the north end of town in a pickup. There was a strong wind out of the north that night. I cut a slice in the mattress and the wind and the movement of the pickup down Main Street did the rest. It was like a Christmas snow storm had hit the town. Feathers danced and darted into every storefront, tree, and sides of the buildings. The banker had neat glassed windows on the bank that he would keep shiny with linseed oil. You guessed it, they were plastered with feathers. He knew that I must have been the culprit, but never accusing me directly when he called me across the street the next week and said, "Bunyard, I know that you had to be involved in this feather deal, but I have to admit that was the best prank that I have ever seen for a Halloween trick." For weeks when store owners opened their doors for business, they found that little feathers had crept under the doors at night.

Closing Procedures

In May 1964, the District No. 82 school board petitioned the state budget review board for additional funds when they realized the district would not be able to raise enough money for the upcoming school year. That summer a school unification election was held which proposed a north and south unified school district for Greenwood County. The vote did not pass this county election. A second unification vote was held three months later, and it also did not pass. In August 1965, Adel Throckmorton, State Superintendent of Public Instruction, ordered the district be annexed into West Elk Unified District #282 in Howard, effective July 1, 1966. Severy was able to keep its kindergarten through grade twelve for four more years.

The high school was closed following graduation in May 1970. For the sixty-one years of the high school, 1910-1970, there were 713 graduates. The last class had eighteen graduates with Sharon Lee Vancil (alphabetically) the last to receive a diploma from Severy Rural High School.

The most common surnames of the graduates were Henderson-12, Coble-10, Johnson-8, Taliaferro-8, Seimars-7, Bahr-6, Fox-6, Austin-5, and Shugart-5.

Severy Rural High School (photo courtesy of Kent Olson)
Greenwood County, KS

#47

Sylvia Rural High School

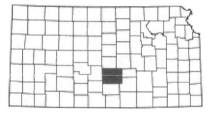

Mascot: Mustangs

Colors: Blue and Gold

Year Closed: 1967

Location: town of Sylvia, western border of Reno County

Town Origins — The Santa Fe Railroad pushed west at a rate of one and a half miles a day. The crews laid track west from Partridge. Depots were constructed at Abbyville, Plevna, and Sylvia. As the westernmost point on the line in Reno County, Sylvia flourished. Sylvia was incorporated in March 1886, and before the year was over, 500 people called it home.

The business directory soon included three general stores, two groceries, two hardware stores, two drug stores, a furniture store, one harness shop, two lumber-yards, two livery stables, a bank, a weekly newspaper, one billiard hall, two meat shops, two hotels, a millinery, a coal and feed store, a restaurant, two churches, and a grade school.

From the 100 year, "Pride in the Past . . . Faith in the Future," history of Sylvia is a beautiful description of the town as reported by a correspondent for the *Leavenworth Times* following an excursion on the Santa Fe line. "The town lies in the beautiful valley of the Ninnescah and is one of the most charming places that one would wish to live."

Education — School District No. 120, indicating that it was the 120th to form in Reno County, became the Sylvia School District in 1885. The first classes started in the fall of 1888 with C.A. Payton as the first teacher. There were sixty-three pupils, and school was in session four months. Mr. Payton's salary for the four months was $42.00.

The first building was wood frame, and rooms were added as needed. No high school work was offered, but later additional subjects were asked to be taught. The first class graduated in 1916. The only other high schools in Reno County at that time were in Hutchinson and Nickerson.

The two-story brick building was located two blocks west of Main Street and was ready for classes in January 1910. It contained a grade school and a two-year high school. The school had six regular classrooms, an assembly room, and a basement where the children could play. The janitor's room was also located in the basement.

Mr. Archie Nelson told of this first school in an interview in 1985. "It was a two-story building and was con-structed in such a way that when the balmy breezes of the pioneer cays blew across the prairies, it had to be lariated down with picket ropes to keep it within the district."

In 1925, as enrollment was increasing, the school board had an opportunity to purchase thirteen acres on the south side of Highway 50. There was no intention of putting up a new building that year. They hoped for a few good crops so that the patrons of the district would be in better financial condition to erect the coveted new high school building. In April of 1926, the rural high school district patrons instructed the board to make a five mill levy for the ensuing year and erect a new high school. The 1926 graduation took place in the Methodist Church. The new high school was dedicated on December 3, 1926.

The two-story, red brick colonial revival building that housed Sylvia High School was built in 1925 for $55,000. The architects were Routledge and Hertz from Hutchinson, who also designed other schools and the courthouses in Gray, Finney, Hodgeman, Edwards, and Comanche counties. The school featured a red clay tile roof, red quarry tile corridors, and large double-hung windows with fanlight transoms. It is as beautiful to the observer today as it was almost 100 years ago when it was built. The building is on the National Register of Historical Places.

Athletics — The great interest in sports by the school and community sparked the need for a new gymnasium. Anton Mothes was on the school board at the time and was opposed. After some consideration, he finally said his oil field was going to play out one of these days, so they had better take advantage and build this new building. The new gymnasium was added in 1949.

The school was the envy of the sports league. Boys football, basketball, baseball, and track were the pride of the school. There were no girls sport teams.

The Snowbarger family had a haymow in their barn, and the boys would play basketball into the nights and all year long, developing an aptitude for basketball. From 1938 through 1967, the boys basketball team won 192 games and lost 43. From 1935-1965, they went to the state tournament nine times in class B and BB divisions. Four straight years, from 1962-1965, the Sylvia Mustangs were at the state tournament.

In 1927, Sylvia started playing eleven-man football. They won fame in a manner that is still in the Guinness World Record Book for losing a game, 256 to 0, to powerhouse, Haven. Haven outscored their opponents 597 to 0 for the year. The legend of that game grew, and explanations are told to this day of what happened. One account was that Haven was to have played their second team, and when they did not, Sylvia opted to kick off after every Haven score and did not play any offense the whole game.

Football was discontinued sometime after that. An eleven-man team was started back up in 1949. By the 1950s, six-man football was played. In 1958, eight-man football was played until the school closed in 1967.

The school's bitterest rival was Alden.

Traditions — Senior trips were taken every year. One year, Harley Melville drove his truck with a tarp over it. The class of 1949 chartered a bus to take all twenty-four seniors to Colorado Springs. They went to the state prison, all of the tourist sites around Colorado Springs, overnighted in Pueblo, and saw the US Mint in Denver.

The 1956, 1960, 1964, and 1967 classes went by school bus for senior trips. Three of these years to Colorado and once to Table Rock in Missouri.

Buses came into the district in the 1940s. They were driven by the senior boys. The math teacher, Mr. Murphy, would drive to away ball games. When the school lunch program was started, the junior and senior high students braved walking or running across the two lanes of busy US Highway 50 to have lunch at the grade school lunch room. No crossing guard, no stop lights, not even a marked crossing line. No accidents occurred, however the close calls were never recorded.

Notable Graduates — There were five Banz brothers—Orville ('35), Floyd ('40) and his twin Leonard ('40), Weldon ('42), and Donnel ('45)— who all served together in the US Navy in World War II. They survived, unlike the five Sullivan brothers from Waterloo, Iowa, who were all killed in 1943 when their ship the USS Juneau was torpedoed in the Pacific.

In 1952, there were four sets of twins in the grade school which had an enrollment of 115 at that time.

One memorable incident happened as senior Merle Etchison was picking on freshman Jerry Clothier. The bullying had gone on long enough, and Jerry used a roundhouse and clocked the much larger senior, who crawled away, never to pick on him again.

Elmer B. Staats ('31) became the Comptroller of the United States from 1966-81. He graduated from McPherson College and was Phi Beta Kappa. With a master's from the University of Kansas, his brilliance in economics led him to Washington D.C. where he served under nine Presidents.

Bud Moeckel ('51), who was married to Joy Shepherd ('51), was one of the stars on two of the state tournament teams of 1950 and 1951. His colorful career included playing basketball at Ft. Hays where he graduated with a degree in physical education. He then coached back in Reno County at Buhler High School. He coached two state championship basketball teams and had a record of 172 wins with 102 loses. He returned to Ft. Hays to coach and teach physical education. He was inducted into the Tiger Hall of Fame and received the Honor Award from the Kansas Association of Health, Physical Education, Recreation and Dance in 1992-93. At his retirement, the university honored him by naming the intramural complex "Moeckel Field" at Ft. Hays State University. His wife Joy also retired after twenty-two years at the registrar's office. These two from the Sylvia Class of 1951 made a significant impact on education for young people in the state of Kansas.

Jerry Kinnamon ('60) won the Kansas state class BB track meet all by himself since he was the only one to score points for Sylvia. He went on to earn track scholarships from Kansas State University and Abilene Christian College. He became an industrial arts teacher and coach at Moran, Hudson, and St. John for forty-four years.

Beryl "Burrhead" Blew ('49) was known by the noise he didn't make. He would work as the city maintenance man for thirty-nine years as well for the Burlington Northern Santa Fe Railroad. His kind and helpful demeanor is still known to everyone who has ever lived in Sylvia. He recalled, "At one time there were numerous freight and steam trains through Sylvia every day. Today (2018) there is only Amtrak. The Dottle Bug was a passenger train going through town as it went daily from Hutchinson to Dodge City."

Beryl served in the army in Korea during the Korean War. He was the first of three generations of his family to serve our country and be stationed in Korea.

Noted Accomplishments

- The band always marched at the state fair in September. They also participated in the league band contests annually.
- The 1946 school newspaper was called the *SHS Mustang*.
- In 1949 the Y Teens club reported in the school paper, "We are also planning a box which we are sending to China to another Y Teen organization. In the box there will be pencils, pencil sharpeners, notebooks, scrapbooks, erasers, etc."

That day which for this generation was not too different than FDR's radio announcement speech that "this day will live in infamy" was November 22, 1963. Like that speech, few will forget where they were when they heard the news. The whole school was directed into the gymnasium for the solemn announcement that President Kennedy had been assassinated. Shock and disbelief for these school children spread throughout the student body.

Closing—The school district unified with Fairfield in 1967. The last graduating class was in May 1967 with seven graduates. Enrollment that year was forty students. The last graduate to receive a diploma from Sylvia Rural High School was Phillip Yust (alphabetically).

There was a total of 852 graduates of Sylvia High School in the fifty-two years from 1916-1967. The most numerous surnames of the graduates were Kessling-29, Clothier-15, Miller-14, Yust-9, Banz-8, Brown-8,

Thompson-6, Stone-6, Kinnamon-5, Smith-5, and Stiggens-5.

Sylvia Rural High School
Reno County, KS

#48

Alton High School

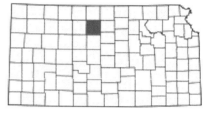

Mascot: Wildcats

Colors: Purple and Gold

Year Closed: 1970

Location: town of Alton, western Osborne County

High School History — On the first year of the 20th century, in 1900, a three-year high school was started in Alton. There were eight students in the first graduating class in 1903. Five of these graduates went on to college. In 1909, the Barnes Law went into effect, and high school became four years instead of three.

Harriet Bock ('12), wrote a very detailed account of the early years of the school for her senior English assignment. She penned, "Mr. George Ruede, our teacher left after the 1908 school year to go to the penitentiary. This statement should not be misunderstood; he did not go as a criminal but accepted a position as clerk. The High School lost one of its sunbeams when he left. During the 1911-12 year the Alton High School was placed upon the list of accredited schools by the State University of Kansas."

Bonds were voted to put an addition onto the south of the present school building, and by this improvement a good structure supported the town. The north half was built in 1885 and this addition was added in 1910. This building housed the grade and high school until the new Alton Rural High School was built in 1925.

There was optimism for the community and for the education of the children as a new grade school was built in 1963. It unfortunately closed in 1983 after only twenty-one years due to consolidation with Osborne and the cost of maintaining the elementary school in Alton.

School Records & Athletics — The school was noted for several records. The most important began in the fall of 1962 and ended in the fall of 1968. The football team won fifty-one consecutive games without a loss or tie. Known for the single wing, the backfield of the flying B's—Brent, Bates, and Brummer—played for those first four years of the streak. This remains the longest record in Kansas high school history (2018). It is the ninth longest streak in United States history. Everett Gouldie was the renowned coach who taught at Alton for eighteen years. His teams of basketball and football played 933 games during this time, winning 710 and losing 220 with three ties. Gouldie always downplayed his role and was quick to give credit for the success to his athletes for their enthusiasm, attitude, sportsmanship, and willingness to follow rules. This winning combination provided many years of happy and exciting moments for the Alton Wildcats.

The greatest rivals in sports were Portis, twenty-one miles to the northeast, and Woodston, nine miles west. To this day there is a sign on a building leading into Portis that reads, "Portis beat Alton in '59." During the 1950s, Portis and Alton battled in basketball with the winner usually going from the regional tournament on to the state tournament. The only state trophy won by Alton boys was for third place in boys basketball. They played in the 1957, 1965, and 1969 state tournaments.

Several football players went on to play college football. Fred Loomis was an all-American guard at Kansas State in 1908. Leo Freeze ('29), Fred McKenna ('30), and Arthur McKenna ('32) all played at Washburn. The McKennas were on the team that traveled to New York in 1934 and held a much larger Army team to only seven points through three quarters.

Girls basketball was a significant sport from the early years into the 1940s. The 1914 girls team won second place in the state tournament after losing to Arkansas City. The sport was dropped for many years, only to be started again for one year in 1965-66.

Faculty — The first teacher to teach in Alton was Abbie McIntire, who was born in 1842 in Alton, New Hampshire. As a teacher she reportedly walked to school from three miles east of town and had to take off her socks and shoes to cross a stream to get there.

Harriet Chace began teaching in 1906 and taught for the next thirty-six years. A popular credit to Ms. Chace was that "she had eyes in the back of her head."

Among the excellent principals was Bernard Tipp, who started as an elementary teacher. He was an administrator and coach in the school for twenty-five years, from 1958-1973. He was remembered as "always representing the best interests of the community."

A popular grade school janitor was Joe Krahl. He was a farmer who moved into Alton and served for thirteen years. "You could always find Joe helping youth with their baseball skills at recess. He loved helping kids learn the game. Lee Guge was the high school custodian for twenty-eight years. A tribute paid to him was, "A man is never as tall as when he stoops to help a child."

Other Memories—The hot lunch program began in 1947. The high school students walked three blocks to the grade school to eat. One student remembered, "We were always looking for a ride, the students were not allowed to drive their cars."

The vocational agriculture department was always outstanding. Four graduates went on to become All-American Farmers. They were Ovid L. Wineland ('39), Harold Hackerott ('40), Thomas "Tim" Hale ('48), and Deryl Carswell ('51).

School Closing—The district unified with Osborne in 1966. The high school was closed after the 1970 school year. The largest class was in 1932 with twenty-nine graduates. The smallest was 1906 with no graduates. The most common surnames to graduate were Brent, Bates, and Carswell representing a total of sixty students, or over 6% of the total of 941 graduates of the school. The high school closed in 1970 with the last class of eight graduates. Edsel O'Conner (alphabetically) was the last graduate to receive his diploma from Alton High School.

The building was bought by a group of community members. It became a Teen Challenge Midwest facility in 2004 for youth.

Alton High School

Osborne County, KS

#49

Longford Rural High School

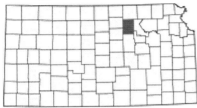

Mascot: Bulldogs

Colors: Orange and blue

Year closed: 1970

Location: town of Longford, southwest corner of Clay County

School History — The town of Longford is on a plateau with wide areas of grasslands surrounding the region. The first school here was called the Logan Township School. Initially, classes were held in the second floor of city hall with one teacher, Chestnut Randal. The need for grade and high school classes led to the construction of a new building in 1912 at the cost of $6,000. Scott Brothers of Concordia were the builders with heating and plumbing by Lewis and Kitchen from Kansas City. The first floor exterior was a light-colored brick laid in black mortar with the top floor consisting of concrete with a stippled effect. The interior was described in the *Clay Center Times*, October 10, 1912, "It is entirely modern in every way with four rooms, superintendent's office and basement."

Early in 1913, the *Longford Leader* reported, "A house warming and dedication took place on January 30, 1913 that included an extensive program as follows: Piano solo, Invocation, Men's Quartet, Recitation, Solo, Reading, Ladies Quartet, Reading, solo, Mixed Quartet, Song, Vocal Duet, Song, and Music remarks."

In May 1914, the high school came under the ownership of the township. Chapman Township taxpayers agreed to pay one-half of the upkeep expenses on the building and grounds, thus sharing the cost of the high school with Logan Township.

Miss Genevieve Hoffman composed the school song, "The Orange and Blue." In 1917, she became the principal of the school. The school already boosted a library of over 400 fiction, reference, and departmental books as reported in the *Longford Leader,* November 22, 1917.

The first graduating class of Chapman Township High School in 1928 included two graduates. World War I had drawn America into the European war. The commencement speaker, according to the *Longford Leader*, May 23, 1918, said, "The best way for young people of high school age to be patriotic was to avail themselves of the educational opportunities offered them so that, if the war should have a long duration they would be able to play a bigger and better part because of their qualifications."

The school became Longford Rural High School in 1922 when a portion of Athelstane Township was annexed to the district. The following year, Durham Township in Ottawa County was annexed. The expanding territory and increase in students led to the hiring of three teachers in 1922-23. Courses in agriculture, along with music and literary societies, were added to the curriculum.

From the Yearbook Archives —

In the first school annual, *The Pioneer*, published in 1925, it was reported that sports were an important extracurricular activity. Both boys and girls basketball and baseball were offered.

A later annual, named *The Constructor*, heralded continued growth and improvements to educational opportunities in the Longford community. The most significant achievement was construction of the new high school building, and classes were moved there February 11, 1929. The students dedicated the yearbook "to the patrons of the school who have made our new building possible." There were eighty-four students in the high school that year.

The *Longford Leader* published a description of the new high school. "The new Longford Rural High School is designed according to the one-story modern brick type. The outside is made of red brick trimmed with black brick."

Depression Era —

The purpose of the commerce class, first offered in 1931, was to prepare students for opportunities in the business field. Courses included bookkeeping, penmanship, typewriting, commercial arithmetic, commercial geography, and shorthand. At this time there were only five teachers in the school. This same year a football field was constructed and eleven students learned the game and played Wakefield, Minneapolis, Talmage, Solomon, and Miltonvale. Though their record was on the losing side, the annual reported "the team had a splendid spirit of good, clean sportsmanship." The school annual that year had advertisements from twenty Longford, two Oakhill, and four Manchester businesses. This would be the last school annual for six years as the great Depression and the depths of economic conditions caused every possible cutback in expenses. It was during this time that the school had its largest classes and numbers of students.

Class composites were not taken in 1937. A scrapbook was compiled with snapshots pasted into a book rather than in a printed format. The football season was described as, ". . . not one marked by victories but a successful one, nevertheless, when considering the experience gained by the large number of freshman and other boys who had no previous experience." In basketball they played in the Clay County League with Morganville, Wakefield, and Green. Other extracurricular activities included class intramurals, tennis, horse shoes, softball, hard ball, and track and field. The orchestra included violins, clarinets, trombone, cornets, drums, and piano. Vocational agriculture and a construction class were added, and no one was surprised when thirty-eight students signed up that first year. There were only seventeen advertisers in this scrapbook which may have been yet another sign of the depths of the depression.

By 1938, there were signs that the worst of the hard times may have been behind this community. The seniors took their field trip to Kansas City. This may have been the first of what became a traditional rite of the senior class passage, to "sneak away" from school for a few days and see the world before returning and completing their studies. The class visited the Liberty War Memorial, city hall, and Swope Park zoo where they saw Jumbo the elephant. Ads in the annual that year included the Faulkner Hotel with a jingle:

There's a friendly "Maggie" in the big white house,

She's neat as a pin, and never harbors a mouse.
If you want a room that's clean,
and food that tastes swell,
Ring the bell of welcome, at the Faulkner Hotel.

By 1945, the annual listed eighty-three former graduates in the military, with one being killed in action.

Sports — Football did not seem to be Longford's strong suit. The 1941 annual described the season as "plenty of brains, plenty of brawn and a swell coach" but could not seem to click together to break the jinx of three scoreless seasons. Finally, a victory over Jamestown, 20-0, came at the end of that season. Sporting orange tops and bottoms, the basketball team suited up nineteen players that year. It would be the last class before the war that would take so may young men just as they were graduating from high school.

By that fall the orange and blue started playing six-man football.

In 1948 a new gymnasium was built. There were no wins in football. The FFA judging team participated in five contests—hogs, poultry, and crops.

By 1951, following a successful 7-1 record the previous year the team played its first night football game on October 31, 1952. That night the Bulldogs pulled out a 34-0 win over Riley. The pep club and cheerleaders introduced a cheer, "Little dog, big dog, flop eared pup, Come on Longford Beat 'em up!"

Eight-man football was the new sport in the fall of 1960. The school annual that next spring showed the team and the picture of the junior class concession stand, which read, "chilliburgers - 25 cents, hotdogs - 15 cents, chips - 15 cents, doughnuts - 5 cents, candy bars - 5 cents, and pop - 10 cents."

Annual Longford Rodeo — The great Longford Rodeo was introduced in the fall of 1956. It became an annual event which continues to this day (2018) It is held on Labor Day weekend and everyone in the community is involved. This fun community event had great participation from the students.

On Labor Day weekend, the 62nd Longford Rodeo celebration was in full swing (2017). Turtle races, face painting, card games in the community center, three rodeo queens, banners decorating the street entrances, the mayor hurrying around town helping, digging holes for the gazebo, a flea market, a freshly manicured, oiled and graveled main street, and the whole community was abuzz with pride and smiles. Multi generations of families continue to reside in this little community along the Santa Fe railroad that runs from Strong City to Nebraska. The tracks that once carried passenger trains, livestock cars, and daily freight trains now see only an occasional grain train and empty coal cars heading back to Wyoming. Mayor Kim Kramer and his wife, Wava (Mullin) Kramer, were in the junior class when Longford High School closed. They returned to farm and also ran the restaurant in town for many years. Kramer proudly tells of the Longford Water Company that touts "the best water in the state, 99.9% pure." The Farmers and Merchants Bank is still on Main Street, though it is only open one day each week.

Mayor Kramer told this story, "We took the FFA to the state fair and were thrilled to find a peep show. We snuck in only to find our vo-ag teacher sitting on the front row! This man, Abe Friedman, was a great teacher. With only thirty-five students in high school its last year, we won first place in judging at the state contest in Wichita. We placed in the top three in national's in Kansas City."

When asked about pranks in school, Kramer chuckled and told of the home economics class. It seemed that cookies that were made in class and kept for later school events were mysteriously disappearing.

Either Gerald Nunn or Jerry Turner was sneaking in after ball practice and making away with the freshly baked cookies. The teacher had planted some ex-lax in the chocolate chip cookies and the thieves soon regretted their "cookie capers."

Jay Kramer ('42), Mayor Kramer's father, reminisced about the history of his school years. "We had eleven-man football. I wasn't worth a hoot, but I enjoyed playing it. Our big rival was Wakefield which was a bigger school. Almost all of the girls took normal training. We had shop and vocational agriculture when the freshman were initiated, castrating lambs the old fashioned way! (with their teeth)

A Teacher's Story — Garry Stenzel, a first-year teacher at the high school the year it closed, told a story of his year in "Looking Back . . . 80 years at Longford School." He had signed a contract to teach in the Clay Center District but found out upon his arrival in the fall of 1969 that he had been assigned to teach at a small town in southwest Clay County.

The school was Longford and I became a Longford Lion. My teaching duties included English 7-12. I was to direct the junior and senior plays and help coach when necessary. I was also given the responsibility of junior class sponsor. The year began on a sour note as the football season was cancelled because of low numbers of students. Soon after that, talk of closing Longford High School began. There was confusion about what would happen at the end of the year and considerable concern among the students about where they would attend school the next year. By the end of the fall of 1969, the decision to close the high school had been made. The junior class play was a success in spite of all my worrying about lines and acting talent . . . One day a student came running into the gym and reported that another student had a splinter in his butt. I said, 'Well, pull it out.' The response was that 'it was a BIG splinter.' Sure enough it was about the size of my little finger. Apparently the student was chasing another student in one of the rooms with a wooden chalk tray. The chalk tray wood was bumped and deposited an arrow like projectile into his posterior. Tom Anderson and I took the student to Clay Center where Dr. Ruff removed the splinter and joked that there must still be a few 'Injuns' in southern Clay County.

Basketball season began and once again there were evening activities. I remember one of our games was with Salina St. John's Military School, and I was amazed to see them all smoking cigarettes in the locker room. Of course, we beat them. Our final game with Wakefield High School was especially pleasing because they had beat us badly earlier in the year, and we managed to beat them 42-40 on a last second shot.

At the end of the year, students at Longford High School had to spend all the money in their class accounts. With the blessing of the principal, we planned an all-school escape to Kansas City (school trip) . . . we visited the state capital building (most for the first time), Kansas City and the Nelson Art Gallery. Most students had never been in an art gallery-museum before and enjoyed it . . . picnic in Swope park . . . stayed in a motel . . . a game at Municipal Stadium for a Kansas City Royals game . . . ball park treats and then the school year ended and Longford High School was no more. It is ironic that I am retiring this year as Longford Grade School closes out its final year.

Graduating Statistics — The largest graduating class from LRHS was thirty in 1935. The smallest class in school history was five graduated in 1964. From 1931-1939, a total of 213 students graduated. Gary Matteson (alphabetically) was the last graduate of the school when the high school closed in 1970.

The high school building today is the home of the Canine International Training facility which trains police and security dogs.

Longford Rural High School
Clay County, KS

#50
Richmond Rural High School

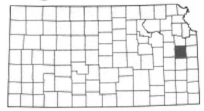

Mascot: Cubs
Colors: Purple and Gold
Year Closed: 1963
Location: town of Richmond, south central Franklin County

History of Town and School — Richmond was the southern terminus of a railroad that ran from Leavenworth called the L. L. and G. It was laid to the southern limits of Franklin County where a loop was built as a "turn around" at this end of the line.

The first school in Richmond was built in 1871 by James Winter. The first public school district was not legally organized until November 1877 with the enrollment of four pupils. In 1881, this school building was moved from the original site to the southwest corner of what was to become the grade school until 1969. By

1883, enrollment was fifty-six pupils and the building was inadequate. A new two-story frame building was built on this location in 1885. The first high school subjects were instituted the next year with algebra and bookkeeping being taught. This building was destroyed by fire the following year and another two-story frame building was built with two additions as the enrollment continued to grow.

In September 1892, a two-year high school course was introduced by the principal, G. H. Crain. From this class, five girls graduated in May 1895. The commencement ceremonies were held in the United Presbyterian Church.

In 1898, eleven pupils completed the two-year course. It was then changed to a three-year course. The class of 1911 was the first to graduate under the full four-year high school curriculum.

Notable Scholars — In 1901, first year curriculum included beginning Latin, algebra, physical geography, English composition, classics, and declamation in the first semester, and the second semester added general history and rhetoric.

Second year, first semester: Caesar's Gallic War-two books, composition, algebra, English literature, and Essay. Second year, second semester: geometry, physics, American literature, and essay.

Third year, first semester: Vergil, geometry, physics, American literature, oration or debate. Third year, second semester: Vergil, Cicero, composition, solid geometry, arithmetic, American history, and oration or debate.

The first Rhodes Scholar from Franklin County was George Ellsworth Putnam from the Richmond class of 1903 (three-year high school). At the age of 15, this was a credit for having been exposed to the above curriculum.

He graduated from Ottawa University and Kansas University where he was an all-conference guard as a football player. George graduated next from Yale with a Master's in Political Science at the age of twenty. He accepted the Rhodes scholarship to Christ Church College at Oxford, England. While at Oxford, he set the World University record in the 16 lb. hammer throw. He returned to Kansas University and Washington University to teach economics. He became the Consulting Economist for Swift & Company in Chicago and served on the Board of Directors.

Among many other notables graduates of Richmond High were

- Guy McCreery, 1898 - Executive Vice-President of GMAC in New York
- Merle Price, 1920 - Captain of KU baseball team
- Lawrence Moberly, 1930 - MA in Chemistry at KU. Westinghouse R&D for 42 years
- Ella Blanche Smith Dahlgren, 1930 - a teacher and principal who apparently invested very wisely, leaving an estate of $3,500,000. She gave generously to colleges, museums, and churches. She had degrees from Emporia State University and Columbia University.
- Francis Kappelman, 1932 – played basketball at Kansas University with Coach Phog Allen and on the 1936, undefeated, all Big 6 team
- Wayne Moberly, 1933 - Chemical Engineer from KU, Phillips Petroleum
- Eunice Stevens Bradley, 1937 - Teacher who started the Elementary Education Department at Kansas State University

- Dr. Chester Spencer, 1942 - Engineering degree from KU with PhD. from Wisconsin in metallurgy. Decorated World War II veteran. Worked at Chase Brass and Copper Co. New York City
- Dr. Arlo Hermreck, 1956 - Chief Orthopedic Surgeon at KU Medical Center
- Mark E. Mersmann, 1959 - CPA with great standing in Missouri, Colorado, and Kansas

Typhoid Reaction—From the town news section in the local paper, there was a story from 1914 under school notes.

> Our gentlemanly school board is having screens put around the outbuilding, thanks to "EX-Ped-agog". Mary Gentry who has been very ill with Typhoid Fever will soon be able to be in school. School opened Monday morning and every pupil was ready for work again. There were 115 present and more are expected to enter soon.

Early Growth—The vote to establish a rural high school was held in 1920, and it carried by 208 in favor and 104 against. The new school district included 26 ¾ sections of land and had a valuation of $1,500,000. The original district was one of the smallest in the state trying to maintain a high school. The time had come since advancing wages paid to teachers made it necessary for Richmond to either enlarge the district or drop out as a high school. Four decades later, the same dilemma would face the people of Richmond.

Bonds were passed for $20,000 for a new high school and building site in 1920. In 1922 the Richmond Rural High School was built on Kallock Street in Richmond.

Hot lunch was served at the Methodist church annex. For many years the lunch hour also was a meeting time for religious education at the Methodist and Catholic churches.

Stories of Richmond—The largest graduation class was 1936 with twenty-five graduates. This could have been due to the baby boom year following the men returning from World War I.

The first school bus was a converted coal truck in the 1940s. There were two buses running in the 1950s, and by this time there were also three grocery stores, a drug store, two banks, and a large co-op elevator in town.

The school newspaper was the *Cubette*. Dramatics, plays, and English were led by Mrs. Jackson for many years. Another outstanding teacher was Miss Pearl Mathias who taught geometry and business classes. Every student knew that they did not mess with Miss Mathias. One memory was shared by a student when he asked, "Miss Matthias, something must be wrong with my typewriter, it does not spell right."

This typing instruction would later come in good stead for a soldier, Vernon Pickert ('47). He recalled, "Many boys were drafted for World War II when they reached eighteen years old. Some did not even graduate as they were called to active duty. I was drafted during the Korean War. I rode a 2800 man troop ship to Korea. Since I was an electrician, the infantry had plans to have me string wire for heavy weapons. A happenstance call was made for someone who could type. That two years of typing with Miss Mathias gave me a desk job for the rest of the conflict."

Following World War II, a navy veteran, Mr. Eugene Bump, came in 1946 to coach and teach industrial arts.

By 1947, his boys basketball team was 20-3. The 1952 team's only loss was in the regional finals at Osage City with the winner advancing to the state tournament.

A memorable quote was attributed to Mr. Larson when his student driver, Connie Keuser ('62), was behind the wheel. "Keuser! There's brakes on this car for a reason!"

A new gymnasium and auditorium were built in 1949.

A love story of lifelong marriages came from the class of 1952. With only twenty-two students in the class, there were three couples that married and are still married to this day (2018). They are Raymond Mersmann and Henrietta Pickert, Eugene OMara and Jane Sigler, and Herb Wolfe and Audrey Metze.

Money was raised for senior trips with paper drives and cake sales. The 1953 class of fourteen took a school bus to Willowbrook, Oklahoma. The boys and girls stayed in separate places, which is noted that that may have been a big mistake because of the late night escapades that followed. The principal, his wife, and Mrs. Selma Cox accompanied the class as sponsors. Nicknames were very popular in this class with names such as Moose, Cookie, PeeWee, Ruks, and Mascot.

The 1955 seniors went to Colorado Springs and did all of the tourist sites from Garden of the Gods, Royal Gorge, and Seven Falls. They played cards all the way, going and coming. Joe Keiser owned the school bus and drove them.

Another class took the train from Richmond, stopped in Welda to pick up their seniors, and traveled to New Orleans. They stayed in the French Quarter and thought of themselves as being very worldly. They enjoyed the beach at Biloxi, Mississippi, and got "baked" before boarding the train for home.

The pranks in this school were noteworthy. Thurman Widner had a mouse on a sting. He would release it to run under someone's desk and then pull it back with the string. On another occasion a cat was released in a light fixture.

The study hall teacher could be easily distracted and the clock at the front of the room could be hand turned to either make the bell ring later or earlier to announce that the class period was over, sooner or later.

Athletics — Basketball practice and games were all played outdoors. Eleven-man football started in 1919. The enrollment at this time was forty-nine in the high school. When Gene Price broke his leg, the sport was discontinued. The boys played baseball in the spring and fall. Sports were played in the Franklin County League against Appanoose, Williamsburg, Pomona, Lane, Princeton, and Rantoul. There was six-on-six girls basketball played up until the late 1940s.

By 1962, there was only one boy in the senior class, and the basketball team lost all of their games.

Endings and Beginnings — By the next year, with the state mandating the consolidation of schools, it became a numbers game. The last graduating class from Richmond Rural High School was in May of 1963. What happened in the ensuing years was one step this side of chaos. In the fall of 1963, the remaining high school students from Richmond scattered to Lane, Princeton, Ottawa, and Garnett. By the next year, a bond issue to build a new high school to be shared by Rantoul, Princeton, Lane, and Richmond failed in a public vote. So, in the fall of 1965, the high school, under the name of Central Heights, was reopened in Richmond with students from

Richmond and Lane attending. The Princeton students joined Richmond in the fall of 1966 in the old Richmond High School building. It was not until 1969 that Central Heights High School was built on the open land northeast of Richmond. The site was chosen by drawing a line between the schools diagonally. Where the line crossed at a midpoint, which was equidistance between the four towns, the school was built.

From 1911 through 1963 there were 650 graduates from Richmond Rural High School. The most common surnames of the graduates were Rocker-17, McCrea-11, Mersmann-11, Pickert-9, Smith-8, Feuerborn-7, and Roecker-7.

The last graduate from Richmond Rural High School in 1963 was Leon Sobba (alphabetically), in a class of nine.

Richmond Rural High School
Franklin County, KS

#51

Howard
High School

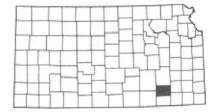

Mascot: Pirates

Colors: Red and White

Year Closed: 1969

Location: county seat town of Howard, central Elk County

First School — The first school in the community was built in 1873. It was a frame building with the lumber hauled from Chanute. The railroad did not come to the area until 1879 to connect the farms and ranches to markets. The coming of the railroad and the establishment of the county seat in Howard contributed to the growth in population. The number of children soon outgrew the small school. In 1881, bonds for $6,000 were voted and a contract with W.M. Crooks and Worth Steele was awarded for the erection of a new building. The new two-story stone school was completed in 1882 for an enrollment of 347 pupils who occupied the lower three rooms and one on the second floor. The rest of the second floor was used for the town hall.

By 1886, additional rooms were needed and a two-story wing was added on the east side of the building. A three-year high school was organized in 1886.

The following was published in the *Howard Courant*, March 8, 1899:

> A bill to establish a county high school at Howard passed both houses of the legislature. It had a great deal of opposition in some parts of the county and did not meet with unanimous approval of the people of Howard. It made a great disturbance and was the principal political issue for two years. It was defeated by the values of the County.

Under the guidance of superintendent L.E. Landis, a four-year high school was promoted in 1900. This allowed graduates to enter colleges and universities.

This building served the community until 1916 when it was replaced by a new red brick high school building with the construction cost of $40,000. This "Good Old Howard High" building was used until 1977 when it closed, and a unified school was built at a new location and renamed West Elk High School.

To Enter High School—All one-room school students and the town kids took tests at the end of the eighth grade. The results of these tests were the indicator of whether a student could pass and go on to the high school. An account from the 1904 school annual described the annual test:

> Four years ago this remarkable class had its beginning . . . During the first year the minds were fresh in more ways than one. With trembling members and quaking hearts they obeyed the summons of their superiors. 'Twas on the 17th of May, '01, that so many fell as a result of the "annual test" and the wailing for their death could be heard even in the Professor's office.

Early Athletics & Organizations—In 1904 the first football team was organized. The first game was against Eureka and ended in a loss of 26 to 0 for Howard. Football was not resumed for a number of years. A basketball team was also organized in 1904. Out-of-town games were played at Moline and Eureka.

The 1946 boys basketball pep club was called the Petterettes. This boys team lost at the state tournament to Pretty Prairie.

In 1905, two organizations were formed for the purpose of aiding student members in the practice of public speaking, debating, and appearing before the public. The clubs were called the Pythian and the Philomathian. Annual contests consisted of a debate, orations, essays, original stories, and declamations.

Early in 1905, Howard Challenged the Southern Kansas Academy from Eureka, allowing Howard the privilege of submitting the question and reserving the right to choice of sides. They submitted the question, "Resolved, that the South's treatment of the negro since emancipation is justifiable."

Howard chose the affirmative and worked up a good argument, and its success was due to the services of the coach, Mr. A.F. Sims. A very good audience was in attendance at the Howard Opera House. Victory was won by the high school, two for the affirmative and one for the negative. Members of the team were Robert Reid - Pythian, Dorcus Bascom- Pythian, and Rodney Thompson - Philomathian.

Yearbook Stories — The school annual had many names through the years: *Royal Purple and Gold, Gold Bug, Herald, Herald Hard Back, Drawoh, Pirate, Pirateer, Key-Noble, Caveat Emptor, Chest of Memories*, and the *Forty-Niner.*

The 1904 yearbook also describes the introduction to chemistry:

> But OH! The pleasures, the privileges of the year '04. With the beginning of the first term we entered the laboratory. The full effects of sulfuric acid was realized and many Stimmel-ating shocks were received . . . On several occasions we were allowed to turn our attention to athletic sports, the dignity of the class was placed in safe keeping and we yelled with all our might . . .

The 1952 yearbook tells of freshman initiation in the fall of 1949:

> We wore gunny sack dresses, braids, painted faces with lipstick and had to kneel before the seniors and say something about being "lowly freshman." We wore limburger cheese and garlic around our necks. To some of us it may have been our first experience with garlic.

By 1947, there was FFA, Y-Teen, FHA, Hi-Y, mixed choir, and orchestra. The orchestra consisted of three violins, a cello, and a bass violin. There was band, glee club, and the annual staff.

Closing Howard High — The last class graduating from Howard High School was in 1969 with twenty-five. There were 1,716 total graduates dating back to 1887. (The graduating classes from 1887-1917 were from less than the standard four-year high school.) The largest class was thirty-three graduates in 1941. The last graduate from Howard High School was Louis Wiseman ('69) (alphabetically).

The most numerous surnames of the graduates were Smith-25, Miller-24, Thompson-19, Perkins-18, Barnaby-13, Morgan-13, Osborn-12, Young-12, Kling-10, Roberts-10, Wells-10 Anderson-9 Carter-9, McDonald-9, Barnes-8, and Gray-8.

Howard High School
Elk County, KS

#52

Coolidge High School

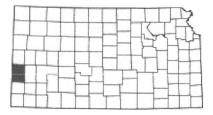

Mascot: Blue Devils

Colors: Blue and White

Year Closed: 1969

Location: town of Coolidge, western edge of Hamilton County, 2 miles from the Colorado border on the well-traveled Highway 50 and also on the Santa Fe Trail

History of the Area — The Santa Fe main railroad west goes directly through the town of Coolidge. A 27-train roundhouse was once located there. The Texas cattle town, Trail City, is just west on the Colorado border.

Trail City was renowned for businesses having a front door in Colorado and a back door in Kansas. Legend has it that if the law from Kansas was seeking a suspect, they could run in the back door in Kansas and out the front door into Colorado. Trail City is where the drovers and cowboys from Texas could gather their herds of cattle under a railroad trellis and have them counted on their way north to the grazing lands of Wyoming and Montana. Each head of cattle would be assessed two cents for this passage under the Santa Fe tracks and was paid to the railroad.

One of the first Harvey Houses built along the Santa Fe Railroad was built at Coolidge in 1881. Harvey Houses were the brainchild of business man, Fred Harvey, and catered to the growing number of train passengers with a hotel, good food with a dedication to customers, decent treatment of employees, and preservation of local traditions. They promoted tourism in the American Southwest. The famous waitresses came to be known as Harvey Girls, and they brought with them higher standards of civility and dining to the region widely known as the "Wild West." There were a total of seventeen Harvey houses in Kansas, including Topeka, Lakin and Coolidge.

German immigrants brought wheat to the area. Dreams of entrepreneurs, ranchers, farmers, and businessmen boosted the area's population from 1880-1910. A limestone opera house and lodge building erected during this era still stand. Coolidge had a peak population of 3,000 and there were five newspapers to serve the community.

In 1942, a Japanese internment camp, Amache, was located just across the Colorado border at Granada. It had as many as 7,500 Japanese internees during World War II.

The cattle trail, railroad, Harvey House, round house, Trail City, and the internment camps during World War II each played a part in forming the educational beginnings and enriching the students of Coolidge.

Community Leader

Ruth Schwerdfeger came to Coolidge at the age of nineteen with her new husband. He worked for the railroad and farmed. In no time, she became a community volunteer and leader. She served forty years as the mayor, councilwoman, and mayor again. Ruth had four children. All graduated from Syracuse after Coolidge High School closed. Ruth was raised thirty miles northwest in the area of Towner, Colorado, where she graduated from high school in 1952. They had no school buses and the parents were hired to pick up and drive the students from their area to and from school. Some of the students would stay in the town of Towner to "room out" with community people during the week and do chores for their board and room.

Ruth was raised on a farm/ranch that had been homesteaded by both sets of her grandparents in 1916 and 1917. They survived the Depression, the Dust Bowl years, and the droughts of the 1950s. The land is still in the family's name.

Athletics

The biggest sports rival was Kendall on the eastern edge of Hamilton County. The favorite sport in school was basketball. Teams in the league were Kendall, Deerfield, Shallow Water, Holcomb, Pierceville, and Manter. Eight-man football started in the fall of 1960. Holcomb started football that same year. The first game for both schools ended with CRHS losing 6-0.

Student Memories

When the school closed the students moved to Syracuse High School. Mike Lennen recalled the following:

> There was a wonderful program for assimilating these Coolidge students into Syracuse. I came that year to finish my senior year in Syracuse. At Coolidge High School we had outstanding teachers and superintendent Patrick McMurphy. Many of the teachers came to Coolidge from Colorado. Lloyd Frakes was the basketball coach and history teacher. He was incredible in allowing dialog with his history students. Though we were one hundred and eighty degrees opposite politically, this education taught me how to discuss and learn from others how to negotiate differences. Mr. Don Stegman was a very good debate coach and we had pretty decent debate teams. Mrs. McNitt was such an excellent music and band instructor.

Jake Thornburgh ('63) also played in that first eight-man game in 1960. He continued his education at Brigham Young University, as would his brother Eugene Thornburgh ('62), and sister Karen Thornburgh Harper ('59). Jake was to become the special assistant to the Surgeon General of the United States while serving as a medical doctor in the Army. He recalled this about CRHS:

> We had about eleven boys in high school so we all had to play in all sports. Everyone was an athlete. We had 12-15 in marching band. I marched from the fifth grade through high school playing my alto saxophone. My sister, Karen Thornburgh Harper ('59), played the tenor saxophone. My brother Eugene Thornburgh ('62) played the trumpet, as did my cousin Mike Lennen.

I always wondered why the mascot was the Blue Devils instead of the Red Devils. I found later that this name dates back to the open range days of the 1880s when fences were being placed around some of the ranches. Pillow case hooded Hamilton County Blue Devils were accused of cutting many of the ranchers' barbed wire fences. Thus the name "Blue Devils" did have some significant meaning.

My father, Eugene Thornburgh ('29), had a propane business in town as well as being a rural mail carrier all during the depression and dust bowl years. He was a major league scouted ball player. After having pitched twenty-nine consecutive innings on succeeding days, he was given a tryout. His arm failed because of fatigue and a baseball career was cut short. We lived in town and walked to school. He was named the "largest small businessman in the state of Kansas."

We had no driver's education at school. We were given the keys and told to go drive. Eugene's sister, Larue Thornburgh Lennen ('44), was quite a driving spirit in the community and contributed to the arts and culture of the community and surrounding area.

Coolidge had graduates that went into medicine and law. Others became teachers, business leaders, ranchers, state political appointees, and university professors.

Farming families who survived the worst of the terrible "Dirty Thirty's" dust bowl years sent their children to Coolidge Rural High School. The Harper family is one whose sons, Robert Harper ('56) and James Harper ('57), achieved great heights following graduation from Coolidge. Both graduated from Kansas State University. Robert's degree was in electrical engineering. He became a primary contributor in human cholera implant technology. He was the person who innovated the music and mo-

tion for the rides at Disneyland, and he worked on the Surveyor for the moon landings. James, a Ph.D. agronomist, became a soybean specialist. He would travel the world as a writer, speaker, and innovator in soybean research.

A Recollection by Karen Thornburgh Harper ('59):

We had no such thing as ACT or SAT testing in high school. When I applied to college I needed to take tests to determine my qualifications and background. I was able to quiz out of many courses and was accelerated into upper level classes. All of this was a credit to my wonderful background, small classes, and opportunities at CHS. We all could be cheerleaders, homecoming queens, play in the band, school plays, debate, and be involved in all of the sports. Most of our teachers were very good and dedicated and had such an interest in the one-on- one learning that we received. In college, we would sit around in the dorms and talk. No one could compare to my high school involvement and experiences.

The post war years in Kansas were an era where small towns and their high schools thrived with a small increase in numbers of students and energy. There seemed to be an emphasis on teacher's education and there were many new teachers to help education in the high schools across the plains. The teacher colleges in Kansas thrived with regional enthusiasm at Pittsburg State, Emporia State, and Ft. Hays State.

Mr. Stegman was the English teacher and debate coach and had a lasting impact on the Coolidge students. Gina Barret ('63) was an outstanding debater. She shared a remembrance of those times and the molding of young minds:

I so vividly remember one of my debate topics my last year was on Capital Punishment.

When I moved to LA and in those adult years as we met new people, we always talked about our high schools. I was always a popular social oddity when I could win every "my home town is smaller than yours" bet, and I could name everyone in my graduating class. It was fun being different in that way. I often watch how kids grow up today and realize how lucky we were to have such a great combination of work and freedom. We all had to work hard, especially for kids, as we cared for farm animals, helped build or repair fence, and drove all sorts of farm vehicles. I got tan in the summer driving tractor. My dad always bitched that Sally Smith drove a tractor better than I did.

When we weren't working, we ran free in the fields and ditches, invented our own games, played with our dogs and cats (I got into animal rescue and have never quit), and rode horses. We got ourselves into trouble and usually got ourselves out of it. Not always though.

I read books. By the fifth grade I had read every book for kids in the local library and the librarian and my mother were sorting out adult books for me to read. In those days, books didn't have serious sexual content so there weren't many I couldn't have. I was addicted to Walter Farley's stallion books, of course, as well as every other animal hero book.

One of the Smith sisters, Sally Smith McLaughlin ('63) shared this memory:

I went to country school C-4 some eleven miles north of Coolidge. We had eleven children in our family and supplied many of the children for that school. Our farm was just over the border into Greeley Coun-

ty, so Coolidge would not send their buses to pick us up for high school. We rode with my older sister as she had her license, or our parents took us both ways. I only had two in my class as an eighth grader. When I arrived at Coolidge, I felt overwhelmed as there were eight freshmen. In later years I always joked that I had more siblings than were in my graduating class.

We were a wheat farming family, so all of us learned to drive a tractor early and worked along beside our father. He would challenge us to excel. Ten of the eleven of us would go on to some form of college work.

My favorite teachers were Mrs. D'Arcy who taught geometry and Mr. Don Stegman who coached debate. Even to this day my life is a continuing education. I crave learning at least a little about things I know nothing about.

One day at a boy's track meet in Syracuse when I accompanied my dad, he looked at the boys trying to run and said that he bet I could out run all of them. After several prodding's, I finally hitched up my skirt in a bloomer style, removed my shoes, and lined up in my stocking feet on the cinder track. I did out run all of the boys.

Our senior trip was to Denver and Colorado Springs. My dad and mom, Bud and Margie Gerard ('40) Smith, and Mr. and Mrs. Don Stegman were our chaperones.

When the school closed and Coolidge unified with Syracuse, our family went to Syracuse for one year. Since we lived in the northern part of the district, we opted to send the remaining Smith children across the state line into Colorado to attend Plainview High School.

First to Last — The first Coolidge High School graduating class was in 1922. A new high school building was constructed in 1948. When the 1963 Kansas Legislature passed the ruling that all school districts in the state had to comply with at least two of three parameters (200 square miles, at least 400 students, and a valuation of at least $2 million dollars), the only one Coolidge could meet was the valuation criteria. The district was one of seven in the state that appealed to the legislature for an exemption, but the request was denied. Coolidge High School closed after graduation in 1969. There were nine students in the last class with Rose Smith (alphabetically) being the last to receive a diploma.

Coolidge High School
Hamilton County, KS

#53
Russell Springs High School

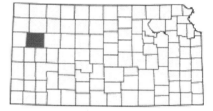

Mascot: Hornets
Colors: Black and Orange
Year Closed: 1966
Location: Russell Springs, center of Logan County

The Early Years — Settlers in the 1880s voted to make Russell Springs the county seat. The community was the center of commerce and activity for the farmers of the region. The year of 1886 was the great flood tide of immigration. They were following the advice of Horace Greeley, "Young man, go west and grow up with the country."

Russell Springs became District 17 in the county and the first school building was built in 1887. Early residents knew of an earlier subscription school in the business district. The two-story frame building was replaced with a two-story brick building that was dedicated in 1931. Several outlying districts joined Russell Springs and became the Russell Springs Consolidated School District.

When the railroad went north through Oakley, there became a continual debate on where the county seat should be placed. After three elections over four decades, the center of government was moved to the larger city of Oakley in 1963. With no railroad through this town and the years of homesteading, drought, economic challenges, the Great Depression, the Dust Bowl, and World Wars, the community dwindled.

A Teacher's Story—In a 1979 account in *KANHISTIQUE* magazine, Minnie Mischke Peterson, a Long Island, Kansas, (Phillips County) native, wrote her story titled, "I'm Going to Be a Teacher":

> That spring my friend, Ethel Howard, learned that there was a vacancy in the school at Russell Springs in Logan County, Kansas. She had taught there at one time and one of her uncles, Charles Woods, was on the school board . . . she wrote to Mr. Woods about me. To my surprise the Russell Springs school board hired me on his recommendation, not realizing they had never even seen me. Neither, for that matter had I ever seen Russell Springs, a town about 125 miles southwest of Long Island . . . So, in September 1912, I journeyed by train to Russell Springs. Despite the relatively short distance, this was not an easy trip. Traveling north and south by train in western Kansas was next to impossible . . . My assignment was to teach grades 5 through 8. The number of pupils per grade was small so I did not find this difficult, considering I had taught all eight grades several years earlier. The principal, Murray Wallace, was a good teacher

and administrator and a man of fine character. He and Miss Ina E. Smith constituted the high school staff. In 1914, after I had been in Russell Springs for two years, Miss Smith took a job elsewhere. To my surprise the school board asked me to take the high school job. I was flattered by the offer but worried about my qualifications. My two years of high school didn't even include some of the subjects that I would be called to teach. . . . Mr. Wallace had confidence in me. I decided to take the job.

The following remarks by Mrs. Joe Wilkinson were made at the dedication of the school house in Russell Springs and recorded in "History of the School District":

> Three towns contended for the county seat, Russell Springs, Logansport, and Oakley. Russell Springs was situated more nearly in the center of the county won in the election and town site Company started building the court house, church and school house.
>
> The church was completed first and the first term of school was held in it and taught by Mrs. Linda Barton. The district was organized in 1887 and J.W.D. Foot was appointed the county superintendent. In 1890 there were two teachers employed and they used the down stairs rooms. The upper story was rented to the Knights of Pythias and used by them as a lodge room.
>
> The salary of teachers was much lower then, for rural schools it was $25 to $30 (per month) according to the certificate and experience. The town school paid $45 and $35.
>
> The school dropped back to a one teacher school in 1895, and so continued for several years. Afterward it came back to two teachers, and in time the high school that many of you have seen grew from a one teacher school until now we have a teaching

force of seven and this beautiful building and equipment of which I am sure you are proud.

There have been many changes since I first saw Russell Springs. There were many more buildings. There were 12-14 business houses, two bank buildings, 2 hotels, and three livery barns, but in all the landscape there wasn't a tree.

Between seven and eight hundred people attended the dedication ceremonies of the new $45,000 Russell Springs consolidated school building at the county seat. The large crowd was unanimous in their praise of the fine building and its arrangement. The consensus was that the school board and Superintendent Torey Avery were to be complemented on the judgement they showed in giving the school children of their district such a well-appointed and well-built school. It was on par with those of other schools in northwest Kansas which ranked among the best in the state.

Torey C. Avery was the superintendent of Russell Springs Consolidated School District for four years. He was a graduate of Emporia State Teachers College and also attended Washburn. A large part of the credit for the fine new building at the county seat should be given to Superintendent Avery. His untiring effort to improve the educational opportunity of the Russell Springs community was monumental.

The area of the district was 102 square miles and it had a valuation of $550,624. The district operated three buses and employed seven teachers with an enrollment of ninety-six in the grade school and forty-four in the high school.

The dedication address at this time was given by Prof. C.E. Rarick of the K.F.H.S.C. (Fort Hays State University) with an appropriate morning program of music by Page, Winona, and Monument High Schools and a solo by Mrs. Virginia Carter, music instructor of the Russell Springs schools. A feature of the music program was the girls orchestra from Wallace, conducted by Rev. P.O. Bergeron. The five girls with their violins and Miss Dickinson gave a mighty fine program of popular numbers interspersed with tap dancing in both chorus and solo numbers. The orchestra had gained favorable publicity in Denver and the towns of western Kansas and were popular wherever they appear.

Russell Springs played in the South 40 League with Winona, Page City, Monument, and Wallace as early members. Edna Avery penned, "Much interest was shown in athletics, music, and drama. Before the new high school was built in 1931, games were played at King's Hall, a large frame building which had a gymnasium and auditorium."

Graduates, from First to Last — The first graduating class was 1913 with Bertha Brown being the first graduate. A total of 246 graduated from Russell Springs in fifty-seven years. Of these graduates, there were seven black graduates. The last class in 1966 had eight graduates. Black students Arthur White ('66) and George White ('66) were the president and vice president of the class. Victor Gieselman ('38) and Virgil Deaver ('41) were killed in action during World War II.

The school was closed in 1966. The largest class was in 1938 with ten graduates. The smallest was 1962 with one graduate. The most numerous surnames among the 246 graduates were Wright-12, Wycoff-9, and Mastin-6. Roxanne Wolfe was the last graduate. During the 1970s, 80s, and 90s, another fifteen Wrights from the surrounding Russell Springs area would graduate from the new Tri-Plains school in Winona.

#54

Randolph Rural High School

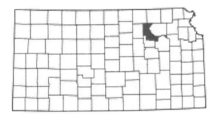

Mascot: Rambler

Colors: Green and White

Year Closed: 1958

Location: town of Randolph, northeast corner of Riley County, Big Blue River Valley

Randoph's Beginnings — The Blue Valley branch of the Missouri Pacific Railroad, which started in Atchison, was planned to run through the village of Randolph. The Panic of 1873 killed hopes of the railroad reaching Randolph. However, the Union Pacific built their own Blue Valley Branch twelve years later in 1885, which ran north from Manhattan to Marysville.

A ferry ran until a bridge was built across the Blue River in 1890. A grist mill on Fancy Creek had three pairs of millstones turned by a four-horsepower turbine wheel built by August Winkler.

First Schools — The first school in Randolph was held in a small building on the east end of Center Street. Very few persons took advantage of school life, and most of them went only a few months during the winter and tried to best the teachers. Every year brought more people to the city seeking education. Something had to be done in order to meet the demand. It was decided that a new school building was the only means that would clear the path.

The new structure was begun in the year 1887, and by the fall of 1888, it was ready for use. The building erected at that time was considered the largest and best equipped in the county. There were forty students the first year. Bookkeeping, algebra and physical geography were taught in the eighth grade.

Attendance increased every year, but the course of study remained the same until 1897-98 when the first-year high school was established. Seven students enrolled as freshmen: Eva Leach, Anna Hawkinson, Arthur Hawkinson, Wesley Fryhofer, Irving Axelton, Andrew Swan, and Viola Secrest. The subjects offered were physics, algebra, word analysis, and bookkeeping. The next year, 1898-99, eight attended high school and physical geography was added to the curriculum.

In the year 1899-1900, the second year, or sophomore level, was established. Since two years of freshmen had gone through the school, most of them returned, and an attendance of nine sophomores was secured. The course of study offered was more of continuation of the first year with the exceptions of Latin, English composition, rhetoricals, and music. Eleven enrolled as freshmen. This brought the total high school attendance to twenty.

The next year, 1900-01, the school advanced once more with the establishment of the third year of high school. Attendance was thirty with seven juniors, ten sophomores, and twelve freshmen. The course study offered to juniors was Latin, general history, algebra, physics, geometry, music, and rhetoricals.

A program for the First Annual Commencement on April 25, 1902, reads:

Class Color - Cerise
Class Motto – Non Finis Sed Initium
Salutatory and Oration: Kingdom by Charles Wesley Fryhofer
Oration: A Remnant of Savagery by Joseph E. Nygren
Oration: The Kansan by Esther Lindstrom
Oration: It Might Have Been by Gertrude Leach
Oration: The Red Man's Fate by Joseph E. Lindstrom
Oration: The Good Novel by Margaret B. Swan
Oration and Valedictory: The American Soldier by C.F. Peter
Miss Margaret Jones, Director
Miss Sadie Blomberg, Accompanist
GRADUATES
Charles Wesley Fryhofer
Gertrude Leach
Joseph E. Lindstrom
Esther Lindstrom
Joseph E. Nygren
C.F. Peter
Margaret B. Swan

This first graduation program is distinct in that all of the graduates had a part in the program. The topics of the orations are insightful of the education of that time. There are but a handful of 21st century high school graduates that would know the meaning of the Latin class Motto of 1902. It translates as, not the end but the beginning. All programs for the graduation ceremonies for the next fifty-six Randolph Rural High School graduations are kept with the school history in the library of the current Blue Valley High School.

A High School for Randolph—In the year 1905-06, Randolph High School became an accredited high school having established the fourth year. The following courses were adopted: Freshman: Latin, algebra, bookkeeping, physical geography, English; Sophomore: Latin, geometry, ancient history, English; Junior: German, physics, mediaeval and modern history, English. Senior: German, physics, mediaeval and modern history, physiology, psychology. Enrollment in the school steadily increased.

From the class history of 1916:

We enjoyed several spreads and entertainments during the term 1916-17 and perhaps just as much as any the tacky party given by the Sophomores on Halloween night. A Halloween never found us more joyful and full of spirit that the one of 1916. Then came the plans for our annual yearbook, the first one ever put out by the Seniors of Randolph High school as we hope not the last. On Friday, April 13, we gave our Senior play, "The Rebellion of Mrs. Barclay" in the second assembly hall and again at Garrison, Saturday April 21.

A graduate, Linnie R. Axelton ('18), wrote back to the class on his 69th year after graduation when he was 90 years old:

Our class was the first to receive a banquet. Before I left for the Navy (and World War I) after graduation I wrote a farewell poem to my relatives and friends. It laid around with my things until November 1978. One evening there was an ad in the Manhattan Mercury from a company in Wichita wanting poems. Just for the heck of it I sent in a copy of my poem. About a month later I received a letter from a poet club in Florida with the copy of my poem that I had sent all approved for publication. It is titled "For My Country." A copy of this poem is enclosed for your alumni gathering.

Randolph became a rural high school in 1923. By 1928 it was the second largest in the county. In 1929 a new high school was built.

Athletics

Athletics—The game of basketball, invented in 1891 by James Naismith, was only about ten years old when the first students entered Randolph High. Weather permitting, the first school teams played on outdoor courts. Later games were moved to the L.A. Hanson Store building (Holmstrom's Feed Store) before the gymnasium was built onto the stone school building in 1921. This stone building served both the grade and high school. Basketball games were played in this gymnasium until 1958 which was the final year of the history of the school. Championship teams abounded throughout the years with two teams making their way to the state tournament according to Charles Setterquist ('39).

Athletics for the girls of Randolph High School was somewhat limited but was recorded by the class of 1917:

> Several years ago the need of some good game became apparent, as there was a definite need of a sport both interesting and vigorous. Basketball was chosen. There were the usual difficulties to overcome, but all arrangements were soon made and girls basketball was instituted in the H.S. to stay. The girls showed a great deal of enthusiasm which resulted in a number of interclass games. On October 10 a game with the boys resulted in a score of 11 to 7 in favor of the girl's regular team.
>
> We had long anticipated a game with a neighboring school, and finally one was secured with the Olsburg girls. We knew about the game a few days ahead of time and all practiced earnestly and vigorously. At last the day arrived and six autos loads of players and rooters journeyed to Olsburg in high schools. Alas, it is with long faces that we tell of that day. Owing to a misinterpretation of the rules by our opponents, the game was called, the score being 8 to 7 in our favor. The Randolph players deserve especial credit for their sportsmanship playing and excellent teamwork. For a while the girls lost a good deal of their pep but are looking forward to a good season 1918-1919. The following are the members of the regular team: Belle Sweaney, Captain, and Ada Sweaney guards, Paulyne Vogelsang and Gail Hinrichs, centers, Viola Tyson and Louise Vogelsang, goalers. B.E.S.

The school annual was called *Canyon Wonders*. The 1937 edition included this report:

> For a school of its size, Randolph Rural High School has one of the best libraries in this part of the state. This library was begun in 1927 with only 437 books. Now this has been increased to approximately 2600 books, all of which are a decided benefit as they are available for the pleasure, education, or research of everyone in the community . . . The types of books contained in the library are reference, classic, ency-

clopedia, fiction, and juvenile. The National Geographic, comprising 32 volumes and including every magazine from 1920 to 1937 is only one of an interesting list of magazines . . . In 1928, the library was for the first time catalogued under the Dewey Decimal system which is used in 99% of schools . . . While the number of books in the library are increasing, the quality of reading material is also increasing.

Football had its place in extracurricular activities during the early history of the school but was dropped as a competitive sport in the 1920's due to a serious injury to a player. Six-man football was later initiated in 1941 and continued as a major sport until the closing of the school in 1958.

In 1922 an addition was made to the building in the form of an auditorium and gymnasium. This was one of the finest gymnasiums in the county at this time.

The Randolph girls team record of 59 wins out of 64 starts was reported in the *Randolph Enterprise* newspaper:

> They capped off this great run by defeating Luray High School team in an invitational game by 46-30. Luray was the champion of the Lincoln Branch League. The Ramblerettes had beaten Vermillion, the champion of Marshall county league 44-42 in a challenge game. M.H. Isaacson, in the five years coached the Randolph girls to 59 wins. The team has lost only 4 games and tied 1 game during those five years. This is Coach Isaacson's last year at Randolph as he has accepted a position as superintendent of the Osborne schools.

Organizations and Activities — The orchestra was organized in 1924 under the leadership of Miss Agnes Brune. It grew to seventeen members. It took first place in the Riley County Music Contest twice and became an active permanent organization of the high school.

Vocational agriculture was part of the curriculum. The 1941-42 FFA Chapter activity report showed extensive participation:

> The vocational agriculture boys have been figuring out ways by which they may make their work more effective and to help with the defense program. Among some of the things mentioned the repair of farm machinery and help with gardens both rank high. Other things the boys have considered are butchering, pruning and establishing fruit trees and small fruits, the building of another hot bed and testing seed.

The yearbook picture that year showed twenty-three boys as members of FFA. In 1948, the vocational agriculture building was added to the west side of the high school.

Men of Science — The *Manhattan Mercury* also covered Randolph news:

> Randolph bears the distinction of being the only city of its size in the United States to have four former residents in the latest edition of American Men of Science volume published every five years including biographical sketches and accomplishments of America's leading scientists. The four to whom recognition has been given are: Hans O. Haterius '19, Frank Holtman '21, and Lyman R. Vawter '42, Edmund Secrest. Together they made their marks in bacteriology, pathology, medicine, physiology, endocrine research, immunology, and artificial reforestation.

Town Under Water—Rumors began in 1932 of a plan for damming the Big Blue River which would flood the valley. This was part of the national effort of stimulating the country's economy by doing public works projects such as the Tennessee Valley Authority and flood control of the streams of America. Over the next three decades, these rumors, government condemnations, court cases, and busloads of citizens to Washington to lobby and protest led to the demise of the town's business community and growth stopped. The beautiful houses, businesses, and schools would all be demolished. Nine cities, 5,000 people, and 55,000 acres of fertile land were eventually destroyed.

A movie, "Stop the Dam Foolishness," ran throughout the valley. The newspaper caption read: "Paper to Drown in Dam Water." The *Randolph Enterprise* closed its doors. Mr. and Mrs. E.C. Newby left behind a legacy of a building that had never locked its doors, day or night.

Closing the School—A paper by Opal Bolton ('50) and Margie Wohler ('39) described the demise of the town and the high school:

> One Randolph is dead—but a new one is rising. By this time next year the Randolph of old will be gone, inundated by the waters of the Tuttle Creek Dam. The same waters will cover the Blue Valley, farms of people who once came to the old town of Randolph to trade. But in its stead, a little more than a mile to the southwest, a new town of Randolph is being built-a town that former residents will only partially recognize.
>
> The quaint little bandstand was relocated which had been built 102 years ago. Everyone who had ever lived in or visited Randolph would remember nostalgically the scene after the town was under water.
>
> Some of the 'promises and fairy tales' that I recall; a wonderful vacation land with millions of visitors, a beautiful well-kept lake with grassed shores for easy access. The result: a lake shore of weeds, brush and mud flats stretching far away from some of the boat docks built at the completion of the lake. Muddy waters, too thick to swim in but too thin to plant. When the graves were to be moved, each grave separately, and the 'remains' placed in a hearse for transportation . . . results rough boxes and remains piled on a truck, many at a time and driven to the new location … the Lord is the only one that knows for sure 'who is where.' Bad memories are hard to forget.

The high school closed with graduation in May 1958. There were fifteen graduates. A total of 729 had graduated between the years of 1902 and 1958. The last graduate was Dean Wege (alphabetically). The most numerous surnames of the graduates were Johnson-27, Peterson-25, Anderson-14, Bergsten-13, Carlson-12, and Wohler-11. The smallest class was one in 1909. The largest graduating class was thirty-two in 1932.

With the unification of districts, Blue Valley High School was formed. It included students from Cleburne, Fostoria, Olsburg, and Randolph high schools. The new Blue Valley High School held classes in the old Randolph High School building for two more years before the forced relocation to a new building on a hill to the west for the fall of 1960. There were twenty-three graduates in 1959, and twelve in 1960. These students graduated from the old building in Randolph, but under the new name of Blue Valley High School.

#55

Havana High School

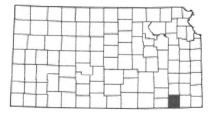

Mascot: Pirates
Colors: Purple and Gold
Year Closed: 1962
Location: town of Havana, southwestern edge of Montgomery County, 2 miles from Chautauqua County, 8 miles from the Oklahoma border

City Origins — The village of Havana was named after Havana, Illinois. The city was founded in 1870 with a general store owned by Lines and Cauffman. Interested people met in the home of D.M. Lines in April 1871 to perfect the school organization ordered by the school superintendent. Havana was designated District #33, which indicated that there were thirty-two country schools organized prior to Havana.

Montgomery County was named after the Revolutionary War General Richard Montgomery who fell at the battle of Quebec City in 1775. Settlers bought claims from the Osage Indians. These settlers came by the droves, and the Indians wanted the settler's money, so they sold the claims cheap. Cost for a prairie claim was $5 and a timber claim was $10. When so many settlers came, the Indians realized they were losing out to the white man. The Indians became upset at the situation and were frightening the pioneer women. Mrs. Caroline Ingalls (of the Little House on the Prairie Ingalls), Rutland Township, was afraid of the Indians as they would come in and take whatever they wanted. Some said they only borrowed, but Caroline Ingalls did not consider it borrowing.

From the one-teacher school of the 1870s, '80s, and '90s, Havana schools grew as the town and the area expanded. With the coming of the railroad, an extension of the Southern Kansas line of the Santa Fe in 1886, Havana became a two-teacher school with over one hundred pupils enrolled. In 1907, another teacher and some high school work were added.

Havana reached peak population in 1920 with 318 residents. Around 1910, L.H. Lines and his wife platted land north of the business district, and in 1914, they sold to Ralph Sercoulomb and wife, six lots, inclusive of this addition, for $300. In the spring of 1915, the Sercoulomb's sold these lots to District #33 for $317. It was here that the grade and high schools were built. At least two additions were added, the last being a gymnasium and a stage built during the school year 1934-35 at a listed cost of $6,790. About one-third of this amount was covered by a federal government grant.

Forming a High School--

With over 100 school districts organized in Montgomery County, the numerous one-room schools would soon need a high school. Havana did not take advantage of the Barnes Law in 1915 which would have enabled the establishment of a rural high school. This would have allowed for the surrounding country schools, by vote, to become a part of the high school. By increasing the square miles of the district, it would have allowed for a larger valuation and tax base to support the high school.

From a small, nine-square-mile district, Havana District #33 increased in size by the action of its neighbors and the reorganization committee of 1946-47 to one of slightly over thirty-five square miles. The first of these additions came in August of 1921when Stone Point voted to disorganize and divide their territory equally between Caney and Havana. When the reorganization committee made their recommendation, effective March 1, 1946, all of Round Mound #93, Eli #94, part of Deer Creek #32, and Sunnyside # 89 became part of the new Havana #33 with the exception of that part of Eli which lay in Chautauqua County (about two and an eighth miles).

In the Montgomery County Schools Yearbook of 1936-37, there were ten accredited high schools in the county: Coffeyville #3, Independence #5, Cherryvale #8, Elk City #311, Liberty #14, Havana #33, Caney #34, Dearing #63, Tyro #108, and Wayside #112. It is interesting that today (2018) there are still four high schools in the county. They were the only four—Caney Cherryvale, Coffeyville, and Independence—considered Class A in 1936. There were 592 colored students in Coffeyville, 436 in Independence, 33 in Cherryvale, 5 in Havana, 9 in Dearing, and 22 in Wayside. Caney, Elk City, Liberty, and Tyro had only white students in 1936.

The 1936 *Purple and Gold* yearbook was the first published by the students at Havana. The forward states, "The first issue of the *Purple and Gold* was edited two years ago. Last year, the school desired to put out a year book but the expense was prohibitive. This year it was decided to put out an inexpensive year book which the students and the community by loyal cooperation have completely paid for it. The staff desires that this issue of the *Purple and Gold* will call to mind in the years to come many of the memories of happy days spent in Havana High School."

The first graduating class from Havana High school was in 1927. There were nineteen students in the school orchestra, a pep club, glee club, and dramatics club. There were boys and girls basketball teams, though there seemed to be more losses than victories. Softball was offered in the fall and track in the spring.

The ten seniors of that first graduating class each had one-line quotes below their names telling a unique quality of each of these seniors. These quotes included Big Flirt, rushes those country school teachers, he's a woman-hater, can he make those A's and how, he just can't stay awake in school, dancing always, a decided farmerette, sighed for many though loved but one, interested in red Chevrolets, and she knows her basketball. Over eighty years later, these lines can be quoted by the class as senior citizens today.

Considering that this was the depth of the Great Depression, the advertisements in the back of the year book to make its publication costs possible were from six merchants in Havana, two from Caney, and two from Independence. One advertisement was from Ralph Sercoulomb, a grocer who had provided the land for the school in 1915. One advertisement was from the Niotaze State Bank, "The Bank that stood the Test," indicating that it had not failed during the late 1920s and 1930s. These merchants are still being recognized for their contribution over eighty years later.

Student Memories — Beverly Lewis O'Conner ('62) share the following story:

I was in the last graduating class in 1962. I told Mr. Gosset, the Superintendent at Wayside at an alumni gathering years later, that I would have had to quit school if I had to go to Wayside when our school closed. Wayside was by far our biggest rivalry. I was a cheerleader and played six-on-six basketball.

My father, Carl Reece Lewis was the janitor. How he loved taking care of the school building. It was his pride and joy. The high school classes were on the top story and the grade school on the lower level. Somehow during the course of the devilment of one night, a cow was encouraged up those twenty-five steps with two concrete banisters to the top of the school. In those times you did not have to go the jail and could undo these wrongs and learn character from them.

Our sports league included Wayside, Peru, Elk City, Longton, and Dexter.

We had no indoor bathrooms until 1952. There was never any kindergarten and no driver's education.

I was raised by my single parent father. I learned to drive at thirteen when my dad threw me the keys and told me to go up town to the store and get some milk. US Highway 75 ran right through town at that time and I was shaking and hoping that I would not be killed. I tried to start the car about twenty-five times and took forever to start it again at the store again. Miraculously, I got my driver's license at the age of fourteen and became a great driver even without any drivers' education being taught in school.

We had a band, but it waned in our final years. Mrs. Margarete Stewart was our vocal teacher. With her orange hair and shrilling voice, she seemed bossy and was very demanding of our involvement.

The beautiful, big, brick bank building stood on the corner in town. It later became the post office. Unfortunately, it was left to vandals and burned down about five years ago.

Our town was a big shipping hub at one time as the Santa Fe ran by here. There was a beautiful hotel by the railroad. We had a passenger train that ran to Kansas City.

The End of Havana High — In May 1962, Havana voted to become a part of the Wayside District with certain reservations and conditions. They assumed no part of the Wayside bonded indebtedness. In 1962, the high school was closed. There were six teachers and forty-seven students in the school.

Havana High School
Montgomery County, KS

#56

Lebanon High School

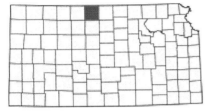

Mascot: Broncos

Colors: Red and White

Year Closed: 1984

Location: town of Lebanon, Smith County

Town History—As early settlers homesteaded in Smith County, a post office and village were established along Middle Oak Creek. The government established the post office. A group of these settlers asked Jackson "Jack" Allen to choose a name for the post office and village. Mr. Allen, a bible student and prominent early day Mason, was the leading literary man of the day, and the settlers looked to him to select the name by which the post office town should be designated. "Why not go to the Bible?" he thought. Searching its pages, he stopped when he read of the Cedars of Lebanon and suggested that name. Nobody opposed, and the name Lebanon was recorded. This was in 1873.

The Center of Everything—Every Kansas elementary student learns that Kansas Day is January 29, 1861, the state's motto is *Ad Astra per Aspera* (Latin for "to the stars through difficulties"), and the geographic center of the continental United States is Lebanon, Kansas. A dedication of the United States Center marker was held on Sunday, June 29, 1941, marking Lebanon the geographical center of the United States. A special historical highway marker just north and west of Lebanon on Highway 36 was dedicated in special services. Dedication of the monument, which is built of native stone, was unveiled with Hugo T. Wendell, the justice of the Kansas Supreme Court, as the speaker. The Morrill triplets—Betty, Jean, and Beth—unveiled the sign designating the highway marker. More than 500 people attended the unveiling.

Lebanon High School—The new and permanent Lebanon High School was built in 1924 on the north-central side of Smith County. The builder was C. Beardslee. H. J. Schuette was the mayor at this time. Both surnames appeared among the graduates of the high school.

The school song, to the tune of "The World is Waiting for the Sunrise," was composed and written in 1928 by five students as they drove to Jewell for a group dinner at the home of Florence Saunders. Florence was the organist at her church in Jewell and became the music teacher at LHS in 1931. The history of this song was provided by Ava Lee (Barcus) Maydew ('48).

Lebanon High School Song
Today, we're singing of our dear high school
LHS-we're all true to thee
We're all, for all, we long for, hope for, pray for,
LHS-we all love thee

Athletics — Athletics were an important part of the school and community. Girls basketball was started early. The first public game played by Lebanon girls was part of the entertainment during the Anniversary Celebration in 1904. The home team was rightly called the "Bloomer Girls," for they were dressed in black bloomers and skirts with high-necked and long-sleeved blouses. Long black hose completed the costumes, and most of the girls played in their stocking feet or wore high top shoes. The 1927-28 team was very successful with their high school principal Ed Jantzen also as their coach. They won a game against the "Terrible Swedes" from Scandia that brought 425 people to the stands to watch. The game was billed as two of the fastest girls teams in northern Kansas.

A girls tournament with Pittsburg Cardill High School was scheduled for February 1928, but a snow storm and mud blocked roads all over Kansas, so they cancelled. Girls basketball continued to be competitive, and they played teams as far away as Prairie View, Hill City, and Almena. Tournaments were held on Saturdays, with games being played in the morning, afternoon, and evenings. Teams came in Friday evening and stayed in homes overnight. At this time, Lebanon doctors would take out tonsils of athletes in Lebanon free of charge.

The first trophy case was built in 1931 and presented by the senior class of 1931. Many hundreds of trophies would be placed on display in the years to come. The boys and girls track records were displayed on the wall of the study hall. Some amazing school records marked the athletes of LHS for their times and distances that will never again be broken.

The first boys basketball game was played in 1924 against Cedar, and it was played at the Lebanon Opera House. The score was Cedar 41, Lebanon 15.

Lights were installed on the football field in time for the October 1, 1931 football game against Esbon. Lebanon won, 12 to 7.

The first undefeated football team in the history of Lebanon was in 1950. Playing their best game of the season, Coach Warren Smith's football team came from behind a halftime score of 14-13 to take advantage of a fumble and go on to win a thrilling 19-14 game. A very potent Alton team was the opponent, coached by the popular Everett Gouldie (Lebanon graduate, 1932). Both teams went into the game undefeated, and Alton was untied. Lebanon was victorious and had the first undefeated season in the history of Lebanon football.

The school had an enrollment of one hundred students, and the team played eleven-man football. In order to fill the schedule, the team played some larger schools, including four county seat towns, one class A school, and one out-of-state school rated first in its class in Nebraska.

The Lebanon Bronchettes were the drill team. They danced with white cowgirl hats and bandannas, performing at football and basketball games. Pride and style coupled by their enthusiasm and spirit for their teams and school was obvious.

A state championship came to the school as the boys were crowned champions at the 1-A finals in Hays in 1977. The victory gave the Bronco's their first state championship in the school history. They were coached by Eugene Johnson who had coached for eighteen years.

Chris Rorabaugh ('77) was selected as the unanimous choice on the all-state tournament team.

In the fall of 1983, Lebanon's last football team ended up with only seven healthy players and had to reschedule their final games to play six-man football.

The newspaper in Lebanon reported all of the school events, activities and sports stories. The editor, "Photoflash Phyllis" Snow, was known far and wide for her flash photography. Pictures were plentiful in the newspaper.

Student Stories

Student Stories — Ava Lee Maydew ('48) shared that she took a twelve-week teaching course right out of high school and taught for forty years in country schools at Esbon and Lebanon elementary schools. Her first country school was Barefoot Nation south of Lebanon. She and her husband Bob Maydew ('47) traveled to Fort Hays to continue their education every Saturday from September until May. Ava Lee got her diploma from Ft. Hays in 1962. This past spring (2017) at the age of 86 she was still substitute teaching and continues to be the spirit of the community and the lifeblood of the Methodist church in Lebanon.

Gladys Schuette Kennedy ('34) always wanted to be a teacher. However, her father needed her at the Schuette Ford Dealership. She went to work for him out of high school at the height of the Great Depression. She did become a teacher, and she was a Girl Scout leader for fifty years. Known in Lebanon as the "Jelly Lady" at the age of 101 (2017), she still plays the church organ at the First Christian Church and drives herself to church (2017). She is a descendent of the Schuette who was mayor when the new high school was built.

First to Last — The first graduating class from the high school was in 1911 with Ada Brown (alphabetically) the first graduate. The largest graduating class of forty was in 1941. The smallest class of four was in the school's last year. The last graduate was Robert Lovewell (alphabetical). A total of 1,635 graduated from Lebanon High School in its seventy-four years as a school. The school was closed in 1984 and became a part of Smith Center USD #237.

Upon closing in 1984, the building was first sold to a farmer who stored farm equipment in it. The next owner was a Dr. Scratch who, with investors, attempted to manufacture pyrethrum products. The venture failed, and the investors took a loss in this startup business. Dr. Scratch's failed business again left the high school building sitting empty. The building was sold to Gloria Snow Bell for $1.00. Gloria is the daughter of Photoflash Phyllis, the town's historian. She now owns the high school in her mother's name. She has much of the town's history in the museum and has restored parts of the building to its former glory.

The most numerous surnames of graduates were Allen-25, Brown-20, Wood-16, Johnson-16, Bell-15, Beardslee-15, Shively-12, Maydew-12, Herndon-12, Stone-12, Harpsnare-12, Hendrickson-9, Shipley-9, Cunningham-8, Rorabaugh-8, Atwill-7, Shook-7, and Gouldie-7.

Lebanon High School
Smith County, KS

#57

Strong Rural High School

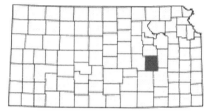

Mascot: Indians

Colors: Red and White

Year Closed: 1975

Location: town of Strong City, Chase County

Origins of the Town and School — The railroad separates the two towns of Strong City and Cottonwood Falls as does the Cottonwood River. The architecturally beautiful train depot of the Burlington Northern Santa Fe Railroad leaves no doubt that the town of Strong City is its own town.

Once the town site was established, the pioneers quickly initiated the educational system. In 1875, Cottonwood Station, as it was called, built its first school house, the North Side School (presuming it was named such because it was north of the Cottonwood River).

The town had been renamed Strong after the vice-president of the Atchison, Topeka and Santa Fe Railroad. The formation of School District #41, which included Strong, occurred in 1883. In May of 1889 there were four graduates.

During the early 1900s, North Side School was closed and students attended school in Cottonwood Falls.

On May 16, 1928 a bond of $30,000 passed. This permitted the construction of Strong Rural High School. The building was designed by Walter E. Glover. Two and one-tenth acres of the Sidler farm were purchased for the building site, and on August 8, 1928, the Sharp Brothers of Emporia began construction.

The company contracted to build the brick structure for $24,570. Later the company added a room, increasing the contract bid by $900. Plumbing, heating, wiring, and fixtures were installed at a cost of $5,300. The building was completed, and on March 27, 1929, forty-six students moved from the Union Store into the new high school.

In 1945, the name of the town was changed to Strong City. The school Spirit song was

While the boys fight for the
glory of our school on the field.
We will cheer for them on the sidelines.
Our school is what we—the Student Body-make it.
Let's be proud of—Strong High School.

Athletics — Basketball at Strong in the 1960s gave the town and the school some glory years and a state high school tournament championship. From the book *Title Towns,* by Steven Farney, the following story is told of this champion-to-be:

Grade school champions! Before today's plethora of youth basketball teams and tournaments, grade school basketball was where most players first experienced the exhilaration of playing on a championship team. Amid the celebration, it was hard not to think of the future. Winning state tournaments is the ultimate goal of basketball players everywhere. It is a recurring dream: young boys nail the buzzer-beating shot, make the key steal, grab the final rebound, and swish the winning free throw. Strong City Indians were dreamers. In 1961, a special group of eighth graders won the junior high league title, and players, and fans alike could not help wonder if Emil Mushrush, Robert Meyer, Steve Brooks, and Carrol Koch might someday be lifting the state championship trophy. As the '65 season approached, these players, now seniors, were quickly running out of time. Oh, yes the Indians also had a newcomer to the group: senior Joe Thimes. He came from neighboring Saffordville which had just closed their high school the year before. Their Coach LeRoy Drier also knew a thing or two about dreams.

This team went on the win the Class BB Championship in Dodge City. Strong's enrollment, at sixty-nine students, was the largest in the field of eight teams in the tournament. In the semi-finals, they met Goff which had only twenty-four students in the entire high school. When making a team, it did matter how many boys that a school had from which to select. Goff had a star by the name of Ed Sourk. The Goff senior had nailed 27 points in the opening win against Prairie View and was figured to be a handful for the Indians' defense. Coach Drier had a plan. Steve Brooks played man-to-man on Sourk and the rest of the team played a 2-2 zone. The plan worked and the previously undefeated Goff team met defeat. Then in a classic final game, Strong City outlasted Monument 48-47. Dreams did come true.

In 1952, reclassification took place in the state athletics association, and the schools in Class B were divided into two classes, B and BB. Those with more than 475 students were in Class AA, 151-475 students were in Class A, 61-150 students were in Class B, less than 60 students became Class BB. This was further modified in 1962, which classified Class AA as the largest fifty-six high schools in the state. Class A encompassed the next 64, Class B the next 224, and Class BB included the remainder of schools in the state.

Closing Strong High School —A total of 511 graduates received their diploma from Strong High School. The first graduate was William Allison in 1929 and the last was Alice Watts (alphabetically) in 1975. The largest class had twenty-one graduates in 1938. The smallest class had four graduates in 1957. There were a total of fifty-seven teachers and eleven principals in the forty-six years of Strong Rural High School.

Strong Rural High School
Chase County, KS

#58

Buffalo High School

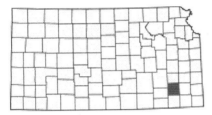

Mascot: Pirates

Colors: Blue and Gold

Year Closed: 1956

Location: town of Buffalo, north-central Wilson County

Early Education—The first recorded school of this area was located northwest of Buffalo where the Buffalo Creek and Bloody Creek join. Cynthia Gould was the teacher, and the year is believed to be 1859. This was a community school before formation of public schools.

In 1866, the first established public school was formed and Cynthia Gould may have taught there also. The post office opened on September 6, 1867, with Chester Gould as the postmaster, thus the establishment of Buffalo. There were two stores in 1869 and a hotel opened by John Van Meter in 1879.

The Missouri Pacific Railroad reached the town in 1886, and under the impulse of new and vigorous life, the little town began growing. Swedish Lutherans settled in the area and farmed and ranched.

George K. Bideau came to Buffalo as the first teacher in the Buffalo schools. He was born in Ohio and came to Kansas in 1870. His mother schooled him at home until the age of twelve. He apprenticed with a physician and studied medicine. He also became fluent in reading and writing Latin. He was one of the first graduates of the Kansas Normal School (later to be renamed Emporia State Teachers College). He taught all grades in Buffalo. In 1885, the school expanded to 120 students with six teachers, and George became the principal.

Addition of a High School—In 1890, bonds were voted for a new school. This consisted of four rooms. The location was between Buffalo and Elm on the east edge of town. The first high school in 1889 was to the ninth grade. In 1895, it became a two-year high school. George Bideau continued as principal during these years. By 1913, it became a four-year high school.

An addition to the school was begun in 1935. Two classrooms, a gymnasium, and an auditorium were added. With this updated, home economics was introduced to the curriculum. The first hot lunches started at this time, also. In 1938, there were seven teachers and a superintendent on the staff as recorded in the yearbook.

Signs of the Times—This was a time and era when nicknames were popular. Names for some of the staff and students were: Whit (Mr. Whitson), Ikey (Irene), Tarzan

(Letha), Polly (Pauline), Shorty (Betty Dean), Romeo (Clyde), Jimmy (James), Skinner (Ben), Slug (Francis), Chick (Billy), Rubber (Max), Agnes (Willis), and Cappy (Loren). The yearbook also recorded the class will and class prophesy. This same year of 1938, the students had a band and a large music choir, and they performed an operetta.

Buffalo had a marching band with flags and majorettes. They performed at half time of the games and at various parades.

Jackie Cutter Orrick ('52) recalled, "Mrs. Ordolf was an all-star teacher who taught English and drama for many years. Another teacher who had a great impact on the students was Mrs. Spare who had been in the women's marines."

Mr. Mohler was a coach and superintendent and served the community for a long time. His wife was the home economics teacher and taught Spanish and Latin.

Buffalo never had any school buses to transport children.

Senior trips were taken each year. The class of 1952 took cars to the Ozarks. The Class of 1954 went to the Lake of the Ozarks. They sold snow cones and candy and worked the concessions at the ball games to raise money for these trips.

The boys played basketball, baseball, and track. The girls played softball and ran track. They played basketball games out of town.

Unification and Closing—With declining enrollment and tight money conditions, the school unified with Benedict and Vilas to form Midway Unified District. The school closed after graduation in May 1955. However, a high school under the name of Midway used the Buffalo

High School building for one more year. The class of 1956 was considered the last to graduate from Buffalo. There were ten graduates with Elizabeth Ann Schubert (alphabetically) being the last graduate from Buffalo High School.

Buffalo High School
Wilson County, KS

#59

Richfield High School

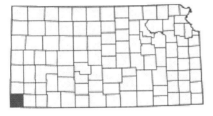

Mascot: Bulldogs

Colors: Purple and White

Year closed: 1946

Location: town of Richfield, northwest Morton County

A High School with an Early Ending—In 1913, a two-year accredited high school was instituted in Richfield with ten freshmen enrolled. Miss Edith Thompson was the teacher. The subjects taught that year were Latin, algebra, US history, English, and arithmetic.

In 1922, bonds were voted in the amount of $10,000 for the building of a combined grade and high school. School was held in the Presbyterian Church while the old building was being torn down and the new building completed. This building was a style of architecture which did not permit the use of the old bell, but the sentiment of the bell was deeply rooted in the hearts of those who had listened to its ringing down through the years. Something of life which they held most dear would be lost without it. As a result, the bell was placed in a tower in the school yard, and the town still lived by the bell.

In May 1924, provision was made for a four-year high school at the annual school meeting. Two teachers were hired that fall for the high school and two for the grade school. The school experienced gradual growth for the next eleven years. In 1931, three grade school teachers were employed. The high school reached its peak during those years with thirty-five students at one time.

Having withstood the horrific Dirty 30s, the Great Depression, and World War II, it could not hold back the out-migration of the population. During the Dust Bowl years, Richfield and the surrounding countryside experienced another exodus, and by 1935 the school had commenced to feel its effect. The grade school was again down to two teachers. The school was fortunate to have two good music teachers during that time. Richfield seemed destined to be a remote town on the prairie when its high school closed in 1946, making it one of the first Kansas towns to lose its high school.

The final nail in the coffin was losing the county court house to the town of Elkhart in 1952. On January 22, 1950, "The Castle of the Plains," also known as the county court house, burned to the ground. A crowd of 700 gathered to watch the inferno, and the flames could be seen for fifteen miles. Following two county-wide elections, the new site in Elkhart was decided at the ballot box and the official court house was moved. Even though

Elkhart is only one mile from Oklahoma and seven miles from Colorado, and definitely not in the center of the county, they had the votes to claim the center for the county's government.

When the Bell Tolled—Lois Kimball Dunn was married in 1945. She lives in the rural area east of Richfield. She has great joy in reliving her historical experiences. Her husband, Wallace Dunn, was a 1939 graduate of Richfield High School.

In 1888, the Richfield elementary two-story building had a belfry that was built above the entrance. The bell was as much a part of the school life as a course of study. On a still morning, its deep, resonant tones could be heard more than five miles away with the ringing of the 8:30 morning bell. The air came alive, adding a certain zest to the atmosphere about the town. Children hurried to their 9:00 classes, and housewives scheduled their daily tasks with the recess and noon bells which called the children to their studies.

What Remains—Richfield High School had its first graduating class in 1924. The school closed in 1946. The building still stands (2018) and is used by the community as a center for morning coffee, card clubs, the city library, reunions, and various other area associations. When the grade school closed in 1975 there were only two little boys in the entire grade school.

To this day (2018) Richfield is the smallest incorporated town in Kansas with a population of twenty-six people.

#60
Selden Rural High School

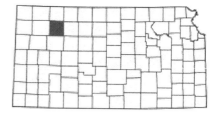

Mascot: Wildcats

Colors: Black and White

Year Closed: 1968

Location: town of Selden, northwest corner of Sheridan County

Origins of the Town & School—Selden came into being in 1888, just after the Chicago, Rock Island and Pacific Railroad was built on a diagonal running from the northeast at Norton to the southwest at Colby. Families and buildings were moved from Old Sheridan, Shibboleth, and Jackson to be near the railroad. The town was named in honor of Selden G. Hopkins who, with five others, made up the town company.

In 1890, crops failed completely, and several bad years left the county scarce for supplies. C. Geisenhener, a county commissioner, was delegated to go to eastern Kansas and Missouri to solicit aid for food, clothing, and seed grain. The response was generous. He traveled on a pass from the railroad.

The first school house was a one-room building with Mr. Aerhart as the first teacher. Soon a two-story schoolhouse was built with two rooms on the ground floor. The second floor was used for church and town hall. This building burned in 1893. This would be the first of three fires that would haunt Selden for the next seventy years.

While a new school was being built, school was held in the back of the Pence and Gray general store. Pence and Gray were also members of the town company in 1888.

The new building consisted of two rooms and served until 1907 when a two-story brick school building was erected. This building was struck by lightning, resulting in another fire, but it continued to be used until a larger school was needed. In 1921 another two-story brick building with a full basement was built. In 1954 a multipurpose building with gymnasium was attached to the building.

Activities & Organizations

Literary groups, singing schools, and spelling bees were early forms of entertainment in Selden's early school history. The Weist quartet, taught by Mrs. Monteith, helped with vocal music at the school. The first band was organized in the late 1890s.

Notable Graduate

Eugene Rohr ('48) bought the *Selden Advocate* newspaper on May 2, 1950. He became the owner, publisher, and editor at the age of nineteen. He became the youngest editor and publisher of an official city newspaper in Kansas and possibly the United States. Upon graduating from high school in 1948 from Selden Rural High School, Gene attended summer session at Ft. Hays College to earn his teaching credentials. He taught school in 1948-49 and 1949-50 at Violet, a country school just west of Selden. In 1950-51 he taught seventh and eighth grades in Selden and ran the newspaper at nights and on weekends.

A Stormy Past

Selden seemed to live in the eye of the storm. A tornado in 1904, followed by a severe wind storm in 1905, damaged the town. The June 3, 1959, a hail storm that centered over Selden destroyed the business district and some of the community's strength and resolve. Over a ninety- minute period that evening, eighteen inches of hail with four inches of rain fell on Selden. Buildings collapsed under the weight, including many businesses. The National Guard and patrolmen were called to duty to prevent looters and sightseers.

Athletics

Selden played eight-man football in a league with Herndon, Weskan, Edson, Jennings, and Ransom. They also played Flagler and Orleans, Nebraska. The girls played basketball and volleyball. In games with Menlo, since they did not have enough for two teams, the girls would play the first game, followed by the boys game. Baseball and track were played in the spring though track was never taken too seriously.

Great basketball and baseball was played at Selden from 1955-1958. A new coach, Jack Bell, came to Selden in the fall of 1955. Tom Thummel ('58) had this to say about the team:

Coach Bell motivated the community and instilled a winning character in everyone with whom he was associated. He was instrumental in getting the new gymnasium built at Selden High School. His wife was Eleanor Bell. She was an excellent English teacher and had the same dedication. We played the triple post that Coach Bell had learned under Tex Winter at K-State. We only lost one game in three years in basketball until we made it to the tournaments. Gove beat us in the regional finals in 1957, and we went to state the other two years. We took second at the state tournament in 1958, but won the state baseball tournament only two months later beating Lucky High from Manhattan in the finals at Peabody. These two sports paved the way for me to go to college at Kansas State and play basketball for Tex Winter one year and baseball for four years.

Traditions — Senior trips were taken most years. Ellis Walker ('64) recalled the senior trip of 1964:

All thirteen of the seniors traveled to the Lake of the Ozarks. Many other seniors from all over the Midwest were also at the Lake of the Ozarks on their senior getaways. It was such a great time to meet and socialize with so many from such a large area. Perry Kruse ('64) fell in love with a girl from Missouri on this trip that would have lifelong attachments. He was the star on our basketball team that had just played at the state tournament that spring. He had agreed to play basketball at Ft. Hays State the next year. He was to only play one year at Ft. Hays as the love strings were tugging him closer to Missouri. He transferred to Southwest Missouri State at Springfield to finish his college career. He married the girl, and they live happily together still some 50 years later (2018).

Fire and Closing — In 1965, the high school mysteriously burned, and the students finished out the last six weeks of the school year in buildings around town. In 1966, the students went to Hoxie, Oberlin, and Rexford for high school. By the time school started in the fall of 1966, a new building had been built as an addition to the grade school and was used for a high school for two more years 1966-67 and 1967-68. The high school closed following graduation in May 1968. The district unified with Rexford. The grade school continued, K-5, with pupils from Selden, Rexford, Menlo, and Gem. Grades sixth through high school were taught in Rexford.

There is no sign of the old high school remaining except the sidewalk and a couple of evergreens that stood on either side of the school steps.

Twenty-seven students received a two-year graduation certificate before the four-year Selden Rural High school was built in 1922. In the forty-seven years from 1922 through 1968, a total of 461 graduated from Selden Rural High School. The graduating classes of 1938 and 1939 both had twenty graduates, making them the largest. The most numerous surnames of the graduates were Mumm-20, Trimble-11, Zimmerman-10, Koerperich-13, Sloan-8, Duesberg-7, Goscha-7, and Schrock-7.

The last class in 1968 had seven graduates. The last to receive a diploma from Selden High School was Betty Zimmerman (alphabetically).

#61

Americus Rural High School

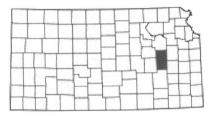

Mascot: Indians

Colors: Red and White

Year Closed: 1972

Location: town of Americus, west-central Lyon County

Town History — Americus was voted, by the people in 1858, to be the county seat of Breckenridge County, later changed to Lyon County. The following year, the county seat was supposedly stolen from Americus and moved seven miles away to Emporia. Ambitious Emporia men conceived of the idea. An account by Tom S. Howell, Emporia historian, had this to say in a story in the *Emporia Gazette*:

During 1858-59 a bitter fight was made over the location of the permanent county seat. Emporia wanted to postpone the election until after the three-mile strip on the south had been attached to the county, but the matter was brought to a vote at the territorial election on October 4, 1858. Americus received 202 votes and Emporia 188, a majority of 14 votes for Americus. At the general election on November 6, 1860 the votes on the county seat proposition were as follows: Emporia 884, Americus 141, Breckenridge Center, Forest Hill 1 and Fremont 73. This put an end to the county seat matter.

The town's fate may have been different if the early days of the county seat choice had gone in favor of Americus.

The KATY Railroad ran from Missouri, through Atchison, through Americus, toward Texas. Another freight train ran from Parsons to Junction City every day. Play along the train tracks was a common activity for young people. Some stories—by those who clearly knew the schedule of the trains—included high school kids taking the tires off their cars and running the rails on the car hubs. Other stories—perhaps by those less knowledgeable of the schedule—told of "borrowing" the hand car to play on the rails, only to be surprised by a train and having to frantically pull the hand car off of the tracks to avoid a crash.

Early Education — A log building built in 1858 was used as a school house until School District No. 2 was organized in 1859. After that, several different buildings were used for school purposes.

In 1869, a two-story stone school house was erected costing $6,000. This building burned in 1886 and school was held in an old cheese factory. Another school house was built in 1887 with two classrooms upstairs and two downstairs. It was in this building that the first years of high school training were taught on the top floor. Grades one through eight were taught on the lower floors. For several decades, a few subjects of high school level subjects were offered, but a four-year curriculum was not available until 1910. Mary Cooper was the only graduate in the class of 1911. Another teacher was added in 1915, and the course of study was enlarged to provide for home economics and normal training. The following year a fourth teacher was added and the new school was erected. This building was used until 1916 when it was torn down and Americus Rural High School was built.

This placed the high school in a class with other schools of its size as far as faculty and building. The classification was not changed by the state accrediting authorities until the local board of education policy for two years prior was accepted by the state board of education.

An unknown author printed this account of the founding of the high school, "While this school stands as a monument to the effort and sacrifice of its friends, yet it is more than that; it is the means for intellectual and social freedom where one may learn to realize more fully his responsibility and opportunity as a citizen of this great Republic and to contribute to its perpetuation as a self-respecting Christian people."

Tidbits and Firsts—The first alumni banquet was held in 1925.

Football was banned in the 1920s due to a serious injury. There was a debate team and orchestra in 1923. A circus was also held that year featuring the Flippety, Flappety, Flappers, all high school girls. There was a short musical program, boys doing vaudeville, a display of basketry, a shooting gallery, and a radio set with a special hookup for the occasion.

In 1924, graduation was threatened because of an outbreak of the mumps.

In 1923, there were ninety-three one-room schools with nine male and ninety-three female teachers in Lyon County. The average enrollment was eighteen with an average attendance of fourteen. The male teachers were paid an average of $93 each month and the female teachers $90 each month.

The first school annual was published in 1948, called *The Scout*.

Fay Duncan was the infamous town cop. He was referred to as Matt Dillon behind his back because he carried a gun. He and his wife ran Duncan's Restaurant. This was the scene of many ice cream socials. The ice came from area farm ponds and was harvested by the teenagers. Nellie Duncan was a fantastic cook and was also the school lunch cook.

A Basketball School—The new high school was built in 1942 by the WPA at a cost of $35,100.44. Its gymnasium was where Americus basketball got its start.

The first trip to the state basketball tournament was in 1955, with the starters being Harold Pickett, Don Edmiston, Bobby Karr, Don Beemer, and Royce Beemer. During this fine season, Americus defeated Hartford 51-42 for the Lyon County tournament championship, defeated Reading 62-61 for the district crown, and then beat Welda 88-68 for the regional tourney championship and a berth in the state tourney. They lost in the first round to Greenleaf 52-47.

The second Americus team going to state was the 1959-60 team consisting of starters Howard Edmiston, Bob Jackson, Kermit Grother, Rich Edmiston, and part time starters Charles Kayser, Gary Vahsholtz, and Gary Gibb. This team won the Lyon County tournament defeating Northern Heights 35-33, the district tourney over Wilsey 51-36, and in the regional finals with a win over Melvern 51-47. The state Class B Tournament was held in nearby Emporia. With opening round wins over Saints Peter and Paul 45-42, and a semifinal squeaker over Mount Hope 35-34, Americus was in the finals against Rozel. The game found the Americus Indians losing 65-57 and ended the season with a record of 24-2.

Spirits ran high for the next year, 1960-61. Losing two starters to graduation, the teams underclassmen were called on to fill the two spots and provide a strong bench, and did they ever! Dan Edmiston and Richard Proehl provided strong defense and excellent ball handling to team up with previous year's starters Kermit Grother, Rich Edmiston, and Gary Gibb. Neosho Rapids was defeated in the championship game of the Lyon County tourney by a score of 46-28. In district tournament play, Americus defeated host Burlingame 54-36, and for a second year in a row, Americus edged Melvern by 67-56 to win the regional tournament. The state tournament did not start off easily as a Rich Edmiston jump shot in sudden death overtime gave Americus a 69-67 victory over Logan. Americus found some breathing room in the second game, beating Midway 72-57 to set up a championship game with Overbrook, another undefeated team. Billed as a "dream" game between the only two undefeated teams in the state, the contest lived up to expectations. Kermit Grother sank a basket at the buzzer to send the game into overtime and then scored again as time ran out to give Americus a 64-63 win and the STATE CHAMPIONSHIP!

Academics & Organizations — Music was also a big part of the high school. The Lyon County Music Festival brought all the high school students into a music competition at Emporia.

The American Future Business Leaders of America was organized in 1958. A student had to be enrolled in at least one business class to be considered for membership.

One student, Lloyd Brown ('52) quipped with a gleam in his eye, "I got straight A's but spent seven years in the same class." It just happened that the band need a saxophone. So when he was in the sixth grade, the bus let him off at the high school, and he practiced with the band for the first period. Then he had to walk the one-half mile to the grade school for the class day.

Traditions — Freshman initiation was the first week of school where even the teachers and a new principal would also be initiated. Gunny sacks, starch in the hair, and onions pinned to the hair were all part of the ordeal for the freshmen. Initiation week ended with the seniors sponsoring an all-school hay ride.

School senior trips went to places such as Rockaway Beach in the Ozarks for the class of 1961. The boys stayed in a separate wing and three of them caught the prized large fish out of the lagoon at night with a string and modified hook. They were to get in big trouble with management as they had the fish in their room. These culprits were Rich Edmiston ('61), Kermit Grother ('61), and Leslie Ames ('61). The 1959 senior class took a ten-day trip to New Orleans. The sponsor for the class that year would not go on the trip as she considered New Orleans an "evil city." The trip also included stops at Elvis's Graceland in Memphis and the Vicksburg battlefield.

Closing Americus High School—The high school closed in 1972. Americus unified with Northern Heights High School, built in the country in northern Lyon County. The towns making up this new unified school were Americus, Allen, Bushong, Admire, and Miller.

The final graduating class from Americus High School had fourteen graduates with Melvin Cecil Reed (alphabetically) the last to receive a diploma. A total of 864 graduated in the sixty-two years of Americus High School history. The most common surnames of the graduates were Edmiston-17, Anderson-12, Myer 12, Weller-12, McAuley-10, Grimsley-9, Johnson-8, Jaquith-7, and Jones-7.

Americus High School Started in 1939 by w.P.A and a bond issue finished 9-22-41

THE AMERICUS HIGH SCHOOL

#62

Edna High School

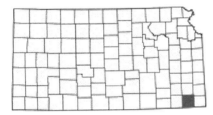

Mascot: Pirates

Colors: Purple and Gold

Year Closed: 1966

Location: town of Edna, south-central Labette County, five miles from the Oklahoma border

Early Education—Labette County was formed and named in 1867. Owen Wimmer, on May 3, 1871, ordered the formation of Wimmer School District, lying in the center of Elm Grove Township. An election was called for the area families at the Wimmer home, but the district failed to organize. A new order was called at the home of P.C. Goodwin. This time the district was organized and given the number 73. In May 1872, the first school board members were elected, and a school building was erected in the fall of that same year. The significance of a school and school board in a rural town just five years after the formation of a county demonstrates the importance of education to this community. The first school was on the site that later was to become the Missouri Pacific Railroad section house. W.J. Millikin taught the first term of the school in 1872-73.

In 1876 a two-story frame building was erected and an addition was constructed in 1901. This building was complete with six rooms that served District 73 until November 27, 1917.

In 1916 steps were taken and bonds were voted on to build a much needed school building in Edna. For several years prior, eight grades and two years of high school had been taught in the old frame building, which had long since served its purpose owing the advancement in educational lines. At this time students could go to a large town of Oswego or Parsons for the extra two years of high school education. Unfortunately, this required most to live and stay in distant towns during the week and come back home to the Edna area on the weekends. The new high school made it possible for more students to attend school in Edna.

The new grade and high school building, which had been built on the space reserved for a public school, was occupied on December 3, 1917. This building had three stories including a basement. It contained fourteen rooms. The lower grades occupied the lower floor and the high school the upper level. The grade school was standardized in 1930. In the school at that time, the following classes were offered: college preparatory, commercial, music, and domestic sciences.

The first graduating class, 1915, had five graduates, and they went into the world to become a teacher, a pharmacist, a refinery worker, and two housewives.

The class of 1920 had nine graduates. Three from this class, or one-third, attended Kansas University at a time when only one in ten in America attended college.

An account written by Nellie Evelyn Froman ('21) reflected the excitement of this new school opportunity:

> All four grades were now taught and the students are proud of the fact that they may graduate at home from an accredited high school. During the construction of the building, students, teachers, and the community at large watched it with interest. When the time came to move from the old building to the new, excitement ran high; and when the shingles on the roof of the old building began to vanish, when part of the walls were torn down, and finally when the remaining part of the lumber was hauled away, we began to feel as though we were thoroughly established in our new home. No traces remain save the memory of those happy days when we were leaving the old for the new, with the realization that through our efforts and those of our faithful teachers, would come the development of intellects better fitted for the problems of life.

Another student, Joe Thompson ('62), shared the following recollection:

> I always said I grew up at the greatest place on earth. Edna was only about eight blocks from east to west, so no one ever took the school bus. I believe the kids that lived in the country were brought to school by their parents, family, or friends. We always had good teachers and school was fun. Verl Shufelt was the superintendent most of my life at Edna. You were well guarded and every mom in town was your mom, so you couldn't get by with anything even if you wanted too. We were very poor but not bad poor. My mother kept us the cleanest kids in town. We always ate well and my mother was a great cook. I got to eat at school which I really enjoyed. My favorite meal was homemade potato salad and hot dogs. The cooks were ladies from right here in Edna.
>
> Even in high school I had no requirements outside of school. I did all my homework at school. One summer my dad bought us a lawn mower. I was eight and my brother was ten. We paid dad back for the lawn mower and had more money that we thought even existed. I never had a job nor need of a job until summer of my freshman year. From then on I worked each summer for farmers close to Edna.
>
> The school year was comprised of (other than school) track, football, basketball, and baseball. Football and basketball were big things in Edna and every game had a big crowd in attendance. In my junior and senior years we played six-man and a couple of eight-man football games. It was at this time our high school had gotten so small we could not field a regular size football team. My junior year we were undefeated league champions. That was a great year. After each game someone would pay for eats and drinks (coke, grape) at our local eating establishment and it seemed like the whole town was there. I was the King my senior year and got to kiss the Football Queen Ann Goodwin ('56) at half time of our homecoming game.
>
> I always considered basketball a YMCA type of sport, so my junior and senior years I played town team basketball. The school year usually consisted of three plays; an eighth-grade play, a junior play, and a senior play. I was the lead in the eighth grade and senior play and participated in my junior play. One year

we had a play to raise money for Christmas lights for the downtown area.

Our initiation into high school consisted of a parade through downtown with all six of the boys dressed up as dancing girls. We had to wear the outfits all day long. Initiation was not bad or mean but was fun. The whole town enjoyed it. Senior trips were great, consisting of a long weekend, and most of the classes went to Branson, Missouri. We still have reunions every five years with a couple hundred people attending. The last one (2013) was smallest we ever had with just over 100 attendees.

With each year as the school had fewer and fewer students, the town also regressed. When I went to high school there were over twenty-two active businesses in downtown which employed over eighty full-time people. Now (2018) there are only five businesses, and that includes the city library with fifteen employees. The high school seemed to be the driving force of our little city. I believe though that the city can be revived. We are in the process of cleaning up and painting five buildings on the main drive and hope to secure new businesses. Edna now has a population of 432 and in 1959 it was a little less than 500. So the population has held, but the businesses have not.

Traditions — The senior class of 1958 went to Rockaway Beach in Missouri. The principal, Mr. Verl Shufelt and Anita Shufelt, Mildred Stewart, and Katherine Russell all drove cars. This class still gets together every year at Branson for an annual summer reunion. The senior class of 1965 took their senior trip to New Orleans. All ten graduates remembered the exciting and educational experience.

Wayne Bozman ('65) recalled the following:

My mother, Dorothy Bozman ('31), and all seven of our family graduated from Edna High School. We had basketball, football, and baseball. Our great coach was Frank Myers. One day one of our football players rode a horse to practice. Coach Myers decided he was going to ride the horse and the horse took off for home with him hanging on for dear life. He was nearly "clothes-lined" and bailed out, much to the laughter and admiration of all of the on-looking football team.

Herb Majors was our janitor. He was one good guy and a spic-and-span clean up guy. He always had our school in such great condition.

We had an old abandoned World War II era airport training field near town. There were always impromptu drag races, with the smoke from the screeching tires and the revving of the engines echoing through the country side. My '54 stick Chevy was the class of all of the dragsters and was seldom beaten in the quarter mile strip.

Della Seger, Immogene Stine, and Opal Spencer cooked together for many years. They were loved by all of the students and were great cooks.

Athletics & Activities — The biggest sports rivals were Thayer and Chetopa. The beloved superintendent, Verl Shufelt, left Edna to become the superintendent at Thayer for three years, then to Chetopa for twelve years, and finally returned to Edna to be the principal at the grade school.

The first school yearbook was published in 1922, called the *Prairie Dog*. In later years the yearbook was published every other year and had the names of *Pirates Log* and *Buccaneers*. The monthly school newsletter was called the *Pirate Plunder*.

Martha Seger Foister ('58) shared the following:

My mother, Della Seger, was one of the school cooks. I played the trumpet in the band and remember vividly the practice and precisions that the marching band performed. My husband John Foister ('54) was also a graduate from Edna. We had a girls drumline and bugle corps. Most of the girls in high school participated. We marched at football games and parades.

Marilyn Sedoris Holmes was an outstanding music teacher here for years. Our music groups, glee clubs, and solo ensembles would participate at Oswego High School and Pittsburg State University every year. This experience was always a thrilling and learning time for all of us.

Spanish was offered as an elective in the 1960s. The school only provided two busses for transportation of the rural students. Driver's education was offered to the freshmen during the last few years of the school.

The End of Edna — The first graduating class had five graduates in 1915. There were 621 graduates in the sixty-two years from 1915 until 1966 when the school closed. The most frequent surnames of the graduates were Baker-14, Stine-14, Cooper-9, Rhodes-8, and Triebel-8. The last to graduate (alphabetically) from Edna High School was Mike Stine. The class of eight students was the last to walk across the stage in 1966. In the fall of 1966, the remaining high school students were transported to Altamont.

Edna High School
Labette County, KS

#63

Kismet Rural High School

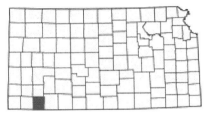

Mascot: Pirates

Colors: Black and White

Year Closed: 1965

Location: town of Kismet, east-central Seward County

Town & Education — The town of Kismet was laid out in the fall of 1907. H.D. Massoni bought land one mile west of town, and his brother bought on Lake Road south of town. They bought this land from A.C. Olin. When Mr. Olin found out both men had families, he said, "All right, I own this land, and I will have it surveyed and start a town, and we will build a school for the children."

Mr. Olin built a Bible school. Children came and went to school on a live-in basis, but it ran for four months and closed. The first public grade school was built as a two-room school.

In 1916, high school studies were added, and classes were held in the combined grade and high school building. The first terms were held as part of School District No. 28.

News of the Day — A town newspaper, *The Kismet Kipper* became a valuable source of information for the community so shortly after the founding of the town. In a 1917 issue, it published the following:

In 1915, the farmers organized a Farmers State Bank which was capitalized at $10,000. A good cashier was sent to run it and the town began to push and boast again. At this time the town consisted of three dry goods stores, two large elevators, two good garages, one up to date depot, two good coal dealers, a pump station on the railroad and one of the best schools in the county as it employed two of the best that can be had, a good telephone exchange and about 30 residents.

During the spring of 1919, a campaign was started with the purpose of organizing a rural high school. Mr. Hess, aided by the Kansas Juvenile Entertainers and the Kismet Glee Club, went to each district that was included in the high school district and explained the proposition to the people.

HURRAH FOR THE RURAL HIGH SCHOOL
One hundred eighty six names on the petition . . . the County Commissioners complied with the law and voted to grant the petition and call an election of the legal voters of districts 31, 30, 28, 17, 15, 12, and 6 to be held on Saturday, 31 May 1919.

~ *The Kismet Kipper*, May 8, 1919

HIGH SCHOOL ELECTION CARRIED

The election on the proposition for building a rural high school at Kismet and voting bonds for some in the amount of $15,000 carried last Saturday by 139 for the proposition and 14 against.

~The Kismet Kipper, June 5, 1919

TEACHERS SALARY HIKE

Kansas educators may demand a minimum of $1000 at their convention next month. Hundreds of young women with certificates are now working in stores and offices because they can get more money. Many educators have deplored the fact that the salaries paid teachers are so low that there is no inducement to anyone to give his time and energy to preparing for the profession.

~ *The Kismet Klipper*, October 30, 1919

KISMET SCHOOL OPENS MONDAY SEPTEMBER 7

With the high school building not completed it is up to the board to do the best they can for at least two months, so they rented the hall over Hick's Grocery for the present.

~ *The Kismet Kipper*, September 2, 1920

Just one week later with the high school not yet occupied and the grade school overflowing with students *The Kismet Klipper* reported the following:

The school board of District #28 is circulating a petition for a bond election for the purpose of building a new fire proof school building for the grade school. This is a very much needed improvement as every available building is being used this year and yet we have not sufficient room to properly handle the pupils. We now have 82 children and only room for han-

dling 50 properly. Let us get behind this movement and push as it will only raise the taxes about $1.30 per year. (September 9, 1920)

With the forming of the Rural High School district came the need for busing. Early 1920s photos show up to five box-shaped vehicles in front of the school. There were two planks on each side, and the students sat parallel as they were transported. A large number of the one-room country schools closed during the 1920s, further expanding the student enrollment at Kismet.

Athletics — Both girls and boys basketball thrived in the early years of the high school. The 1933-34 girls team was undefeated.

The following is a representative story of a farm boy educated through the Kismet schools and shows the background that a small school has on students as they are educated and inspired by teachers to become leaders in many varied occupations in life. Excerpts were taken from the *Kismet Centennial,* 1987 book published by Lola McVey, who was also the editor of *The Kismet Klipper*:

Raised on a farm, Ernest McVey '41 started college but was soon called into the service during World War II. He served 28 months in the Army-18 months in the Philippine Islands from D-Day plus one. He returned home in April 1946 and began teaching music at Kismet Grade School that fall. He met a teacher, Lola Winifred Claar who was also teaching in the grade school in Kismet and they were soon married. Ernest '41 resumed his studies at Bethany College graduating in 1949. He and his family returned to the family farm near Kismet as his parents were retiring. A band picture in 1960 shows Ernest with 40 Kismet band members in their uniforms. A stipulation to play in the band was that the student had to take private lessons either before or after to play in the band. Quite the dedication of both the teacher and the student.

In 1961 both Ernest and Lola returned to Wichita State University. After another teaching position at Great Bend, they returned to Kismet where Ernest took the instrumental music teaching position at the newly formed Southwestern Heights High School. Lola became Speech Pathologist at Meade and Fowler, later including the home district of Southwestern Heights (Kismet). Ernest was still teaching in 1981 until his sudden death. Ernest's great love for Handel's Messiah. He had directed four Messiah choruses in two communities. This prompted 126 people to sing "Since by Man" and the "Hallelujah Chorus" in a musical tribute at his funeral.

Kismet Rural High School
Seward County, KS

Unification and Closing — With the school unification law in 1963, the counties were directed to plan for the unification of the schools in their respective counties. Kismet received permission to cross county lines and reached out to Plains in Meade County. A new high school was built along US Highway 54 with a planetarium and auditorium for 600 people. The new school, named Southwestern Heights, opened in the fall of 1965.

Kismet Rural High School closed after graduation in May 1965. The twenty-four graduates in the class of 1965 made it the largest in any year from the high school. The last graduate to receive a diploma was Ann York Miller (alphabetically). There were 439 graduates in the forty-four years, from 1921-1965. The most numerous surnames of the graduates were Green-7, Fellers-6, Lambert-6, McVey-6, Smith-6, Brown-5, Jantzen-5, Miller-5, Simonson-5, and Thompson-5.

#64

Gem
High School

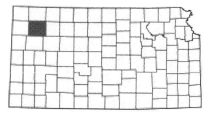

Mascot: Tigers

Colors: Black and Gold

Year Closed: 1965

Location: town of Gem, east-central Thomas County

School Beginnings — Gem was one of the few towns in Kansas that published its own history. A publication by Bill James and Marge Brown titled, *The History of Gem, Kansas* provided background for this story. Gem is located in east-central Thomas County on US Highway 83 along the Rock Island Railroad which runs diagonally from Norton to Colby.

One of the advantages sadly missed by the early settlers of Gem was an education for their children. Until 1884, the job of teaching the youngsters to read and write fell on the parents themselves.

In 1885, there were several families homesteading in the Gem vicinity. They began a movement for the organization of a school district as provided by law and as soon as the school population was sufficiently large, district 33 was organized. A small sod building was hastily built on a site one-half mile west and three-quarters mile south of Gem, which was the center of the district. This school was named Green Valley School House. It served the patrons for two years before becoming inadequate for their needs. A frame building nearer to Gem was constructed for the beginning of the school in 1888 and named Mt. Vernon.

With the addition of several other outlying one-room elementary school districts, in 1905 a new block school was built. It was large enough to utilize the services of three teachers. Due to delays in construction, the school year did not start until January 1, 1906. The school became the Gem Public School and was a graded school. In 1908, an additional year was added to the course. In 1916, a second year was added to become a two-year high school.

In 1921, a new brick high school and grade school was built and named the Gem Consolidated School. It expanded to nine teachers. The high school was on the upper level and the grade school on the lower level. The gymnasium had a stage on one side and a balcony on the other three sides for viewing ball games and stage events.

An Historian's Remembrance —Jerry W. Knudsen ('55), professor emeritus of journalism at Temple University, was a former journalist who specialized in the history of the press in both North America and Latin America. He earned a Ph.D. in history at the University of Virginia, where he was one of the first Jefferson Fellows, and received a Freedom Forum Award from the Gannett Foundation for his long-term coverage of the Pinochet dictatorship in Chile. Knudsen, wrote in the *Prairie Winds Newsletter* of the Thomas County Historical Society and Prairie Museum of Art and History in the Fall 2008, Vol. 35 No 3 issue:

It always amused my classes at Temple University based in Philadelphia, but also with students, that there were only six members in our graduating class at Gem High School in 1950. But what really grabbed my students was stories of the Midwestern custom of the "senior" sneak, which is this case meant all six of us crammed into one car along with our coach and sponsor Robert Berry. We wrecked mild havoc from Topeka, to Kansas City to St. Louis to Memphis. It was simply representative of hundreds of small high schools in western Kansas and elsewhere who in days gone by served their communities well.

We never had enough guys to play football, so in the fall it was volleyball and in the spring baseball and track. In basketball, I think we won one game out of two seasons, and finished one game with only three players when our reserves had all fouled out. But no matter, the day after a game, men would gather at the tire and body shop to talk with animation about what went wrong the night before.

There was one bone of contention, however about whether or not dancing should be allowed in the Gem school. (Remember this was the late 1940's, light years away from social mores of today.) Leading the opposition was the Rev. Irwin Bradshaw, a good and decent man who used to hand out Hershey bars to all kids who could produce A's on their report cards as they boarded the school bus he drove to help make a living. But he had this thing against dancing. I was a student representative at the School Board meeting when this issue came to a head. Ernie Ziegelmiller, who wisely skirted the issue of separation of church and state, focused on the social merits of dancing for young people. "Where did you meet your wife," Ernie asked. There was no answer, and some of us lived to perform an exhibition of square dancing on the Gem High School stage later on.

Looking back on the years, I feel the greatest benefit of Gem High School and myriad of others like it was that we got to know one another. And, knowing each other enabled us to know others in a wider world we were about to enter.

Traditions — John Flannigan ('59) shared this memory:

We always had a school play. We had a very good education with science, English, math, typing, and business. We had music, choir, and even a marching band. There was no home economics, but shop included a woodworking class. My senior sneak was to the Smokey Mountains. With our sponsor, the superintendent and his wife, and all eight in my class, we piled into two cars for this end of the school trek. One of those cars was a tiny 1956 Studebaker.

Athletic rivals were Menlo, Rexford, Selden, Herndon, and Levant.

Closing Gem — The high school closed in 1965. There were 236 graduates in the forty-four years of the school. The largest class was ten graduates in 1962. The first graduate was Twila Houston in 1922. The last graduate was Connie Wilcox in 1965. Zieglemiller was the most prominent surname of all the total graduates with six, but five other of the graduates married Zieglemillers to bring the total with that last name to eleven.

Students were given the choice of where to attend school after Gem closed. A few chose to go to Rexford, but most went to the new unified district in Colby.

#65

Dwight Rural High School

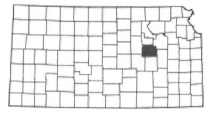

Mascot: Rockets

Colors: Purple and White

Year Closed: 1968

Location: town of Dwight, northern Morris County

Early Education—The first school room in Dwight was in the Grandview (Brooks) Hotel. It was a subscription school opening in September 1887 with the students paying to attend. Bonds for $2,000 were voted for a school building in 1888. In 1906, an addition to this building was completed with another bond voted at $5,000.

A two-year high school was started in 1915 in the grade school building. In 1915, interest grew for a new high school building. Even though many were in favor of the issue, there was much opposition also. Some were apprehensive of the cost in relation to the number of students who might attend. In 1919, a special election was held to issue $20,000 in bonds to erect a new high school. Out of the 459 votes cast, the issue passed by 43 votes When the school opened that fall in the grade school building, there were seventeen students enrolled.

Several new school laws were initiated by the State of Kansas in 1919 that influenced the Dwight schools. The school age law was enacted whereby children who would be six years old on or before January 1 would enter school at the beginning of the school term in the fall. All children between the ages of six and sixteen were required to attend school unless finished with a diploma. Free dental examinations were introduced and provided to students by the state. Every school was required to display the American flag with a proper flag staff outdoors. Every school room was provided with a flag to be displayed.

Dwight Rural High School became accredited with a four-year course in August 1920. The high school board gave notice that the school would accept any student coming from a territory where there was no school. The county would pay the tuition, but if they came from a district where there was a high school, no tuition money from Morris County would be provided.

The school officially opened on September 6, 1920, in the grade school building with twenty-six students enrolled. The first graduation class was in 1921.

Athletics — Basketball was introduced in the older two-year high school as early as 1912. The games were played on an outside court until 1920. Goals were put in the rink for winter playing. The new high school was complete with a gymnasium thus the game was brought indoors at the school in 1921.

An account of one of the first games played was recalled in the *Dwight Advance* in January 1921:

> The Parkerville-Dwight basketball game was played at Dwight. The girls lost 8-11. The boys had a scrappy game—seemed as though both teams were out for blood and got their fill. In the second quarter, Hollshausen was knocked out but got back in the game in the last half. One of the Parkerville boys injured his knee in the third quarter. Final score – Dwight 21 Parkerville 18.

About a week later, the basketball teams traveled by rail to play at Alta Vista. Nearly fifty students and rooters planned to go by auto, but weather set in and arrangements were made to go by rail. The Rock Island Railroad consented to stop regularly scheduled train No. 31 at Alta Vista and Dwight, which made traveling convenient.

Construction on the new high school started in April 1921 and was completed in time for the school to open five months later on September 12, 1921. The total cost was $23,765. The heating contract was $6,407 and the wiring contract was $497. The building was all brick and modern in every respect, with running water, electric lights, and toilets on both floors, two sets of showers in the basement, and water fountains placed conveniently throughout the building. The gymnasium seating for 400 was arranged to be used for an auditorium as well as basketball. It was considered to be one of the finest school buildings in Morris County.

Neighboring towns had introduced football into their high school activities. After some controversy, Dwight introduced football in 1924.

The story of Dwight Rural High School and its history would not be complete without its final six years as a high school. The word dynasty could not be bestowed on any sports program more appropriately.

- Football: 43 wins and 5 losses, four undefeated years, state champions, and twenty-nine consecutive wins.
- Basketball: 135 wins and 16 losses (half of those losses at the hands of much larger high schools in invitational tournaments), five out of six years to the state class BB tournament, and a single loss in regionals in 1965 that prevented the mighty Rockets from earning six straight trips to the state tournament. They were the only team to ever win the state tournament two times and this was back to back in 1966 and 1967.

A team, a coach, a community, and all the Dwight students helped in making this dynasty. A first-year coach out of McPherson College, Ralph Rindt taught his players to believe that "if we ever get beat, it's an upset."

In an account in the *Kansas Sports* magazine, March 1987 issue, 1965 All-State guard, Arden Oleen said, "We never stepped on the court against a team that we felt was better than us. Confident, you bet. But we never took anyone lightly."

The *Kansas Sports* magazine gave further details:

Our goal every game was to keep our turnovers to six or less and hold the other team under 50 points. You never have a bad night on defense, Rindt reasoned. DEFENSE was their trademark as the most points Rindt's Rockets would ever allow in one game was 65. "We worked on our full court press both ways for twenty minutes every night in practice." "Every player who ever played for me was important to me because of the role he would play in our success," Rindt said. "I had every player who was best at one thing. Best Free Throw shooter, Best Defender, Best effort, than anyone else on the team and let them know it. Everyone felt like they belonged and that they were important, because they were.

Darrell "the Horse" Miller ('66) recalled, "Coach Rindt would casually walk down the school hall and put his arm around my shoulder and whisper, 'You are the best rebounder.' You have to believe that this made me think and rebound even better. We wore a coat and tie to every game. We never got into trouble because our teammates depended on us."

Dwight placed five different players on every major All-State First team for five straight years. Seven more earned second team and honorable mentions. Most of them went on to college and played. The three Oleen brothers—Jan ('62), Kent ('64), and Arden ('65) —made up 60% of the Bethany Swedes starters.

Academics—Courses taught were algebra; English I, II, III; elementary science; ancient history; geometry; agriculture; civics; physiology; and commercial law.

In December 1953, patrons of DRHS passed a bond issue not to exceed $158,000 for an auditorium-gymnasium which would provide additional classrooms and shop space.

The music department was a pride of the Dwight community. Groups varying from orchestras to band were asked to appear at clubs and various events. High ratings were received at annual music festivals in Emporia.

The mascot of the Rockets was chosen first because of the school's location along the Rock Island Railroad and the famed passenger train through town was called the "Rocket." Then, in the 1950s, it morphed into the spaceship Rockets logo.

Unification to Closing — On July 1, 1965, the Unification Law in Kansas was passed. Wilsey, Dwight, and Council Grove voted to unify. In April 1968, the Kansas State Fire Marshall ordered the high school closed immediately as the building was deemed unsafe and in danger of collapse. The old building was razed in 1970.

A total of 592 students graduated from the school from 1921-1968. Allen Dasher was the first in 1921 and Stewart Wright the final graduate in 1968 (alphabetically). Though Dwight was a melting pot of the pioneer homesteading farms across the frontier in the 1860s to 1890s, a significant number of Swedish immigrants came to the Dwight community and farmed. Six percent, or thirty of the total graduates had the surname Olson. Followed by Johnson-17, Alpelin-15, Hogle-12, and ten each of Switzer, Morgan, and Holm.

#66
Summerfield High School

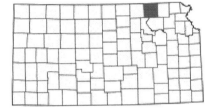

Mascot: Irish
Colors: Green and White
Year Closed: 1979
Location: town of Summerfield, extreme northeast Marshall County

A Border School — Summerfield High School's north wall bordered on the Nebraska state line. Until 1963 there were many students from Nebraska attending Summerfield schools. There were buses that ran across the state line to pick up students that attended Summerfield schools. A ruling from the Nebraska legislature forbid the Summerfield buses from crossing the state line to pick up Nebraska students. Nebraska also refused to pay any state aid for these students to attend an out-of-state school. If

Nebraska families wanted to send their children to Summerfield, they had to pay out of state tuition as high as $3,000 per year. Today (2018), Lewiston, Nebraska, buses pick up students in Summerfield to go to school in Nebraska.

Summerfield Origins

In 1888, work started on the right-of-way and the railroad track was laid for the Kansas City Northwestern and Missouri Pacific Railroad to run from Kansas City, Kansas to Virginia, Nebraska. The main stops from Kansas City, Missouri, and Kansas City, Kansas were Menager Junction, Tonganoxie, Oskaloosa, Valley Falls, Holton, Goff, Seneca, Axtell, Mina, and Summerfield in Kansas, and Bookwalter, Armour, Tate, and Virginia in Nebraska.

The town of Summerfield was named in honor of Elias Summerfield, the superintendent of the railroad. The first train came to town in February 1889. (The last whistle sounded on October 31, 1919.) A school was organized even before the town was granted its charter on October 12, 1889. Eight grades of elementary education were offered in a one-room, wood frame building.

According to 1893-94 records, the school year opened on September 4 and closed on May 25. The school offered ten years of education in eight-month terms (thirty-two weeks). There were sixty students and three faculty. The high school subjects taught were physics, history, physical geography, English, and algebra.

In 1898, five students completed the two-year course, and the first class graduated from Summerfield High School. In 1899, a one-room addition was built above the existing two rooms. The grade school was on the first floor, and the high school occupied the one room upstairs. There was an enrollment of 184 students. The receipts were $1,513.19 and expenses were $1,473.38, of which $920.00 was salary. Enrollment grew, and by 1904, there were a total of 221 pupils.

Tragedy

An account from the *Summerfield Sun* on February 17, 1905:

> About 3:30 o'clock in the afternoon the pupils of the high school room noticed that the floor of the room was getting exceedingly warm, the room becoming so warm that the window had to be opened. About fifteen minutes to four the professor discovered that the fire had broken loose just back of the coal box and immediately stepped to the hall and rang the fire alarm. The greater share of the scholars thought it was merely a practice drill as did all the teachers except the professor, but as soon as they had reached the outside they were told to get what wraps they could without getting into too much danger. One of the larger scholars was then sent to town to give the alarm and a crowd was soon at the scene of the fire and everything was done to save the building but this was soon found to be a useless task and they then turned their attention to saving the books, and wraps of the scholars.
>
> Professor McKinley is to be highly commended on the proficiency with which he had drilled the scholars . . . Attendance the day of the fire was about one hundred and thirty and it is no easy matter to clear a building . . .

Rebuilding & Growing Summerfield

A temporary school, the Summerfield Subscription School, was established in the United Presbyterian Church. Tuition was $25.00 per pupil. The school held classes in the Eureka Hotel. Students in grades seven through ten were able to complete their school work for the year. Twenty-five pupils attended. Six students graduated from high school that year.

Immediately after the fire, work was started on a red brick building. It was completed in 1905 at a cost of $12,000. The high school course was lengthened to three years. During the school year of 1905-06 effort was made to replace things lost in the fire. The following items were purchased: 250 classics, a 14-foot wool bunting flag, an Edison mimeograph, a globe, and eight framed artotypes (an early form of photography producing copies made with carbon pigment).

In 1910, the first four-year high school course was offered. There were two high school teachers. Normal Training was added to the curriculum in 1915. From 1915 until the 1940s, Summerfield High School trained many young teachers for the rural schools of Marshall County. A large number of them went on to successful careers as teachers. Some of Summerfield's best teachers were homegrown.

A petition was passed around and signed by 135 voters, only five of whom were women. This petition called for an election to vote bonds in the amount of $6,500 to erect an addition to the present building. The election took place on August 23, 1915. Of the 117 votes cast, 116 were for and one was against the proposal. The second floor belonged to the high school. There was a large assembly room or study hall across the west end of the building. Three rooms were designated for English, math, and science classes.

A belfry with a large bell was an important part of the schoolhouse. Remembering the tragedy of the 1905 fire, two fire escapes were provided for the second floor.

Bob Frazee ('47) recalled this incident from 1944:
There was a fire drill and all of the students were standing out in the playground. The superintendent gave the announcement that it was alright for the students to go back inside the school house. Several of the boys said they were not going back into the school as there was a fire in the belfry. An astonished superintendent called the fire department and the fire was extinguished without any major damage. It was thought that a sparrow had brought a twig for a nest that had a hot ember and it started the fire.

In 1916, W.H. Seaman, County Superintendent reported that, "The two most progressive schools in Marshall County are Waterville and Summerfield."

Academics & Athletic Activities — Through the years the school kept in step with the times. The students participated in scholarship, spelling, dramatic contests, and sports contests and held their own against other schools in the county.

In 1908, Summerfield had its first football team. The story is that Fred McClure attended a football game in Manhattan and came back so enthused about it that the boys organized a team. The first game was against Beattie. Summerfield was defeated 80 to 55. When Beattie came to Summerfield for the return play, there was a surprise ending to the game. James Duggan, one of the Summerfield players, fell on the ball and completely flattened it, flat as a pancake. That was the only ball Summerfield had so the game ended abruptly.

Nicknames were very popular as everyone had their nicknames printed in the early football team pictures. There was a boys baseball team by 1909 and a basketball team as early as 1911. There was a girls basketball team as well in 1911.

The fiercest rivalries were with Axtell, Beattie, and Waterville. Many teachers and coaches got their start in Summerfield and moved on to other schools. Rick Thomas ('55) said, "I had four different coaches in football and basketball in my four years of high school."

Being a member of an athletic team in these early days of the school was very different than today. To play games at Axtell and Beattie, the students traveled by a horse-drawn buggy or wagon. When playing Frankfort, Marysville, or Waterville, they packed their suitcases and traveled by train to their destination. They played a game in the afternoon, stayed all night, and came home on the train the next day.

The teams were not as well provided for in those days. Whatever equipment was available was used to the best advantage of the team. Often a player leaving the game gave his helmet to a player going in.

A picture of the 1919 team shows that only one player had shoulder pads. All but two of them had regular football pants. None of them had helmets or special football shoes.

Sports were not the only interests of the school. The County Oration and Declamation contests were held yearly until 1936. There were yearly scholarship and spelling contests.

Many clubs existed in the school. The Athenians and Zelagathians (Dramatics) entertained each other with programs. The Parliamentary Law Club studied Robert's Rules of Order, the aim to learn to conduct an orderly business meeting. There was a Letterman's Club and Kayettes.

There was another group called the Torture Club. The members played ukuleles and they enjoyed their meetings immensely

The earliest school newspaper was called *Flashlight*. Later school newspapers were called *Megaphone*, *Blarney*, *Echos*, and *Cat's Purr*. In 1937, *The Shamrock* was published and with the exception of a few years during the war, published every year after that time.

Student Stories — In 1928, Solon E. Summerfield, a nephew of Elias Summerfield (the town's namesake), started a scholarship at the University of Kansas. The scholarship was for a complete four years of study at the University of Kansas. In 1938, Donn Gordon Mosser ('38), a senior at Summerfield, was awarded the scholarship. It was the first time a Summerfield student won the scholarship. That year Solon Summerfield, who was the head of the Gold Stripe Hosiery Line in New York, wrote:

For it isn't by money you measure a school,
Or the miles that its borders extend.
For the best things you gather, whatever the school,
Are contentment, enjoyment and friends.
If you live and you work and develop your school,
In spite of the fact it is small
You may find that your school-your own little school
Is the very best school after all.

-from the 1942 *Shamrock*

In 1937, one year of typing was added to the curriculum and taught to juniors only. That year a bond was defeated by nine votes to erect a building to house a school auditorium, as well as vocational agriculture and home economics facilities. When the plan was defeated, the school gymnasium was remodeled to serve as a home economics room.

In 1940, the school was modernized and water was piped in. The next year a stage was added on the second floor. By 1946, a hot water unit was added, and showers were installed for the girls.

There were no football field lights, so all home games were played in the daytime. Bob Frazee ('47) recalled the following:

> We played both eleven-man and six-man football games, depending on the size of the other school's team. We took cars to transport the team to out-of-town games. The girls played 3-on-3 or six-girl basketball. Basketball games were played in the city auditorium, which also was used as a skating rink.

A noteworthy rock band called the Impalas was made up of Summerfield boys. They were Terry Stedman ('67), Laird Bookwalter ('67), Henry Burcher ('67), and Steve Tegtmeir. They became a very popular band in the region in the 1960s and 70s.

Tom Bookwalter ('62) designed the distinguished Kansas State University Powercat logo in 1989.

A New School — On October 8, 1948, an election was held. As a result, the school was divided into a grade school district and a rural high district.

State officials directed that if Summerfield intended to maintain a school, there must be new facilities. On May 3, 1953, a bond issue of $245,000 was approved to construct a building to house both units of education.

The new school was made of masonry block with an exterior of tan brick facing. It was built on the north end of Main Street on the east side. It had four standard elementary classrooms and high school facilities for bookkeeping, typing, science, homemaking, shop, vocal and instrumental music, study hall, library and hot lunch. The dedication ceremony was held on November 23, 1955, on the Wednesday before Thanksgiving. A crowd of more than 600 people came to see the new building.

There had been no hot lunch program in the old school. This offering started in the new school. No more running home for lunch or carrying lunch pails. The cost for school lunches for the 1967-68 year were grades 1-6 at 25 cents, grades 7-8 at 30 cents, grades 9-12 at 30 cents, and adults 40 cents. An announcement in the school paper in 1972 stated that the school breakfast would cost pupils 10 cents.

Unification to Closing — During the following years, education became more expensive. The school district boundary lines were to be redrawn and unified into larger districts. After much discussion and voting, Axtell, Beattie, and Summerfield were united as a district with each retaining its own school. This plan was not accepted by the majority of the voters. Beattie withdrew and asked to be unified with Marysville.

The districts were redrawn and Bern, Axtell, and Summerfield were organized into District #488.

The last year Summerfield operated as Rural High No. 3 and Grade School District No. 137 was 1966. There was an enrollment of 76 in high school that year.

Regina Smith taught first grade in Summerfield from 1934 until 1980. During these forty-six years, she taught the majority of the students that graduated from Summerfield. She was an institution and loved by all.

In May 1979, the high school closed due to declining enrollment. The last graduating class of thirteen students received their diplomas from Summerfield High School with Betty Whitmore (alphabetically) accepting the very last diploma. A total of 978 graduated from Summerfield Rural High School from 1898 through 1979. The most numerous surnames to graduate were Young-15, Volle-15, Johnson-13, Eastman-12, Frazee-12, Sejkora-12, Miller-10 and Smith-10.

Summerfield School
Marshall County, KS

#67

Ensign Rural High School

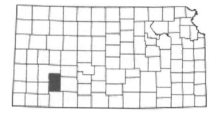

Mascot: Wildcat

Colors: Red and White

Year Closed: 1979

Location: town of Ensign, eastern Gray County

Town and School History — The town of Ensign is on the railroad line that runs northeast to Dodge City and Southwest to Sublette, Satanta, Hugoton, and Elkhart. US Highway 56 parallels the train track that cuts diagonally from the middle of the state to the southwest corner of the state. It is a popular shortcut for travelers heading for New Mexico, Arizona, and California.

The Ensign grade school was built in 1915. The high school students met in the hardware store until the cornerstone for the high school building was laid on November 19, 1920.

The school's strongest rivalry was with Montezuma, twelve miles away.

Notable Graduate— A notable graduate of Ensign was Norris Sayre ('37). He was a local boy who returned home from World War II. He attended college at Kansas State University and then came back to Ensign to open the grocery store for several years. He returned to K-State to finish his education, then came back to Ensign to teach. He moved up to principal and later to superintendent.

Unification Woes— When the school unification law handed down by the Kansas Department of Education was delivered, a school district had to meet two of three requirements. Ensign met only one.

1. 200 square miles in the district. Ensign had 178.
2. 400 or more students in kindergarten through twelfth grade. Ensign had 139.
3. $2 million in assessed valuation. Ensign had no problem here.

A possible solution was to add a few more miles to the district. This would have involved getting a few areas to the north and east, not belonging to any school district, to agree to join the Ensign district. A few of those residents petitioned to come into the high school district, leading Ensign to believe that it had met the first requirement by having more than 200 square miles in the district. The state sent a man around to the schools to discuss unification, so the community dutifully gathered in the high school gymnasium to listen to him. When the man was introduced, he stood up and said, "I'm sorry, I cannot discuss unification with you. An injunction has been filed by Dodge City." Dodge City did not want just a portion of the Gray County district, they wanted it all, and with political pull, they got it.

Mr. Sayre continued to update the curriculum. The graduates continued their education at colleges and trade schools. School was much the same as before except for the cloud of unification hovering over the community.

In 1969, the state legislature passed a law stating that all remaining non-unified school districts in Kansas would be disorganized July 1, 1969. Districts facing mandatory unification were Florence, Ensign, Kanarado, Coolidge, Odin, and two districts at Leoville.

Over sixty people from Ensign, including parents, teachers, and students, went to Topeka to back Mr. Sayre as he pleaded Ensign's case. The chairman of the education committee, Senator Joseph Harder, interrupted Mr. Sayre after one sentence saying, "I'm sorry Mr. Sayre, we've run out of time. Would you like to leave your notes?"

The citizens of Ensign school district voted to close the high school that spring. They voted to unify with Cimarron and became USD 102. As part of the Cimarron District, the high school in Ensign remained open until 1980. The community had never had any school buses, but now they had to transport students to activities. The new district gave Ensign two buses for their students.

The year following the closing of the high school, the students who were seniors went in different directions. Some went to Dodge City, Fowler, Montezuma, and Cimarron. Three outstanding athletes chose to drive to Ingalls rather that play at Cimarron. With students going in four different directions, it was not long until folks took their younger children out of the grade and middle schools and sent them with their older siblings. The only school bus that was permitted to come into old District #4 (grade school) for a few years was Cimarron. Following the closing of the grade school, the Fowler and Montezuma buses came in to pick up children.

Credit for Ensign Story — Betty Pegran Herrman graduated from Ensign High School in 1947. Her husband, Les, coached the little league baseball team for sixteen years. He had the John Deere dealership in partnership with his father in Ensign for forty-two years. Betty's father was a mechanic in town, and her grandmother owned the local café. At eighty-seven years of age (2017), Betty Herrman lives in the neighboring town of Dodge City, and this history of Ensign was shared with gracious, vivid memory. Asked to name a few outstanding graduates of Ensign High, Betty said, "Why, I'd like to think they all changed the world."

In Betty Herrman's ('47) words, "Losing the high school killed the town."

The high school closed in 1980 after fifty-nine years. A total of 643 graduated from Ensign High School. The first graduate in 1922 was Harvey Bratton. The last graduate to receive a diploma in 1980 was Lori Trent (alphabetically). The most numerous surnames of the graduates were Miller-21, Herrman-14, Stauth-14, Sutton-13, Kimbrel-12, Reinert-10, Johnson-9, Beggs-8, Moody-6, Richardson-6, Scroggins-6, Etling-5, and Harrell-5.

Ensign School
Gray County, KS

#68

Gove Rural High School

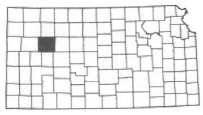

Mascot: Vikings until 1948, then Panthers

Colors: Black and Old Gold

Year Closed: 1968

Location: center of Gove County

Area History — The area that became Gove was part of Trego County until the 1880s. The county struggled to get the required 2,000 in population to become an official county. E.A. Benson from Davenport, Iowa, purchased 250 sections of land in what was to become the town of Gove City. He laid out the town site with the help of surveyor C.J. Ferris.

Both Gove County and Gove City were named for Captain Grenville L. Gove, a Union soldier from Compa-

ny F, Eleventh Kansas Cavalry. He had been involved in chasing and skirmishing with Confederate General Price along the Kansas-Missouri and died in Olathe, Kansas, in 1864. The town was not on a railroad line but was near the center of the county. The promoters made no secret that it would be a candidate for the county seat. E.A. Benson was the instigator in getting a sod hotel building constructed just west of the present court house for the workers to live in while working on other buildings in the town. The Bensons "served a big free dinner in the sod building. It was served cafeteria style and was one of the best dinners anywhere around. Families loaded in their wagons and came from all the homesteads. A dance was given that evening. Everything was free, and this generosity was perhaps one of the deciding factors when a count seat was voted on in the fall." The first church services and the first school were both held in this sod building. While workers were living in the sod building, they were constructing a two-story hotel made of stone and known as "The Benson House."

The Benson house was completed in the spring of 1886. Stone for the house was quarried from section 30, Township 12, Range 28. The name "Benson House" and "1885" were carved in stone on the front. The building was used as a hotel for a few months in 1886 until Gove purchased the building for $1,000 on June 1, 1891. With the alterations, additions, and improvements, it has continued to serve as the Gove County Courthouse.

Education — The first attempt to obtain a secondary school for Gove County was made through legislative channels. A special enabling act authorizing a ballot at the general election of 1896 was the method prescribed by the general high school law of 1886. The law applied only to counties having a population of 6,000. Gove County, with a population of 2,126, tried to organize such a county high school. In the November election the proposition was defeated 231 to 97.

A second special act for the establishment of a county high school at Gove City was enacted on February 29, 1903 (interesting date as it was not a leap year and there was no February 29 that year). This required the county commissioners to make an order establishing a county high school, when petitioned by a majority of the legal voters, and providing forty-five percent of the legal voters did not protest. Upon receiving of a petition with 384 signers, the county commissioners ordered a county high school established at Gove City and named six trustees: George Royer, Gove Township; J.M. Sturman, Payne Township; Hiram Richardson, Larrabee Township (Larrabee was the Governor of Iowa and friend of Benson and may have had some stake in Bensons land purchases in the county); M.E. Wilkinson, Jerome Township; A.A. Madden, Lewis Township; and E.C. Prather, Grinnell Township.

High School — Gove County High school opened September 14, 1893. It offered courses in college preparatory, normal training, and general education. The school opened with an enrollment of nine pupils and was maintained in the red brick grade school building in Gove City. It became Gove Rural High School in 1915 in accordance with the Barnes Law of 1915 which provided for the establishment of a rural high school.

A new high school was constructed in 1920-1921. This two-story, red brick high school was located in the southeast corner of Gove City. It was built for $45,000 and was ranked with the best in the state. This well-built school still stands nearly 100 years later and houses the Gove County Historical Association. It opened for classes in September 1921 with an enrollment of fifty students, thirty-eight girls and twelve boys.

An addition was built onto the southeast corner of the high school in 1949 at a cost of $35,000. This expansion housed the science room on the top floor, and boys and girls dressing rooms on the main floor of the gymnasium.

The Gove High School Panthers took second place at the Class BB state basketball tournament led Bobby Randle ('66).

Student Stories—Bob Randall ('66) shared this story:

> My dad was the county engineer, and we spent our free time traveling on 1,200 miles of the county roads. I had twelve in my class of 1966. We had taken second in the state basketball tournament in both 1964 and 1966. Entering the final game for the title in 1966, we were undefeated.
>
> We had no football, but we played baseball in both the fall and spring. We had a nice band and I played the trumpet. We marched in the Ft. Hays Band Day parade quite proudly, all sixteen of us. We had four rows of four and played quite well. We had no idea that we were the smallest band and strutted with pride.
>
> We had a great debate coach, Milford Messer. He taught us boys to wear black socks when we were presenting at a debate instead of the normal white socks that we all wore to school.
>
> Our rivals in sports were Grinnell, Grainfield, and Park, all schools on the northern rim of Gove County. They were on US Highway 40 and eventually Interstate 70. The Grainfield gym had the out of bounds line painted against the brick wall. The balcony hung down

over the floor. The term "cracker box" was shared by all of us.

A great community, they would drive their cars to the ball park in the summer every time those lights went on. The cars would ring the field and honk their horns with a great catch, a score, and any hits by the home baseball team. As the summer sunset faded, this nightly scene of cars arriving, the smell of the freshly cut alfalfa and wheat fields, and the thousands of fireflies of the evening are imprinted on my memory.

So this little school gave me a great education for life. Debate, music, and sports have carried me well for many years.

Unification and Closing—In 1965, Gove School District No. 1 became part of the Unified School District No. 292 Wheatland, consolidating with Park and Grainfield. Classes continued to be held at GRHS until the last graduation in May 1968. There were 469 graduates from 1924-1968. The last graduate receiving a diploma was Charlene Zimmerman Koster ('68) (alphabetically). The most numerous surnames of the graduates were Smith-18, Powers-15, Zerr-14, Beesley-12, Evans-11, Lewis-11, Mendenhall-11, Wilson-11, and Johnson-11.

Gove Rural High School

Gove County, KS

#69
Milford High School

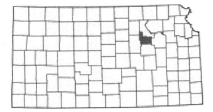

Mascot: Panthers

Colors: Purple and White

Year Closed: 1965

Location: town of Milford, northern Geary County

Settling Milford—The early settlers came to claim land as part of the Kansas-Nebraska Act which opened the territory in 1854 to land in which the Indian title was extinguished. The early pioneers established the town of Bacheller (later renamed Milford). The town was incorporated by act of the territorial legislature in 1858. The first store opened the next year. This was followed by a grocery store, dry goods, marketing and drug store, lumberyard, sorghum mill, cigar factory, slaughter house, and a cement plant.

School History—On June 30, 1921, the citizens of Milford Township voted to establish a rural high school district: Milford Rural High School, District No.1 of Geary County. This included the city of Milford, most of Milford Township, and a few sections of Riley County. The members of the first school board were L.B. Streeter, E.M. Wilkins, and John Miller. These names are reminders as to the involvement of parents and leaders in the community, as in 1924 and 1927 there were Miller and Streeter graduates.

Prior to 1921, two years of high school subjects were offered in the upper room of the Milford Grade School. It was because of the Barnes Law in Kansas that the possibility of forming the rural high school at Milford came to pass the voting ballot.

The first graduating class of 1924 had five graduates. This class chose the school colors of purple and white, and these remained the school colors until the school closed in 1965.

According to Rosanne Ballou ('48), the Milford Panthers won first place in the first district basketball tournament in 1930, arranged by what is now the Kansas Athletic Association.

The Girls Reserves were organized in 1937 and were active until the late 1940s. The Kayettes club replaced Girls Reserves in 1948 and continued until the school closed. The Kayettes earned many plaques, which were placed in the school trophy case for the service organization.

Iris Farlow Shandy ('46) recalled the following:

Because our country was at war during our school years, we came to know what restrictions and rationing meant. Ration stamps were needed for gas, tires, shoes, sugar, and meat and many other products. Even our favorite candy bars and gum were in short supply. Patriotism flourished as a great scrap iron drive was held with the freshman-sophomore classes pitted against the junior-senior classes.

In the spring of 1944, high winds took most of the roof off of the school building. The gymnasium area was the most exposed to the elements and heavy rains left water standing on the gymnasium floor. Holes were drilled into the floor to drain the water and kept the floor from being damaged. With most of the roof gone, school had to be conducted elsewhere. Dividers were placed in the old church, and classes were moved there for the rest of the school year.

According to Shandy, "Everything was crazy. Skipping class had by this point reached a state-of-the-art status. A group of boys went row boating on the river and a couple of girls hopped the Dottle Bug and spent the day in Junction City. Keeping track of everything and everybody took it out of Mr. King, our weary principal."

During the war years, so many teachers and community members served in the armed forces or worked in the military plants that it became difficult to find teaching staff. Some of the replacements were not of the highest caliber, but school did go on. The boys basketball team continued without a coach. There was no football and no band.

School Leaders—One board member, Mrs. J. B. Walters, served from 1940 until the school closed in 1965. She worked passionately for the school and helped hire a new principal. A former navy officer, C.M. Smith was hired in the fall of 1946. For the next two years the school was transformed into "ship shape." Mr. Smith came along at a very crucial time for Milford High School. Discipline and rigor happened overnight with his leadership. He was an exceptional administer, a teacher, and a coach.

Of his tenure, Rosanne Walters Ballou ('48) wrote the following:

> When Mr. Smith said "jump," we just said "how high" and did what he directed. He introduced us to some discipline and order and even to study. We were gradually growing up and thinking about the future and he helped in several ways as he did not tolerate goofing off well.

Smith's first year as coach, he led his boys basketball team to the championship of the Clay County Tournament. The Junction City paper wrote, "The Milford School this year only had eleven boys enrolled and ten of them were out for basketball. Coach Smith declared a half-day holiday starting at noon to celebrate the victory."

Wakefield, just across the Republican River to the west, was the school's most heated rival. "We referred to them as the 'English,'" said Ballou.

Philip Walters ('46), was the son of a school board member. Walters attended Kansas State University and excelled academically. He finished number one out of his chemistry class of 400 his freshman year. A picture was taken with his chemistry professor for the *Royal Purple* yearbook for his achievements. Philip was killed the next fall in a tragic auto accident coming home while driving on a sandy road through Ft. Riley.

The next principal was Mr. Arthur Jones from 1948 until he also died in an automobile accident in 1959. His wife, Mrs. Goldie Jones, was an outstanding math teacher until the school closed in 1965. As senior class sponsors, they accompanied numerous senior trips. Mrs. Goldie Jones became the only member of the Junction City Area of Retired Teachers from Milford. A graduate of Lucas High School and of the University of Kansas in 1926, she taught for eleven years in Winchester, Robinson, and Maple Hill before coming to Milford.

Traditions — The first yearbook was published in 1948. This also was the year of the first homecoming celebration for the high school. The queen was Dorothy Jane Arkell with attendants Joan Budden and Roseanne Walters.

A highlight each fall was the Halloween Carnival. This carnival was held annually to help raise money for the senior trip. It was enjoyed by many for miles around. The school decorated and each class was assigned activities. Booths were run by the students. Milford and Junction City merchants were generous in donating prizes for the bingo table. Prizes were sometimes given for costumes. Throughout the years, Milford had very little trouble with vandalism or pranks on Halloween. Many thought it was because the young folk were too tired to be out after the carnival. Much work and many hours of getting sponsors may have curtailed some of the usual Halloween shenanigans pulled in other towns at these times.

The senior and junior plays and the all-school play were well attended. A musical program was held for the general public. The junior-senior banquet was one highlight of the school year. During the 1930s and 40s, no dancing was permitted, but in later years the freshmen and sophomores were welcome to dance after the banquet. New or best dresses were a must for the girls, and the boys were handsome in their shirts and ties.

School Improvements — In 1953, the patrons of this district voted for a $60,000 bond issue and a metal gymnasium was built just south of the school building with a breezeway between. The first basketball game in the new gym saw the defeat of the Milford team by their arch rival Wakefield. For a time, the size of the crowds led one to believe an even larger gym was needed. In February 1961, during a heavy snow storm, the gymnasium was destroyed by fire. Every citizen of Milford who heard the alarm was on hand to help fight the fire and carry out equipment, trophies, and anything that could be saved. For a time it was feared that the school building would also burn, but it was not harmed. Yet another gymnasium was built with minor changes and was ready for the basketball season the next school year.

During the summer and prior to the start of school in 1956, the school board purchased a school bus. This was the first bus owned by the district, and it was used to pick up a small group of students from Ft. Riley and students between Ft. Riley and Milford. Mr. Calvin Faulkner, a teacher and athletic coach, became the first bus driver.

The Inclusion of Fort Riley Students — In May 1958, Jerry O'Brian became the first Fort Riley student to graduate from Milford. He told this story of his high school days:

> During my senior year, Bill Noble and I would wrestle around quite a bit and even on the school bus. One day while we were wrestling on the bus, waiting to go to lunch, we broke one of the windows. We realized that we needed to report what we had done so we told the principal, Mr. Jones. He said that since we were honest about it and had told him what we had done, that the school would take care of the repair. Of course, boys being boys, after lunch and on the school bus we started wrestling around again. And yep, you guessed it, we broke another window! Not only were we young and foolish, we were naïve for we thought if we reported our second misgiving right away we would not have to pay for the repair. As soon as we got back to school, we reported to Mr. Jones that we had broken another window. Guess what, adults look at these things differently. We each had to pay to have one of the windows repaired. Did we learn a lesson? Sort of. We would still wrestle around, but NOT on the school bus anymore!

Fort Riley students began attending Milford High School because of a happenstance meeting at the Fort commissary between Verdis Brighton, who was delivering meat, and SFC General O'Brian. A conversation about high schools led to Principal Jones saying if SFC O'Brian could get ten students from the Fort, he would send a bus to pick them up to come to Milford to high school. Coach Faulkner drove the bus that first year in 1956 to pick up sixteen students, one of which was Jerry O'Brian ('58). Thus started a lifelong relationship between Jerry and his new school and classmates. Having moved with his family at least eight times, he found Milford his true home in the states. Following graduation and working at the Milford grain elevator, Jerry joined the Navy and made a career. While serving as a naval officer, he has traveled from all over the country to attend his school reunions.

An End for Milford — The town of Milford is now under water. Over fifty years ago the Corp of Engineers moved the town to the east to make way for the Milford Dam and Reservoir. On this narrow nose of the northern tip of Geary County which is only six miles wide, the school district was bordered on the east by the enormous Fort Riley Military Reservation and to the west by the Republican River. Good farm land along this basin provided a rural community with many small family farms.

It was with heartache the school closed in 1965. A total of 297 graduated from Milford Rural High School in its forty-two years of existence. The most common surnames of the graduates were Miller-10, Kidd-9, Wilson-8, and Cleveland-7. The last graduating class of ten walked across the stage and received their diplomas from Principal Lynn Wallace and Board President, Mrs. J.B. Walters, in May of 1965. The last graduate was Lyle Reaka (alphabetically).

The buildings and grounds were purchased by the Corps of Engineers for the construction of the Milford Dam and reservoir. The gym was purchased from the Corps by a church-sponsored school. It was moved to the church grounds at Enterprise, Kansas. The red brick building was torn down in 1965-66. Bricks from the school building may be found embedded in the doorsteps of many houses in New Milford.

Milford School
Geary County, KS

#70

Mt. Hope High School

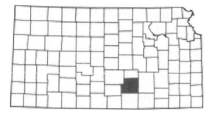

Mascot: Pirates

Colors: Blue and Gold

Year Closed: 1966

Location: city of Mount Hope, northwest Sedgwick County

County Population Note — Sedgwick County is the second most populated county in Kansas. Johnson County and Sedgwick County together make up well over one-third of the population in Kansas.

Early Education — The first school house in the area was a log cabin. It was a structure on a one-acre tract of land about three-quarters of a mile west of the present town. The three R's were taught in this school - reading, writing, and arithmetic. The exact year the school started is not known, but the school board minutes of July 31, 1877, show expenditures of $211.75 for the previous school term spent on the teacher's wages. When the school was established, the town of Mount Hope was only a federal mail drop at the residence of the postmaster, T.H. Randall. Mr. Randall was also on the school board. The books that were used were personal copies belonging to the students. The school term was three months long, and Mr. Pyle, the teacher, received $20 per month for his services. The next few years saw rapid growth of population in the township and businesses in the city. These developments pointed to the need for expansion of school facilities.

The land had been purchased from the grantor, once again Mr. T.H. Randall. A second school house was constructed. It was a two-story, barn-like building which often shook so much in the Kansas wind that school was dismissed on windy days. From the local newspaper, *The Mentor*, on March 28, 1890, "School was dismissed yesterday noon on account of the wind being so high that there seemed to be danger of the building blowing over. Its appearance and safety concerns created the desire for the community to have another new school."

In June 1896, a school election voted 170 to 18 in favor of bonds for a new school. The ground breaking was in August 1896 to lay the foundation for a new school building. An October newspaper account indicated that J.P. McCormick and Mayor E.W. Jewell made heavy sacrifices in time and effort in order to promote the project. The schoolhouse was surrounded by maple trees excepting about half an acre on the north left for a playground. The edifice was in the shape of a vertical cross with four porches, one story high, with a room in each of the four wings. The hall where the four rooms met housed the library. Above the library was another room and above that the cupola for the bell tower. In 1907, the district designated the room above the library for the new high school. The school house was dedicated in November 1896 (three months after starting construction) and completed in June 1897. A shed to shelter horses for those who rode to school was added on the school grounds.

An anonymous hand-written note included with the school history archives says, "Each room had an organ (or overtorium) and pupils and teachers sang songs each morning. Jerald Fanlkey, one of the teachers, was a musician and sang heart fully."

A paper titled "School Architecture" refers to the building of a school:

> Before presenting the Plans and Elevations of school buildings, I have deemed it important to make the following suggestions in regard to a few practical points.
>
> 1. Site for the Houses: Healthfulness is an important consideration. Avoid swamps, stagnant pools and low places. In this State every school-house should be so situated as to have access to the south wind during the summer . . . It is far better for children to walk a little farther to a beautiful spot, than spend six hours each day where the surroundings are uninviting. The site itself should be an education.
> 2. Front of Building: The best front is that toward the east. It is important that a school-room have one end unbroken either by windows or doors for blackboards and teachers stand . . . If the building faces south the wind sweeps through the entry along the aisles whenever a door opens thus continually blowing dust about the room and into the lungs of teacher and scholars . . . But, other things being equal, AN EAST FRONT IS THE BEST.
> 3. Out Houses: Every school-house designed for both sexes should have two outhouses. Many a child delicate and sensitive organism contracts permanent physical injury, and becomes the victim of untimely death, by delaying to obey the calls of nature at the proper time. The too prevalent custom is to build one out-house with two compartments. It is far better, however, to build a separate out-house for each sex, on the rear of the lot at some distance apart . . .
> 4. Lightning Rods: As the best summary of directions on this subject and the most authoritative, I give below the very valuable opinion of Prof. Joseph Henry of the Smithsonian Institute, Washington D.C. as stated in a letter addressed to N. Capen, Esq. of Boston, Mass. dated May 4, 1870 . . . A rod of this kind may be put up by an ordinary blacksmith . . .

A High School — In 1904, a group of seventeen students who had graduated from the eighth grade paid $75 each to secure the services of a high school teacher, the Reverend B.F. Buck. The subjects taught were algebra, English, bookkeeping, literature, and ancient history. There was officially no high school, but the following year, 1905, saw the establishment of the first district high school.

In 1910, the first graduate of Mt. Hope High School was Hazel Fishback, the only member of the class. By 1912, forty-seven students were enrolled. By 1914 there were sixty enrolled. By 1915 there were sixty-two enrolled.

A bond election was held in May 1913 which carried 213 to 26. High school leaders claimed that a new $12,000 school building would be ready for occupancy by the time school started in September. July 1 came with the closing on a two-acre patch of ground at the time planted to alfalfa west of the school house. Bids were let, and construction of the school for $10,000 was started. The building was turned over to the high school board in time for the start of the fall term (60 days). The final construction for the high school commenced in 1925 for $41,610. Thirty car loads of brick were required. Classes were held in the township hall until the new facilities were ready in January 1926. One of the most important features, and the greatest addition to the school, was the gymnasium and auditorium. All grades were held in this building with the grade school on the lower floor and the high school on the second floor.

High School Life

Three buses were used daily in transporting both grade and high school students to and from school. These were often driven by teachers for supplemental pay.

The boys played football, basketball, and track. There were no girls sports. The biggest rivalry was with Andale. There were often extracurricular scuffles between over-exuberant fans and students. Another big rival was Haven.

The school yearbook was called the *Pirate*. The final and last yearbook in 1966 was dedicated to all MHHS alumni:

> Although this high school will cease to exist, it will be kept alive by the cherished memories of all those who have walked through these doors. A part of every heart will linger forever in these sacred halls.

That year there were more boys in choir than there were out for football. The band had forty-eight students and the orchestra had twenty-two. There were twenty-eight girls in Y-Teens.

Academics

By 1962, both Latin and Spanish were taught by Mrs. Carroll. There was an outstanding music program under the leadership of Mrs. Johnsmeyer. The music festival at Andale was always a big event. If the musical ensemble or solos were good enough they would go on to Wichita to perform. The band would march annually at the Kansas State Fair in Hutchinson. Christine Vollweider ('62) recalled in a letter back to her alumni gathering:

> I wonder if Nancy Moss Carnes ('62) remembers the many hours we spent trying to make a mirror in Chemistry? And that we almost blew up the school from the chemicals we were using. And who couldn't forget Mrs. Rankin and her blue and black dresses. I think those were the only ones she owned! Oh yes, Martha Johnsmeyer brought the best out of me in music. She and Eunice Dow were the best. Does anyone remember all the music practices? Our parents didn't like it, but we came home with "1"s.

Industrial arts was taught by Mr. Vernon Pough for eight years, from 1957-1964. It offered drafting, light metal, welding, small engines, and woodworking. Mr. Pough recalled, "Halloween! That was a wild time. One year chickens appeared in the school."

Traditions

Senior trips were a rite of passage for the seniors. A school bus was driven by the janitor and his wife to accompany seventeen seniors to Colorado in 1952. They visited a prison and traveled on to Carlsbad

Caverns in New Mexico and to Juarez, Mexico. By the 1960s, the trips were a one-day event to Davis State Lake. Funds for these trips were mostly from concessions and ball games, magazine sales, and picking up dropped corn in the fields behind the corn picker.

Vera Mae Beal Davis's days at Mt. Hope High School were highlighted by this memory, "Who put the cow in the school? Whoever was behind the stunt remains a mystery, as well as how the guilty parties were able to pull off the feat."

The pranks were the usual cow and chicken tricks in the school. Jim Bardshar, who is now a successful farmer, was usually the instigator of these fun productions during his time in high school. Jane Rassmussen ('64) recalled one story in a letter back to her alumni gathering:

> A moment I'll never forget—about half of us seniors ('64) were in study hall, and we always did something to Mrs. Carroll. One day Johnnie Dulop jumped out of the library windows. Mrs. Carroll (who did not know there was a balcony under the windows) went running and screaming down the hall to the office. By the time she returned, we had Johnnie back in the room, which was no small feat! My, could she yell, and in Spanish too!"

Notable Graduates—Jim Kissick ('43) became a colonel and flew Flying Tigers in Asia. Calvin (Vin) Kissick ('64) would become the pilot for Air Force One.

Bill Chance ('51) went to West Point and played football. Ben Johnsmeyer was also a West Point graduate.

Closing the School—The last graduating class was 1966 with seventeen graduates. The last graduate to receive a diploma for Mt. Hope High School was Leah Jane Weve (alphabetically).

In its fifty-seven years from 1910-1966, there were 826 graduates from Mt. Hope High School. The most numerous surnames of the graduates were Dick-26, McCormick-16, Grier-15, Johnson-12, Kissick-11, Garrison-10, Jorgensen-10, Goodman-9, Moore-9, Jones-8, Smith-7, and Hill-5.

The school unified the next year with Burrton (thirteen miles north). In 1972, the district had an election on the proposal to build a new high school in the country, just outside the city limits. It was defeated. Mt. Hope split off from the district and unified with Haven USD #312 to the west in Reno County.

Mt. Hope High School
Sedgwick County, KS

#71

Hanston High School

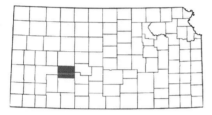

Mascot: Elks

Colors: Black and Orange

Year closed: 2006

Location: town of Hanston, east-central Hodgeman County

Town Origins & Early School History —

The spur of the Santa Fe Railroad, running from Larned and ending in Jetmore, ran through Hanston and was built in 1890. The rail line was originally staked to be in about the same place as present-day highway K-156, which is located near the town. The Hann family offered to give the right-of-way to the railroad if the town would be called Hanston. The Hann surname was a part of the community for the next 125 years.

In 1911, the first high school in the county was known as the Niederacher High School, named after George Niederacher, the landowner who donated the property on which it was built. Up until this time, the county's educational system was solely composed of a network of small, one-room schoolhouses and a couple of town grade schools in Hanston and Jetmore. There were forty-eight of these elementary schools, although not all existed at the same time. They educated only grades 1-8. After the founding of Niederacher, students from these elementary schools could attend the high school, but it was a subscription school, so they had to pay tuition to attend.

In a few years, the Niederacher High School name was changed to Hodgeman County High School. Hanston Rural High School was established in 1926 and was later called Hanston High School. The first graduating class was in 1927 with eight graduates. The "new" high school was built in 1949.

Student Stories —

The school rivals were the members of the 50-50 league—Burdett, Rozel, Windthorst, Offerle, and Spearville.

These are some of the memorable experiences shared by graduates in the final yearbook in 2006:

> Donald Sebes ('57) – Mr. Duncan was the principal and he sent us seniors to the photo studio to get our pictures and we decided to stop at the Red Haven restaurant to get a Pepsi. We weren't supposed to do this and unknowing to us, Mr. Duncan was watching out the school window. We didn't get in to trouble but Mr. Duncan asked us how our Pepsi's were just to let us know that he knew.

Pat (Osborne) Housman ('51) – . . . when she was a Junior in High School, in 1950, she had to go to the school board to get the first High school dance approved. After some discussion the board approved the dance, but it was to be called, "school party games."

Paul Hubin ('47) – . . . attended the Peaceful Ridge Country School until 1943. He drove a 1929 Ford Model A to school. Leland Salmons rode with him. In the winter he had to drain the radiator when he got to school because it had a leak and couldn't hold any antifreeze and would have frozen if he didn't. Paul had to bring a 5-gallon bucket of water with him to school since the school didn't have a well and they wouldn't have had any water without it.

Fay (Goller) Powell ('33) – Faye along with Al Schwint were the first cheerleaders in 1931-32 at Hanston High school.

Madonna (Hendrickson) Cossman ('48) – The cooks baked on old kerosene stoves. They put the food on the bottom burners and only lit 2 or 3 so that the food wouldn't burn. The stoves didn't have any temperature gauges on them. The school had a lot of mice and they would get into the trash cans. She would have to step into the trash can and stomp them to kill them. Everyone else was too afraid to do it.

Allen Selfridge ('67) – One of Allen's favorite memories was when the school performed 'Oklahoma', which was directed by Mrs. Sandra Walker. He said, "it was a great experience and Mrs. Walker was a special kind of teacher."

John Ney ('70) – We had bad luck during grade school when the circus came around. They decided to skip our class going every year for some reason. Finally, our senior year, we decided to skip school and go the circus. The principal found out and came to Dodge City and dragged us home.

Paul Wasko ('81) – I remember when my brother, Kurt, and sister, Donna, won the Homecoming King and Queen and they still had to kiss.

Dustin Lee ('00) – I remember how Coach Slaton's wood shop class would always turn into "Game Film 101 Class."

Leasa Salmans ('91) – I remember when the 1989 Boys basketball team went to state. The community dribbled a basketball all the way to the Hays Park and then the 1978 State team members dribbled from the park to the Coliseum. I thought it was really neat that those guys came back to do that.

(These former state tournament players from the 1978 and 1989 teams returned in March of 1991 to participate in the school's spirit.)

Irene (Bamberger) Holmes ('35) – Making pies in home economics class. My boyfriend, Veryl Holmes, would always come over to eat the leftovers. I always made sure there was a piece of pie left just for him.

Consolidation Efforts – As the populations changed and shifted around the county, the one-room school districts began to consolidate with neighboring districts or dissolve completely. Buses brought the rural children into Hanston. By 2000, due to rapidly declining enrollment, the Hanston and Jetmore districts began to discuss the possibility of consolidation. However, no agreeable solution was found during the next five years. In the fall of 2005, Hanston began sending its elementary students to Burdett as part of a contractual agreement with USD No.

496 Pawnee Heights (located in Pawnee County). The following school year, 2006-2007, all Hanston grades were merged with the Pawnee Heights school system. The elementary students attended school in Burdett, middle school students went to Hanston, and the high school students went to Rozel. The two schools have kept their contractual agreements and both school districts retained their individual USD numbers and their respective boards of education. This new school district was collectively called the Pawnee Heights Schools.

Five years later, following a failed consolidation vote on April 6, 2010, Hanston and Pawnee Heights districts elected to go their separate ways. This opened the door again for negotiations between Hanston and Jetmore to create a unified school system for Hodgeman County. As part of the agreement, the boards agreed to retain Jetmore's mascot, the Longhorn, but the school colors would change. To honor the histories of both districts, black was selected from the former orange-and-black Hanston Elks, and red was selected from the former red-and-white Jetmore Longhorns.

A quote from 100 years earlier in the *Jetmore Republican* paper of August 24, 1911, would stand again as Hodgeman County now had one county high school:

> What we need is the cooperation of the entire community to make the school a success and our people should stand together as a unit and help Prof. Davis in every possible way to place this institution where it should be among the educational institutions of the state.

School Closing — The school closed in 2006. A total of 942 graduated in the seventy-nine years from 1927-2006. The last graduate was Benjamin Wilkens (alphabetically).

The most numerous surnames of the graduates were Salmon-58, Hollings-20, Korf-19, Miller-18, Hertzel-14, Hann-12, Hahn-11, Ewy-10, and Holmes-10.

Hanston High School
Hodgeman County, KS

#72

Schoenchen High School

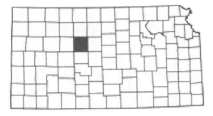

Mascot: Bluejays

Colors: Blue and White

Year Closed: 1968

Location: town of Schoenchen, Ellis County

Volga German Background — The southern half of Ellis County was homesteaded and settled by many Volga Germans in the 1870s and 80s. The villages of Antonino, Munjur, Pfeifer, Loretta, and Leibenthal all had a Catholic church and some schooling opportunities. Schoenchen was the only town that established a high school. It had an unusual cooperative arrangement with the parochial school in town. These villages were very similar to those in Volga Russia and in Germany where the population came from. Most of the farmers lived in the villages and traveled out to work at their farms in the daytime.

The founders of Schoenchen were originally a part of a group of Germans who came from farms in the Lower Volga River region of Russia. They had come to Russia at the invitation of Catherine the Great in the last half of the 18th century. They were descendants of the Germans who had accepted Russia's offer of free land and exemption from military service in 1782 and 1783. In 1762 Catherine II, a German princess, deposed her husband Peter III, a German prince, and took the Russian imperial throne. Catherine published a manifesto inviting Europeans to immigrate and farm Russian lands while maintaining their language and culture. When the exemption from military service was revoked in the later part of the 19th century, many of the Germans in Russia, including those from German Mennonite communities, immigrated to the United States. Some came to the village of Liebenthal, five miles south into Rush County, Kansas, but a disagreement there caused thirty-five families to relocate and form their own church and settlement at Schoenchen. This new settlement was founded in April-May 1877 and included members who all originally were from Neu-Obermonjou or Schoenchen, Russia.

Education Matters — The community of Schoenchen always placed a high importance on the educational needs of their children. The first "schulmeister" (teacher) was John Diecher who taught classes from his home that included religion, reading, writing, and singing. When the founders of Scheonchen found that schools could be operated through tax money, they organized their own school in 1880 and built the town's first public school. It was a thirty-foot by thirty-foot native limestone structure. Because the students and teachers were Catholic, the priest also took the opportunity to provide religious instruction during school hours. The district operated on a parochial-public school basis. The Sisters who taught grades 1-6 were paid by the parish, and the Sisters who taught 7th and 8th grade were paid by the district.

From 1921-1926, a two-year high school was started in the first public school building. The grade school and high school had 120 students and was taught by four Catholic sisters. In 1926, bonds were passed totaling $25,000 for building and equipping a high school. It was constructed of modern American brick and contained sixteen classrooms and a gymnasium. Tuition was paid for students in at least five surrounding neighboring communities of Leibenthal, Loretta, Pfeifer, Munjor, and Antonio. Rent was paid to the parochial school for use of some of their buildings for the public school.

The first graduating class was in 1928 with six graduates—Joachem Enslinger, Celestine Werth, Paul Werth, Rudolph Windholz, Aloysius Zimmerman, and Bertha Zimmerman.

In 1938, a new gymnasium was constructed of native limestone. This eighty-three by seventy-six-foot structure was adjacent to the high school and served as a social center for community activities.

By the early 1940s, the schools had 150 students from the first grade through high school. The high school had a preference for business training courses.

In 1940, due to enrollment growth, the auditorium was converted into classrooms and a new auditorium was built by the WPA (Works Project Administration). The parochial school next to the church was changed to a public school and the district paid rent for the use of the parish buildings.

From the school's beginning, classes were conducted in religion before the start of the school day. Monsignor Riedl was renowned for his zeal in these education sessions. The father also taught religion classes on Saturday mornings for two hours. He was tragically killed in an auto accident and the whole town mourned his death.

A new state law in 1953 curtailed the instruction of religion in a public school.

A Student's View — Lillian Hermann Leiker ('52), at a delightful 83-years of age (2017), shared her memories. There were thirteen in her class, including her husband to be, Lester Zimmerman ('52). They moved to Wichita to work for Boeing to save enough money to moved back home to buy a farm. Tragically, four years later, Lester died. Lillian raised six children by herself. She sold Avon products for forty-two years, until she was eighty years old. In her own words, "I was very successful."

Lillian recalled:

In high school we took the REN Scholarship tests every year with a #2 lead pencil. REN stood for the counties of Rush, Ellis, and Ness. The tests were given to all students. The first, second, and third place students were recognized as the scholarship winners. Being modest, I was a winner in Algebra, English, and Home Economics, though Home Economics was not my favorite. Baseball was the sport for all seasons for the school and the town. It was played year around and on Sunday afternoons.

The district only had one bus in which it bused high school students in from Pfeifer and Vincent schools.

Activities included school plays. These were enacted by each class and performed for the community.

The rival schools were McCracken and Bison. Though the students did not compete athletically with the larger school, Victoria, to the east, they seemed to always have "an axe to grind" with Victoria.

I played volleyball but was not permitted to play on the team because I had glasses which cost a lot of money if they were broken. I graduated as the valedictorian of my class.

Lillian was raised on a farm with six siblings. They are all still alive (2017) and range in age from seventy-five to eighty-eight years old. She proudly said, "And we all like each other!" She still owns the family farm and says she always will, "come hell or high water!"

The family raised cattle, chickens, and geese when she was growing up. Her mother had this thing with geese, claiming "They didn't eat much grain and were self-sufficient." She would sell many at Thanksgiving as their meat was not as dry as turkey.

All of Lillian's six children are living, and two of them are successful cattlemen. They all gather at Table Rock in the Ozarks each summer for a grand family reunion. She says, "Great families and great people were raised and educated in Schoenchen."

School Closing — The last graduating class from Schoenchen Rural High School was in 1968 when the district unified with District 489 in Hays, twelve miles north.

Schoenchen Rural High School
Ellis County, KS

#73

Quenemo Rural High School

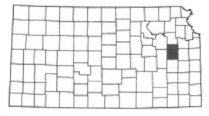

Mascot: Buffalo

Colors: Blue and White

Year Closed: 1978

Location: town of Quenemo, east-central Osage County

Area Lore & History — Through beautiful valleys, surrounded by tree-clad hills, flows the Marais des Cygnes. The river glides along swiftly, having only started one county to the west. At a bend along the river a village of Quenemo was established. One historical legend is told of a beautiful Indian maiden astride her pony dashing along the river to the Indians in the area crying "The Whites are coming." The whites may have named this little town after this same beautiful Indian girl. Yet another account is that it was named after a Sac and Fox Indian Chief who resided here and was buried in a plot southwest of town in a mission cemetery.

The headwaters of the Marais des Cygnes River were formed thirty miles upstream, north of the town of Reading in Lyon County. The Great Flood of 1844 was known to the Indians as "Big Water." It was along this beautiful waterway that the government established the Indian Agency. It was nothing more than a seat of the Sac and Fox tribe. The chief of the tribe was Keokuk. The mission was located southwest of Quenemo. It consisted of two large buildings capable of accommodating 300 pupils, but the largest number ever enrolled was about sixty. From 1860-1868, the Agency was the government building or headquarters. It was merely a lounging place for Indians. The treaty of 1868 was made by which the government secured the land on which Quenemo now stands, and the following year the Indians were removed to Indian Territory.

Numerous more floods would occur in 1886, 1898, 1909, 1951, and 1965.

In a history of Quenemo, Mattie M. Largent, 1900 graduate, wrote the following in the *Quenemo Republican*:

> From 1860 to 1868, the Agency was merely an Indian Agency where hundreds of Indians swarmed, drawing their annuity from the government, and lounged around their wigwams wrapped up in their blankets or roamed the great prairies in search of large game. There were just enough white men here to do the government's business with the Indian. And Lo, the poor Indian, often fell short of rations for some of the government's agents were schemers, and unscrupulous and some to them amassed great fortunes.

In 1868 a treaty was made with the Sac and Fox Indians whereby the government secured the territory upon which Quenemo now stands, and the following year was noted for the removal of the Indians to the Indian Territory (present day Oklahoma). But they did not like their new home so well as they did their old one, for they thought as much of their old home as the people of the present time; and would we not also revolt if we were forced to leave our homes? So they concluded to come back, and in the following spring a part of the tribe was again seen in their old homes. But fate had turned against them, for the government again sent them to their new homes, but had some trouble in getting them to stay, for it was about fifteen years later that the last band was moved.

The country at this time was being settled by families of the Caucasian race. The first public school for white children was opened in 1869 and taught by Miss Anna Craig.

In another account in the *Quenemo News*, George Largent wrote, "The first school was a subscription school taught in an old frame Indian-house south of town. There were no blackboards, charts or maps, and very few books. The course of study was limited not even covering all the common branches, but work was thorough."

First School House — In 1871, a $7,000 bond for school purposes was passed and a first brick school house with two rooms was built. The first graduating class was in 1893 and consisted of two graduates, Frank Shinn and Jesse Cloud. During those first ten years, fifty-five graduated from the school. These were considered graduates of the school even though it was less than a standard high school. The 1871 school had only two rooms and was for elementary schooling. Additional years were possibly added around 1883.)

From George Largent in the *Quenemo News*, "In 1896, while Mr. Deardorf was the principal, the course was revised and a regular 2 years of Latin were taught at the High school. The standard of education kept advancing and in 1903 the principal and board adopted a 3 year High School Latin course. Everything that the course covered was fully approved at the State University and for these years the pupil graduated with the highest honors was presented with a free scholarship good for one year in any college in Kansas."

In 1916, a $22,000 bond was passed to build what was then called the Rural High School, erected on 4th Street. The building was later condemned. In 1960 another bond for $243,000 was passed for a new high school.

Miss Margaret "Mattie" Largent taught at Quenemo for fifty-two years. Nearly everyone for the next half century had her for a teacher. A 1900 Quenemo graduate, she got her normal training and then graduated from Kansas State Normal School. She is in the Emporia State Teachers Hall of Fame.

Two more teachers, Lucy Windett and Paul Sims, were later also inducted into the Emporia State Teachers Hall of Fame.

Town Rise and Demise — From the 1880s until 1920, the thriving town of Quenemo was the winter home of Lucky Bill Newton's Circus. With his five sons, they were known throughout the United States for the quality of their circuses. Other prominent businesses were a three-building sanatorium and the Wilsons Brothers Mill. A post card from 1920 showed eighty-one businesses in Quenemo.

It may have been the flood of 1951 which ultimately led to the demise of Quenemo. The Corps of Engineers built Melvern and Pomona lakes for flood control. The rerouting of Kansas Highway 68 was a final straw as it was extended from Pomona west as K-268, thus bypassing most of the automobile and business traffic to the north and not through Quenemo.

Stories of the School — The school paper was called *The Buffalo Bugle*. One article written by a student in the 1930 issue was titled, "Be Reasonable" – "'I'm very sorry' said the personnel manager, 'but if I let you take 2 hours off for lunch today, I'd have to do the same for every other employee whose wife gave birth to quadruplets.'"

The school record for the 100-yard dash was set in 1932 by Jasper Cade at a time of 9.9 seconds. Den Stadel ('70) set the school record in the shotput at 45' 6" and in the discus at 136' 8". He would later be a star at the University of Kansas and was a strong candidate to participate in the 1980 Olympics which the United States boycotted.

The 1938 Annual called *The Blue Bird* shows a very large marching band.

Another article in *The Bugle* recounts a school trip to the American Royal in Kansas City in the 1950s:

> Arthur Godfrey of radio and television fame was the guest of the Royal and performed on his horse. It was a great show. On the way home, one of the buses broke down. We were about an hour away from home and it was getting late so that a service provider could not be reached. So, the other bus towed the bus with a log chain all the way home to Quenemo. Laughter and excitement ensued.

Athletics — March 1960 will always be remembered as the year Quenemo won the boys state basketball tournament. The team headed for Dodge City riding in Principal L.J. Haughn's Corvair. The star, Dennis Bolin ('60), a 6' 5" senior, led the team to victories over Selden, Mullinville, and Cassoday to win the title. He scored 38, 41, and 37 points in those games which was exactly half of the team's total points. To this day (2018) this record still stands with the Kansas State Athletic Association as being the most points ever scored in the State Championship Tournament by one player. Dennis would later become a very successful businessman in Emporia with the Dolly Madison Company. This team was coached by first-year head coach Dennis Montoya. Much of the credit for coaching would also be given to Mr. Lafe Haughn. The team's trademark was their 1-2-1-1 zone, full-court trap defense. Mr. Haughn would later coach at Emporia State and lead them to the fourth-place finish in the national NAIA tournament.

The earliest recorded record of a football team was 1919. In the 1947 yearbook, the following account was reported:

> 1946 for the first time in many years Quenemo High fielded an eleven-man team. We did not get started until late and therefore, could not get into the Osage County League . . . We embarked on a tough five-game schedule by playing Pomona . . . they were no real competition . . . the game 38-0 in favor of Quenemo . . . we walloped Melvern 18-0 . . . ventured to Edgerton . . . toughest game of the year . . . Willis Kramer '47 was knocked unconscious . . . one of their players had a broken arm and several (5 or 6) were unconscious and had to be worked on during the game . . . we emerged as the winner 25 to 6 and Edgerton folded their season

after that game . . . They said we were too big and tough (our team averaged 160 pounds which is not too bad for a high school team) . . . we journeyed to Waverly . . . we were beaten 66 to 0 . . . Veryl Fagen '47, one of our halfbacks, was hit in the last play of the game and did not regain consciousness until 6 o'clock that evening . . . our wonderful coach, Mr. Fleck, is in his first year as coach and principal at Q.H.S.

In 1965, Quenemo, Melvern, and Olivet were unified into District #456.

The 1969 yearbook was dedicated to teacher Paul Sims, "An individual who has gained the respect and admiration of the entire school and community of Quenemo. He has been teaching here since 1958. We feel that a leader of his caliber brings honor to himself and our school! Mr. Sims (Chief) had introduced tennis to the community. He taught industrial arts and political science. He financed the tennis courts for the town."

The final year book, *The Buffalo*, published that it was a very sad year. The last graduating class was in 1978 with a class of eight. The last to receive a diploma from Quenemo Rural High School was Debra Walters (alphabetically). A total of 802 had graduated from Quenemo High School. The most numerous surnames of the graduates were Logan-14, Windett-11, Reed-10, Wilson-9, Larson-7, Meier-7, Stadel-7, Bennet-6, Cloud-6, Driver-6, Largent-6, and Miller-6.

Quenemo Rural High School

Osage County, KS

#74

Neosho Falls High School

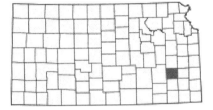

Mascot: Bulldogs

Colors: Black and Gold

Year Closed: 1960

Location: town of Neosho Falls, northeastern Woodson County

Town Origins — The history and establishment of Neosho Falls is one of great hope, vision, and dreams. The statewide floods of July 1951 affected this town more significantly than any other town in the state.

One of the first works of the early settlers was to build a dam across the rapids on the Neosho River, thus the town became genuinely "The Falls." On April 6, 1857, Col. N.S. Goss and Isaac Dow arrived in a one-horse rig from Iowa. At this time, the area was the reserve of the New York Indians and not open to pre-emption. These two men were instrumental in almost every endeavor and progress in establishing the town of Neosho Falls. Goss was appointed the first postmaster. Dow was on the County Supervisors.

Isaac Dow was reared and educated in Maine where he learned the trade of millwright from his father. In 1852, the Dow family moved to Cedar Rapids, Iowa, then to Waverly, Iowa. It was there that Isaac met Nathaniel S. Goss. Goss was the older of the two men and had just recently suffered the loss of his beautiful wife. The two men decided to go to the new, raw country of Kansas.

First School — In 1858, the first school in Neosho Falls was on the private property of H.E. Curtis, who afterward figured in the war as a colonel of a colored regiment. A public schoolhouse was built in 1869, and the first classes taught in 1870. This school proved inadequate, and in 1871, a large addition was made to it at the cost of $500. The following year a building was purchased for $1,000. This, with the original building valued also at $1,000, made the total school building valuation $2,500.

A grist mill, two hotels, and other businesses boomed. The new community prospered and the population grew rapidly. A climax was reached on August 16, 1858, when Neosho Falls was formally declared the county seat.

As written by Wallace Duncan and Charles Scott in the history of Allen and Woodson counties, "The county seat advantages belonged to us by natural right, and in 1870 we reached the dignity of corporation with a population of thirteen hundred souls, O.P. Houghawout being the first mayor."

However, after a long conflict, the county seat was finally fixed at the very center of the county in Yates Center.

In the spring of 1861, after he had taken the Woodson County census, Isaac Dow went with a company of commissioners appointed by the Governor of Kansas at that time to locate lands in Kansas. By the time Dow returned that fall, war had broken out between the North and the South. Dow finished his school land task, and a company of volunteers was started at Neosho Falls with B.F. Goss as their captain. This first unit from Neosho Falls was called the Neosho Falls Union Rifles.

Duncan and Scott further wrote, "The removal of the round house and change in the M.K. & T. division of the railroad followed by the loss of the land office in 1876 deprived the growth of the town. But the office building was purchased in 1878 and Professor J.J. McBride organized the first high school grades, and in his teaching transmitted the finest intellectual inspiration our educational system has ever known. He was a graduate of Ann Arbor and had many fine qualities . . . more than to any other person, the reputation we have gained of being the 'Athens of the county.' The teachers who came after him fostered the tone that has made our school the very best possible to the size of the place, and the spirit of our people has been unusually refined for so small of town."

Visit from the President — In the spring of 1879, it was learned that President Rutherford B. Hayes planned to take a fall tour through the West. At a meeting of the fair board, the secretary, R.P. Hamm, suggested the head of the board of directors invite President Hays to visit the fair in Neosho Falls during his tour. Major Geo. Snow was chairman of the four-county committee. He started the ball rolling by writing to James Harlan, a Republican senator from Iowa. Harlan had been Secretary of the Interior under Abraham Lincoln. In due course of time, the invitation was extended, and to everyone's amazement, the president responded in a letter that he would be honored and accepted the invitation. This piece ran in the *Yates Center News*, October 2, 1879:

> The fair was a grand success in every particular. The entries largely exceeded those of any previous year, 710 having been made before Saturday evening preceding the opening. The display of horse and cattle was the largest and best ever made in the State; and while this was an off year in fruits, the display was very credible . . . by 10 o'clock it was estimated there were 30,000 (some estimated 40,000) people at the fairgrounds. Quite a lot of people came in on the trains that were running that day . . . as the procession crossed the river and approached the archway into the park, the President doffed his hat to the Goddess of Liberty, Miss Emma Snow. "Uncle" Ept Beardon, a white-haired darkey who had at one time been a slave, crowded to the front with one of his boys. As the President approached, Uncle Ept shouted, "Three Cheers for President Hayes!" The President stopped the coach and shook hands with the proud old darkey . . . Gov. St. John, on behalf of the people of Kansas, gave the welcome address to the President . . . a call was made for Mrs. Mary Hayes . . . President Hayes gave a rather lengthy address . . . At the conclusion of the speech the President introduced Gen. Wm. T. Sherman, calling him the man who led our armies from Atlanta to the sea . . . presented the President with a remarkable chair, without it's like or equal in the world manufactured from horns of Kansas steers . . . A young fellow who was a stranger there was particularly trying to get near the President or attract his attention. He finally appealed to Senator Finney of Neosho Falls and told him what he wanted. Senator Finney elbowed his way through the crowd, taking the young man with him to the President. The stranger then told Mr. Hayes this tale: "Last week, my wife gave birth to twins, her first children, a boy and a girl, and I have come 325 miles from home in order to see the President and ask him to name them." Mr. Hayes promptly replied, "Name them Rutherford and Mary!"

In 1898 bonds were voted for a new school house, and a modern brick structure was built.

Notable Student—That same year, 1898, another Iowa born, Neosho Falls raised and educated man, Thurlow Lieurance, was appointed by Governor John W. Leedy to Chief Musician of the 22nd Kansas Infantry. At the age of twenty, he had just been mustered out of the army following the Spanish-American War. This musician would go on to overcome polio and be one of the most prolific composers of the time. His work writing the music for over 100 Indian songs is renowned. His most popular composition, "By the Waters of Minnetonka," is still played by orchestras. Glenn Miller, Paul Whiteman, and Lawrence Welk featured the music. Lieurance attended high school at Buffalo and graduated from Cherryvale.

Best and Biggest Little City—By 1900, the records indicated that enrollment at the high school was sixty-three pupils and the grade school had ninety. The grade school number compared to the high school number is indicative of the many one-room country schools of the time.

The commencement announcement for April 22, 1908 showed sixteen graduates.

The Neosho Falls Chamber of Commerce brochure heading proudly called the town, "The Best and Biggest Little City on Earth." The following is also from the brochure:

> Many good business enterprises thrive here and consist of the combination Grocery-Market, 2 cafes, 2 Grain Buyers, 2 Barber shops, 2 Produce firms, 3 Service stations, 3 Bulk Plants, 3 Feed Stores, a Hotel, Combined Restaurant and Bowling Alley, "The Chicken Inn" for chicken dinners serving parties or families, 2 Carpenters, 2 Interior Decorators, a Furniture Repair and Wool Work Shop, 2 Coal Dealers, A Welding and Blacksmith Shop, an Allis-Chalmers Implement Firm , a hardware Store, a Funeral Home and Mortician, a Post Office, a weekly picture show, a Dance Hall, a Telephone exchange, a Salvage Plant, a Lumber yard, a Licensed Graduate Veterinarian, and the M.K.&T Railway operates 2 daily mail-passenger trains, rail and motor freight daily except Sunday.

Flooded Away — In July 1951, the day came when the hopes and dreams of the little town were swept away by the rising waters of the Neosho River. The flood would rise to the second floor of the high school. This proud edifice would be restored, but never regained its prominence and enrollment. The little town was destroyed.

Gerald Connan recalled, "I lived six miles away near Piqua to the southeast. Every morning I would hop on the MKT (Missouri, Kansas, and Texas) train to ride to school. After school I would jump back on the "puddle jumper" and ride back home in the evening. It cost $2 for two weeks. After my junior year in 1943, they discontinued the train and I had to go to Iola to finish my high school. My dad hired my uncle to drive me to Iola so I could finish school. I hated to miss out on basketball, but I had no way to get to school after the train stopped."

Mrs. Louise Roberts was superintendent starting the fall of 1951, following the flood, and she held the position for eleven years. Mrs. Roberts taught in the Neosho schools for a total of twenty-four years.

The high school was discontinued following the 1959-60 term, and the pupils went to Yates Center. The school term of 1965-66 was the last term as school District No. 8 was held here until 1967. It was under the Yates Center District No.366. Mrs. Ann Ireland and Mrs. Louise Roberts were the last teachers in the Neosho Falls School.

Neosho Falls High School
Woodson County, KS

#75

Hickok School

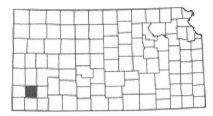

Year Closed: 1953

Location: eight miles east of Ulysses, Grant County

A One School County — There has only been one high school in Grant County. The last country school to close housed all eight grades in the village of Hickok seven miles to the east of Ulysses. It was located along the railroad. The building still stands and is used as a home today (2018).

Grant County was organized in 1887, and the town of Ulysses became the county seat. Both were named after the former president. Grant County was home to many "booms and busts." Breaking up the prairieland, homesteaders planted wheat seed, changing the landscape forever. The great wheat crops of the late 1920s brought the need for grain storage and shipment. Thus, the elevator at Hickok on the rail spur was the location where the small community was organized in 1928. The severe dust bowl years of 1933 to 1936 dropped the price of land to nearly nothing. Changes in farming technique and the resump-

tion of "normal" annual rainfall of sixteen inches annually gave hope to the return of productive farming by the late 1930s.

The discovery of gas in the county led to the building of the first carbon black plant at Hickok in 1937. This Peerless Company Plant became the county's first gas-related industry. Panhandle Eastern ran a pipeline to connect with the Hugoton field. When it was discovered that the "wet" natural gas in this field produced a superior quality of carbon black, United Production built another plant at Ryus in 1940. It was expanded in 1943, making it the largest such installation in the world.

The county is on top of the world's greatest "ocean" of water known, the Ogallala Aquifer. It was not until 1937 that the first wells going down some 290 feet were able to touch this underground sea. Wells that could pump up to 1,000 gallons a minute were drilled which could irrigate a quarter section of land.

Sugar beet production became an alternative crop in the late 1930s. Following the war, great wheat crops in 1947 and 1948 led to the boom of the grain elevator business. The Sullivan Brothers, who had been prominent in the business since the 1920s, expanded their operations at Hickok, Milepost, and a huge concrete elevator storage operation at Coolidge. George E. Gano and Jess Rixon built an elevator in Hickok in 1928. They built the railroad siding for it at a cost of $1,535. The elevator had its own electric light plant. It had two driveways, two dump pits, and two legs. George E. Gano sold his interest in his three Gano elevators to Bunge Corporation in 1947. This elevator burned in 1948. The Barton Construction Company built a new concrete elevator with a capacity of 200,000 bushels for Bunge Corporation shortly after the old elevator burned.

Maxine Rixon Simmons, the daughter of Jess and Della Rixon wrote the following story:

Something else occurred in the community of Hickok which is of historical interest. Shortly before the school was to open in the fall of 1928, there appeared, a mile and a half west of Hickok, a school house. Overnight 'Old Town School,' yes, the frame schoolhouse which had been located in Old Ulysses had been moved to this location. No one would admit who moved it, but it was so nice to have the schoolhouse in which to start school in September 1928. Because of its original location, it became known as 'Old Town School, District No.1, Hickok. Many students attended there. The first teacher was Mrs. Elva Johnson, for two years, then C.W. 'Preacher' Hampton one year, Vern Johnson for two, then Dan Ray for two years, and in 1935, I graduated from the 8th grade. Shortly after we graduated the new brick building was built, which still stands in the same location, but now is a dwelling.

The original schoolhouse was purchased by Guy Zongker and moved to Ulysses to become a garage. The property was purchased by my parents in 1944 when they moved to town, and would you believe that 'Old Town School' is still being used today? It is my mother's garage—very little has been done to change it either on the inside or outside. Not many people can say that they own the building in which they went to grade school, but I can.

Last Class — The elevators and the carbon black plant brought workers to the Hickok area and supplied a steady number of children for the Hickok school. With consolidation of the one room schools and the encouragement of the state to eliminate the country schools, the school was closed in May 1953 and the students were transported to Ulysses.

Carol Kennedy Sterling ('53) graduated from the eighth grade from Hickok with three in her class in 1953. This was the year that the school closed. Her family lived one-half mile south of the school on a farm. Her father was a mechanic in town, and her grandmother ran the local café. Her parents always drove her to and from school. The children took their lunches every day. There were never more than fifteen students in the school during these later years. Her father, Lester Kennedy, was on the school board and helped build the new brick school in 1935.

The teachers were mostly older women who only taught for a few years and then moved on to other teaching positions. Each grade level would be called to the teacher's desk to get their assignments and individual instruction. Some of these teachers were Earline Endicott, Arlene Young, and Ruth Hampton.

The school had a piano for music and individual desks for the students. There was a small library and a stage where the Christmas programs were held.

Math and spelling contests were held with the other one-room school in the county. They also had track meets in the spring when all of these outlying one-room schools brought students to Ulysses to have a field-day and competition at the high school track and football field.

The school was two-story structure. On the lower level basement, one half was occupied by the furnace. The other half was often used for roller skating during a rare Kansas rain and in colder winter months.

A pictorial history of the Hickok school shows eighty-six students in the eighth grade posing in front the school in 1949. There is no record of the numerous eighth grade graduates from the Hickok school. The building still stands and is presently a residence.

Carol Sterling ('53) said, "I believe we were very well prepared for high school coming from the Hickok School. I still own three quarters of land where wheat and milo are the primary crops. I raised four children with three living in Arkansas and one in Ardmore, Oklahoma."

Author Note—As a sidebar to this story, when I mentioned that I was a veterinarian from Iowa, Carol remarked, "I know a veterinarian from Iowa. His last name is Woodbridge but he now lives in Ardmore, Oklahoma, and is married to my daughter."

This same son-in-law veterinarian, Rick Woodbridge, and I were classmates at veterinary school at Kansas State University in the early 1970s. What a serendipitous encounter.

#76

Utica Rural High School

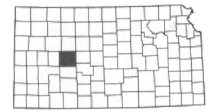

Mascot: Dragon

Colors: Kelly Green and White

Year closed: 2005

Location: town of Utica, northwest corner of Ness County

School History — The first school in Utica was a subscription school and a fee was charged to those who wanted to attend. The one-room frame house east of Utica, later known as the Ramser House, served as the school building. The teachers were Mr. Sherry and later Mrs. Carpenter. She stepped down to serve as a railroad depot agent as she was one of the few in the community who was qualified.

In 1888, a frame building was constructed on the same location as the present grade school building. It was a two-story building, 24' by 52' in size. Only the first story was used for the school. The upper story was the meeting place for the lodge, church, and other community activities. Later, all of it was used for the school.

In 1920 and 1921, the frame building was replaced by a brick one that consisted of four large rooms plus a classroom, a store room, a library, and two stairways. The building was constructed by Butler, and it was considered a nice building for this time.

The high school was built in 1922 and 1923. Mr. Bliss was the contractor. The outstanding feature of the building was the gymnasium. It was the largest gymnasium and had the largest seating capacity of any school building in this part of the state. Due to the facilities, Western Kansas Educational Association events—such as scholarship contests, musical festivals, and basketball tournaments—were held at Utica. The school hosted invitational tournaments with as many as sixteen teams.

Students at the high school were offered class choices from 35.5 units in the curriculum. A large-capacity activity bus provided transportation for the students to places such as the state fair where the thirty-piece band performed each year, though there were never any school buses that picked up the rural children for the school district. Three houses were purchased for teachers who sometimes had difficulty finding housing.

Remembering Utica

As many as 700 former students have attended the school reunions, held every five years. Although Utica High School was one of the smallest schools in Ness County, it offered many advantages that larger schools could not provide. Per the graduates, each student received more personal guidance from the counselor and instructors than could be provided in larger schools.

There was quite a distinction in the school when there were five sets of twins; four sets of girls and one set of boys. One set of those twins were the Jacka girls, Donita and Wanita, who attended country school through the sixth grade. They came to Utica from twelve miles out in the country when their older sister Kay got her driver's license and could bring them all into town. Their class of 1964 had twelve girls and one boy, and they had all been together since the sixth grade. That class of girls was undefeated in basketball their senior year. Donita said, "I never learned as much in my life as I did in those six years at Sunnyside country school."

A sign in the school read:

The Mission of Utica High School is to produce students who display the attitudes, competence and knowledge to become productive adults.

Student Stories

A rich heritage of Utica was recalled by Roy Thornburg ('55):

My grandfather came to this area in 1885 from Winchester, Kansas, on a hunting expedition. He built a sod house and bummed around the area for a short time. He went to Wyoming and became a section foreman for the Missouri Pacific Railroad. He came back in 1903 and started a ranch and raised Angus cattle. This ranch and the Angus continue to this day (2018). My father Francis Thornburg ('29) and Uncle Howard Thornburg ('29) and three sons, Lance ('82), Marlin ('84), and Rodd ('87) were all graduates of Utica High School.

I graduated from Ft. Hays State University, as did all three of my sons. We used our Utica education and background in our business endeavors. We all had been in 4-H and learned how to speak, run a meeting, and many aspects of agriculture. I had gone to country school at Smokey Hill Vale #18 in Gove County. I remember the day when the Jacka twins were born as they were our neighbors. I came to high school in Utica and became part of the marching band. I played the cornet. We marched at Ft. Hays, Dodge City, and at the state fair in Hutchinson. We got to see Roy Rogers, which was a neat experience, in the 50s. My wife, Ailene O'Toole Thornburg, taught school in Utica for twenty-five years.

My degree at Ft. Hays was in agriculture. I used this in my business for fifty-eight years as I ran a bulldozer to supplement the farming operation. I was fortunate to be on the Goodland Vo-tech board and used my industrial arts and welding knowledge to contribute on this board for many years.

Our senior trip was to the Lake of the Ozarks. My parents drove one of the cars and we spent a week boating. There were fifteen in my class in 1955, ten boys and five girls. The senior trip was such a great experience as this class bonded and has had a lifetime of memories.

Dennis Atwell ('67) shared his memories:

We did not have a vocational agriculture department, but the industrial arts training was exceptional with Mr. Redimer as the teacher. We added the shop and music rooms onto the school during my time. I was very active in 4-H and was involved in swine production. My Utica training in leadership and industrial arts provided me well at Kansas State University with my Agriculture major. Our families have been great supporters of community and the farming area of Ness County. My dad, Merritt Atwell ('39), served on the school board for twenty-seven years and became the head of the Kansas Small Schools of Quality organization, which advocated for the school in smaller communities. The area schools like Ransom, Healy, Weskan, Tri-Plains, Jennings, Golden Plains, and Bazine all had wealth with oil valuation and the bigger schools from cities in eastern Kansas wanted part of the tax valuation from the oil in production across rural Kansas.

My younger brother, Brian Atwell ('79) was paralyzed from the chest down in a tragic pickup accident on the way to school on a country road. My mother, Thelma Stutz Atwell ('40), a teacher at Utica, was following one mile behind and made the call for an ambulance. It was nine days before graduation. He was the star athlete in school in cross country and the center on the basketball team. He was six-foot-three and quite a born leader. He spent nearly five months in intensive care and hospitals. The accident rallied the community in support for the family and all of the school activities. He went to Barton County Junior College for three years and then Ft. Hays State University for three years to graduate. He became a leader and advocate for the Americans with Disabilities. Brian managed a company called LINK (Living Independently Northwest Kansas). Going to Utica to school gave him an ability to manage his handicap and contribute to others with disabilities for the rest of his life.

Closing the School — A total of 854 graduated from Utica High School from 1915 until the school closed in 2005. In eighty-six years, there was quite a wide range of surnames of the graduates. Some of the most numerous were Johnson-18, Babcock-16, Och-13, Atwell-12, Martin-11, Basinger-11, Jones-10, Sturtz-10, McCartee-9, Holmes-9, Wheatcroft-9, Mitten-9, North-8, Jacka-8, McBee-8, and Crabtree-8.

The largest graduating class was twenty-three in 1961. The last graduating class in 2005 had five graduates with Dillon Schwindt (alphabetically) the last graduate of Utica High School.

Utica High School
Ness County, KS

#77

Delphos Rural High School

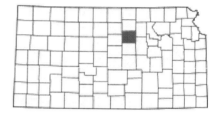

Mascot: Maroons

Colors: Maroon and Gold

Year Closed: 1966

Location: town of Delphos, northern Ottawa County

Area History — Delphos was founded in 1867 by Levi and Dan Yockey. The two brothers moved to the area from Delphos, Ohio, and named the community after their hometown. They, like many settlers, came to this area for a fresh start after the Civil War.

Recorded history relates that the town was relatively quiet in the late 1860s. Indian raids, kidnappings, droughts, blizzards, and grasshoppers were all plagues that affected the earliest homesteaders and farmers.

Schools in Delphos date back to a log cabin just west of town on Yockey Creek. This cabin also served as a church and was only used as a school from 1870-1872. In 1873, a building was erected on Custer Street at a cost of $2,100. Only a year later, during a blizzard, it burned to the ground. A new building for all grades was soon built with the first graduating class in 1883 of seven women graduates. The brick school building was built in 1915 and an addition was added in 1935.

The city auditorium was used for all-school plays, basketball, and graduation ceremonies. It was the only building in town with a gym-sized floor and a stage.

The last "new" school was built on the north edge of town and was ready for classes in 1952. The final graduating class was in 1966 as forced consolidation of Kansas schools was legislated. USD 239 was then formed, with Minneapolis, seventeen miles away, getting the high school. For several years, as a possible time of appeasement in Ottawa County, all of the freshmen went to the former Delphos School and the upper three grades went to Minneapolis.

Athletics

The sports team was always known as the Delphos Maroons. By one account of a former student, Dana Hauck ('67), "It would not be politically correct in this day and age, but although it was never to my knowledge displayed as a mascot, the maroon was a term for a runaway Negro slave. Accordingly, the school colors were maroon and gold."

It becomes apparent that even though education and the amount of knowledge increased a lot over the course of time, young people in these rural areas didn't change all that much. They worked and studied hard, most grew up on the farm or had farm jobs, they played and competed hard in sports, participated in every club and activity, and were involved in all the usual pranks that young wild students like to pull.

Rites of Passage

Freshman initiation in Delphos was a rite of passage. The following account by Dana Hauck ('67) describes what many freshmen experienced during their first week of high school:

Freshman initiation carried on in the same manner until the school closed as far as I know. It would be described as outright unlawful hazing today, but in my opinion, after it was over, if you hadn't experienced it you had missed out on a lot of bonding together and fun. During initiation week, the seniors would split up and go pick up three or four freshman in each car. They would throw us in the trunk of the car together, drive around town, and then head out into the country several miles, all the time making U-turns and backing up and going in different directions making sure we were disoriented. Then they opened the trunk and let us out to find our way back to town. In my mind anyway, it was somewhat more difficult because there were no mercury vapor lights at every farmstead and almost no towers with flashing lights. But most of us knowing the country fairly well, would eventually recognize a landmark or someone's house and get headed the right direction back towards town. There was a different theme all five days of initiation week. On one day, which I recall was the least enjoyable at the time, both boys and girls had to go to their respective bathrooms, strip down from their clothes, and wear an empty gunny sack that had contained oats from Clarence Cain's seed house with a hole cut out for the head and arms. Talk about itching!

This account of initiation was so colorful that the complete story deserves retelling just for the history of the time:

Another day, we were all assigned a comic strip character we had to dress as. I remember I was Brenda Star and had to wear a short tight skirt with high heels and a red wig. I was thankful that I didn't draw what one of my fellow classmates did, Baby Huey! He spent the entire day at school wearing nothing but a large diaper made out of a tea towel or part of a sheet and carried a baby bottle which he had to suck on when commanded by a senior. On Friday, they tied us all in a line with a long heavy rope and then tied it onto the back of a senior's car and led us downtown and around the square where we knelt down to the seniors at each corner with nearly everybody in town parked around the square honking their horns and clapping. Back at the high school we went through a paddling line and walked through a deep tub of molasses followed by a tub of chicken feathers. This was followed by a watermelon feed and we were finally full-fledged students of DRHS.

A couple of more stories from this legendary Delphos area cattleman, Hauck, definitely shows liability was not much of a concern in the 1960s:

The year I was a freshman in the fall of 1963, and barely turning fourteen years old, I was allowed to pull the entire student body on two hay racks hooked in tandem behind my dad's John Deere 4020 for the annual FFA hay ride. It was out to Chaney's pond about five and a half miles from town. By the time I was a junior, there was an all-high school picnic at the Ottawa county state lake some twenty-three miles away, northeast of Bennington. Donnie Tasker and I, along with our girlfriends, Janet and Marcia, rode in the seat of Don-

nie's dad's single axle, sixteen-foot bed grain truck with only grain sides (no stock racks) while the entire student body rode in the back. The superintendent and teachers followed with the food.

A final story was about the annual Armistice Day game with the school's most bitter rival, Glasco, fourteen miles to the northwest.

The game was on the real day now known as Veteran's day, of November 11, and not on a Monday for the convenience of a three-day weekend. The game was always held at noon on that day. Of course, in that time probably the majority of men in the community had served in the military in either WWII or Korea and the American Legion had a huge membership, their own building, and was very active. On Armistice Day evening, they always held the Legion Carnival. There were several kinds of games of chance—a cake walk, games set up in the city auditorium, and a Ferris wheel and merry-go-round set up in the street. There were still two pool halls on the square and plenty of cereal malt beverages were consumed.

Delphos High School
Ottawa County, KS

#78

Bluff City High School

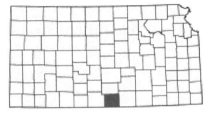

Mascot: Tigers

Colors: Purple and Gold

Year Closed: 1967

Location: southern Harper County, five miles from the Oklahoma border

The following was from the yearbook of the 1935 high school annual provided by the family of Charlie Jelinek:

In 1890 while our grade school has always been efficient about a need of a higher education it was apparent at an early period in the history of the town.

Area History — James Glover, the first settler of the area, noticed that some of the best citizens moved away to give their children the benefit of a higher learning.

They seldom came back, and the thought came to him, "Why not a Township High School?"

Through his connections with the Alliance Political Party, Rep. Geo. Coulson prepared a bill to authorize Stohrville Township to establish and maintain a high school and did not apply to any other township in the state of Kansas. Two years later, the law went statewide.

Thus, James Glover can rightfully be called the "Father of Stohrville Township High School."

High School — In 1925, the splendid high school was established. The founders of Bluff City dreamed of a population of 10,000. It did rise to about 1,000. Then the railroad shops and roundhouse moved to Anthony and the opening of the Cherokee Strip caused Bluff City to lose a large portion of the population. A great part of the business section was destroyed by fire.

Athletics & Activities — The 1959 Football team was the 86 League Champion. This was a league made up of eight schools: Bluff City, Sharon, Argonia, Grenola, Zenda, Milton, and Milan. The 8 stood for eight-man and the 6 stood for six-man football. The league had originally been made up of these schools which played six-man football. In 1957 they all switched to playing eight-man football, thus the 86 League.

Ben Horyna ('59), a member of that championship team, recalled, "Our coach was Herb Ewing. He coached football, basketball, and track for the boys and basketball for the girls. He taught social studies and physical education." Ben went on to become a teacher-coach and counselor in Kansas high schools for forty-one years.

Music included band, glee club, and choir. Band was discontinued in 1957 as there was no teacher available.

Another graduate, Cynthia Misak Evinger ('66), recalled that nearly everyone went to college. "Our educational background may have had some limitations due to curricular limitations, but we did fine in college and nearly everyone graduated."

Education did seem to be a prominent vocation as Bluff City graduates went on to teach at Wichita State University, University of Iowa, and the University of New Mexico.

School Closing—The high school closed in May 1967. Most of the students went on the attend high school in Anthony. For the next five years at Anthony High School, the valedictorian and salutatorian were all from Bluff City. That first year at Anthony High School, three of the starters on the basketball team were from Bluff City. This small high school had some excellent students as well as athletes.

The first graduating class was in 1926 with three graduates. The final graduating class was in 1967 and with four graduates. Myrl Misak (alphabetically) was the last to receive a diploma from Bluff City High School. A total of 398 graduated in forty-two years, from 1926-1967. The largest classes were in 1935 and 1937 with sixteen graduates each year. The most numerous surnames of these graduates were Jelinek-20, Cooper-18, Baker-13, Misak-13, Mayo-10, Scheel-10, Vardy-7, Anton-6, Stubbe-6, Shellhammer-5, and Ziegler-5.

#79
Windom Rural High School

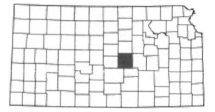

Mascot: Tigers

Colors: Orange and Black

Year Closed: 1966

Location: town of Windom, west-central McPherson County

Area History—The town of Windom was located along the Santa Fe Railroad. There was passenger service to McPherson daily. One could ride to Galva for 10 cents to go to visit or to a ballgame in daytime but had to walk back home in the evening.

The train that ran from Florence to Ellinwood was called the Doodle Bug. There were "turn tables" in those towns so the Doodle Bug would come from the east in the morning and from the west in the afternoon and deliver mail from both directions daily. This allowed for twice daily mail delivery.

The "Swedes" lived mainly south of the tracks and farmed in that vicinity. The rest of the farmers in the surrounding countryside were mostly from German and English backgrounds.

Windom School

Windom School — An account written in 1914 by Roy Myers for Professor D.C. Steele catches the earliest school experience in Windom. It is titled, "The Progress of the Windom School":

More than thirty years ago, even at a time when the site of our pleasant little town was still a natural prairie, the same rugged spirit of progress which bade the pioneers come to the prairie fastness aid to them "You must educate your children."

These people banded together and built, not on the present site of the Windom school but near the corner, one fourth mile south of it . . .

Two years later, when the first signs were seen of the railroad, and the men who were to found Windom, or Laura, as it was then called, had wakened to their possibilities, beneath the roof of their first school house . . .

Then the patrons of the school, who ever watched its progress said "Such effort needs compensation. Truly they want to learn and they shall have the opportunity." They met in a triumphant meeting and arranged to erect a modern building. During the spring and fall of 1911, the new building was erected. In fact, the people seemed glad to invest in this new project, for $7,500. The building arose, modern in every detail, being composed of four large rooms, splendidly heated and lighted, besides cloak rooms, halls, etc.

Now began the new era of the Windom school. Three teachers were hired instead of two. The grammar school was divided into two sections under the care of two competent teachers. The entire high school, was composed of 25 students, seven of which it is sad to say did not finish the year's work. Placed upon this new basis, the advance of the school was rapid. Although a full year's work was done in a period of eight months, yet it was not an accredited high school.

During this first year, athletics was fostered and the basketball boys especially fought many mighty battles.

The second year of the new era began with a new corps of equally competent teachers composed of four members, two of which now gave their whole-souled efforts to the progress of the eighth grade and the High School. The efficiency of the school was now so recognized that simply it was enough to promote its students from eighth grade to the high school. This so linked the school together that not one of those who completed the eighth grade had failed to enter high school. The good backers of the school now bought several splendid books and botany paraphernalia.

25 members had now sought admission into the progressive High School, all but two which finished, leaving a splendid record. One morning the professor stood before the students and read from a letter as follows, "Windom High School is credited by the State University as one of the Third Class." Great joy this brought to the students.

Athletics took on a new form, tennis being the major game. Very soon the players proved that they could play with the best of them.

On the first of September 1913, the present year began with a total enrollment of 96 students, 35 of whom were in the high school . . . Windom High school had been credited as one of the Second Class-truly a remarkable achievement. At the beginning of the school year the school was presented by the proper officials with an efficient physics laboratory equipment, indeed a great aid to the students . . .

Far from the south have come many students with the sunny smiles of old Sweden. From the northern hills students have emerged from their native fastness. Yet any doubting the ability of the teachers and students or the good will of the school supporters are invited to pay them a visit. Nothing so pleases the occupants of the school as to be blest with a visit.

Windom High School was fed students from the country schools. Every eighth-grade student would go into the county seat and take the county tests to be able to advance to high school. Each May there would be a parade in McPherson with the eighth-grade graduates riding on a parade float as the communities would gather to celebrate their graduation.

Another account of the school was written by Leona Spear Ellwood ('22), for the last edition of the school yearbook, the 1966 *Tiger*.

We started as the Tigers back in 1909 with "The Orange and the Black." We adapted our colors and mascot from the old Princeton song.

We were upstairs in the old frame building, but by 1913, the first class had graduated and there was a new building—a neat four room brick structure with a tile room and central heating. Steam heat! More and more our farmers were buying cars and there were air planes. The high school occupied the two west rooms. There were only two teachers, but students were taught Algebra, Geometry, Latin, Science, Hamlet and even Russian Literature.

In 1918, it was decided that we must have a gym, and a new brick gymnasium was built . . .

By 1923, we were ready for football. Our gear and helmets were the puniest and the coach had to fill in a play, but it was eleven-man and we had Thanksgiving games. We were real "Up Town."

Now there was talk that others should be brought into our District so that more could take advantage of high school education. After much debate and decision, our friends on the north and our Swedish friends to the south united with Windom to become Windom Rural High School.

Too many injuries made football dispensable, so all emphasis in sports was directed to basketball for both boys and girls. In the thirties, we had girls who played with the great 'Babe' Didrikson. Alberta (Williams) Hood played on a pro-team. Our emphasis until the forties, had been on sports. Now music's place in our curriculum became important. Under the direction of Mrs. Uarda Thompson with her imaginations, inspiration and determination, our local vocal groups and soloists became tops in our league and district.

In the later forties, we started playing football again. This was six-man football, a new game for small schools.

Our enrollment had been as high as 91 and as low as 27. Our faculty had grown from one to 10.

Our graduates have served in every branch of their country's service all over the world. Our girl graduates have served in the WAVES and Army Nurse Corps....

We have placed outstanding graduates in the fields of business and education. Our graduates, with their mid-western resourcefulness, are scattered from the Atlantic to the Pacific.

Yes, we even spawned a Rhodes Scholar, J. Dennis Andes, Class of 1929.

Athletics & Traditions — November 8, 1956 was a record day for Windom High School as they hosted Kanopolis for the first eight-man football game to be played in Kansas. "And Kanopolis was good," said Gene Reinecker, a teacher and coach at that time. The cars were lined up a half mile south of town trying to get into the game.

The first bus for the district was an old army vehicle with planks on concrete blocks for the students to sit on.

The rivals for Windom were Little River, Marquette, Galva, and Inman. Senior trips were always a highlight and brought many memories for the students. Some of those trips were to Kentucky and Tennessee.

The 1947 senior class went to Lincoln, Nebraska where the principal, as chaperone, went to visit friends and family on the side. The 1948 senior class rode in a grain truck to Mexico by way of Brownsville, Texas. The girls stayed in motels and the boys stayed in the truck. The 1950 and 1951 trips were chaperoned by the Burkholders. They told the kids that to eat shrimp properly you had to eat the whole shrimp, tail and all! The 1957 senior class of three went to New Orleans. The 1958 class went to St. Louis and south. They saw *South Pacific* on stage, which was a treat as they had performed it as a junior play under the direction of Mrs. Uarda Thompson.

Girls basketball was dropped as a sport as there was a medical doctor on the State Board of Education that said that basketball might cause problems with the reproductive system. It was later revived, but they played the six-on-six, half-court game. A great player was Alberta Williams who later played for the Wichita Thurstons basketball team. She was an all-American and was recognized as the best center at a Dallas invitational tournament with the Wichita team.

Bob German ('51) later coached at one of the rival schools of Marquette. On his first game back in Windom as an opposing coach, someone turned loose two dozen pigeons in the gymnasium at half time. No one has confessed to this day.

Mrs. Uarda Thompson was a legendary music teacher. She also taught in the neighboring country schools. She had a saying that, "Not everyone is a soloist, but everyone can sing." The musicals all had wonderful costumes. Some of the musicals she produced were *South Pacific*, *Guys and Dolls*, and *Oklahoma*. The students won many "superior" ratings at music festivals.

The boys basketball team took a road trip to Chester, Nebraska, which was the home of eight-man football. The coach, Gene Reinecker, had arranged a home and away series with their team. They played the game in an old opera house in Carlton, Nebraska.

Coach Reinecker told the principal that if the district would provide the equipment, he and the shop class would wire the school with a public address system. When the project was completed, he hurried to Principal Bob Burkholder's office to report that the system was ready. Only they both heard over the intercom, coming from the shop the kids playing with the system, saying, "Now hear this, now hear this. All principals eat shit!" Coach rushed back to the shop and said, "Now hear this. All principals eat shit!" The students didn't look up, but there were many subdued grins from both the coach and the students.

School Closing — The high school closed in 1966 with a graduating class of ten. The last graduate was Cynthia Williams (alphabetically). The largest class was twenty-two in 1935.

A total of 612 graduated in the fifty-four years from 1913-1966. The most common surnames of the graduates suggest some of the Swedish heritage of the area. Among the graduates were Peterson-24, Anderson-16, Raleigh-13, Nelsons-11, Swenson-10, Neel-10, Carlson-10, Geiman-9, Johnson-9, Lindholm-9, Pearson-8, Bengston-8, and Elwood-8. The name Meyers had 32 graduates from Windom High School.

#80

Marienthal Grade School - St. Mary

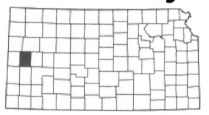

Mascot: Warriors

Colors: Maroon and White

Year Closed: 1997

Location: town of Marienthal, eastern Wichita County

Wichita County is one of only five counties in Kansas that never had a high school close. Located in a very low-population area, the centrally located county seat of Leoti serves all high school students in the county.

Marienthal School, in 1997, was the last rural elementary school in the county to close.

History of Marienthal — The town's rich history started as early as 1890 with the westward movement into Wichita County. Land under the Homestead Act at $4.50 per acre was less expensive than in the counties east such as Rush and Ellis. German-Russian immigrants came further west, settling along the Missouri-Pacific Railroad at town sites of Coronado and Halcyon. By 1892, twenty-six families had settled in the vicinity of what would become Marienthal.

Before long, the question of building a Catholic church arose and fostered rivalry between the towns of Coronado (five miles west) and Halcyon (three miles east of Marienthal). The problem was solved by a compromise which suggested that a new town be founded about midway between the two rival towns. Marienthal, named after a town in Russia where many of the settlers originally lived, became the new town. It took shape in the spring of 1893 when the first church was built.

Education — The school began in 1910 in the remodeled church rectory. The first teacher was Pearl Metheney. He was followed by Fred Metheney in 1911. With the school board in agreement, Father Edward sought Sisters (nuns) to be teachers. However, there seemed to be none available. By 1914, through an appeal to the Bishop in the city of Wichita, Sisters were sent to Marienthal.

By 1930 the little school in Marienthal was inadequate to house the number of children who attended regularly. The local school board was neither willing nor in a position to enlarge the school since more than half of the children came from other districts. It was finally agreed that the parish should pay for the new school to be built on church grounds. By 1936, the population of the parish rose to 465. The need for a new school to replace the two old, inadequate buildings had long been apparent. Hence, a meeting was held February 19, 1958 and a resolution was drawn up to build. The first classes were held in the fall of 1959. The school had four classrooms, a spacious auditorium-gymnasium, and a kitchen off the gymnasium. Bishop John B Franz, D.D. dedicated the new school building October 15 of the same year. Three years later in 1962, the debt was paid in full and $18,000 was put on loan to the diocese.

Most of the eighth-grade graduates from St. Mary School would go to high school in Leoti.

Student Stories — For the outlying elementary school children, going into the larger high school in the bigger town could be a terrifying experience. One such experience was documented by Phyllis Rowland, in an article titled, "The Crazy Hazing Days of 1946."

The note was given to all freshman that day-the first Thursday of the new school year, September 6, 1946. I trembled as I read: 'Heed our decree, freshman, or suffer the consequences! Tomorrow, freshman boys will wear women's skirts and blouses to school. Girls will wear men's overalls.

All garments must be worn backwards. All freshmen must hang a string of onions around their necks. Everyone must walk to school, from the First State Bank at the main intersection, down Broadway, all the way to the high school. Freshmen initiation will formally take place at 3 p.m. in the gymnasium.

The program at the Friday afternoon assembly was "entertainment" by freshmen who were to perform in whatever was demanded by upperclassmen. A group of lowly freshmen were required to scrub, with a toothbrush, a strip all the way across the gym floor. When my turn came, I was told to stand at center stage and crow like a rooster. Not such a difficult request, but to me it only emphasized my standing as a green country kid, My weak response was more of a peep than a crow.

For eight years I had loved school, but this—my first year of town school—was a gigantic many-eyed monster, with all eyes staring at me.

The initiation ensued and the students all survived. This just seemed to be the rite of passage and the faculty and administration played along like it was a time honored ritual. There did not seem to be a worry about the scared little freshman regardless if they came from town or one of the country schools.

Jeff Ritter ('71) share the following story:

The grade school was part of our Catholic Church. It was taught by nuns. The upper elementary grades were considered public school and received state aid. The church leased the school to the public school. We had religion classes for twenty-five minutes early each morning before school hours which was the agreement with the state. My dad Jerome Ritter ('44) graduated eighth grade from Marienthal School. Two of my three siblings did also, with my youngest sister graduating from Leoti after the Marienthal School closed in 1997. We got to play all of the sports and participated against the other grade schools in the area. When entering Leoti High School, I was not overwhelmed by the classes and the much larger numbers of students. My education at the Marienthal grade school was very excellent.

#81

Wilson High School

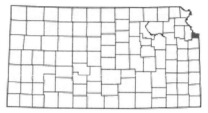

Year Closed: 1925
Location: Wyandotte County

The Smallest County in Kansas—Wyandotte County is known to all Kansans as the smallest area-wise in the state. Nestled along the Missouri River to the north and east, and bordered on the south by the Kaw or Kansas River, it covers only 159 square miles. The county's entire geographic area was not large enough to have been considered adequate under the 1960s state education law to maintain a high school (200 square miles was the minimum).

Wyandotte County was named after the Wyandot Indian tribe. This tribe migrated from Ohio in 1843 to this region along the Missouri River. They assimilated with the Anglos, and many of them were Christianized and became involved in the early organization of the government of the territory. One of these Wyandots was elected the first territorial governor.

Kansas City University was located at 33rd Street and Parallel Avenue. Included on this seventeen-acre campus was Mather College, School of Theology, College of Music, Kansas City Normal School, School of Elocution and Oratory, Kansas City Hahnemann Medical College, and Wilson High School.

Mather College was situated on the university grounds in this Kansas City suburb. It owed its existence to Dr. Samuel Fielding Mather, a descendant of Cotton Mather. About a year before his death, Dr. Mather made a proposition to the board of trustees who were appointed by the general conference of the Methodist Protestant church (different from the Methodist Episcopal and Free Methodists). Mather's proposal was to convey to the board certain valuable tracts of land in the suburbs of Kansas City. The trustees directed that a building or buildings should be erected before October 15, 1897 at a cost not less than $25,000. The offer was accepted on the last day of May 1895, just a few days before Dr. Mather died.

Wyandotte's High School—Wilson High School

occupied a building which was erected in 1907 at the cost of $25,000. It offered six courses of study: classical, philosophical, science (prerequisites for college), English, and a teachers course. A business course was also provided for students not expecting to attend college.

Called Wilson Hall, this first building was occupied by Wilson High School in September 1908. The building had a large room used as a gymnasium in the basement with lockers and bathrooms. The late Mr. W.S. Wilson, for a number of years, was the President of the Board of Trustees and contributed to its erection.

The catalogue for 1910-11 gave the following enrollment: Mather College 30, Wilson High School 149, School of Oratory 198, Normal School 10, Hahnemann Medical College 68, School of Theology 13, those counted twice 23, making a total of 435 as reported in the *The Kansas City Kansan* newspaper on January 30, 1923.

The Kansas City Kansan

Parents contribute to Save Wilson High School; PATRONS GET BEHIND INSTITUTION AND PREVENT CLOSING; KLAN GIVES $200

Wilson High School will continue, school officials announced today following a second meeting of parents last night at the school. Of the $3000 estimated as needed for teacher's salaries, the remainder of the year, a total of $2000 has been pledged. A subscription of $200 was made last night by Wyandotte Klan No. 5, Ku Klux Klan. The money was enclosed in a letter sent to Wilson High School in care of the principal, C.O. Braden. The letter stated the Wyandotte Klan had been informed that the school needed funds, and desired the officials to accept the money in order to further the good work of the school. The money was accepted by the school authorities and parents . . . the committee to discuss the advisability of establishing a new rural high school will meet tonight at the School ... a survey of the seven rural school districts in the northeastern action of Wyandotte County will be made with the purpose of establishing a rural high school according to Miss Olive Thompson, County Superintendent. The districts are Welborn, Nearman, Vance, Hazel Grove, Pomeroy, White Church, and district No. 5 known as Muncie.

The Kansas City Kansan, January 26, 1923

The tax money paid to the school, which had been operating under the Barnes School Law, had been exhausted, and unless the additional money is obtained, the school cannot remain open. The plan will only be a temporary measure for the remainder of this year.

The Kansas City Kansan, September 2, 1923

The University is under the direction of the United Brethren and Methodist Protestant Church . . . Students from the rural district may enroll in the High School free of charge. Students within the city limits of Kansas City will be required to pay a tuition fee of $25 a semester.

The Kansas City Kansan, September 7, 1924

WILSON HIGH WILL ENROLL: Department of Kansas City University to Sign up Tomorrow; Class Work, September 10

Enrollment at the Wilson High school, Thirty-third street and Parallel Avenue, the high school department of the Kansas City University will begin tomorrow and close Tuesday, David L. Megil, principal announced last night. "All Classes will enroll during these two days. About 100 students are expected at the school this year," Megil said. Class work will begin September 10. Megil is the new principal at the school this year. He is a graduate of the University of Kansas.

The preparatory school lasted only one more year. With the passage of the Barnes Law, there was insufficient funding. Welborn Rural High School was located just to the west in the county and had started with one class in 1923 with plans to add one more class each year. Welborn saw a sudden increase in students when Wilson High School closed in May 1925 following graduation.

The Kansas City Kansan, July 5, 1925

WELBORN HIGH BEGINS 4 YEAR TERM

. . . Students going from Wilson to Welborn will be required to take an accrediting examination before entering, as the work done at Wilson this past year was not accredited by the State Board after it had been found out that, "practice" teachers [who] did not have certificates were in charge of some of the classes. This decision of the State Board nullifies all work done during the last year and students going to another school will be required to pass examinations before school is accredited: the new school had been fully accredited by the State Board and all courses necessary for the students to have before entering the universities and colleges will be offered.

Preparations are being made to take care of a hundred students in the High School next year. Most of the classes will be held in the $40,000 building which was put into use this last year, although the old building may be used for some of the work.

"One of the best school cafeterias in the state is maintained at the school," Miss Thompson (county superintendent of schools) said. She added "that this helped the enrollment of the school a good deal, as the students were able to get hot lunches every day."

Only one class list from the spring 1924 graduation was located, and fourteen graduated from Wilson High School that year.

Struggling financially (even accepting money from the Klan), using practice teachers, and the Barnes Law all led to the closing of Wilson High School following graduation in May 1925. Wilson Hall still stands today and is used as an early childhood school.

Wilson High School
Wyandotte County, KS

#82

Gridley Rural High School

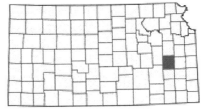

Mascot: Yellowjackets

Colors: Black and Gold

Year Closed: 2003

Location: town of Gridley, southwest corner of Coffey County

A Flint Hills School — In "The History of Gridley" column printed in the *Gridley Light* in December 1967, Norma Birk wrote the following:

> The first school was built by Steve Povenmire and Cornelius Stuckey in 1911. It was a two room brick building built of brick made near Gridley. The bill was paid for by the receipts of a dance held in the school before it was partitioned. The high school was organized in 1912 under the principalship of Morris James. The same building housed both the grade and the three

year high school. In 1913, H.W. Mudge became princi-pal. He and his wife, Bertha, made up the entire high school staff. Bertha Werts and Gertrude Chamberlain made up the grade school staff. Later, a second story was added and the school became a four-year high school in 1915.

The Gridley Rural High school was organized in 1922. Since the enrollment exceeded the capacity of the exist-ing school building, high school was held in the upstairs of Bahr's Hardware for two or three years. One hundred bonds of $500 each were issued in 1921 for construction of the high school. Payment began on January 1, 1934. The final payment of the bonds was on March 26, 1937. A new gymnasium was added in 1954.

The chairman of the committee to promote a new high school was H.P. Monroe. He wrote a column in the *Grid-ley Light* on August 8, 1919, titled Accredited High School:

> It has been pretty generally reported that Gridley will not have an accredited high school this year. I wish to say that the report is without any foundation-not a word of truth in it. Gridley will have an accredited high school and I hope and believe a better one than we have ever had. We have the teachers and all the equipment necessary and are looking forward to a very successful year.

"Build a new high school or lose the students" became the discussion by 1920. The threat was that without ade-quate facilities the boys and girls would go away to an-other school. The Rural High School board let the con-tract for the new building on June 12, 1922, to T.L. Zollars of Independence, Kansas. The ground breaking was on June 15 and the expected finish date was October

1, 1922 (106 days later). The heating, plumbing and wir-ing contract was let on August 23, 1922.

High school classes were not to start until the expected completion date of October 1. The school board had tak-en precautions by having several buildings to rent on a temporary basis and proceeded with school work. The teachers were already hired and were to soon take up their duties. The following was reported in the *Gridley Light* on August 18:

> The teachers hired are the best to be had and it is a positive fact that the pupils of the new school will re-ceive the proper instruction. These teachers were picked from a list of seventy-five applicants, and only those of the best recommendation were considered.

The school year did start on October 2, 1922. Because the school building was not finished, the classes began over Henry Bahr's store with fifty-six students. Students were asked to bring their grade cards and any text books that the student was willing to sell. Courses offered that fall were English, Latin, science, history, civil govern-ment, physiology, psychology, and agriculture.

A box supper was held in mid-October to raise money for athletics. The boys showed an interest in football as more than twenty reported for practice. The girls wanted to show what a girls basketball team could do as soon as they could find a place to play.

An outside speaker, Professor Hanson, addressed the student body in late October 1922. He had been in China since 1903 and gave an interesting account of conditions in that country as reported in the *Gridley Light* on No-vember 2, 1922:

> He showed how the Chinese had obtained a dominant position in the Dutch East Indies, and cited facts pre-

dicting their leading position in the future. He told of the splendid opportunities for men and women to become leaders in shaping Chinese future. His speech was much appreciated by the pupils.

The November 10, 1922 *Gridley Light* featured a headline—significant of the time—titled "The Armistice."

> Saturday, November 11, is the Fourth Anniversary of the signing of the Armistice, when the implements of destruction were silenced in November, 1918. Sacred to every American and to every Kansan is that memorable document which said to the nations of the world that law takes precedence over the reign of force, and that the barbarian and savagery of the ages before civilization shall have no place in the modern world. The Governor of the Great State of Kansas has set apart Saturday November 11, 1922 as a state holiday for fitting observance and proper celebration

> Owing to the fact that the farmers do most of their trading on Saturday, the Gridley stores will be unable to close. All work will cease however, at eleven o'clock a.m., for five minutes in observance of the great moment when the guns ceased to thunder on the battlefields of France. The banks will both be close during the entire day.

The New High School—The new gymnasium was not completed until January 1923. A basketball schedule and practice commenced for the rest of the winter months. By February 1923, the school board decided to lengthen the school day, closing at 4 p.m., beginning February 12. This was to be done on account of starting the high school late in the fall.

On May 29, 1923, a large crowd was on hand for the first commencement at the new high school with eight graduates. John Povenmire ('23) was the valedictorian and Clara Kaufman ('23) was the salutatorian. The speaker urged the class to continue with their education to fit themselves for modern problems in this age of speed. The remarks were indeed timely and appropriate.

By the fall of 1925, enrollment reached sixty-five pupils. A high school orchestra was organized that fall with Miss McDaniel as the instructor. She had fifteen members in the orchestra the first year. Proceeds from the one-act play, *A Can of Suspension*, followed by a box supper, raised $45 to pay for a set of drums and straps that had been purchased for the school.

The final bonds were paid off on January 1, 1937. A community celebration was held for the burning of the last bonds. That same year, a Manual Training department was established with twenty-two boys enrolled. The first-year boys learned the use of different tools and making small articles. They worked the lathe and turned out lamps, candlesticks, and smoking stands. Many made small cedar chests. The second-year class made large walnut chests and refinished furniture brought from home.

Miss Ruth Mudge (her brother owned the grocery store in town) had come to Gridley to teach Domestic Art and Science in 1925. She would continue and also teach art and history in 1927. By 1929 she was named principal. She had advanced degrees from the University of Chicago and the University of Iowa.

The home economics department was led by Mudge in the 1920s and 1930s. In addition to advanced sewing, there was study of the home and family relationships, household expenditures, and etiquette. Students in the foods class demonstrated their culinary ability each day by serving well balanced and appetizing hot lunches for the whole school. This program was started in 1933 by Mudge and her students. The charge was ten cents. This was only an estimate as it was determined that, if necessary, the charge might increase to twelve or thirteen cents. Those who brought produce, eggs, and other commodities from home would have their costs for the lunch reduced. The freshman girls would do the dishes on a one-week rotation schedule. They would receive their meals that week free. The department was the only one in the county to function so efficiently. By the end of the first year, the average for lunch was thirty students. The enrollment that year was seventy-eight students.

School Traditions & Athletics — In 1932 and 1933, the juniors cooperated and postponed the buying of class rings. The gold market had escalated to the point that the cost was prohibitive.

In the fall of 1933, a boys physical training class was introduced to replace football for one year. The boys were divided into groups and played different games as the season changed, from soccer, kittenball, touch football, basketball, and track. Boxing gloves were purchased and each boy had the chance to learn the rudiments of boxing. It was a one-year experiment for boys physical education.

By 1935, a 12-6 victory over Burlington was the highlight of the football season. Burlington played LeRoy to a scoreless tie and Gridley defeated LeRoy 19-0. The scores in Burlington games prior to that were mostly favorable for Gridley.

In 1935, six students made the All-State Band. They were Agnes Romary, Victor Beavers, Cloyce Johnson, Cecile Holton, Eileen Newland, and Jackie Dewitt.

Elmer Wells ('31) was an outstanding athlete. He went on to Pittsburg State and became an all-conference tackle on the football team. He graduated with a degree in physical education. In 1937, he brought his highly-touted Randolph basketball team back to Gridley to play the Yellow Jackets. He knew that Gridley usually had one of the best teams in this part of the state. Elmer "Burley" Wells presented a problem of loyalty for the locals as he was an old friend to many. The school won out in the long run and also on the score board with a 32-21 victory for Gridley.

From a *Gridley Light* advertisement, January 14, 1937, for the Mudge Market:

ORANGES 2 Dozen, medium size 25¢
HEAD LETTUCE per head 5¢
BANANAS 6 pounds 25¢
GRAPEFRUIT per dozen 25¢
SPUDS (Egg McClure) per peck 39¢
CABBAGE per pound 3¢

Eleven-man football was played until the 1950s. At that time eight-man football became necessary for the fall sport because of lack of boys. Baseball was played until 1959. Girls basketball was played into the 1930s. With the mandatory inclusion of Title 9 legislation, girls basketball was started again in the 1970s.

The new field house with a large industrial arts facility and remodeled home economics rooms was completed in 1956. The Home Economics department had three complete kitchens with a range, a refrigerator, and all the cooking utensils for teaching. A separate kitchen was provided to prepare the long-standing hot lunch program at the school. There were twelve sewing machines and tables for teaching. Industrial Arts education began in 1955 with the anticipation of the new facility.

Busing was started in 1952 with the buses owned by Willis Beyer. His business was the Beyer Motors Company. He hired the bus drivers, which was a great savings for the school district. He was an ardent supporter of the schools and the community. He was credited and instrumental in the paving of the streets in Gridley and bringing water into the town. He had attended the University of Kansas and refinished cars at his business. Three of his boys followed him in his business and all were graduates of Gridley High School.

The biggest rival was Burlington, the much larger high school in the county seat town. The Gridley Yellowjackets made it to the 1952 Class B State Basketball Tournament by defeating Hope, 59-55, in overtime at the regional finals. The season came to an end by losing the first game to Powhatton, 58-50, in the enormous sports arena in Hutchinson.

Senior trips were held annually. In 1954, the school bus journeyed to Colorado Springs for a five-day trip with twenty seniors and Superintendent Musick as sponsor. More than once, Mr. Musick suggested that the bus could turn around for home if misbehavior continued. The 1960 class chartered a bus for Branson, Missouri. Money for the trip came from concessions at school activities and car washes.

Mr. Milo "Pete" Peterson was an outstanding music, band, and choir instructor for over fifteen years. He was renowned for having the football players march at halftime performances in their football uniforms.

An Extended Unification & Closing—The

school district unified with Leroy in 1966. Gridley High

School closed after graduation in May 2003. The last class had eight graduates. The last to graduate from Gridley High School was Nathan Morray (alphabetically). The school had a total of 1,384 graduated in eighty-eight years from 1916-2003. The most common surnames of the graduates were Beyer-51, Birk-51, Bahr-35, Kraft-29, Young-25, Raaf-17, Williams-16, Johnson-13, Wells-13, MacKaskey-10, Mudge-9, Povenmire-9, Huber-9, Dewey-9, and Moore-9.

Gridley Rural High School
Coffey County, KS

#83

Hudson Rural High School

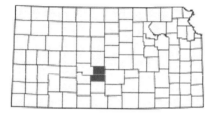

Mascot: Wildcats

Colors: Purple and Gold

Year Closed: 1966

Location: town of Hudson, northeastern Stafford County

Town Origins—The farmers and tradesmen who settled Hudson in the 1870s were mostly immigrants from Germany or second-generation settlers from Missouri and Illinois. The residents of the area met at the post office to discuss the establishment of a school. District #75 was formed and a school house built. The Missouri Pacific Railroad came through the area in 1888, bringing more settlers.

An addition to the original building and a second teacher were added in 1906. Enrollment increased rapidly, and this enlarged school building was inadequate for the numbers of students. In 1911, a red brick, two-story building with basement was erected.

School lasted six months with a two-week break at Christmas. The boys came to school after the fall harvests were completed. There was no age requirement for beginners, and parents decided what age their children should be when they went to school. Each child furnished his own slate and was asked to bring the old Sears and Roebuck catalog from home because this was the pre-toilet tissue era. Beginners were taught English. Most youngsters learned to speak English after they started school because German was spoken in their homes. In 1914, the first high school class graduated from the two-year high school.

Expanded High School Education—During the summer of 1923, there was a realization throughout the community that a separate high school was needed. The classes in the red-brick building were bulging. In the October 11 issue of the *Hudson Herald*, an announcement informed the public that a mass meeting was to be held in the high school room of the school house to discuss the proposition of a Rural High School for Hudson and its community. Everyone interested in the education of their children and grandchildren was urged to attend.

An election was called for on March 25, 1924. When the heated campaign was over and the votes were counted, the proposition was defeated. Rev. Zwilleing's column in the local newspaper on March 27, summarized the situation succinctly:

Remember education is always an honorable and worthy cause to work for and what was not accomplished at this first Rural High School election may be accomplished at a later date.

In the fall of 1924, the superintendent of schools, R.C. Maddy, informed the students that they were going to present an operetta, *The Captain of Plymouth*. None of them had ever heard of an operetta, but no matter. The story of the courtship of Miles Standish was familiar and everyone pitched in. Singing parts and speaking parts were given out and rehearsals began. On nice days the rehearsals took place in the school yard. Later the scene changed to Witt Hall where the stage and auditorium were used for final rehearsals and performance. It was a grand affair for the whole community. The quality of the music and the entire performance made everybody proud of their school and their children.

During the next two years, School District No. 75 added the third and fourth years to the high school curriculum. By 1926, a bond election passed for the new high school. That year a graduating class of seven seniors received their diplomas. On July 22, 1926, an official announcement was received from the State Department of Education in Topeka that the Hudson High School was fully accredited. On August 26, the new building was completed, a lot of accomplishment in only eight months.

The new building was complete with a home economics room, a history-English room, a physics lab, a study hall, and a gym and stage in the sub-story level. The new building had no indoor toilet facilities, so the two old "White Houses"—a couple of eight-holers out back—remained equipped with big sacks of lime, standard equipment in those days. The 1926 building served as a good community center with box suppers, cakewalks, and special programs on holidays.

In 1927-28, the junior class gave two plays, the proceeds of which were used to put a ceiling in the auditorium. The boys of the entire school, under the direction of Superintendent Maddy, aided in the task. The girls prepared a meal at noon under the guidance of the home economics teacher, Grace Maddy. Mr. Maddy painted the class emblem, the Owl, on the ceiling as a signature of the class which financed the project.

Athletics & Activities—In 1923, Hudson participated in the first known county-wide track meet. The result was that Hudson came out on top in the grade school section.

The Hudson schools continued to have a very active music department and athletic program. Six-man football was first played in September 1939. It drew big crowds throughout the 1940s. In 1949, one of the "dream games" between the six-man football teams of Hudson and Montezuma was held in Macksville for the state champions in the Sixball Bowl. Hudson won 7 to 6 in a game played in snow and rain that made play for both teams almost an impossibility. The record sheet for the state champions read, "During the last five years, Hudson High School has won forty-four games and lost two. The combined scores were 1,855 points to the opponents 386."

The school band performed at all the games, and community support was behind the team and band all the way. The annual band trip to the state fair in Hutchinson—to march down Main Street and in front of the grandstand for the evening performance—was the highlight of the season. They also traveled to Wichita, Hays, Alva, Oklahoma, and other towns to march in their events.

Modernizing the School — A new auditorium was built in 1953 with a stage, basketball court, restroom facilities, and dressing rooms for the athletes, as well as a lunchroom with a kitchen for a hot lunch program. In 1954, a new one-story high school was added to the auditorium.

On July 1, 1966, the Hudson district unified with St. John to become Unified District No. 350. In December, sealed bids were taken to raze the old two-story, 1911, red brick elementary building, which had also held the first high school classes. Many citizens of Hudson hated to see the landmark torn down and hauled away. The large iron bell in the belfry had rung to call children in to school on time and in from recess for over forty years.

Traditions — Senior trips were the highlight of graduation year. Cars and coaches transported the students to Bagnal Dam, Missouri; Rock-Away Beach, Kansas City; St. Louis Cardinal games; Colorado Springs; Denver; Carlsbad Caverns; White Sands; El Paso; and even to Juarez, Mexico where the students attended a bull fight. One imp from the class of 1961 bought enough M-80s in Missouri on his senior trip that he still had an ample supply to use, at times, fifty-six years later.

Pranks and acts of wonderment were not uncommon. Sulfur dioxide (smells like rotten eggs) was accidentally expelled throughout the school, much to the surprise of the innocent aspiring chemists. Watermelon rinds under a car's spinning tires, a cow inside the merry-go-round, a Model A on blocks, and girls trying to convince the German teacher that they were color blind as they looked out the window at the teacher's "green" convertible (which was really red) are just a sample of the stories told years later by graduates.

The band director was one for all times. Mrs. Molly Cloud Houston got uniforms for the band and majorettes, complete with hats. With only twenty-five students in band, she recruited the upper grade schoolers and took the band to the state fair. She also added girls carrying batons to make the band look bigger. It so happened that they were marching through the state fair grounds and were following the huge and popular Kingman band. The kids were too shy to attempt to march and play their instruments at the same time, so the drum major just played the bass drum for the down beat and the snare drums played to accompany the bass. As they turned the corner, there was Mrs. Houston demanding that they play a march in step. As they crossed the railroad track, the lead trumpet player stumbled and bloodied her lip and nose as she fell face down. There were no more songs attempted on that year's trip to the state fair.

Notable Graduates — The Class of 1952 was quite talented academically. There were four boys who went on to college and graduated cum laude or magna cum laude. Two became college chemistry professors, one an engineer, and one an architect. Ronald Spangenberg ('52) remains a practicing architect at his company in Wichita at the age of 84 (2018).

One class member was Richard Payne whose dad was on the school board. His dad would always tell people that "Yes, Richard graduated too." Richard told his dad that someone had to be social in the class. Richard went on to be a very successful banker.

Yearbook Memories — A summary in the *Re Echo* (yearbook) preserved some of the "remember when" memories through the four decades of the high school's existence:

Did you ride a horse to school? In 1932 Earl Murphy rode a horse eight miles to school.

Remember those cold days riding to school in a buggy or wagon wrapped in blankets.

In 1928 Earl Krankenberg rode a bicycle 3 ½ miles to school. One morning with the temperature a frigid 16 below zero he froze two fingers.

Remember when the school term lasted 6 months?

1920's-30's Do you remember when there was no running water in the school and we all drank out of the same bucket from the old well that was pumped by hand?

1920's Remember when the airplane landed in the field just west of Hudson? Some of the high school boys skipped school to see the plane. Those who did not return to class were expelled.

1920's Remember the janitor holding his watch in one hand and the school bell rope in the other to ring the bell right on the minute. Everyone lined up in front of the school building and marched in to the beat of the triangle. The older high school boys decided they were too old to march in with the "kids", so they hid the triangle, which they returned to Mr. Maddy the superintendent when they graduated.

1920's Hudson had 11-man football. They first played in overalls. "Fat" Jennings, Produce Buyer in Hudson, also a professional football player was the coach. In 1926 new football suits were purchased.

1929 The "Owl Yearbook" was printed with the Owl as the school emblem.

1930's Remember when Fred Ellis brought his pet squirrel to school and would conceal him in his shirt during class.

1930's Remember when the boys would dip the girl's pony tails into the ink wells. And when the ink wells had something else besides ink in them? (Pew)

1949 The St. John News article appeared: "Whenever the folks up at Hudson want something done, they follow the simplest, most direct, and most effective procedure known to man—they just up and do it. They are transforming the city park into a modern athletic field. When complete it will be lighted for both football and night baseball. Farmers gathered with tractors, graders, fresnos, and other equipment to level the field and prepare for the lighting system. It was all done in the usual Hudson fashion-by everyone pitching in and doing the job."

1940's Hudson High School baseball team wearing their usual overalls and white mill caps defeated Hutchinson High School baseball team.

1940's The school emblem changed to the "Wildcat".

1940's Rural High School Districts were formed. Hudson Rural High School became District Number 2 with their own separate school board.

1940's Remember the challenge football game between Hanston and Hudson played under the lights at Brown Field in St. John? Hudson won a thrilling 34-32 game.

1948 Hudson Sixballers and Coach Paden won the State Championship by defeating Montezuma with the score 7-6. Remember the storm that developed during and after the Game? Montezuma folks were stranded in snowdrifts on Highway 50 but were rescued by Santa Fe train crew during the night and returned to Kinsley.

Remember Bill Ochel as school custodian, and how he enjoyed pulling a joke on students and faculty by also being "a good sport" when students pulled a prank on him. Bill Ochel placed "plastic vomit" in the kindergarten room while the students were out to lunch. The joke backfired because when they saw it they over reacted—what a mess for Bill to clean up!

A teacher was supposed to lock the school safe after leaving the principal's office but forgot to lock it. Mr. Ochel found it open and threw papers all over the office and told the teacher that someone had gotten into the safe and ransacked the place. The teacher got down on all fours and wailed until Bill told him the truth and the teacher chased him all over the school yelling and vowing that he was going to get him.

Bill Ochel, the custodian, telling the principal John Deckart, his wife was on the phone. Mr. Deckart answered the phone with "Hello, honey" only to find he was speaking with the County Superintendent.

When some high school boys climbed on top of the school building and filled the toilet vents with chat Mr. Ochel only remarked, "them ornery devils".

1948 A skit was presented for entertainment at the Hudson Alumni Frolic of 1948. Arvel Mueller was the salty old sea captain in the skit. He portrayed his part of the captain with a wooden leg so well that people wondered when he had lost his good leg. Another event at the same party featured Joyce Schrader and Stan Hallman's talent at jitterbugging.

1952 The Colorado State 6-man football champs challenged the Hudson 6-man state champs to a game. The game was played at Brown Athletic Field in St. John under the lights The St. John paper reported: "A crowd of 3500 attended the game. It was one of the most exciting games ever witnessed in the Brown Park. Wiley (Colorado) played championship football but was not enough to stop the Hudson powerhouse who won the game 38-14.

Many other "remembers" about Hudson High school are recorded in the *Re Echo* which gives one of the best documented stories of a high school as any in the state of Kansas. This was a very vibrant and committed community for any educational opportunity and gave their students incredible support.

Closing — The last graduating class from Hudson High school was in 1968 with nine members. The last graduate to receive a diploma was Kenneth Wondra (alphabetically). A total of 440 graduated in the forty-one years of the high school, 1926 through 1966. The most numerous surnames of the graduates were Fischer-26, Spangenberg-16, Teichmann-16, Nolte-11, Siefkes-7, Hinz-6, Alpers-7, Hallman-7, Bauer-6, and Heyen-6. These names were mostly of German decent and made up more than twenty percent of the total graduates of the high school.

#84

Woodston Rural High School

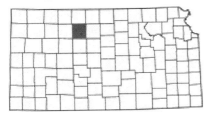

Mascot: Coyotes

Colors: Purple and Gold

Year Closed: 1968

Location: town of Woodston, eastern edge of Rooks County

Early Education in Woodston—Woodston was established along the Missouri Pacific Railroad in 1885 as a railroad town between Bull City (Alton) and Stockton. The town was named for Stockton businessman, Charles C. Woods, who was instrumental in getting the railroad to Stockton.

A new two-story brick school building was opened in the fall of 1907. Two bonds had been passed to raise the money needed to build the school. The votes garnered unheard of unanimity, the first 129-0, and the second 136-0. Enrollment in the first year totaled 136 students in nine grades. Education included one year of high school from the start.

In 1908, the school had ten grades. The school board planned to add one year of high school each year until all twelve grades were available. However, in 1909 the voters of the district rejected the increase in mill levy necessary to accomplish this. So in 1909-10 and 1910-11, the school had nine grades. Funds were finally approved and by 1913-14 the twelfth grade was added, and the high school became accredited.

The first yearbook was published in 1915. *The Quill*, prepared by the senior class, was printed by the local newspaper.

The Barnes Rural High School Act of 1915 made it possible to organize a rural school district comprised of many country elementary school districts providing a larger territory from which to draw students and tax support. A petition to the county commissioners to hold an election to organize a rural high school district was rejected late that year. The reason it was rejected is not clear. Possibly the outlying elementary schools did not want to be taxed and lobbied the commissioners.

Six more years would pass before the new three-story Woodston Rural High School began on September 12, 1921. Commencement for the class of 1921, which did not attend school in this new building, was held on May 26. The building was dedicated that same day. The festivities included music, recitations, and short remarks by the school board, faculty, and patrons of the district. The address was given by W.D. Ross, former state superintendent of public instruction and leader in the rural high school movement in Kansas. His address, according to the newspaper editor, "was one of the best talks that we have ever listened to."

School Modernization & Unification — A new auditorium and grade school were built on the south side of the high school building in 1958-59. The Woodston schools were unified with Stockton school district in 1966. Classes continued in Woodston High School building until 1968, after which Stockton became the high school attendance center. The grade school closed in 1974.

Boys sports were always strong, and participation was very active for football, baseball, basketball, and track. Girls basketball teams dominated in the 1930s.

A yearbook picture from the mid-1930s showed twenty-four students in the orchestra, with five violins. All five boys in the orchestra were wearing bib overalls. The Boys Glee Club that same year had nineteen boys with each dressed in a dark suit and tie. Ms. Gertrude Bonecutter was the music teacher and led a superb music program for the students.

Student Stories — Bob McCall ('40) served in the Army Air Corps in World War II in England. He drove the school bus for Woodston and later for the new unified district from Stockton. His eyes twinkled as he told this story: "I came home to Woodston after the war and married. I had a blacksmith business, farmed part time, and drove the school bus. I had been in England two years, six months, and twenty-one days for the wartime. One incident stands in my mind about a bus trip on the highway going to Stockton. The front wheel and tire came off completely, but I was able to keep it on the road with a full load of kids."

World War II took a heavy toll on Woodston families. The Taylor family had four boys—Murray ('28), N. William ('30), Russell, and Fred—in the service at the same time. Russell was killed on the Saratoga in the Pacific as it was dive bombed by the Japanese. His brother, William Taylor ('30), was on the same ship and survived. Only a week before, a third brother, Fred, had been on the Saratoga but had been reassigned. Another killed in action was Emma McSnavely ('40) an army nurse.

Edna Dibble ('42) was Woodston Postmaster for forty years. She became the second wife of Bob McCall ('40) as they had both lost their spouses. She shared this story:

> We took our senior trip in May of 1942 to Colorado. Gas and tires were not yet rationed, so our little caravan of cars headed west on the two-lane roads. I still can envision the Colorado Prison and a cheese factory we visited.

Closing the School — For many years the student newspaper was one of the finest printed by a small high school in Kansas. After the closing of the local commercial newspaper, the student publication contributed much to the community as well as the school. The quality of education was high for a small school, and many graduates went on to distinguish themselves in their chosen fields. The schools were a vital part of the life blood of a community, and a loss of the school was a major step in the decline of this country town.

The largest graduating class was twenty-four in 1938. The smallest was five in 1957. The high school had become part of the Stockton District in 1966 and the last graduating class of fourteen graduates was in May 1968. The last graduate to receive a diploma from WRHS was Kathy Welker (alphabetically). There were 715 graduates in the fifty-five years from 1914-1968. The most numerous names of the graduates were Dibble-13, Jones-13, Dunlap-13, McNutt-11, Murphy-11, Glotflty-10, Miller-9, Palmer-9, Buttermore-8, Melton-8, and Palmer-8. Over four percent of those graduates had Scottish surnames of McCollough, McNutt, McNeal, McReynolds, McCall, McDowell, McGhghy, McGinnis, and McIntire. It's an interesting figure considering that the area was not a particularly ethnic settlement when Woodston was first founded in the 1880s.

Woodston Rural High School
Rooks County, KS

#85

Talmage High School

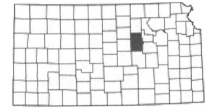

Mascot: Eagles

Colors: Maroon and Gold

Year closed: 1943

Location: village of Talmage, northwest quadrant of Dickinson County

Area History — The village of Talmage was eight miles from the county seat of Abilene. The countryside was settled by German, Swiss, and Dutch with many coming from Pennsylvania and settling mostly northeast of town. Some had sold their farms in the east and were able to pay cash for their new land in Kansas. Others came from the "old" country and homesteaded. Their first church was the "River" Brethren Church (later the United Brethren). Many of these families had surnames with four letters such as Zook, Book, Gish, and Lady. There were many English to the west of town, Baptists to the North, and numerous families named Chase to the southwest.

The Santa Fe Railroad built the Superior Branch in 1887, and Talmage was platted next to the railroad in 1888. The town was named after the popular evangelist Thomas DeWitt Talmage, an author, Lyceum lecturer, and Editor of the *Christian Herald Magazine*.

The following was taken from the school paper titled *School Echo* with the editor and chief, the English teacher, Mrs. Walter Kuiken:

"Listen! My children and you shall hear—the history of the school of Talmage, so dear," In 1873, settlers coming to Kansas from the eastern states . . . a little, black, frontier school house was spied 10 miles northwest of Abilene, the cattle-trading center. The building was a wooden structure unpainted, long, and rectangular, with "district 29" inscribed above the door. It was situated on the northwest corner of the crossroads, north of where the town of Talmage now stands and was built by Harvey and Jim Moore for $1700. Mr. Thomas "Doc" Iliff donated an acre of land for the building and the school became known as the "Iliff School" . . .

The pupils of that first school ranged in age from 6 to 20. There were 7 grades . . . reading, geography, arithmetic, spelling, grammar, and writing . . . often said the pupils went to school until they knew as much as their teachers . . . term of school was approximately four months. Most of the students walked to school some up to four to five miles . . . boys would carry girls and small children across streams.

By 1900 the community had expanded . . . felt the need for a larger and better school building . . . addi-

tion was built. In 1907, a movement for consolidation had begun . . . and the two year high school started.

In 1908, a south addition was added. A four year high school was started . . . lasted only long enough to graduate one class . . . the district deemed it unprofitable to maintain a 4 year high school.

. . . for several years no additions were made to the building, nor any major changes effected in the schedule until 1926 when the four year high school was again instituted. Mrs. Taylor was the first principal of the new four year high school.

Talmage High School—The first class to graduate from the high school was in 1927 as there were no seniors in school the first year. The class was composed of Thelma Koelling, George Chase, Helen Ingalls, Marie Young, Dean Chaffee, and Harvey Watt.

The district voted to erect a new building. Legal issues delayed the construction until the summer of 1929. Five acres of land were purchased from Mr. Briney as a site for the new building. The old building was torn down and converted into a private residence. The new building was ready for use at the opening of the 1929 fall term. Enrollment was 100. There were six on the faculty. The building was well equipped with a fine gymnasium, well ventilated classrooms, and a nicely lit stage. Many luxuries were provided with accessories for athletics and community functions. "A new modern building has replaced the little frontier school house but the spirit of learning is still the same and the ultimate purpose of the school has not changed-the education of the child is its goal." (Mrs. Walter Kuiken)

William Allen White and Margaret Hill McCarter were among the famous writers who were commencement speakers. Thomas DeWitt Talmage was a good friend of T.C. Iliff, the town founder who donated the land for the school. He was also one of the frequent lyceum speakers. Lyceum courses were used for many years for bringing in many and varied programs to the schoolhouse as the community center. The business in Talmage began to diminish during the war years. Because of improved roads and automobiles, townspeople started shopping in Abilene, and Talmage stores were gradually sold out and closed.

The high school was closed in the spring of 1943.

Talmage High School
Dickinson County, KS

86

Bucyrus Rural High School

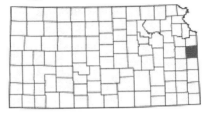

Mascot: Bobcats

Colors: Red and White

Year Closed: 1953

Location: town of Bucyrus, north-central Miami County

Area History — Early education in the area began with the development of the community. Bucyrus Rural High School became a four-year, accredited high school in 1920.

The following was written by Jeanie Hellabower Laskie ('09) in the 1920s:

Many home seekers were attracted to the Great Plains known as the Kansas-Nebraska Territory.

In December 1857, two brothers, from Virginia came to this particular place. These brothers were David and Did Heflebower. They homesteaded their claims and later purchased several sections from the government. On the following February, Billie and Tommie Holden came from Ohio and settled on adjoining farms. From Illinois, came William Waterhouse and George Wicklines . . . Here the families lived the first hard years of the homesteaders, under the vast skies, girted by an immense and remote horizon.

Settlers of this era witnessed the many attempts on the part of political leaders of both the North and the South, to make Kansas a Free-state or a Slave-state of the Union. The Free-state leaders finally won the long struggle and Kansas became a Free State on January 29, 1861. In 1862, the government passed the homestead law in Kansas. This marked the opening of vast areas of land to the home-seekers . . . A one room school building was erected by Uncle Billie Holden and his brother Tommie. The chosen site was one and one-half miles southwest of Bucyrus. The interior of the building was of native lumber and vastly different from our own comfortable, modern school-home.

The equipment consisted of seats, which were backless, benches of the crudest type, a small stove, and painted blackboards for writing space and slates with slate pencils. This building was destroyed by Bushwhackers in one of the many raids during the early years of the Civil War.

. . . In the early 1860s a second school building was planned at the site of the present school and was deeded to the school district by E.H. Kirby . . . The school year was divided into two terms; a four month winter term and a three months spring term. There was no fixed course of study as a guide for the teacher and pupil. The progress depended almost entirely up-on the judgement of the teacher, and the children advanced accordingly . . .

. . . among the social activities of the neighborhood were spelling bees, home dances, bob sled parties, husking bees, house warmings and singing schools. These people were mindful of their religious development as well as the material side of life. Mrs. Did Heflebower and J.C. Lovett started the first Sunday School in the school house. Church was held there too, whenever a minister happened along, regardless of denomination.

This same building was the home of the Wea Grange, established in 1873. Thus the little school house served for school, church and Grange for five years . . .

As the community grew in population and became more prosperous, the school building became inadequate to meet the demands; so a new building was planned. The old one was purchased by E.H. Kirby and he moved it to his farm to be used as a part of his barn. This new building was started in 1884. Before the building was completed, the funds were exhausted; the board of education at that time was composed of Chas. Kirby, J.C. Lovett, and David Heflebower; consequently, the problem for further resources was a grave one. After futile attempts at neighboring banks, the board obtained $500 loan from George Robinson. The building was not finished in time for the next session of school therefore, the children attended one term of school in the old building as it stood in Mr. Kirby's barnyard. For the new building, real seats were provided, windows were placed on either side of the room, the walls and ceiling was ceiled, and much more writing space was provided by the use of more painted boards, and the stove from its station in the center of the room furnished the heat.

. . . For many years the young fold of Bucyrus received their education in the two room wooden building, south and west of town, the school consisted of grades only with two instructors, the community watched their accomplishments with pride. Opening exercises were enjoyed each morning by the group singing familiar tunes played on the organ by some of the pupils who had musical training . . .

Expanded High School Studies — Jeanie Heflebower Laskie ('09) and Mrs. Marie Weir wrote in a paper account titled *Our School and Today:*

In the year 1906, members of the graduating class expressed desire to study high school subjects and to receive advantages of high school training. In accordance with their wishes, ancient history, algebra, composition and rhetoric, and agriculture were offered and were taught by Mary McCarthy. The following summer, the third room was added to the building and Mr. Fred N. Lewis was hired to teach a high school course. In accordance with the school board, what Mr. Lewis taught was called a three-year high school course. On May 15, 1909, the first high school class consisted of three graduates—Billie Thompson, Eva Knight, and Jennie Heflebower.

The new superintendent, Mr. E. Rex Moody, encouraged the community to form a Rural High School. In 1918, bonds were issued for the construction of a new brick building which was designed to house both the high school and the grade school. The vote carried by ninety-two votes. The building was completed in September 1918. The new building gave many advantages to the children—separate classrooms, an auditorium with a stage, the gymnasium, and the telephone. The flu epidemic was prevalent the fall of 1918. There were only seven weeks of school from the first of September, 1918, until the first of January, 1919. A student, Ross Roberts, in the junior class, had enlisted in the service of his country for World War I the summer of 1918. He died on November 28, 1918, of influenza in Camp Polk in North Carolina.

Activities & Academics — The first yearbook was published in 1920. It highlighted dramatics, literacy, and the printing of the school newspaper, the *Bucyrus Community Echo*. The following words are from the inaugural school yearbook:

Under the direction of Mr. H.L. Euler done by the fourth year English work . . . excellent stories, essays, poems, and editorials have been written and enjoyed very much by the pupils. This annual which you are reading is our first attempt in its field. We feel honored in knowing that we are the first attempt of such an enterprise at Bucyrus, and hope that it will please you. By Geneva Windmood

One of the first two graduates of the four-year high school in 1920, Thomas Craig ('20), wrote in the yearbook, "It is a pleasure to know that this class is the first one to be graduated from the four-year Bucyrus Rural High School course. The two members hope to live a life which will be enjoyable to themselves and others."

Kansas had a fall teachers' meeting for many years. School would not be held for several days, usually in early November. An article in the November 12, 1929, *Bucyrus Community Echo* provides an early story of physical education:

Teachers Relate Meeting Events. Interesting Reports of the State Convention are given by Instructors. Four tell of the Kansas City Session. That the annual State teacher's convention was highly beneficial is the report of all the teachers of Bucyrus Grades and High

School. The meeting was held October 30 until November 2 inclusive . . . The theme of the convention was "Increasing professional spirit by rendering professional service." . . . James Reeves, a physical director from New York City says that while the longevity of life is increasing yet statistics show that adults at the age of forty now have less chance of living until they are fifty, than at any previous time. He declared that physical education should form the basis for all education.

Athletics — In 1919, a football team was organized which proved to be a good one. Tennis was played in the spring months as the gymnasium was large enough to make a fair-sized court.

Increasing Course Offerings — In 1920, the school became a four-year accredited high school and a class of eleven began in vocational agriculture. Each boy chose a project that he desired. Besides these projects, the class studied shop work, carpentry, and animal husbandry. They emphasized the work of dairy cattle, hogs, beef cattle, wool, and horses.

The new Bucyrus Rural High School had a splendidly equipped laboratory for physics, general science, and agriculture. It also had a library of excellent books, not equaled by any school of its size at the time. By means of entertainment, the school had placed in the building $100 worth of best pictures, a Victor portable stereopticon, a suspended globe, a Chippendale model Edison machine, twenty-five records, and a Rotary Neostyle Mimeograph.

A Musical Community — From the *Community Echo*, November 12, 1929:

Miss Doyle, pursuant to instructions of the Board of Education is opening classes in various instruments. Belonging to these groups are woodwinds, brass, and strings. Each group will meet for one half hour period two days a week . . . by this method all the children are given an opportunity to learn to play an orchestral or band instrument without the expense of private lessons.

Another headline in the same issue of the *Community Echo* is titled "Readings, orchestral Selections, Negro Act -Give Variety Program":

As the main feature of the entertainment Friday evening, two one act plays were presented by the members of the junior class . . . orchestra played three selections . . . Richard Myers gave two selections . . . As an advertisement for the minstrel, which will come later this month, Harry Pratt and Gilbert Knap staged a few jokes . . . It has been several years since the high school has offered a negro minstrel . . . Mr. Eastwood will produce "Jubilee Minstrel" . . . the humorous repartee between the interlocutor and end man and the musical numbers will furnish a full evening program. The act will open with snappy Negro song by the mixed chorus . . . in the repartee is a number of good jokes and the songs are quite appropriate.

The band looked splendid in their new suits and hats as they played for the May 1949 May Day Program. The 1946 yearbook showed twins, Fay and Ray Bendorf. There were a girls and a boys basketball team, with seven boys out for basketball. Coach Paine, who was new that year, was quoted as saying, "They mastered the 'art and science' of cooperation to great degree, and became a team a school could be proud of." In tournament play, the team won third place trophies and lost only to the tournament winners, Edgerton and Louisburg, which both advanced to the Regional Tournament.

Joe Knight, the grandson of Marie Winkler Knight ('36) said, "Bucyrus was always a music school. With Wea only three miles away, we stood out in music and they seemed to have more talent in sports."

Barbara Hook Dougan ('49) said, "I played the slide trombone. Our voice teacher, Mrs. Jack Marriot taught us how to make speeches and public speaking. I always believed I had an excellent education. We had a marching band and competed at the district music festivals in Lawrence. In 1951, there were two solos and a clarinet quartet which placed. In 1950, four girls placed in individual solo work. We did not have buses or Drivers Education."

After graduation in 1949, Barbara moved to Olathe to work in county government. She drove a school bus for thirteen years for Stillwell and Blue Valley. She became a rural mail carrier out of Stillwell for eighteen years and was a crossing guard for Stillwell for ten years. "I loved kids, you never know what they are going to say," she said. Undoubtedly the kids loved Mrs. Dougan too.

School Closing—From the beginning of the two- and three-year high school in 1909 until 1919, there were thirty-six graduates. From 1920 until the school closed, another 226 graduated. Two Bucyrus High School boys, Jack Heflebower and Edwin Rosner, answered taps in World War II. They had been drafted and did not finish high school before going to the service and into the war.

There were three graduates in the last class of 1953 with Eldon Wren (alphabetically) the last to receive a diploma from the school. The most numerous surnames of the graduates in the forty-five years education at Bucyrus were Roberts-6, Whitaker-5, Winkler-4, Witt-4, and three each for DeCock, Furgason, Kirby, Laskie, Lindemood, and Vohs.

Bucyrus High School
Miami County, KS

#87

Sharon Rural High School

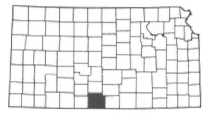

Mascot: Cardinals

Colors: Red and White

Year Closed: 1984

Location: town of Sharon, eastern Barber County

A Barnes Law School — The Sharon High School was organized under the Barnes High School Law in the summer of 1910. At this time there seemed to be some misgivings as to the outcome of the venture. The high school opened in the fall of 1910 with Prof. J.F. Johnson as the principal. He was retained as principal the second year.

In 1912, Prof. W.M. Seaman was given charge of the high school. The school grew so rapidly that a third instructor was employed at the midterm. In the fall of 1913, the same faculty was in charge, but much strengthened by one more instructor. At this time the school carried classes in three, four-year courses, fully accredited by the University of Kansas. By 1914, the district encompassed approximately four-square miles, the high school having enrolled sixty-seven students, or one for every five of Sharon's population.

High school enrollment had reached beyond the capacity of the old building by 1924. The financial burden for building and support of the school was too great for District No. 28 to continue. W. Harsbarger came to the rescue with a proposal to reorganize to a rural high school instead of a district high school. Three months later, the rural high school was formed and bonds for an addition to the old building were issued.

This school building burned to the ground in 1959 and a new high school was opened in the fall of 1960. At that time there were as many as eighty businesses lining Main Street. Today (2018), there are only eight.

Traditions — The school song was to the tune of the "Washington and Lee Swing." Sports teams played in the Great Plains League. Rivalries were Cunningham, Attica, and Nashville-Zenda. The boys basketball team was the Class B State Champions in 1960. The football team won the 1977 eight-man state championship the second year of the state playoff system.

Lennes Rankin ('57) shared the following:

> We lived on a farm away from town and I had to ride the school bus. We milked cows and had stock cows so there were always chores to be done. I had no

way of staying after school to play football though I did play basketball.

My son Brian Rankin ('84) graduated in the same class as Martina Schiff McBride ('84), the famous country music singer. She has been the Country Music Association, four-time "Female Vocalist of the Year." She was raised on a dairy farm and learned to perform singing with her father, Daryl Schiff, and his band. She maintains a home in Sharon and often has this as her home-base as she performs a national touring circuit.

A wonderful teacher for many years was Mrs. Margaret Johnson. She was a renowned science and biology teacher and everyone loved her. She was at Sharon High School for nearly thirty years. One day when we were in science class, the bottles in the chemistry lab began to rattle and the flag on the wall was wiggling. Mrs. Johnson admonished a classmate, Sonny Byers ('57), "Sonny, would you please stop your leg pounding because you are shaking the whole school!" We were actually having a freak earthquake. We never let Sonny live that one down.

Every student that graduated from Sharon High School raved about the school lunch program. The cooks, Virginia Hrencher, Betty Boor, and Thelma Skinliver, with their supervisor, Margaret Moser, made a lifetime memory of great food provided by these ladies who cooked for twenty to twenty-five years each. In 1989 the school consolidated with Medicine Lodge. When it closed, many of the people of Sharon thought of themselves as the "red-headed stepsister."

School Closing—Sharon had been a self-sustaining school district, but Medicine Lodge benefited from the valuation. Many raucous meetings were held before the consolidation was completed. The school closed following graduation in 1987. The last class had ten graduates. Joe Schmidt (alphabetically) was the last to get his diploma from Sharon Rural High School. A large percentage of the students went east to Attica in Harper County instead of the county seat, Medicine Lodge, after the school closed.

There were 923 graduates in the seventy-six years from 1912 to 1987. The most numerous surnames of the graduates were Riche-42, Traffas-23. Dick-19, McGuire-14, Mans-13, Smith-12, Blick-10, McDaniel-10, Laudick-9, and Shelite-9.

#88

Waldo

High School

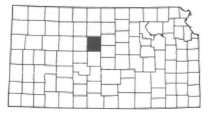

Mascot: Warriors

Colors: Red and White

Year Closed: 1964

Location: town of Waldo, north edge of Russell County

Early Education — Waldo Rural High School was located nineteen miles from the county seat at Russell, Kansas. The first school in Waldo, known at the time as Pleasant Run School District 50, dated back to the school year 1880-81. It was a combination subscription and county school and was held in the home of Mr. C. Caprez with Mrs. Crane as the teacher. The district received $55.06 from the county treasurer and $5.30 in subscription funds according to the County Treasurer's report.

A. Zeigler, John Pangburn, Abe Michael, and C. Caprez were among the active people promoting the construction of a new school building. It was eventually built on the Haskell farm, south of the creek, about one-half mile south of the present town of Waldo. Sixty-seven youngsters and their teacher crowded into the stone building in 1887-88 school year. The district voted in 1888 to build a new building. This 24-feet by 30-feet building was a frame construction located on the present school site. It was built at a cost of $957.

High school work was introduced in 1904-1908 with an enrollment of five students. The old school building, used by District 121, Osborne County, was moved to the school grounds to accommodate the high school until the new stone building was completed in the spring of 1911. This limestone building was torn down in 1958. Both grade and high school were moved into the new building and the old frame building was sold and moved. The first graduate of Waldo High School was Mamie Pangburn, Class of 1912.

The high school was fully accredited under the Barnes School Law in February 1914. There were three teachers in the stone building by this time. Gradually, as it became necessary, more teachers were added. New fields and subjects for study were added to the school curriculum which included athletics, music, manual arts, business, and other subjects.

In 1929, the "old" auditorium, manual training, and music rooms were built. Ray Wagoner, the school superintendent, was the architect for the red brick building. It was situated north of the two-story limestone rock school. This red brick building was torn down in the early 1980s.

Education Mid-Century

Waldo was a member of the tough Lincoln Branch League which, for a short time period, included all high schools in Russell County with the exception of Russell High School. Some of these schools were Luray, Lucas, Gorham, Dorrance, Wilson, Bunker Hill, and Paradise. The Lincoln Branch League was named after the railroad branch of the Union Pacific that traveled east-west from Salina to Colby. It also had a daily passenger and mail train that passed west in the morning and back east in the afternoon. This passenger train was called the Jittney.

In 1957 the new modern grade school and high school building was constructed all on the ground floor. This was a time of growing enrollment following the baby boom years. The optimism and effort of the community provided a modern and progressive setting for the education of their youngsters. The Rural High School District #3 board members at this time were Kenneth Ward, Everett Keller, and Kenneth Day.

Declining Enrollment and Closing

1959-1964, school went on as usual, but with an ever-declining enrollment. At the close of the 1962-1963 school year, Verlin M. Rogers left the Waldo school system. He had served as superintendent for fifteen years. When the school opened in the 1963-1964 school year, there were only twenty-three students enrolled. When the high school closed in May 1964, the final curtain dropped on Waldo High School after sixty years and 427 graduates. The last graduate was Doris Johnson (alphabetically) in a class of three graduates.

The largest graduating class from Waldo was nineteen in 1934. The smallest was one graduate in both 1912 and 1913. The most numerous surnames of the graduates were Bean-15, Mullender-11, Caprez-9, and Murphy-8. These surnames represent long-time families in the area who also contributed in establishing the educational system, school board involvement, and other areas of community leadership. Pangburn and Caprez were two of the four names mentioned who were instrumental in the 1880s in the formation of the school.

#89

Stilwell Rural High School

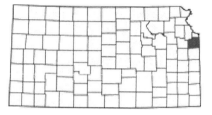

Mascot: Mustangs

Colors: Purple and White

Year Closed: 1970

Location: southeast corner of Johnson County

Area History — Stilwell Rural High School was located on today's 199th Street, just east of Metcalf in a community with some of the oldest educational history in the state of Kansas. This area was settled in 1857 in Aubry Township with many different people coming from Germany, Ireland, and England. The census of 1860 showed a population of 288 with only eight that could not read or write. Education was important in Johnson County from the time of the first settlers who were determined to provide a strong educational foundation for their children. School houses were often the second community building built, right behind churches. Eventually one-hundred school houses dotted the Johnson County countryside.

The village of Aubry was located near the center of the township and was the trading center for the farmers. Times were prosperous and new families settled in the area. In 1860, fifty-four families lived in the township and about sixty students attended school.

In 1861, things changed dramatically. The Civil War broke out and the area became a battleground. The assessor, Oliver H. Gregg, wrote later in the *History of Johnson County* about riding in the area to estimate the value of the land through the country during the war:

> The majority of the houses were empty, the fences down and fields overgrown with weeds; no travelers were seen on the roads, no cheery whistle of farmerboy, or crack of teamster whip, none of the ordinary sounds of healthful farm-life—only the desolating marks of war and the stillness of danger. The few citizens remaining had the guarded air and watchful, suspicious glance of men who carried their lives in their hands.

If most people had moved away and the few remaining citizens felt they "carried their lives in their hands," it is most unlikely that they sent their children to school. However, O.H. Gregg's wrote in 1874, "At the close of the war, Aubry soon recovered from the effects, and is now one of the most flourishing and prosperous townships in the county."

Today only a historical marker outside Stilwell Elementary School reminds people of the harsh times during the Civil War. It reads, "QUANTRILL'S RAIDS AND THE MILITARY ROAD 1862."

In the Spring of 1862, William Clarke Quantrill, confederate guerrilla, led raids in and about Aubry, taking an uncounted toll on lives and property. Union troops seeking the raiders camped often along the military road (now Metcalf) from Fort Leavenworth to Fort Scott. Union retaliation provoked Bill Anderson of Aubry to join Quantrill. Later he became known as Bloody Bill.

First High School — Seven one-room country schools, in addition to the Aubry Grade School, were built in the six-by-eight-mile township from 1871 through 1873. In 1907, when the Aubry School had been in operation for almost fifty years with grades one through eight, the community decided to organize a high school. To make room for the school, a third room was added to the west side of the existing Aubry School. The high school used the room on the second floor while grade school was taught in the two lower rooms.

The community was proud of its high school. From an advertisement in the *Olathe Mirror* in June 1908:

> Stilwell will introduce a high school course next year and here teachers will be employed. M.B. Samuel goes back to Stilwell again this year and receives $77 salary. He will have the two years high school work.

Unfortunately, the community did not get a chance to enjoy the enlarged schoolhouse for very long. In April 1910, right before the first high school students graduated, the whole building burned to the ground. Fortunately for the pupils, they had not re-entered the building after recess, though the Principal, Mr. Finn, had his hand on the bell rope to call them. The teachers on the upper story, Miss Phelps and Miss Conbouy, cut off from escape by the stairway, came down the fire escape.

Commencement for the four graduates of the first graduating class, 1910, was held in the Baptist Church.

New Town, New School — When the original school was built in 1858, it was located in the middle of the Aubry Community. Twenty-eight years later, the Missouri Pacific Railroad came through the area half a mile east of Aubry. A new town, later named Stilwell, developed around the railroad depot. When plans were made for the new school, it was natural to choose a site closer to the more populated town. The new site was located on the south side of Missouri Avenue (now 199th Street) and a few hundred yards east of State Street (now Metcalf Avenue).

From the Olathe Mirror:

> Messers Gus Zimmerman and Tom Conbouy of Stilwell were in Olathe Monday on business connected with the building of the new schoolhouse for Stilwell. This building, which will take the place of the Aubry schoolhouse that was burned several weeks ago, is to be a commodious, up-to-date structure and will be located in the Conbouy, Miller & Goebbel addition to Stillwell.

In August, the school board bought two acres of land from Conbouy Estates for $250 per acre. Soon, they went from planning to building. The *Olathe Mirror* in November reported, "The work on the new schoolhouse has begun." By March the new schoolhouse was finished. The 32' by 62' building was made of red brick and the upper level had wooden siding.

During the first years of the building's life, high school was held in the two upper rooms while the grade school occupied the two lower rooms. The primary room of the grade school had grades one through four, and the grammar room had grades five through eight. This building still stands today (2018), but its history is much more interesting than just being a 108-year old structure.

The new schoolhouse was huge but was quickly outgrown. With nineteen students attending in 1910, the enrollment had doubled by 1920. The original subjects taught—English, spelling, mathematics, history, Latin, and civics— were expanded with seven new subjects added to the curriculum: manual training, home economics, agriculture, general science, biology, physics, and typing.

Building for the new high school commenced in 1919 across the street to the north. The six classrooms were complete in the summer of 1920. Different than most high school structures of the time, this was a one-story brick building. The price was $33,000, $30,000 of which were raised by issuing bonds. The *Olathe Mirror* described the newly finished building:

> The building is modern in every respect, large and ample classrooms, library, domestic science room, manual training room, well equipped laboratory, splendid gymnasium with dressing rooms equipped with showers. The gymnasium is a combination auditorium and gymnasium. It has a good stage with dressing rooms and will seat five hundred people at any time. A room had been built for moving picture machine and moving pictures will be used in the schoolhouse . . . What a magnificent building for 40-50 students and three teachers. No wonder the community is proud of the building and the school is to be recognized as one of the best.

The new building served Stilwell Rural High School District #2 for fifty years. The gymnasium was changed in the early 1950s and again around 1960.

Athletics — Sports at the high school level played a big role in student education. Max DeWeese, principal of Stilwell High School in 1912, was proud of his fine boys basketball team. He recalled, "We beat both Bucyrus High school and Belton High school."

In 1920, Stilwell High School joined the newly organized Johnson County League and later won many trophies. Three years later, the basketball team had a smashing year. They won all the league games and received the championship trophy. The baseball team did great as well and won a league first-place trophy.

Community Center — The little town of Stilwell was the center of the surrounding community. If you were a student at a nearby one-room school, you came to town for your eighth-grade graduation. You enjoyed sports events and plays at Stilwell High School, and maybe you were clever enough to be in a township-wide spelling bee.

There was no newspaper in Stilwell, but the students at the high school started their own newspaper in 1918 named *The Exponent*. It was to become the oldest high school paper in Johnson County. It was published until the school closed in 1969. The school paper reported important events for the high school. It also covered events at the Stilwell grade school and the one-room schools. The paper also reported on people who were visiting the schools.

The grade school students were lucky to have the high school just across the street—like an extension of their own school building. They could walk across 199th street to play basketball in the high school gym or eat a hot lunch in the home economics room, and they celebrated eighth-grade graduation and other special events in the gym.

A school orchestra was developed from a very humble beginning. In October 1932, five students became interested in ensemble playing. With three violins, a cornet, and the piano, this small group laid the foundation for an orchestra that ultimately included more that ninety percent of the student body. Instruments were furnished by interested persons, parents, students, and the school district. Mr. Lynds was the director of the orchestra throughout its existence. As reported in the 1938 school yearbook, "With the orchestra, a purpose has been developed which provides for worthy use of leisure time, encourages musical expression, and provides some training in orchestral playing."

This same yearbook described the Dramatics Club:

Our Dramatics Club was organized during the first weeks of school. The purpose of the club is to teach the members to feel at ease when on as well as off the stage and to develop and train voices for good speaking. Taking part in dramatic contests teaches the members cooperation, honesty, and fair play. Members of the club are very much indebted to Miss Bricken for her able and conscientious leadership as our sponsor.

It was customary for the junior and senior classes to present class plays which furnished the opportunity for stage appearance and a means of carrying on other activities of the school. The earnings from the junior play were used to defray expenses of the annual Junior-Senior Banquet. The senior class plays helped pay the expenses of the baccalaureate and commencement programs with the proceeds.

The plays in 1937 were very ably directed by Mrs. Rice who deserved credit for their success. Members of the two classes took this opportunity to extend lasting appreciation to her for thoughtful assistance rendered.

The Junior Play on November 19, 1937 was *Beads On a String* by Myrtle Girard Elsey. The Senior Play on April 15, 1938 was *A Little Clodhopper* by Walter Ben Hare.

The 1938 yearbook described, "The organization of the chorus was divided into boys and girls chorus each of which met twice a week in the last period of the school day. The purpose of the chorus has been to foster the love of good music, to develop the vocal abilities of the students. To promote the better use of leisure time . . . The chorus is directed by Miss Bricken, who has shown a great interest in practicing with and in helping to develop each ability. Thank you, Miss Bricken."

Athletics — Basketball was a major sport at S.R.H.S. The first organized games were played out-of-doors prior to 1912. W.D. Smith ('12), who later became the school treasurer in 1938, played on that early basketball team. The first indoor game was played in 1920 in the new building. In the fifteen years that Mr. Rice coached at Stilwell, his teams won three league championships and rated second place three times. In 1928, after winning the regional tournament at Kansas City, Kansas, Stilwell was privileged and honored to enter the state tournament at Ottawa.

In 1958, the grade school board leased four acres to the north of the high school from the high school board. When the school boards signed the agreement in which

Stilwell High School leased the land for a new grade school in 1958, they planned for the future. The agreement was arranged to be in force for fifty years, until 2008.

The future turned out differently. The two schools only got to co-exist as neighbors until 1970 when consolidation of high schools with Stanley left the high school vacant. After one year of consolidation with their arch rival, Stilwell joined the Blue Valley High School. The abandoned Stilwell High School building stood for a few years until it was demolished to make space for a new east-wing for Stilwell Elementary School in 1975.

From 1910-1970, there were 454 graduates of Stilwell High School. Of these graduates, the most common surnames were Smith-18, Conbouy-10, Dugan-8, Hiatt-7, and Vaughn-7. The last graduate from Stilwell Rural High School was Ronald Gene Phelps ('70) (alphabetically).

#90

Towanda High School

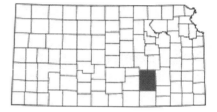

Mascot: Chiefs

Colors: Red and White

Year Closed: 1963

Location: western Butler County

Area History — Towanda was an Osage Indian name for "many waters." It was this abundance of water in this marshy area that drew the first settlers to this area.

In a 1953 historical paper about the history of Towanda, Evalina Edmiston wrote:

> Martin Vaught said, "The year of 1860 was the driest I ever saw in Kansas . . . to add to our woes, along in August came a myriad of grasshoppers."
>
> J.R. Mead arrived in the area in 1863. At that time there were 150 people in Butler County. Towanda was

the last town this side of New Mexico. The Big Spring at Towanda and the wide grass bottoms about it, formed an inviting camping spot. There the Indians pitched their tents and let out their ponies. Mead traded blankets, trinkets, and other things for their robes and furs. The Indians came from the south and west and as many as 1500 camped there. There probably were 20 different tribes. In 1863 from the south came Kickapoos, Shawnees, Delawares, and others who settled on the Walnut and Whitewater Rivers . . . These Indians were the friends of all wild Indians on the plains, and as long as they remained, the southwest frontier was safe from attack by the savages.

The grand rush for land came in 1870-1871. By the close of 1871 practically every quarter in the county had been filed. After the grasshopper plaque of 1875, many left to go 'back home' and did not return.

Education — According to Mrs. Samuel C. Fulton, the first school was held in Towanda in 1867-68. It was built of logs. The first two-story brick school was built in 1886. This school was almost totally demolished by a tornado on March 31, 1892. As there were only a few weeks more of school, the structure was propped up with boards and the term was completed.

The school was rebuilt as a three-story brick school house. Ever-increasing enrollment and need for space drove the push for a new, larger building. In 1900 the standard wage for a teacher was $30 per month. Room and board was $10 per month. In 1902 the superintendent received $50 per month. The total levy for school purposes that year was 16 mills. The estimated value of the property was $3,000. Total paid out for school purposes was $900.81.

Before the oil boom of 1903-04, enrollment was so high that various buildings and rooms around town were used for teaching. In 1911, bonds for $15,000 were voted to erect a new, modern building. The building was constructed of pressed brick and was two stories high. It contained six recitation rooms, two spacious corridors, a laboratory, an office, two large play rooms in the basement, a dry system for ventilation, a furnace, and coal rooms. The building was heated with hot air ventilation and lighted with electricity. The library contained many volumes, most of which were carefully selected. The laboratory was to nurture the best results in education. Basketball, baseball, and field work were organized and made a part of the regular schedule of the students.

The following was written in *The Chieftain*, the first yearbook from the new Towanda High School:

Until 1911, only one years' work had been offered in the High School, at the beginning of 1911-12 two years' work was given, in 1913 three years' work, and not until 1914 was the term increased to nine months in length and four years' work offered in each of two different courses - College Preparatory and General, including Household economics, and Agriculture. The High School is now accredited under the Barnes Law, approved by the State Board of Education, and participates in the county fund set apart for such schools . . . So in this second year (1915) of our existence as a Barnes High School the students herewith chronicle such items and events as seem most interesting, hoping that wherever this little book may be prized as a souvenir of the preliminary successes of your institution, a realization of a dream come true - M.H. Read, Principal 1912-15.

In 1923, bonds were voted for a new high school building at the cost of $75,000, and in 1925, two new areas of teaching were offered, home economics and commerce. The subjects taught were Latin, algebra, ancient history, physics, English history, rhetoric, geometry, literature, and zoology. Students had no choice and were required to take all of these courses.

Athletics — In 1935, the Class B Basketball Elimination Tournament was held in Towanda on March 1-3, 1935. There were twelve schools competing with four of them receiving byes for the first round. The teams in the tournament were Rosalia, Leon, Andover, Potwin, Burns, Latham, Whitewater, Benton, Atlanta, Cassoday, Midian, and Towanda. Towanda lost to Midian in the finals and the winner proceeded to the state tournament.

The motto of the class of 1941 was "Backbone, not Wishbone." Was this an omen to the upcoming war declared just six months later? During World War II, M.G. Starr wrote an open letter to local boys in the service. It was carried in the Towanda paper:

> To the Boys in the Army and camps - Just to let you know that even Pat Starr and his folks think of you all. Yes, sure miss you boys and often inquire about you and look ahead to the days when you will all return. You wonder how old Towanda is getting along. Well, the weeds got plenty big here with no boys to cut them. The school house yard was cut yesterday; It sure is nice to see out once more (Pat lived across the street).

Student Stories — Memories from the class of 1953: "Remember when some cheerleaders rode home from an away game with their boyfriends instead of on the school bus? Superintendent Tommy Monninger chastised them because they had also gone to the El Dorado night club. Wonderland? They all had to write and deliver apologies in study hall, and Janice Bell, who dated James Coats, said ruefully, '. . . and we shouldn't be going to night clubs, where we step in and Wonder where we're going to land!'"

This same class of 1953 took their senior trip to Carlsbad Caverns and Nuevo Laredo, Mexico. Mr. Arnold played poker with the boys while crossing Texas. "Some of us got sunburned at Galveston! Now that senior trips are no more, we realize how lucky we were back then."

At the reunion of the Class of 1951, a Halloween was recalled when some kids scattered corn stalks all over the school ground and thought they would not be caught. "HA! Names were called the next day, and a bunch of us left class to clean it up. However, this prank couldn't compare with the earlier one of putting a goat on the school roof."

Many classes had their heroes, queens, and characters that made them special. The class of 1959 was no exception. Frank Shoemaker ('59) was born in 1941, just before World War II in Neosho Falls, Kansas. He had six uncles, two cousins, and a future stepfather that all served in the war. When his family moved to Towanda, he was in the fourth grade. In an interview with Peggy Windler at the Towanda Museum (2017), Frank gave a colorful remembrance of that era:

> That museum you're working in there right now, well, when I was in the 4th grade my Uncle Chet lived in Towanda and he used to take me down there to that rifle range and we'd shoot .22 rifles, right there in the basement of that museum. Mr. Arnold, the superintendent, started a PeeWee basketball tournament in

Towanda, and you had to weigh 100 lbs or less. All of the boys wanted to play in that tournament, and a lot of them were a little heavy. One in particular I remember was Norman Mosier, he'd run around the section there where the cemetery is and ol' Clay Hill was. He'd run around that thing 2 or 3 times and he'd come back and weigh . . . he ran until he weighed 100 lbs so he could play. We used Clay Hill as a backstop for target shooting. We'd go out there and wax our cars, and just hang out up there. We used to take our cars out there and we'd polish'em and wax 'em and take pictures of 'em . . . I had a bunch of cars. Some of my favorite ones was a '41 Ford convertible, and I had a '49 Oldsmobile Rocket 88, and a '53 Studebaker coupe. Ol' Dale Schmidt and most all the kids had Fords, flathead Ford V8s, and Chevrolet 6-cylinder. I come to school driving a '49 Olds Rocket and that was the first automobile with an overhead valve V8, it was a pretty hot car back in them days. And ol' Schmit said, "What'r you doin' drivin' that ol' bus like that? He says, "Man, that's an old woman's car." And I said, "Well I bet that'd blow the doors off that Ford." So we went out and raced and sure enough, I blew the doors off that Ford. Two weeks later there he came and he had a baby blue '50 Olds Rocket 88 convertible with a white top. Really a sharp car. We had a lot of fun in school, there, I tell you. We really enjoyed it. I always told Mr. Arnold, "I may not have come out of there being a math whiz or an English professor, or anything like that, but we sure learned how to get along with people and I think that's worth a lot." We had a lot of fun in this old town.

As a teacher, coach, and superintendent, Mr. Gene Arnold left an indelible mark on a generation of Towanda students. Frank Shoemaker recalled:

He was a cool guy, but he used to put us boys in trouble all of the time. One time it snowed really badly and they excused all of the country kids. They didn't have to come to school that day. Well I lived out in the country, so I got my ol' car fired up and I come to town and picked up some guys. A lot of us skipped school cause it snowed so much, and we went ridin' around Towanda. I looked in the rearview mirror and there was Mr. Arnold right behind us. Next mornin' we went to school and he called us in the office. He said "OK, if you can get to town to run around you can get to town to come to school." So we had to wash school busses and wash dishes in the cafeteria and I don't know what all kinds of jobs he gave us. So, we had to pay the price for that one.

Senior trips occurred each year but the one that may be the most renowned was the one for the 1959 class to Mexico City. Eighteen seniors with Mr. Arnold as their sponsor boarded a school bus. An account written for the *Western Butler County Times* gave a log of this remarkable trip:

The group traveled through the Arbuckle mountains, to the Alamo in San Antonio, then to Laredo and through customs at Nuevo Laredo, Mexico, to board a train. On the train they met a Spanish girl, and Mr. Arnold invited the class to her home for dinner. Then they rode on to the National University, Chapultepec Castle, a gigantic stadium seating 100,000 with walls made of lava from an erupting volcano and an Olympic size swimming pool. They toured the pyramids of the ancient Aztec civilization, the palace of Fine Arts, heard a rehearsal of the Mexico City Symphonic Orchestra, visited homes, learned the Cha Cha, ate tacos and tortillas, played bongo drums, and taught the Mexicans to rock and roll. On the return trip they boarded their bus in Laredo and headed to Corpus Christi and the Breakers Hotel, which was right on the beach. Swimming at the beach provided the first look at the ocean and the taste of salt water for many of the group. Deep sea fishing provided a sea food dinner with their catch. After dinner they ate birthday cake for Mr. Arnold and sang happy birthday to him. He then awarded prizes for the day's fishing catch. The prize for the most fish caught went to Norman Mosier and Gary Jones with nine apiece. Frank Shoemaker got the prize for the biggest. Of course, some claimed the one that got away was bigger, but they had no proof. Then to Waco, the Tam 'O Shanter Courts, more swimming, and to Enid for one more night so everyone could rest and also have one more night of swimming. Upon arrival in Towanda, they were greeted by a large and warm reception. The trip provided memories, loads of fun, an accent and a few Spanish words in the vocabulary, and a better understanding of how people in other lands live, whether they are rich or poor. Such an experience and thanks were extended to everyone in the community, parents, and teachers for help in making this trip possible. Those making the trip were George Shepard, Norman Mosier, Carl Brush, Walter Weller, Frank Shoemaker, Jim Rowland, Jim Laymon, Gary Jones, Karilyn Wagner, Susan Geymann, Delores Williams, Janet Geer, La Vaun Healy, Sharon Marshall, Sharon Wiens, Marie Wells, Dona Lovern, Mr. and Mrs. Reeves, and Mr. and Mrs. Arnold.

Mr. Howard Oliver was the last music teacher and had a very large choir, boys chorus, band, woodwind trio, brass ensemble and a nine and twelve girls ensemble.

School Closing—The school closed after the 1963 graduation with twenty-two graduates. The last graduate was Judy Wohlgemuth (alphabetically). A total of 596 graduated from Towanda High School in its fifty years of existence, 1914-1963. The school was unified with Benton, Oil City, Silverton, and Banora to form a new school built north of town which was named Circle High School.

#91

Rozel High School

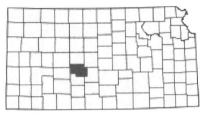

Mascot: Tigers

Colors: Purple and Gold

Year Closed: 1966

Location: town of Rozel, Pawnee County

The School of Hard Knocks — Rozel's first high school was built in 1912. The gymnasium was added twelve years later in 1924. The school burned to the ground on October 17, 1948. The following account appeared in the *Larned Daily Tiller and Toiler* on Monday October 18, 1948 (a single copy of this newspaper cost 3 cents).

$100,000 Loss In
Rozel School Fire

Sunday afternoon Blaze
Destroys Rural District
Building in Two Hours

The cost of the new building was $100,000 but insurance would only cover $32,000. The new vocational agriculture building under construction at that time was not damaged. Contents destroyed included band instruments valued at $1000 owned by the boys and girls of the school and about $1000 worth of typewriters, also owned by the pupils. A few musicians of the band saved their instruments by taking them home after the band played at Ft. Hays at the Saturday afternoon football game. Forty five tons of coal in the basement was ablaze for several days after the fire started.

Also saved was the football equipment used by the six man football team in the game with Windhorst Friday afternoon to give it an airing after the game, but all other athletic equipment in the gymnasium was destroyed.

A bond for $32,000 was completed two years before this for the shop, music room, and bus garage. Of these, the bus garage was the only addition that was not damaged in the fire.

A tornado on May 5, 1949 stuck Rozel, then a town of 216 people, leaving two injured. There was another account in the *Larned Daily Tiller and Toiler* on Wednesday Nov. 10, 1948:

Back to School at
Rozel This Week

Three weeks of enforced vacation ended Monday. Rozel boys and girls were back to school in temporary quarters Monday morning after a three-week vacation following the fire which destroyed their school building on Oct. 17.

The community building south of the school building and the new vocational building on the school grounds are now housing the grades and high school and will be used until a new building replaces the ruins of the 36-year old structure. Rozel schools are really making a new start in their make-shift quarters, as all the schools records were destroyed in the fire. The records were kept in a safe in the office of Supt. George W. Adams. The fire-seared safe was retrieved from the rubble a week after the fire but when it was opened the records were so badly charred by the intense heat they are of no value.

On May 20, 1949, the *Larned Daily Tiller and Toiler* also reported on the tornado:

A tornado can leave some unusual tricks behind. Mrs. L.E. Arnold is the only resident known to have profited from the storm. A five dollar bill sailed into Mrs. Arnold's window during the big blow. It is believed to have been the first time a tornado ever left a tip.

Mr. and Mrs. Guy Patterson gave another account of the tornado. With their youngest daughter, Sue, the couple huddled in a mud and water filled ditch in front of their home during the tornado while five other Patterson children took refuge in the ditch on the other side of the street. "We counted the heads over there as they came up after the storm passed and were we relieved when all five came up," Guy told the neighbors during an exchange of experiences.

The school closed on December 6, 1916 until after the Christmas break because of a diphtheria outbreak. The first graduating class was in 1917. That year there was a literary society and a girls basketball team.

History of Athletic Excellence — Rozel will forever be known as the only school in state history that won the boys basketball state tournament in back-to-back years in two different classifications. With a new coach at the school in the fall of 1958, Richard Boone, straight out of Pittsburg State University, came to town. He had been raised in and graduated from Haviland, only sixty-two miles southeast of Rozel. Though he would only be the coach for four years, he became a legend in the school's history. He reportedly had been in the barbershop before school started that fall and had seen some of his players come into the shop. By their height, he claimed to know instantly that they would be great for his team. And great they were. In his first year as coach, they led Rozel to the Class BB State Championship in Dodge City. Enrollment grew, and with sixty-one students in the high school, Rozel's classification became B. Competition with larger schools did not phase the Rozel boys as they repeated, in 1960, by winning the Class B State Championship trophy.

Football was played as six-man, then eight-man, and finally eleven-man with unification in 1967. The school's rivals were also members of 50-50 League: Burdett, Offerle, Windthorst, Hanston, and Spearville. Half of the six schools in the league were from south of Highway 50 and the other half from north of Highway 50, thus the name, 50-50 League.

Coach Boone left for Arizona in 1961 and became a college dean but returned to Pawnee Heights to coach the girls basketball team thirty-seven years later in 1998 and 1999.

Notable Graduates — One of the renowned graduates from Rozel High School was Harold Patterson ('50). He was a great athlete and a three-sport letterman at the University of Kansas. He was the second Kansas high school graduate on the KU 1953, runner-up national champion, Jayhawk basketball team. The other player was the big man and high scorer, B.H. Born, from little Attica, Kansas, 125 miles to the southeast of Rozel. The legendary Dean Smith from Topeka High School was a graduate assistant with that team. Patterson then starred for the Montreal Alouettes and the Hamilton Tiger-Cats in the Canadian Football League for nine years. He held the record for a 1956 game when he gained 338 yards on pass receptions until it was broken in 1967. He still holds the record with 588 yards pass-receiving in the Grey Cup. A nephew of Harold's, Gary Patterson, also came from Rozel, but technically did not graduate from Rozel as it had already consolidated with Burdett to form Pawnee Heights in 1967.

Unification Efforts — In 1967 the school was unified with Burdett, eleven miles west, and the district was re-named Pawnee Heights with the high school located in the former Rozel high school building. In 2005, under a contractual agreement with Hanston, that district sent their students to the elementary school in Burdett and their high school students moved to the newly named Pawnee Heights High School in Rozel. This was a total of twenty-two miles from the townsite of Hanston to Rozel on buses.

A total of 611 students graduated from Rozel High School. The last class was in 1966. The smallest graduating class was in 1920 with only one graduate. The largest class was eighteen in 1939.

Rozel High School
Pawnee County, KS

#92

Republic High School

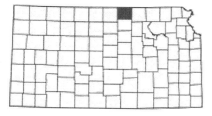

Mascot: Wildcat

Colors: Red and White

Year Closed: 1973

Location: northwest corner of Republic County, less than five miles from the Nebraska boarder.

Area History — At the time that the four-year high school began in 1910, there were 135 grade schools and country schools in Republic County. The county population peaked at 18,562 in 1901. The population at the 2010 census showed only 4,980 county residents.

In 1887 the question of an adequate school building was brought before the people in Republic. The school-house built after a vote that year was a white frame, two-story building with dark trim. This school was used for ten years. The first graduating class was in 1901 with the graduation program held in the Baptist Church. Classes were held in this building until the "new" two-story brick building, a twelve-year school, was opened in the fall of 1910. The new school had room for domestic science, agriculture courses, and also restroom facilities.

A Normal Training School — Normal training also was offered, and some outstanding rural teachers came from that program. This training was for students who were educated to be teachers in the rural one-room schools of that time. Mrs. Sybil Davidson Rahe ('32) taught the first and second grades at the Republic School from 1956 until her retirement in 1982. She wrote an account of normal training in December 1997 at the request of her children:

During my Junior year I started preparing to take classes to get a Normal Training certificate to teach school. Republic was widely known for its Normal Training for rural teachers. Many students from other districts came to Republic for the training. I was 15 years old and Miss Gladys Peterson and Miss Hildur Dahlstein, both Swedish teachers from Lindsborg College (today Bethany) took an interest in me. Miss Peterson was the teacher who influenced me a great deal to start going to Sunday school and Church. Reverend Gertrude Pettiblon was the minister at the United Brethren Church at the time.

After Leonard graduated in 1931, it was arranged that I should walk one mile and ride 2 ½ miles into school with Florence Haptonstall. This I did most of the time. No buses then! If I missed her, which wasn't very often, I walked. I passed my teachers exams in the spring of 1932, but did not get a school to teach. There were as many as 20-25 applicants for every teaching position as it was the start of the very serious depression and drought years and everyone wanted a job. I graduated from high school shortly before my 17th birthday in 1932.

The "new" high school, by this time thirty-seven years old, was condemned in 1947 by the state. However, classes continued to be held in the building for a while. The classes were moved out of the condemned building over Christmas vacation in 1948. For two and a half years students attended classes in various buildings across town until the new elementary and high school building was opened in the fall of 1951. Four or five classrooms were devoted to grades 1-8, depending upon the enrollment. Usually there were two grade levels in each classroom.

School Traditions—The first yearbook was called the *Patriot* and was published by the senior class of 1918. In the first six years having a high school, fifty-three graduated and seventeen of those went on to be teachers.

The school paper in May 1927, known as the *Rep-City Wild Cat*, printed the valedictorian and salutatorian addresses. The boys and girls track teams had just returned from Belleville where they competed against the other eight high schools in the county. An article of the senior sneak was classic for the times:

Thursday May 12, laying aside their dignity, and bedecking themselves in overalls and straw hats, the Seniors sneaked away from their old high school and vamoosed to Superior Park for the day. Armed with a worthy old musket, they entered the portals of R.H.S and kidnapped their sponsor, Mr. Simpson, and carried him along. They spent the morning in trying to slide down the slippery slide and playing baseball. Each of the Seniors had contributed to the dinner and the Seniors proved themselves very capable in disposing of the food. After this most bounteous meal they journeyed to the cement plant and explored it very thoroughly . . . This was very interesting as well as instructive. They were furnished with two guides and they attempted to explain everything. After this they returned to the park and soon returned home, tired and happy.

The football team of 1929 had seventeen players. They posed in their uniforms with two coaches looking smartly dressed in their three-piece suits and ties standing on the school steps.

Phyliss Hofts ('46) was the head cheerleader and later a teacher for a year and the school secretary. She shared stories of Republic:

One 'hot' basketball game with Hardy was played in city hall. My father, Jim Thomas, thought the referees "had made an error" on a call, so he jumped out on the floor to protest. My brother, Kent Thomas, (who went on to play football at KU and into the service before dying young with diabetes) was playing. He picked Dad up by his overall straps and put him back in his seat. The law came that night to escort Hardy out of town. All games were interesting with large and vocal crowds.

Our senior sneak in 1946 took us to Denver, Colorado in the back of Ralph Morehead's grain truck covered with a canvas tarpaulin. Needless to say, we were "wind burned" but had a wonderful time in the big city. We were chaperoned by Cal and Violet Sutherland and Ralph and Violet Morehead.

The class of 1942, the first graduating class after the war had started, was a renowned group of seniors. The boys all knew where they were headed. One of those boys was Glen Hofts ('42) who later married Phyliss. Upon enlisting in the navy, he used his beautiful voice and was recruited into the navy choir. The locals crowded around their upright radios on Sundays to hear Glen and the navy choir sing as a representative to our country's spirit during those war years.

Don Symmes, also in the class of 1942, became a favorite son of Republic. He came to town as a teenager with his family, traveling in a tour car. They were regarded as gypsies as they would stop in different locations to stay only a short time and then move on. Don was captivated by Republic and refused to go on with his family. He stayed and roomed at the hotel. He was supported by some of the area farmers and townspeople. He was the ring leader for every fun activity. He graduated and went on to college at Kearney State in Nebraska and received his doctorate in California. He was notorious for making calls in the middle of the night to his friends in Republic just to chat. Symmes organized the fiftieth class reunion from his residence in California, and the reunion was one for the classics. There was a county tour that stopped at all of the old memory spots. There was a talent show and a fishing trip. The reunion was topped off by a banquet and an orchestra, all sponsored by this little boy who stayed on to be adopted by the town and his high school classmates of Republic.

Athletics — The *Republic Booster* newspaper, dated November 28, 1946, had a picture of the undefeated football team which had seventeen players as well as their two coaches in their coats and ties. The team was undefeated.

Wildcats Undefeated This season
Results of all games:
Republic 40 Courtland 0
Republic 41 Agenda 26
Republic 57 Hardy 6
Republic 53 Burr Oak 6
Republic 33 Chester 0
Republic 26 Jamestown 7
Republic 53 Jewell 25
Republic 77 Scandia 22

With the close of Republics football season, the Wildcats were undefeated and made fourteen straight wins in their last two seasons.

The same paper had the movies showing in Republic at The New Community Theatre for the next two weeks featuring Warner's *Night and Day* with Cary Grant and Alexis Smith and Sam Wood's *Guest Wife* with Claudette Colbert and Don Ameche.

The subscription rate for the *Republic Booster* was $1.00 and the single copy was five cents.

School Closing — There were a total of 714 graduates from Republic High School when it closed in 1973. The students from Republic began attending high school in Belleville. The most numerous surnames were Elliott-19, Sankey-13, Daughtery-13, VanNotwick-12, Hurley-9, Smith-8, Cooper-8, Fuller-8, Mitchell-8, and Millin-8. The largest graduating class was twenty-six in 1940. The last graduate was Lynn VanNotwick (alphabetically).

#93

Barnard High School

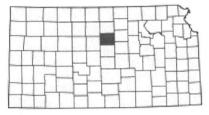

Mascot: Cardinals

Colors: Red and White

Year Closed: 1966

Location: town of Barnard, northeastern corner of Lincoln County

History of Schools in Barnard — Barnard High School was organized in 1905 with twenty-seven students enrolled. The old school building burned down in 1908. Classes were then held in various churches around the city. The term was completed without loss of educational efficiency. A new school housing grades 1-12 was constructed that year from red brick and limestone.

Departments and offerings were added during the next few years. Athletics began in 1916. Domestic art and science became part of the curriculum in 1918. A Normal Training course was added in 1919. Music courses began in 1920 and commercial law and penmanship in the spring of 1921. Manual training and laboratories for physics and agriculture were soon to follow. (Source, 1920-21 Barnard Annual)

Barnard Rural High School became its own entity with the dedication of a new brick high school in 1948. It was connected to the old school to the east. The 1951 *Cardinal Annual* stated, "Due to the foresight and insistence of the people of the community we are fortunate and thankful to be able to take part in the activities connected with this magnificent accomplishment."

Consolidation Protest — One of the most interesting peaceful protests in the state of Kansas happened that summer of 1966. It came from air and land. Leaflets were dropped throughout the county seat town of Lincoln and a fifty car and truck caravan protested and lobbied the issue that if Barnard had to lose its high school and come to Lincoln, the public demanded better roads to transport the students. The county commissioners and elected officials had not experienced this kind of grassroots protest. The commissioners—Fred White of rural Lincoln, Lawrence Mettlen of Sylvan Grove, and Ted Metz of Lincoln—expressed mild irritation and amusement at the attack. "It's the most ridiculous thing that has happened in my eight years as county commissioner," said White in an interview with the *Wichita Eagle* newspaper. Ridiculous or not, signs reading, "We're for a Better Safer Road for our School Buses," rode high in a Chevrolet pickup and VW vans. Edsels and pickups with campers paraded around the courthouse square. At 10am, a single plane passed over the city and dropped several thousand leaflets headlined "Here WE Come!"

Metz, whose district included Barnard, said in the *Wichita Eagle*, "The whole thing is a publicity stunt by three or four people over there-who are good people and friends of mine-but they don't know all of the facts." He expressed doubt that there was much concern on the part of very many of Barnard's 200 residents or that much of a demonstration would materialize.

After the protest, the rural roads of the county did get a face lift. Literally, the squeaky wheel got the oil and all rural residents noticed a more concerted effort to improve the roads.

Traditions & Athletics

The school song was:
Barnard High. Barnard High
We will fight for Barnard High
She's our high school
We'll stand by, you bet
We will sing, we will shout,
We will hang the banners out,
As we fight for the red and white.
For it's hep, hep, hep, everlasting hep,
That's what you find at Barnard High.
So where e're we go, you will always know,
That we're fighting for Barnard High
Keep them fighting,
Yes, we're fighting for Barnard High.

Girls sports included softball and basketball. A very active band performed at the Kansas State Fair parade, complete with a majorette and flag girls. Students complained about wearing the hot, scratchy uniforms all day. A large, mixed choir was led by Mrs. Canfield.

From the *History of Barnard High* booklet in 2016, under the heading of "Yester-me, Yester-you, Yester-day," Charlie Kelley ('66) penned the following:

Music was my favorite subject. I can remember Mike Donabauer ('65) sang "How Are Things in Glocca Morra?" I could never hit the tenor notes. Armin sang "The Impossible Dream." Mrs. Canfield had everyone singing. I remember Ray Coover ('66), Joy Wolting Hart (graduated from Lincoln in 1967 after the school closed), and David Simmons (graduated from Lincoln after the school closed) all sang at plays and school events. We all participated at the regional competition. Mike Biggs ('64), Mike Donabauer ('65), Armin Kelly ('65), and Steve Simmons ('65) became The Barnard Beatles, wigs and all.

Consolidation & Closing — In the 1960s, discussions across the state arose regarding consolidation of schools to better meet student needs by offering a broader curriculum and more academic opportunities. This affected many schools and entire communities. By 1966, Barnard, Vesper, Beverly, and Lincoln High Schools consolidated and became USD #298. The last class graduating from Barnard High School was 1966 with an all-boys class of nine. The last graduate receiving a diploma from Barnard High was Kenneth Srna ('66) (alphabetically). The grade schools continued to be held in their respective communities for a few more years.

In the school's fifty-eight years of existence, from 1909-1966, a total of 668 graduated from Barnard Rural High School. The largest class was twenty-seven in 1932. The smallest classes, with one graduate, were in 1911 and 1913. The most numerous surnames were Loy-18, Wallace-13, Keeler-12, Myers-10, Cornellisson-9, Kelly-9, Biggs-8, Marstellar-8, Adams-7, Hart-7, and Jackson-7.

Barnard High School
Lincoln County, KS

#94

Zenda High School

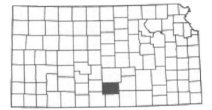

Mascot: Gorillas

Colors: Blue and White

Year Closed: 1966

Location: town of Zenda, southwest Kingman County

History — Zenda was first called Rochester—after Rochester, Minnesota—in the mid-1880s. At the time there were twenty-eight other places around the country that were named Zenda. At one time there were nine high schools in Kingman County. Today (2018) there are only two.

District #5 was started in Zenda in 1919. Seven freshmen in a small room above the Eureka Theater, now the Zenda City Building, met for the beginnings of a high school in Zenda. The first furniture was long tables and some chairs. Since it was impossible to have sports, a good dramatic club was organized. Several plays were presented in the theater. The three-act play *Diamonds and Hearts* was perhaps the best.

In the fall of 1920, the new high school building, which still stands (2018), was ready for students. There were three years of students, or a three year-high school, by 1921.

Traditions — Chapel exercises were held perhaps once a week or every two weeks. Classes took turns entertaining, or outside speakers were invited. School parties and picnics were other fun projects. The first senior class staged a good play, *Stop Thief,* coached by Miss Whitmer. Football started in 1957 with an eight-man team. Rivals were Nashville (KS) and Norwich.

The senior trips were a right of graduation. One senior trip was to Nashville, Tennessee, the Grand Ole Opry, and then to Miami Beach. A coach and his wife drove the drivers' education station wagon. A single teacher, Dortha Duerson, drove her own car for the trip. Miss Duerson was very well liked by the students. She also helped with the yearbook and was the faculty appointee to the very active Lions Club in town.

Early Consolidation and Closing — In March 1947, plans were made to consolidate the following rural one-room schools with District 82: Happy Hollow, Pleasant Hill, and Sunnyview. The Happy Hollow School was moved to Zenda to make another room for the school. A basement was built during the summer of 1947 and the building was placed on top of it. This made District 82 a three-room school. In early 1956, a basement and two

rooms were added to the north part of the brick grade school. Then the school became departmentalized.

A total of 466 students graduated with a Zenda High School diploma. The last graduating class was in 1966. The last graduate was Kim Westerman (alphabetically).

#95

Esbon
High School

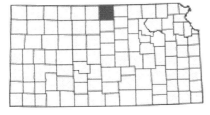

Mascot: Tigers

Colors: Black and Orange

Year Closed: 1983

Location: town of Esbon, western Jewell County

Area History — The Esbon town site was located on the main line of the Chicago Rock Island and Pacific Railroad. It was 245 miles west of Kansas City and 445 miles east of Denver on the beautiful, rolling prairie. Esbon became one of the most thriving and prosperous little cities in the northwestern part of Kansas.

Education — The Esbon School District #98 was organized in the early 1870s. Per the *Annuals of Kansas*, in

1874 Jewell County had 113 organized school districts. The first school building was a sod house. In 1880, a five-month term was conducted with Arthur Chapman as the teacher.

When the town was established in 1887, the area was known as Ezbon Township after Ezbon Kellogg. He was the son of A.B. Kellogg, one of the first settlers in the county and the first county treasurer. Up through the 1890s the spelling was E-Z-B-O-N. When the first newspaper was established in June 1892, it was named *The Esbon Leader*. From that time on, the letter S seemed to replace the Z.

Charley Whitney, writing in the *Jewell County Monitor*, printed the following in the January 8, 1903 issue about the town of Esbon:

> Esbon is located on the main line of the Rock Island in the western central part of the far-famed garden spot of the State-the one time banner corn county of the world-the county of Jewell.
>
> In the matter of public schools, Esbon should feel proud, as her educational institution is one of the finest in the county.

In August 1903, Jerome Hills was awarded the contract for a big two-story building for District #98. The *Topeka Capital Journal* wrote a very descriptive article about Esbon, "A brief description of Jewell County's most progressive town . . . another big improvement taking place is the erection of a fine new public-school building."

The next fall, 1904, those pupils who had earned common school diplomas (eighth grade) were admitted into the first class held for the high school. The principal's salary was $100 per month. This was a two-year course for the original high school training.

The first class of four graduates to finish the four-year course was in 1912. Each member of this class was very successful. They became a YMCA Director, a successful banker, a house wife, and a medical doctor-surgeon at Research Hospital in Kansas City.

Ivanoel Gibbins ('18) would also become a medical doctor. She was the superintendent, John Gibbins, daughter. She served for thirty-six years in India as a missionary physician and surgeon in the Punjab area. There is a hospital in the Punjab named after her. The Philadelphia Presbyterian Church was the primary benefactor. She was awarded a gold medallion by King George V for her meritorious service.

Jewell Monitor December 29, 1910:

> As a grain and livestock market, Esbon stands up well toward the head. During the past year, 11 cars of wheat, 121 cars of corn, 7 cars of horses, 128 cars of cattle, 129 cars of hogs, 53 cars of hay and 27 cars of other products have been sent out on the Rock Island. The town nestles close to the railroad, but it keeps 3 drays busy taking care of the incoming and outgoing freight.

In May 1920, voters in the Esbon school district voted bonds for a new school building. The *Esbon Times* reported, "The contract was awarded for $48,849.83 to the low bidder Glen Percy of Mankato."

Fiftieth Anniversary—The year 1937 marked the fiftieth anniversary of the town. The Esbon High School annual *Esbonite* gave the following information:

> . . . The present school building was erected in 1920 and has been in use ever since . . . This year the school started with an enrollment of 65 . . . And ended the year with 60.

From the February 24, 1947 issue of the *Esbon Times*, ". . . a special election held in Esbon Saturday the proposition to establish a Rural High School for the west side (Jewell County) carried by a majority of more than 2 to 1." This brought more townships into the school district, making it not only the largest in the county in area, but also the largest in valuation.

A bond election for a new high school building was held in April 1955. The cost of the new building was $220,000. The new building was completed and classes started in 1956.

Athletics—The Esbon High School boys basketball teams played in the 1927 and 1970 state basketball tournaments. The Esbon Lady Tigers went to state in 1925 and 1982. The boys also won the 1947 State track meet.

The 1953 football team started a thirty-five consecutive win streak. This streak came to an end on the last game of the 1958 football season.

In 1975, the Esbon headlines were that Margo Gillet, an Esbon senior girl, went out for footballs at EHS. Margo was the first female to participate in varsity football in Kansas schools.

Balloon Landing—Esbon drew national attention when Malcom Forbes's hot air balloon was blown off course and landed in Melvin Shipley's farm northwest of town at 5:30 PM on October 22, 1973. Mr. Forbes began his cross-country flight on October 4, from Coos Bay, Oregon, destined for the Atlantic Ocean. His goal was to become the first balloonist to cross the continent in a hot air balloon. The next morning busloads of students from Esbon and Lebanon schools, as well as many other spectators, came to the Shipley farm to see the balloon lift off at 8:45 AM. The flight ended for Mr. Forbes successfully on November 9, 1973 in Chesapeake Bay.

Enrollment Decline & Closing—In the 1920s, Esbon High School was one of eleven high schools in Jewell County. Declining enrollment, changes in agriculture methods, and the disappearance of the family farm caused these high schools to close, one by one. Sixty years later (2018) there is only one high school remaining at the county seat in Mankato.

The Esbon and Burr Oak districts voted in April 1983 to consolidate their schools by a 4 to 1 margin. The high school classes were moved to the former Burr Oak High School and the newly organized name was White Rock.

A total of 745 students graduated from Esbon High School in its seventy-two years, from 1912 until 1983. The most numerous surnames of graduates were Frost-25, Underwood-14, Beam-13, Johanek-12, Lewis-12, Steinhover-10, Fogo-10, Sloan-9, and Thompson-8. The last graduating class in 1983 had eight graduates with Glen Underwood (alphabetically) being the last to receive a diploma from Esbon High School.

Esbon High School
Jewell County, KS

#96

McCracken High School

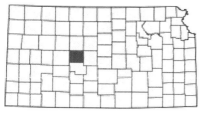

Mascot: Mustangs

Colors: Blue and Gold

Year Closed: 1984

Location: town of McCracken, northwest Rush County

Town Origins—McCracken was named after J.K. McCracken, a railroad contractor, in 1886. The welcome sign leading into the town reads, "Its biggest asset is the people that call it home." Pioneers settled in, breaking out limestone of "post" rock to build homes, businesses, and fences. The bank built in 1902 was made of "post" rock and it is the stateliest building on Main Street. There were many pioneers from eastern states with a German settle-ment northwest of town and an Irish settlement southwest of town.

The community lost a great number of their soldiers in the wars of the 20th century. Their names are still revered in the area—Paul West-World War I in France, Fay Burch-World War I in France, Gilbert Campbell-World War II on Savo Island, Walton Gilbert-World War II in the Philippines, Glen Gordon-World War II in the Pacific, Francis Lovitt-World War II in France, Harley Raymond Janke-World War II in Italy, Glen Gordon-World War II in the Pacific, Eugene Davis-World War II in Germany, and William Harp-Vietnam War.

A school house was built of brick from Brick Hill on the Big Timber Creek and was completed in December 1887. Businesses in town at that time included a general store, carrying clothing, groceries, flour, barrel salt, and feed. Two general merchandise hardware stores carried agriculture implements, sewing machines, windmills, building materials, and coal. There were two doctors and druggists, a jeweler, the Bank of McCracken, the Pacific House, a furniture dealer, livery men, a contractor and builder, a shoemaker, restaurant and bakery, photo gallery, and a company handling farm loans.

A college was started just seven miles northeast of the town site called Entre Nous. It was started by the Connecticut Yankee, Howard Barnard. Its purpose was to train teachers for Kansas schools. The book, *Yankee on the Prairie,* by Allan R. Miller, depicts the rural teaching methods and one man's dedication and contribution to Kansas teacher education:

Books, Schools, Education are the Scaffolding
By Means of Which
God builds Up the Human Soul.
-Entre Nous College, 1911-1912 Graduation Souvenir

Education— The high school was built in 1911. The first graduating class was in 1913 with seven graduates.

The first curriculum when the four-year high school began was First year-freshmen—English, Latin, algebra, Greek Roman history; Second year—English, Latin, algebra, geometry, medieval and modern history; Third year—English, Latin, geometry, physiography, American history; Fourth year—English, Latin, physics, botany, and one elective.

The R.E.N. (Rush-Ellis-and Ness Counties) league scholarship contests conducted by Emporia State Teachers College were held annually. The following were some of the results for the league and the state contests:

1938: 2nd League, 4th State	1950: 2nd State
1939: 1st League, 5th State	1951: 2nd State
1940: 1st League, 3rd State	1952: 4th State
1941: 1st League, 3rd State	1953: 1st State
1942: 1st League, 3rd State	1954: 2nd State
1943: 1st League, 1st State	1955: 1st State
1944; no league, 1st State	1956: 1st State
1945: 1st League 9th State	1957: 1st State
1946: 2nd League, 4th State	1958: 1st State
1947: 2nd League	1959: 2nd State
1948: 1st League, 2nd State	
1949: 1st League, 2nd State	

The original school mascot was the Blue Birds. In 1958, the mascot changed to the Mustangs and the school colors became blue and gold.

The original high school building was torn down in 1958 and was replaced with a new building where classes started on February 1, 1959. The band mothers sold plates with images of the old McCracken High School.

They were on display in the window of the City Café. That February the first play at the new school was a one act play that received a 1 rating at the district speech festival. Members of the cast, all from the class of 1959, were Arlene and Marlene Wilson, Karen Walker, Joyce Showalter, Donna Knight, and Peggy Harper. There were only five graduates the first year of the new high school.

Athletics—On December 19, 1958, the McCracken basketball team opened with a R.E.N. league game against Bison with a capacity crowd. The game was the first contest ever played in the new gymnasium. It was a large brick structure and was ideal for R.E.N. tournaments. The top scorer for McCracken, with eighteen points, was Bobby Peters ('60). Bison won the game.

When league high schools were closed and unification caused the R.E.N. League to disband, McCracken joined the South 50-6 League. By the 1970s, they joined the Lincoln-Branch League.

Fifty students were enrolled in 1963. MHS again won first in state scholarship that year. There were seven out for six-man football. In October of 1963, they defeated Offerle by a score of 42-6.

The McCracken Madrigal Singers, led by their teacher Barbara Reinert, became renowned in the area for their performances. In 1972, seventeen madrigals departed on a charter bus for a five-day trip to South Dakota. They sang at the high school in Rapid City and then toured the Black Hills and the Bad Lands.

The McCracken Mustangs won the state basketball tournament in March 1972. This team had been invited to the Tournament of Champions in Dodge City. With an enrollment of fifty-one students, it was the smallest school entry. The largest was by Shawnee Mission North with an enrollment pushing 2,000. MHS led most of the game before falling 53-51 in the first-round. McCracken then edged Dodge City 59-58 in the loser's bracket game. They then defeated Chapman, 54-38, for third place.

School Closing — The district became unified under state law with the county seat city of LaCrosse. With one school board, the decision to close McCracken was based on declining enrollment and the cost of maintaining McCracken High School. The Concerned Citizens Committee filed a recall petition for a board member. A claim of breaking the open meetings law was thrown out by a judge. An attempt to have the district withdraw some of their land and join the Bazine district was thwarted by the President of the USD #395 School Board from Lacrosse. He commented at a meeting that the board had no legal authority to allow a portion of the district to withdraw. Also, McCracken could not have old school district No. 28 again. USD #395 refused to have buses from Bazine USD #304 come into their school district to pick up students.

The subject of a land transfer to the Bazine district was presented by the Alexander and McCracken patrons to Bazine's school board. Approximately 125 McCracken area residents and Bazine USD #304 patrons gathered at a special Bazine school board meeting to discuss the possibility of a land transfer from Rush County USD #395 to Bazine USD #304.

The Bazine board rejected the plan that would have placed the sixth, seventh, and eighth grade students in McCracken and the high school students in Bazine, citing the cost of transportation and public opinion as the major factor for the rejection. The Lacrosse board voted not to allow any district to bus their students to another district.

The school closed in 1984 with 651 students having graduated from McCracken High School in its seventy-four years. The biggest classes were in the 1930s with twenty-seven graduates in 1935. The most numerous graduate surnames were Higgins-28, Irvin-14, Casey-12, Schuckman-11, and Conrad-9. The Scotch-Irish surnames of the graduates were also very prominent with twenty-five graduates having the last names of McCormick, McMullen, McCaskey, McGaughey, McKittrick, and McKinney.

On May 21, 1984, Richard Wittman (alphabetically) was the last graduate of McCracken High School.

McCracken High School
Rush County, KS

#97
Jamestown Rural High School

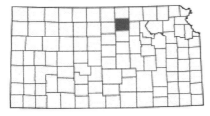

Mascot: Jayhawks
Colors: Blue and White
Year Closed: 1980
Location: town of Jamestown, north-western Cloud County, 10 miles from Concordia (county seat)

First Schools

It was one of the brightest towns in the county, and one of the most sightly spots of ground to be found anywhere. It was at the junction of two branches of the Missouri Pacific and on Buffalo Creek. It was only five years old, but had about 500 enterprising people, two railroads, two grain houses, a bank, lumber yard, shops, and stores befitting a town of its size. It has just completed a splendid two-story school house, worth $5000 when fully furnished. It has an excellent water-power flour mill on the Buffalo.

"Jameston," from *History of Cloud County*

Charles Gould chose to drive his cottonwood sapling stakes and attached his name, thus claiming his homestead, a part of which is now the north side of Jamestown in 1872. Whether the direct lineage can be identified, there were Gould graduates from Jamestown in the first graduating class in 1896, as well as in 1904, 1910, and 1912. As soon as he could, Mr. Gould built a small brick house for his protection. Two years later, in 1874, one term of school, the first in Jamestown, was held in that stone house. Eight years later, in 1880, a white, wooden, two-story, four-room school house was proudly put to use by the community. Bonds for a total of $800 were voted for the purpose of building a new schoolhouse. Within four years, the enrollment was so large that the Christian Church was rented and the higher grades attended classes in the church building.

In the summer of 1884, a school building was erected. The structure served the district faithfully for more than three decades even though it was virtually impossible to heat. It was so cold that it was dubbed the "White Sepulcher." For thirty-four years it was the educational center of the community. High school commencements began during this time. It was from this school that the first seniors graduated in 1896.

In the fall of 1911, Jamestown teachers announced that the time had come for all to gather their books and other personal effects. Moving day was upon them. They marched en masse to the community's new, three-floor, red brick building, just one block from the "White Sepulcher." Here the community's continuing commitment to excellent education commenced. School, in what was then a completely modern facility, started in the fall. Students graduated from this building for the next forty-four years. The last high school and gymnasium for Jamestown was built in 1957.

Stories from Students

In an early account from her grandmother's letters, Kathleen Anderson ('57) shared the following:

In 1920 there was quite a fuss among parents about rehiring the current superintendent because he attended card parties and under his regime the high school pupils learned to dance.

In 1924, my aunt who graduated from the University of Kansas applied for a teaching job in Jamestown, but she was declined by the school board. Many of the members belonged to the Klan and she was a catholic. The letter continued, "Klan sentiment is so strong throughout the state, fostered by our Klan governor that there is no chance for a catholic in the public schools."

A great aunt of mine was teaching first grade in Jamestown in 1932 and made $125 per month. The depression took a toll on the schools, too. A 1933 letter said, "There are many teachers who did not get a school this year and those that did took a heavy cut in salary. We have cut two high school teachers."

Don Dotson ('54) shared his sports memories:

My first year in high school we played six-man football. I was the quarterback for the team. The field was 85 yards long and the quarterback was not allowed to run past the line of scrimmage unless he took a handoff from one of the two other halfbacks. We had no lights, so all the games were played in the after-noons except at Jewell. Every other year we got to play under the lights, which was a thrill.

During WWII, Concordia, eleven miles away, had the largest German prison camp in the state. Prisoners came in jeeps and worked in the hay fields with our family. Many could speak some English. We stacked hay on a flatbed truck all day. They were really nice guys. I drove the tractor at the age of ten with the baler. The Germans were amazed at this kid doing such work. My mom did the cooking and the Germans loved the beer we offered them before we ate.

I bought a Wizard motor bike for $158 and was still under age and had to have it tagged. I would take it to Concordia and drive all around even though I was under age. My next bike was a Cushman and I, some 60 years later, am still a member of the Cushman Scooter Club.

My mother, Ruby Champlin Dotson ('29) and I had the same first grade teacher, Miss Laura Murray ('02). Miss Murray was an extraordinary teacher and lived with her brother Steve Murray ('07) who was the postmaster in town. Neither ever married and were great contributors to the Jamestown communities.

My cousins Gary ('54) and Bruce ('54) Champlin were more studious than me and both went to K-State and became an aeronautical engineer and veterinarian. We were all in the same class.

The senior trip was to Colorado. There were eighteen in our class and we traveled west and got into a terrible snow storm at Colby. It was the first of May as sleet and the biggest snow of the year hit the area. We all were in cars as we plowed on west to Manitou Springs, the Garden of the Gods, a steel factory in Pueblo, the Denver Mint, Lakeside Amusement Park, and to a musical at Rock City.

Asa Grennan ('62) also shared stories:

We were from a poorer family, but it didn't mean anything. It seemed everyone was equal regardless of income. Everybody seemed like family. During my school years Jamestown had three implement dealers, two car dealers, two restaurants, a movie theater, barber shop, and businesses lined Main Street. This changed during my high school years when we drove. Concordia was eleven miles away and it seemed you really had to plan a trip there as it was so far away. I believe the thing that helped destroy the small town was transportation. The roads and vehicles improved, and it became so easy to go the larger towns that the small towns could not compete for the business.

School Lunch Program —
The school hot lunch project sponsored by the Young Woman's Christian Association, a local organization that operated in the school for two years from the fall of 1944 through the spring of 1946. The project was very popular with the parents and pupils. Due to various circumstances, it was forced to close. The YWCA planned to sponsor the project the next year as many requests were made for the continuation unless food shortages and restrictions made it impossible. The wonderful cooks were Mrs. Hulda Elniff and Mrs. Pearl Hutchinson.

Athletics —
Jamestown High School athletic teams competed in the Pike Trail League which was made up of schools from Randall, Jewell, Scandia, Courtland, Simpson, and Cawker City. Some students participated in eight-man football, volleyball, basketball, and track and field.

The End of Jamestown —
The first graduating class of 1896 had one graduate, Olive Gould Nelson. There were no graduates again until 1901. Whether these first classes were two-year high school graduates cannot be determined. Including the early years, a total of 963 graduated from Jamestown in the eighty-five years from 1896 through 1980. The largest graduating classes were in 1926 and 1938 with twenty-four graduates each. The most numerous surnames were Nelson-37, Johnson-23, Peterson-19, Lundblade-16, Gray-15, Christenson-11, Vollan-11, Anderson-10, McBride-10, French-9, and Smith-9. The last class of six graduated in May of 1980, with the last to receive a Jamestown diploma being Laura Schwerman (alphabetically).

#98

Hunter Rural High School

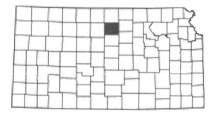

Mascot: Huntsman

Colors: Orange and Black

Year Closed: 1966

Location: town of Hunter, southwestern corner of Mitchell County

History of the Town — Hunter was originally located four miles west of its present location. In 1916, the town was moved to take advantage of the Salina-Osborne Railroad (1917). Today (2018), these rail tracks are part of the Santa Fe Railroad.

Hunter was declared a city of the third class by its county commissioners at Beloit (the County seat) on January 9, 1919. At one time there was a population of 250.

Though the years never showed a large increase in population in the town, many of the same family surnames remain in support of "their hometown." There is a spirit of community support among the rural and town residents. The Lutheran and Methodist churches are well attended. There remains an American Legion and Auxiliary, Lions Club, Extension Homemakers Unit and 4-H Club, church organizations, unified school, and other community activities. Many former students of Hunter schools have made prominent places for themselves wherever they reside. Alumni meetings, Memorial Day programs, and reunions are well attended.

Active communities surrounding Hunter in the early days were Blue Hill, Green Valley, Round Star, Ash Grove, Victor, and others.

The following was taken from the *Mitchell County Centennial History* book:

> Many rural High Schools were being organized across the country by 1917. In realizing this need in the community, Hunter voted bonds for a High School. Two teachers were hired and classes began in the fall of 1917. A permanent course of study was organized. The close of that year saw 45 students at work in the basement of the local Methodist church. A splendid new building was being constructed. When completed this new school with its equipment and organization was rated second to none in Mitchell County for a rural High School. The second year started with three teachers and fourth was added in its third year.

Hunter Hope was the only community doctor. He assisted and coached the athletic teams, which added much interest to the school system. When school began, not only did local students attend, but four came from Sylvan Grove and one from Beloit.

Building a School

Building a School — For the Bond Election 1917, a notice in the local newspaper read:

Dear Voter
Our future education depends upon your vote next Monday December 10.
We have made arrangements to attend high school at Hunter, Kansas. A great many of us are unable to attend high school away from home.
To carry the high school proposition next Monday, means only 2.50 per $1,000 on the valuation of your property. What would its defeat which would deprive many of us of our education mean to us?
Please give us your support, thus maintaining our high school at home, your town, and at our town, Hunter, Kansas.

Another article in this same paper read:

Hunter High School
Our hometown of Hunter Kansas is nestled on the Southern slopes of range of Blue Hills (elevation 1900 ft.) a picturesque view from the south especially. These Blue Hills have a deep-blue haze about them, both summer and winter. Much blue stem and buffalo grazing for cattle, added to the wheat, and grain sorghums, alfalfa and other crops make this area, a good farming community.

The first year, twenty-four students completed the term. In the fall of 1918, nineteen students returned as sophomores, enrolling in the building downtown (later occupied by the recreation hall), and recited part of their classes there and part at the church. A big improvement was that they had their own individual desks. The worst handicap of the year was the flu epidemic, with no school for two months due to the illness. By the time the ban was over, the professor informed the students they could move into the new high school. On January 1, 1919, a cold, snowy day, each student picked up their desks and materials and waded the snow drifts to the new school. The structure was made of native stone quarried from Tom Haden and Cap Berry's farms in the community. Much of the labor was donated to make the fine two-story building with a gymnasium in the basement and facilities for showers.

The first graduating class was in 1920 with students who had started the school as sophomores. Audrey Bilger (alphabetically) was the first graduate in this class of five girls. The largest graduating class was twenty-six in 1944.

Student Stories

Student Stories — Harold Heller ('41) had started college at Kansas State when the war broke out. He became a Merchant Marine and served in the Army Air Corps. Landing in the Philippines in 1944, he sent word back to Virginia Bressel ('41), one of his classmates, that he was surviving on the island, which had an elevation of one foot. He reported conditions as very primitive. The food was so poor and the quantity so limited that soldiers were stealing each other's rations. The only way to prevent others from swiping was to spit all over it when it was first handed out.

Virginia had taken the Normal training and became a one-room school teacher. Following the war, Harold returned to Hunter and married Virginia in 1945. They had a farm east of town. The family soon started as Terry Heller ('65) was born in 1947. There were two more children born to the couple who would later graduate from Sylvan Grove after the Hunter High School closed in 1966.

Athletics — An eleven-man football team was pictured in 1925 with a colored halfback in the back field. The 1922-23 girls team picture had seven girls lying on their stomachs, propped up on their elbows with their hands on their chins, and their index fingers pointing upward. They had great smiles and their bloomer-type uniforms and athletic shoes looked very fashionable.

Vesper may have been one of Hunter's rivals in athletics as they played both football and basketball. No other towns really stood out as primary teams to beat. Nearby Tipton did not play football. The Hunter Huntsman mascot was uniquely dressed in a pilgrim hat and English-style hunting outfit carrying a musket. The athletic teams were independent and played in no league. They played Sylvan Grove, Paradise, Waldo, Beverly, Vesper, Lucas, and Luray.

Terry Heller ('65) remembered:

> Our senior trip was to Chicago. All thirteen seniors rode the train from Salina and spent nearly a week in the Windy City. Our new coach, Mr. Dick Switzer, was our class sponsor. He was originally from Abilene and had played football at the College of Emporia. He was just a few years older than our senior class and had a wonderful rapport with the seniors.

Professor Claude A. Summers was the principal and taught in Hunter for twenty-two years until the grade school closed in 1970. He was an incredible teacher and could have taught any class or subject. Terry Heller summarized this teacher's significant teaching talents as follows:

> If I would have just listened to him, I wouldn't have had to go to college. We just called him Prof. His primary teaching subjects were math and geometry, but he also taught all of the sciences. We were very respectful of him though in chemistry we were always trying to make bombs. Our school had really tall windows and one of these chemical experiments turned into a debacle. With the help of Keith Otting ('66) and Ruth Geering ('65), these young scientific minds had taken an old empty duplicating fluid jug, added an experimental substance in the bottom, and suspended a test tube inside with a copper wire. I was holding the screen open with a yard stick and Keith and Ruth were about to drop the jug out the window when Mr. Summers unexpectedly came into the science room. He calmly said, "What are you guys doing?" I yelled back, "We don't have time to talk about it Prof!" as the dangling jug exploded, spraying its contents all over the outside bricks below the window. We spent the next two days scrubbing the bricks to remove all of the discolored debris stuck to the building.

Professor Summers' wife, Margaret Summers, taught home economics until the high school closed in 1966. She then became the home economics teacher at nearby Sylvan Grove. Having her there for the transferring Hunter students provided them with a friendly, familiar face that helped make the transition easier

Highway 181 reaches Hunter from both the south and west. Wagon Wheel Park is used for summer picnics. The slogan on the sign is:

> In case you are coming our way. The "Welcome Mat" is out, we'd be happy to have you stop by and enjoy "our town" of Hunter Kansas.

#99

Shallow Water High School

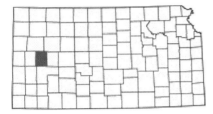

Mascot: Tigers

Colors: Red and White

Year Closed: 1969

Location: town of Shallow Water, south-central Scott County

Town Founding—Shallow Water was founded much later than most of the rural communities of Kansas. It came into being because of a railroad dream and venture by a man named McCue from Garden City. He proposed a transcontinental railroad across the High Plains from Canada to the Gulf of Mexico. Construction of the Garden City Great Northern began at Garden City. The rails were laid into south Scott County. Herbert Mott, who owned one of the first tractors in Scott County, was hired to operate it for the railroad. During one of the worst heat spells of the summer, a twenty-mule-team pulled an elevator grader.

These recollections, by Bill Mott, were published in the *History of Early Scott County* by the Scott County Historical Society, 1977:

> McCue had a January 1 deadline to reach Scott City. Mexican crew members worked in a blizzard laying ties on frozen ground to meet the deadline. A need for water led to digging in the area. They found that only a few feet down under the surface water could be reached. An 8' x 8' shelter was constructed with the word "Shallow" printed on the side. The community began in 1912 when H.J. Mott was given a half section of land by Friends, or the Quaker church.

The railroad paralleling U.S. 83 did not see completion all the way to Canada, but it did give service to the community. A grain elevator, post office, and store were opened by 1916. Ads were placed to encourage settlement in "our fair city."

Some recollections of the time period were that Herbert Mott was too good of a businessman to be a Quaker preacher. "When his group sent flyers to Nebraska and other areas to encourage settlement in Shallow Water, they gave a glowing report of the town. They mentioned hundreds of trees found in the area, but failed to say that they were seedlings that had been hauled in to fulfill the boasts! Many of the original abstracts in Shallow Water read "AQUIRED THROUGH FRAUD AND DECEIT." (Published in the History of Early Scott County by the Scott County Historical Society.)

Education — The first grade school was started in a small building that was moved into town in 1912. A second teacher was added in 1918 to begin a two-year high school. The next year another teacher was added to become a four-year high school. The first graduating class of two graduates was in 1922. The original building was replaced by a two-story, stucco structure. There were two rooms upstairs (for grades 3-8) and two rooms downstairs (for the high school). The first and second grade classes met in a small building east of the big school. There was an outdoor basketball court in back of the school. A portable stage for programs could be pulled onto the outdoor court. Graduation exercises were held in the church along with community sings, plays, and other programs.

Shallow Water consolidated in 1924 with the district to the west to form Shallow Water Consolidated District #10. There was much opposition to this move at the time. A school bus was used the first year of consolidation. The bus was a disc wheel Chevrolet with a wooden body. The heater was only a pipe that ran under the seats.

Plans for a new high school were drawn in May 1939, and a new adobe building was completed in 1942. WPA labor did the work, mixing adobe from suitable soil found north of the building. It was the only adobe high school building in use in Kansas and maybe the largest adobe school building in the world. It had the distinction of being the only high school built in Kansas by the WPA.

The thirties, the depression, dust storms, and the impending World War caused a dramatic decline in the number of high school students in Shallow Water. Class sizes diminished markedly. There were no graduates in the 1945 and 1946 classes. There were only seven students in the entire high school by the end of World War II.

In 1950, a three-person school board presided over the staff, which consisted of a superintendent (teacher), two teachers, a custodian, and a cook. The area farmers took turns donating beef for the school lunch program. Enrollment gradually increased as the farm students returned to schooling.

Music, woodworking, world history, general science, math, English, typing, boys basketball, baseball, track, and girls basketball, softball, and track were part of the curriculum. Home economics, biology, constitution, and psychology were added in 1955. Industrial arts, mechanical drawing, bookkeeping, commerce, chemistry, shorthand, geometry, algebra I and II, and social science were added in the 1950s with increasing enrollment. There were three full-time buses bringing students in from the rural areas.

Athletics — There was no football as the numbers of students were not sufficient to field a team. Sports and physical education were offered during regular school hours. Baseball and softball were played in the first six weeks in the fall and the last six weeks in the spring. The chief rival was Holcomb, though it was a larger school. Whenever there was a sporting event, the whole town would show up. There was always talent to entertain the crowd.

The girls basketball team was undefeated in 1957 and went undefeated for three straight years in softball. The red satin and white uniforms were quite stunning, and the teams played with pride for their school and community.

Kay Patton Moeller ('59) talked about her time in school:

> Competition in music consisted of mixed chorus, girls glee club, girls trios, sextets, triple trios, and boys

quartets, octets, and ensembles. The band performed, as well as a brass ensemble and several solos in vocal and instrumental. We traveled to the Western Arkansas Valley League Music Festivals every year at the same school (Kendall) because it was the largest school facility in our district. We had several talented pianists with Verlene Mohler accompanying the competition performances and Gloria Bontrager ('54) accompanying most of the school performances. Miss Mays, our director for many years, was always given high marks for music selection in all of our competitions.

Our main focus was on morals, music, and sports. The annual was published each year, which was completely put together by the students. They were sold for one dollar as a down payment and the remaining two dollars was due when the books were available at the end of the school year.

This reprint is from the *Shallow Water School Tiger Tales,* by Deva (Duff) Cupp ('66), and was titled, "Always do Your Best!"

Sitting in her third grade classroom, I soaked up her every move—sweet perfume to this little country girl, intent upon becoming a teacher myself one day. We began each day by saluting the flag. She taught us how to say the Flag Salute and really mean it—she stressed that it was One nation under God. "There was no comma after 'nations' boys and girls! She'd insist. "Let's say it again and this time, let's say it like we mean it!" for some reason, that makes all the difference in the world to me still—giving a richer meaning to words repeated every day.

She received a life-time Kansas Teacher's Certificate after two years of college and spent her entire teaching career at Shallow Water School. Her style of teaching was to make learning fun! Whether drilling for a spelling test, learning the states and their capitals, or playing a rousing game of Chinese checkers-she made learning an adventure! She had a closet full of games and often took the time to play with us during rainy day recesses. She taught us how to play Fox and Geese, Red Rover, Steal the Bacon, and Capture the Flag, often joining in our delight!

She shared her love of literature through books that taught moral values and lessons. Listening as the gentle hum of her voice buzzed around my ears like flies, I lay on the cool classroom floor, noting the distinct sweet aroma of "school house" wax, and dreaming of the day I too would read to youngsters each day after lunch. Little Britches taught me the value of giving your boss a full day's work of honesty and integrity. I experienced the pain of caring as I wept openly along with Miss Kamp and Ralph Moody when his dad died. From Twenty and Ten I learned of the evils of Hitler's Germany and of the importance of remaining loyal to a just cause even at the risk of death! I laughed along with Henry Huggins as he scared all his friends by chortling, "I'm the ghost of Henry Huggins."

Miss Kamp invited the third and fourth grade girls to her house for supper and a slumber party. Knowing all the little secrets about her house, I crept up on a number of unwary classmates, chortling "I'm the ghost of Henry Huggins!" reducing them to shrieks of terror and delight! After several such episodes, I heard Miss Kamp croak wryly, "You'll be the ghost of Deva Duff if you don't get quiet and go to sleep!" If I'd learned anything from Miss Kamp, it was that she never threatened anything she wasn't willing to carry through on… I've often wondered if that was the beginning of the end for Miss Kamp's sleepovers.

My college training for teaching was often dry as chalk dust but I held onto the dream of a little girl who had already learned most of what she needed to know about teaching from watching her third and fourth grade teacher in action.

Imagine the delight, twenty-four years after attending my last class under Miss Kamp's secure hand, to be given the opportunity to teach at Shallow Water School-next door to her! Each day after school, I'd stop by her room to visit and often asked her for advice concerning difficult situations! Once again she reminded me of the importance of laughter-of making learning fun! On what I thought was my worst days, she could make me laugh as she'd snort derisively, "there's not a court in the land that would convict us!' (For doing away with misbehaving boys and girls, I suppose!)

Her last days of teaching were difficult as she rapidly lost more and more of her mobility. She spent most of her last year at SWS on a motorized cart, her speech was becoming slurred, and the simplest tasks became monumental tasks-but she taught! She taught about the tenacity, hard work, the love of life, laughter, and tears!

Her last day of teaching, Miss Kamp's student aide knocked on my door and handed me her precious set of Little Britches books with a message, "Miss Kamp wants you to have these." Unwanted tears sprang instantly to my eyes as I realized the significance of her gift! (Now I share my love of literature each day with my students as I read aloud to them-and I still cry openly along with my students and with Ralph Moody when his father dies!)

It's early evening . . . as I heave against the massive back door of the school. I'm met once again by a familiar old friend-the distinctly, sweet aroma of "school house" wax! The halls are silent, friendly . . . as yet unscuffed. I flick on the light in my old third and fourth grade classroom-now my classroom and speak to my Lord, "Thank you, Father for knowing the heart and soul of a little nine year old girl and for caring enough to make her dreams come true! Thank you for giving me a role model like Miss Kamp! May my life inspire young people to follow the plans You have for me!"

In an account in the S.W.S. Tiger Tales 2000 edition Harold Trout ('40) remembered:

My first basketball coach was Miss Kemper. I was in the third grade and we played on dirt courts. On Wednesday nights, nobody was using the school so we got to practice in the gym . . . Shallow Water was a nice little town then . . . what I miss about the past is the moral values, no speed limit, no patrolmen, no driver's licenses, and my youth . . . the thirties were a very difficult time. The dust storms started when the wind changed and there was this big black cloud. When the dust storms hit, you couldn't see a thing and you couldn't raise any crops. There was so much static electricity in the air that the electric lines would glow red. There was so much dust that we had to stack our plates upside down in the cupboard to keep the dirt off them and we had to plug the windows with rags.

School Closing—The adobe high school was placed on the National Historic Register in 2005.

The school's largest class was fifteen graduates in 1966. In the forty-eight years of Shallow Water High School there were 260 graduates from the school. There were no graduates in 1945 and 1946. There was only one graduate in 1928 and two each in 1922, 1923, 1924, 1929, 1931, 1943, 1944, and 1948. The most numerous surnames of the graduates were Miller-11, Graham-8,

Whitson-7, and Duff-7. The school closed after graduation in 1969. The last graduate was Kyle Yardley (alphabetically).

Shallow Water High School
Scott County, KS

#100

Kanopolis High School

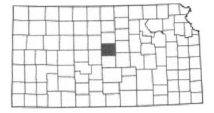

Mascot: Bulldogs

Colors: Orange and Black

Year Closed: 1967

Location: town of Kanopolis, eastern Ellsworth County

A 1908 Account of Fort Harker — The town of Kanopolis was also the site of Fort Harker. Though this army post preceded any schools in the area, an account of a woman written fifty years after her arrival in Kansas seems appropriate to the history of the area and for preservation of the times. The following was written by Mrs. Henry Inman in 1908 for a presentation to her Ellworth's Women's Club:

The anniversary of the birthday of Kansas is so very near that it suggests my giving the W.K.D. Club a reminiscence that I pledged Mrs. McFarland so long since. When with you on January 28, 1907, I was ill, really not able to be one of your number, so hastened home to care for myself and trust I am not too late in the fulfillment of my promise.

It necessarily takes me back to 1856 and my home, Portland, Maine and where a series of entertainments was given by the influential ladies of the city for the benefit of the so-called "Kansas Sufferers." Each night for a week I represented one or more characters in tableau, as past allotted to me.

The affair proved a financial success. The money was forwarded and made good use of, but had I then known how my future was to be identified with Kansas and her people how much keener my interest would have been, however, the Civil War came on not so very long after this, I married and at its close Col. Inman was ordered West. This was in 1867. And in January 1868, I left my home for Ft. Harker, Kansas.

In that day the facilities for traveling were not accompanied with the comforts of the present time, but all went fairly well until we reached East St. Louis. There was not a bridge then over the Mississippi River, and at midnight I walked over the ice to a boat which took us to St. Louis proper.

From there we journeyed on to Salina, Kansas where our train was awaiting to bear us on to Fort Harker, then the terminus of the Union Pacific Railroad. It was snowing slightly, but the storm increased, and although Secretary Coburn denounces the word "blizzard," with apologies to him I can substitute no other to express the conditions of the storm we rode into.

I had seen picturesque ones in New England, but never where the snow seemed to come from every direction, up as well as down; and when seventeen miles east of Salina we became snowbound. The drifts proved too much for our faithful engineer and his engine. So we were left on the open prairie to the mercies of the elements, with complete time for reflection, and one entire side of our train buried in snow. One passenger car was all we boasted, and I often recall the personnel of that one . . . "Uncle Sam" provided bacon and crackers and the tin wash-basin . . .

The commanding officer at Fort Harker (for the storm had reached there) anticipated the situation, knowing I was on the train dispatched to Salina if possible to get word to me to this effect.

I had brought several mince-pies (New England ones), carefully packed in my trunk that when my first meal was served in my new home, some one familiar dish would be in evidence . . .

Late that afternoon our conductor came with the cheerful intelligence that smoke could be seen in the distance which meant our troubles were nearing an end. A platform car with twenty men provided with shovels literally shoveled us out . . . This time we stopped at Brookville, fifteen miles east of Fort Harker, where I was met by friends from the Fort with an ambulance drawn by 6 mules and as many soldiers as escorts, for we were now in a hostile country. But we reached the Fort without further trouble . . .

This was the memorable winter of 1868. And I was surprised on my arrival to find Colonel Inman already in the field with General Custer and the famous Seventh Cavalry with General Sheridan in command.

Pioneers were struggling at this time to make homes for themselves and children, continually fighting against the odds, as day after day they were driven into the Fort for protection against strolling band of Indians who were ever seeking revenge, yet always with the courage to return to the claim and begin anew the life they had so zealously taken up . . .

In all his glory I have seen the Indian prepared and painted for war; the war-dance at midnight, when from their fires the entire country seemed ablaze; have watched them brought in captives after rescuing a girl of fourteen, whose father, mother and only brother had shed their life's blood in the effort to protect the little family. The child was cared for and finally sent to St. Mary's Mission.

"Lone Wolf", a Kiowa chief, who quite recently visited Washington D.C. in behalf of his interests, is still living. He visited the Fort in 1868 or 1869 to hold conference with Government officials, and presumably to smoke the "Peace Pipe." He had with him 150 squaws, papooses and young warriors, who sat about on the ground the entire day in sullen silence and afforded us the one opportunity in our lives to observe their characteristics and study faces; but truth to say I discovered no Mini-ha-ha, as Longfellow has immortalized.

From curiosity alone, I invited "Lone Wolf" to dine with me and my family which, accepting, through his interpreter, he seemed eager to do. I laid aside all conventionality, however, and instead of placing him on my right, gave him the entire end of the table. His one idea seemed to be to imitate, and he soon substituted the fork for his knife, while his manners improved as the meal went on. After this we took him to our living-room where the piano interested him immensely. He had never seen one before, and both the mechanism and music held him spell bound. The familiar saying, "Music hath charms to soothe the savage beast," became verified in his case, for a time at least, for while listening his weather-beaten face was pitiful to see. He

was really affected, and I felt sorry for him. But my sympathies took flight when he tried to enter into a business contract with Colonel Inman and offered him no end of ponies, buffalo hides, and other of his possessions for his "white squaw," but clung tenaciously to a tomahawk with which he professed to have killed many warriors.

The frontier life was confined mostly to Fort Harker and the surrounding country. History records the past and present, and I consider it a privilege to have been here in the early days, I can now fully understand what it means to settle a new country . . .

. . . I am a loyal Kansan, but perhaps not as enthusiastic as my husband (Colonel Inman), who often remarked "that after returning to the State from a journey elsewhere he felt like getting down and kissing the soil." . . .

The Army abandoned Ft. Harker in 1872. For five years it had become one of the most important military stations west of the Missouri River. Over the years, the threat of Indian raids in the region diminished as the territory was settled and the railroads moved west. Ft. Harker at its most active had 700 soldiers and possibly twice that many civilians and 400 horses and mules.

In June 1880, the United States Senate passed bill S. 194, an act disposing of Ft. Harker as a military reservation of public ownership and giving the 10,240 acre tract of land to the Interior Department for sale. The land was bought by Col. Henry Johnson and resold to Dr. Hodge who in the summer of 1885 formed a group of seventeen Ohio capitalist investors. They envisioned this area to become a metropolis much like Cincinnati and Cleveland. It was to be the center of Kansas and thus the name Kanopolis was chosen.

Their dream never quite materialized. The city of 500,000 that they had advertised failed to grow. By a vote of the people, the county seat of Ellsworth was chosen twelve miles to the west.

Salt Mines — The first salt mine opened in 1890, one of the earliest in Kansas. At one time there were three mining companies working some 1,000 feet underground in the area east and south of Kanopolis. The sandstone blocks used to build the hoist house and boiler house came from the hospital at Old Fort Harker. The mines attracted many Mexican workers and they assimilated into the schools and town. After a lengthy naval career, Johnny Miller ('58), worked in the salt mines following graduation until retirement. He recalled, "There were many Mexicans that worked here in the mines. They were great people and good classmates. We were all in the same boat. They became leaders and some of the most popular kids in our classes."

Early Education — Kanopolis Dam was built as a result of the Flood Control Act of 1938. Work began in 1940 but was halted in 1942 because of the war. Three and a half years later the work began again, and in 1948 the flood gates were closed. This was the first reservoir by the Corp of Engineers in the United States. The dam spanned across the Smokey Hill River.

In 1887, land was donated by the Kanopolis Land Company, and a three-story brick schoolhouse was built in 1888. The Kanopolis school system became more advanced with the completion of a new high school building in 1922. It was built from the plans submitted by Charles Shaver, a local boy who became a noted Midwest architect. According to available records, the first four-year high school class to graduate was the Class of 1919.

Prior to that there had only been a two-year course of study.

In 1954, a new grade school building was erected, adjoining the high school building. When the old grade school was torn down, a proud historical landmark was lost.

The school song, to the tune of the Notre Dame Fight Song, was proudly sung:

> *United we stand, so loyal and true,*
> *K.H.S. we're cheering for you.*
> *Can't you see it's bound to be*
> *Dear old Kanopolis to victory.*
> *We're from a school that's ready to win,*
> *We've got a team that never gives in.*
> *We're not worried never blue, the Bulldogs*
> *Will pull us through.*

A memorable sporting event in Kansas involved the Kanopolis football team. On November 8, 1956, the Kanopolis team traveled to Windom for the first eight-man football game to be played in Kansas. The cars lined up a half mile south of town taking the teams supporters to get into the game. Windom survived a very close, hard-fought battle and won 7-6.

Stories from Students — Lonnie Hayden ('56) worked in the brick plant following graduation. He remembered Mrs. Bertha Powell, a fifth and sixth grade teacher. He told this story:

Had 'shaken baby syndrome' been known at that time, I would have been a victim. Mrs. Powell was mean and everyone who went to Kanopolis had her for a teacher. Yet, she was probably the best teacher I ever had.

She would read to us after lunch, even before class was supposed to start.

Lonnie Hayden was no angel in high school as the pranks and interesting events seemed to always lead to him. A couple of tales included a stray skunk that was found in Mr. Hofer's car and a Volkswagen that found its way onto the flat roof over the study hall. Lonnie and his buddies would make noontime runs to Ellsworth to meet up with some girls, only to race back to high school to innocently make it to afternoon class. They had it timed to the minute. One day they were a few minutes late in getting back. When the principal stopped the three boys at the top of the steps, he reprimanded them and said, "I know what you have been doing and never do this again." So the next day they just stayed in their cars in the school parking lot under a tree and turned up the car radio and thought they had fooled the principal. Only time got away from them and they missed the bell and were late yet again. The principal met them again and would not believe their story of innocence.

Pedro 'Pete' Rubalcaba ('57) was a very popular and handsome boy and vice president of the class. He had bought an Indian brand motorcycle. He came to school the next day all bruised with cuts all over his face and arms, looking like he had been beaten to a pulp. Lonnie Hayden met him and asked what happened. Pete said, "Oh, I got beat up by that darned Indian."

Lonnie shot back, "What do you mean, we ain't got no Indians around here."

School Closing—There were 602 graduates of Kanopolis High School. Of these graduates the most frequent surnames were Perez-16, Torrez-11, Thompson-10, Smith-9, Cisero-8, Jacobo-8, Munoz-8, Merrill-7, Bray-7,

and Hurley-7. The salt mines employed many immigrant Mexicans whose children graduated from the Kanopolis schools. Other common surnames of graduates were: Marez, Gravino, Rubalcaba, Orozco, Vasquez, Diaz, Rivera, Lamia, Quartaro, and Ysquerra. Many of these students were married in the community and brought with them a rich heritage.

The high school was closed in May 1967 and consolidated with the Ellsworth school district. The last graduate was Nanette Stoppel (alphabetically).

Kanopolis High School
Ellsworth County, KS

#101

Florence High School

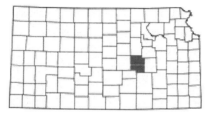

Mascot: Wildcats
Colors: Red and White
Year Closed: 1971
Location: town of Florence, east-central Marion County

A Railroad Town—Few towns in Kansas have such a rich history with railroads than Florence. The Atchison, Topeka and Santa Fe reached this townsite in 1871. Florence was purposefully founded on the diagonal from Topeka, Emporia, and on southwest to Newton at the intersection of the Cottonwood River. There were five miles of side tracks within the town as the railroad established a machine shop, a large depot, and a round house. The railroad could switch engines around the block until 1934.

Only six years after the ATSF was built, Fred Harvey bought the Clifton Hotel near the depot. The railroad was short of money, so Harvey invested in the hotel. He established the first Harvey House Restaurant with sleeping rooms. He hired Chef Bill Phillips from the Palmer House in Chicago to come to Florence for the unheard of salary of $5,000 per year to manage the restaurant in 1878. The railroad later repurchased the hotel from Harvey. The Harvey House closed in 1901, though part of the hotel is still open as a museum today (2018). The Santa Fe owned the buildings and Harvey owned the business and the furnishings. This agreement was all done with a handshake. In the 1890s there were eight passenger trains daily through Florence.

Education—There was a fire at the original high school in Florence, a stone building, in 1911. It was extinguished, and the school was reopened in the same structure. It was used for the grade school for sixty years after a new high school was built. In 1954, the lunchroom was moved to the second floor where the old auditorium had been located. A fire marshal, with the help of then Superintendent John Wiebe, found some old charred timbers in the foundation under the lunch room and managed to get the building condemned in 1968. This led to the closing of the school until the charred timber issue could be resolved.

Athletics & Traditions—The athletic teams played in the Cottonwood Valley League with Marion, Peabody, Hillsboro, Hope, Herrington, and Council Grove. The arch rival was Marion, which seemed to be everyone else's rival in the league as well. There were no girls sports until the near closing of the high school due to the

Title IX legislation when track, volleyball, and basketball were added.

Florence played eleven-man football and had the distinction, very early in the century, of playing the Kansas Agricultural College in Manhattan and beating them. Florence organized an Alumni Association in 1913. It is the oldest high school alumni organization in the state and celebrated its 105th anniversary with a banquet in 2018.

The 1927 yearbook showed a debate team and the National Honors Society as clubs within the high school.

Senior trips throughout the 1950s and early 1960s were usually to the Lake of the Ozarks in Missouri and the Kirkwood Lodge. Mr. Ben Barrett, a most beloved teacher at the high school from 1940-1971, was often the faculty sponsor on the trips. Money for these trips was raised with car washes, concession sales, and school plays.

The homecoming queen in the fall of 1966 was Kris Reid ('67). She was crowned at halftime of the Florence-Trinity football game. The two captains, Russel (Bud) Hanes ('67) and Mike Robinson ('67) placed the crown on the Queen. Her attendants were Susan Stauble ('68) and Carrie McClure ('68).

Student Memories — Michael Robinson ('67) was a football captain in his junior and senior years. He talked about life in Florence:

My great aunt was the Spanish teacher. I had been out the night before chasing cattle on horseback that had gotten out and were running through the cornfields. There were four of us boys that had worked most of the night to get them back in. We had gone home and got some sleep and didn't get to school until about 10 o'clock the next morning. The principal met us at the door and was about ready to "lower the boom" on us until my great aunt, Maxine Robinson, who was the Spanish teacher came to our defense.

Mr. Barrett was the most awesome teacher in history. He was not real exciting but really a super guy and taught us all to love history especially military history. His son, Tom Barret ('67), was in my class

The senior trip was the highlight of many of our lives. Vivid images and details still come out as we gather these fifty years later. The principal, who was one of our sponsors, alarmed all of us one night in Denver. He ran out into the hallways of the motel and was panicked that he wanted to know where the fire exits were located. We went to Cave of the Winds, the Royal Gorge, and a number of Denver sights. There were seventeen in my class and we rented a regular bus from someone who was the chauffer. Of course, there were a few problems created by sneaking out after hours. As I recall, it was mostly the girls that got us guys into trouble. There were clean shenanigans, and we all got home safely though the stories seem to get bigger each year they are told.

My dad, Claire Robinson ('42) and mother, Joanne Crowfoot Robinson ('45) were both Florence graduates.

Bob Harris ('58) recalled, "The lockers were all on the second floor at the high school. There were never any locks on them and nothing was ever stolen. I did the announcing at the ball games and kept score at all of the games."

Charles Dannenfelser ('58) told the story of four generations of his family attending school in Florence from 1870 through 2002:

We were proud of our town and our school, very proud. The flood of 1951 was a very big blow to us. It caused first the loss of the highway that went right through the middle of town. With it went the Riverside café and station, the Sunnyside station and café, and numerous businesses. Families left and never returned. It was a sad time, but we came back, only then to face the loss of our schools. The years have not been kind to our beautiful little Kansas town.

High school was about sports, egos, cars, and girls. Football didn't bring much for me, but playing quarterback was an honor to some degree. Basketball was better for me as I got to play as an underclassman . . . our senior year brought some glory while taking third in the state tournament, losing to the eventual champion Natoma.

My father, Noel Dannenfelser ('28) and mother, Dorothy Stovall ('30) were graduates from Florence also. We had four generations of family in the Florence schools. I would like to be able to see more of the early history. The twenties must have been something!

Notable Graduates — Sharon Margene Savage ('62) became Miss Kansas in 1964. She participated in the Miss America pageant in Atlantic City that year. She was a student at Kansas State University and a member of the Kappa Kappa Gamma sorority. She toured with the USO throughout Germany, France, and Europe in the fall of 1964 and wrote post cards home to Florence with greetings about how much she loved the experience and thanked the community for being able to represent them on this wonderful tour. She was tragically killed while riding with her mother east of Emporia in a convertible in a head-on crash in May 1965. Sharon was talented in piano, organ, clarinet, voice, art, dancing, speech, and dramatics. Her ambition was a singing career and to work as a specialist with exceptional children.

Bob Harris ('58) recalled, "Margene was in my 4-H Club in which I was the leader. She was such a gorgeous and kind girl. She was a natural leader. Her death still is remembered as such a tragic loss to our town and the state of Kansas.

Busing & Consolidation — There had been wagons with horses busing children up until the early 1920s. In 1924 the district bought its first school bus. There was a Reo dealer in town, and this first school bus was a classic Reo bus. The district ran three bus routes—one to the east of Cedar Point, one to the south nearly to Burns, and a third to the west and north. When Cedar Point schools closed in 1968, Florence gave up a significant amount of land to Chase County and the Cottonwood Falls school district. The bus route toward the Cottonwood area was eliminated.

Burns school district to the south became the first consolidated district in the state of Kansas. Florence was the fourth district in the state to consolidate. As late as 1950, there were still thirty-five rural school districts in Marion County.

In about 1954, County Commissioner George Marlet convened community leaders in towns north of Florence. Under his intense leadership, they discussed a centralized high school in the far northern region of Marion County. It brought together the communities of Lost Springs, Ramona, Lincolnville, and Burdick to form a rural high school called Centre High School which opened in 1957. In 1969, Tampa joined Centre High School.

Closing — The district consolidated with Marion in 1971. The high school was closed in May 1971 under the guise of saving money for the taxpayers. The junior high and grade school were to remain in Florence. Within two years, the grade school was closed and all K-6th grades were moved to Marion. The next year the Marion school district built a new grade school to accommodate the increase in students. A second bond was passed for a $10 million addition to the high school in Marion. A third bond for a new gymnasium and auditorium was sold to the voters as a brick building but was actually constructed of a tin or metal exterior. With these three bonds for over $30 million total, the schools in Marion were eventually rebuilt at the taxpayers' expense. The community felt deep bitterness about the closing of the high school in Florence and moving the remaining students to the county seat town of Marion. It is still prevalent today, some fifty years later.

The largest graduating class was in 1925 with thirty-five graduates. Florence reached its peak population in the 1920s with between 2,000 and 3,000 residents. There were 1,439 graduates in the seventy-eight years from 1894 through 1971 when the high school closed at the end of May 1971. The most numerous surnames of the graduates were Robinson-31, Williams-24, Smith-20, Savage-20, Waner-13, Johnson-11, Miller-11, Allison-9, Haach-9, and Myers-9.

There were 175 students in grades one through twelve in Florence at the time of the school closing. The last class of 1971 had eighteen graduates. The last graduate to receive a diploma from Florence High School was John Zook (alphabetically). The majority of the students attended Marion High School in the fall of 1971.

Florence High School
Marion County, KS

#102
Grant Township Rural High School

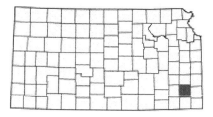

Mascot: Blue Devils

Colors: Blue and White

Year Closed: 1967

Location: ½ mile from the town of Stark, northeast Neosho County

The School with Three Names—Though it was considered the Stark School, it became the Grant Township Rural High School in 1929 when bonds were passed for the new school outside of the town proper. The high school in Stark at the time became the grade school. In 1960, the school unified with Hepler and Walnut and underwent yet another name change to become the Joint Rural High School. Thus, over sixty years of high school in Stark, there were three names—Stark, Grant Township Rural High School, and Joint Rural High School.

In 1929, the new high school building was a two-story, tan brick building. There was a tempting bannister from the top floor to the first floor which was forbidden to be used as a slide. The penalty for sliding down this eight-inch oak banister was to have to eat lunch with the principal. Principal Woodworth had frequent lunch partners.

Athletics—The new gymnasium was built to the north of the school after the war. Athletics were limited to boys and girls basketball until 1957. Notable outstanding boys teams were the 1946 team, led by guard Don Sailors, and the 1955 team which lost to Arma (who advanced to the state tournament that year).

Lavon Michael Heilman ('50) was a player on a winning girls basketball team:

> We only lost one game in the four years that I played. Our coach, Webster Olson, had told us to all make sure we were in bed before 10 o'clock the night before our game with Moran. We had beaten them quite handily the first time that year and may have been just a little overconfident. Needless to say, we got beat. Without that game we would have had four undefeated years while I was in high school.

The school had no football team until 1957. The practices and games were played across the road to the south in a cow pasture for the first two years. Max Page ('59) brightened as he recalled, "We knew where the fresh cow manure was and always tried to tackle the opposing players in that area if possible. The field was then built to the east of the school, but we still had no lights to play at night."

The school played in a six-man league that included teams from Hepler, Walnut, Galesburg, Thayer, and St. Paul.

School Activities & Traditions — The school had an active orchestra until 1945. Oralee Collins Beggs ('45) played the piano, and James Heddan ('45) played the trumpet. There was always a marching band, and it marched regularly at the homecoming parade at Pittsburg State. In what seemed like a twenty-mile march, the band played at the Neewollah (Halloween spelled backward) celebration each October in Independence.

Senior trips throughout the 1950s and 60s were to Rockaway Beach, Missouri. Larry Lindberg ('64) recalled, "What happened at Rockaway, stayed at Rockaway!"

Lavon Heilman ('50) remembered, "Our trip was to Noel, Missouri. There were fourteen of us seniors and a sponsor."

Howard Woodworth ('38) was later named the principal. He taught industrial arts and drove the school bus. His wife, Nellie Haddam Woodworth ('39), son James Woodworth ('62), and daughter-in-law Janet Markam Woodworth ('63) were also Grant Township Rural High School graduates.

Student Stories — Sacrifices were made by most students to help the family expenses following the Great Depression and the war years. Lavon Heilman ('50) remembered, "I would walk the one-half mile at noon each day of the school week from the high school to the restaurant in town. I would wait tables for forty-five minutes and received a hamburger and twenty-five cents and walk back to school in time for the afternoon classes. This helped the family and allowed me not to have to pay for the school hot lunch."

Max Page recalled the following story:

Driver's education was offered at the school in 1952, and the first car was a leased Chevy from the local car dealer. One of these driver's education teachers was also the teacher and coach Roy Meyers. He was known to come by the study hall in first hour and handpick four boys to drive. We would drive to Erie where he would go the courthouse and send the boys over to Richie's Rexall Drug to get a Coke. The girls in the study hall were always really jealous of us getting to go and drive those special mornings.

In the fall of 1955, four brave freshmen boys led by Max Page ('59) decided to hold the door to the bathroom and not let anyone in. It so happened that four senior boys approached the bathroom door to find it held shut. At the standoff, the seniors broke the door down at the hinges. Mr. Woodworth again had a disciplinary opportunity. Of course, there was silence as all of the boys in the school were called on the carpet. The second time around, the interrogation provided one, and then all of the culprits to confess their involvement. For the next two weeks, the principal had the company of eight boys for lunch.

Mrs. Marie Kahler was the English and home economics teacher. "She knew how to keep order," recalled Joanne Lindberg ('65). "As I look back in my later years, she was the best teacher I ever had. It seemed like she was here 100 years, but when the school closed after the 1967 graduation, Mrs. Kahler went onto Erie High School to teach for several more years."

Lavon Michael Heilman ('50) reminisced, "Mrs. Kahler would take me out of other classes every Thanksgiving, Christmas, and Easter to help bake the pies for the special hot lunches for those special holidays. From the time I was a freshman on, she thought my mother had taught me to make pies better that anyone in the school."

In one of those ornery moments that seems to always bring out the cleverest pranks, Bill Vandervort ('56) almost confessed, "There was a coal bin down in the southwest corner of the lower level where coal was shoveled into the room and used to fire the boiler. After it was discontinued as the fuel of choice, the concrete-walled room sat empty. It seems that three or four boys took a cherry bomb and suspended it from the ceiling. They then stuck a cigarette in the end and lit it. They escaped back to class to wait for the excitement. About ten minutes later, a sonic boom reverberated throughout the school and the steam registers vibrated. Our English teacher's eyes became the size of saucers, and I think her hair surely was standing on end. She screamed and ran down the hallway to run into Mr. Woodworth as they seemed exasperated as to the cause of such an explosion. All these sixty plus years later, I think there is still an unsolved mystery inside these walls as the case is still open." Bill winked after telling this story.

School Closing—After the school closed in 1967, the remaining students were bused to Erie. The vacant building, which stood stately in the company of three generations of students, sat empty. Some of these old fortresses in other towns were sold to start-up businesses for office or storage space. Some were torn down. Some seemed to stand until they died with broken windows and trees growing up through collapsed roofs. Others were retrofitted into museums with high school trophies, uniforms, yearbooks, and memorabilia.

For Stark/Grant Township/Joint Rural High School, the old school building took a much different reclama-

tion. In 1993, following the visit back to her fortieth year class reunion, Arthena Carlson Massoth ('53), a Leavenworth schoolteacher, along with five of her conscripts from the Stark area, began the restoration of their dear high school building. The spark was ignited and as many as fifteen alumni and friends began the arduous journey of recapturing the once regal building and making it into a community center. A touching account of the methods and the renovation of this 13,000-square foot school was published in the spring 2015, *Southeast Kansas Living Magazine.*

The school closed following the 1967 graduation, which had fifteen graduates. The last graduate of Joint Rural High School was Robert E. Wright (alphabetically). There were 717 graduates in the fifty-four years from 1914-1967.

The most numerous surnames of the graduates were Smith-17, Harding-14, Goff-12, Richwine-11, Bennett-10, Defenbaugh-10, Kelsey-9, Williamson-8, Carlson-7, Dunham-6, Wilson-6, and 5 each for Kennedy, Myers, Olson, Sailors, and Simmons.

Grant Township Rural High School
Neosho County, KS

#103

Horace School

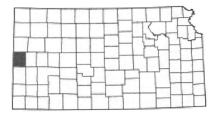

Location: town of Horace, Greeley County

No Closed High Schools in Greeley County —

On the western edge of Kansas on the Colorado border, the town of Horace, Greeley County, and the town of Tribune (county seat of Greeley County) were cleverly named after the popular *New York Herald Tribune* editor and politician, Horace Greeley. Greeley County is one of only five counties in Kansas that has never had a high school close. For this account, Horace, being the last elementary school to close in the county, was chosen.

The following is from an account by Winifred Smith in the *Centennial Book of Greeley County*, 1988:

In 1873 the Kansas State Legislature created Greeley County along with 21 other counties. It was an unorganized county with an area of 780 square miles and a population estimated at 20. In 1886 it was attached to Hamilton County to the south for judicial purposes. Greeley County became a temporary county in 1887.

In the October 26, 1888 issue of the *Enterprise,* a plains farmer wrote, ". . . soon we will be called upon to select the place for a permanent county seat . . . The aspirants are Tribune and Horace.... Tribune became the county seat. Greeley County was organized in 1888."

Horace School District #1 was formed in September 1888. As was common for the rural counties, the elementary schools were the first public schools in these communities. High schools were commonly established after the turn of the century. Whether Horace ever offered ninth grade cannot be found in the history of the school. Tribune grew as it was also on the railroad line and became the center of commerce and trade.

Each fall in the early school years before schools could open, each school had to be fumigated for the purpose of disinfecting the building. In some of the rural teachers contracts a statement was inserted that the teacher do the janitor work, cleaning floors, carrying in coal from the coal house, starting the fire, keeping it going, and cleaning blackboards (now called chalkboards because they are no longer all black).

During the cold weather teachers went early to get the fire going before pupils arrived but if she picked up pupils on the way those pupils too, shivered along with the teacher. The stove was usually a big, flat-topped, pot-bellied one that stood in one corner of the room with a protective jacket around it. In another corner was a big stone jar for water with a community cup (possibly each pupil later brought a cup of his own); happily everyone survived without any ill effects. For many years double desks were used. Now single desks are used which are often moved together in groups.

~Winifred Smith,
Centennial Book of Greeley County, 1988

One teacher said that during the winter months her pupils brought soup for lunch; it was heated on the flat-topped stove and they enjoyed hot soup at noon.

Another teacher recalls that although her home was in Horace, she stayed during the school week with a family that lived northwest of town several miles. She drove a horse and buggy to school and hauled three of the family's children. Two of them sat in the seat with the teacher and one sat down on the floor in front of the buggy next to the dashboard.

Another teacher related that she rode by horseback to school for six years beginning about 1916. Part of those years, even in blizzard conditions, she rode the horse for five miles. Other years she rode seven miles, depending on which family she was boarding with.

During the bad winter of 1911-1912, some children wrapped burlap sacks from the toes of their shoes to their knees to keep their feet warm and dry while walking to school.

About 1931, the Horace Grade School assembled at 9:00 am. It was a mild morning on March 26 with beautiful snow falling. Within fifteen minutes the wind had risen and a full-blown blizzard was raging. The temperature dropped to two degrees below zero. Outside toilets were no place to send children when one could not see for the swirling snow. There was a partially dug, unfinished basement under the schoolhouse where there was a furnace and coal. This was where the children were sent when nature called. When four o'clock came, the storm was still raging. No one was allowed to leave unless adults came for them. Some of the teachers and pupils from the country spent the night at the schoolhouse. The next day, after the storm had abated, the country students were taken to homes in town. It was three days before the rural parents were able to make it to town to get their youngsters.

During the Model-T era, a teacher recalls hauling the children of two families to a rural school. One day after leaving the home of the second family where she picked up children, the Model-T stopped. When she got it started it would go backward but not forward. She backed the car to the farmer's house where he fixed it and they went to school. She declared the Model-T would jump snowdrifts.

There were social and fun times mixed in with the hard times. Rural children played ball, ante over, hopscotch, and marbles during intermissions. The town schools had more athletics. The girls basketball teams wore big black baggy bloomers. At the time, the students thought were great.

Sometimes two rural schools would get together for pie suppers, box suppers, ciphering matches, and spelling contests. All county spelling contestants came to Tribune in the spring for a county spelling contest. There were literary meetings that were fun as well as educational. At these meetings, debates were held, readings were given, and musical numbers were entertained.

Horace School

Greeley County, KS

#104

Alamota
Grade School

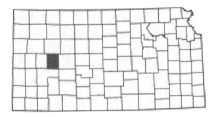

Mascot: Tigers

Colors: Red and White

Year Closed: 1980

Location: town of Alamota, Lane County

The Town of Alamota—Named after the hills and bluffs of white magnesium limestone along Walnut Creek, Alamota is the Indian word for white rock. The first post office in Kansas was established in Lane County in 1877. This village sounds like Laura Ingalls Wilder's home in the valley of the south fork of the Walnut Creek. Lane County is one of the only five counties in Kansas that never had a high school close. This history of Alamota School is an account of the last rural elementary school to close in the county.

This story is primarily taken from a spectacularly in-depth history of Alamota School written by Kathy Steffens Nett, a 1960 graduate from Alamota School.

Alamota School was District No. 1 in Lane County in western Kansas, approximately seventy-five miles from Colorado. The district was later to become No. 6 in the 1947-48 school year. From a column in the *Dighton Herald* on February 27, 1936:

> Last Thursday work began on the new grade school building at Alamota. The project comes under the WPA program. The building will cost in the neighborhood of $6,000. Schools built under the present WPA and PWA programs are not only a monument to the present administration in Washington, but they will serve the people of the community for generations to come.

Frances Morehead, Alamota's first teacher, recalled many years later her impressions of the new school:

> The building consisted of a full basement, furnace room, kitchen, coal room, and a big room that was used mainly for play and for eating "bucket lunches." The upstairs had two cloak rooms, two rest rooms, a large library with folding doors, and the main classroom –all geared up for a one-teacher set-up. There was a water fountain in the classroom, a real luxury! There was water most of the time, although Alamota never did have an oversupply of water.

Mary Steffens wrote of her memories at Alamota:

> I started the first grade in the fall of 1950. It was Mrs. Vulcan's first day too. She wore a red dress and brown

"granny shoes" designed for women who had to be on their feet all day. She had pretty brown hair, wire rimmed glasses, and a sharp nose.

At that time every county had a county superintendent of schools who oversaw all of the schools. Grace McKelvy McGuire was the Lane County Superintendent from 1944-1951. She started teaching at Alamota in the fall of 1951. For the next 12 years she taught at Alamota which was longer than any other teacher in the school's history.

Mrs. McGuire and Mrs. Vulcan took their students on field trips by train ride east to Beeler and another to Ness City. They also visited the Wonder Bread plant in Hutchinson, a bottling plant in Dodge City, a weather station, and a potato chip factory. This valuable exposure and education expanded all the children lives and experiences.

Mary Steffens remembered, "I was fascinated by the precision of the bottles as they were filled, capped, packed, and loaded onto trucks. Each student was given a loaf of bread at the Wonder Bread plant. This was a treat to some of the students whose moms baked and rarely had 'store bought' bread."

There were sports, though all of the practices were outdoors. Mrs. McGuire promoted and played softball with her students. In October each fall, she brought her radio to school and allowed the students to listen to the World Series during class. She taught everyone to keep score. The boys and girls from fifth through eighth grade made up the baseball team. They played the other one-room schools throughout Lane County. They often won the tournaments and had many trophies to show for it.

In the fall of 1958, buses were added and parents no longer had to transport their children to and from school. This came as the two other country schools, Hackberry and West, in the southeastern corner of the county closed their doors and unified with Alamota. This added sixty-nine square miles to the district. This required an addition to the school which was the first since the school had been built twenty-two years earlier by the WPA. This addition included a cafeteria-kitchen, a stage, one classroom, bathrooms, and a principal's office.

There were fifty-one students in 1962. The largest graduating class was eleven in 1960.

One student from each class attended spelling contests at Shields in 1962-63, and Alamota took first place.

Girls teams won volleyball and basketball trophies. The boys baseball team, in the fall of 1968, won all of their games with scores of 9-8 over Shields, 27-3 over Amy, 27-3 over Manning, and 17-5 over Shallow Water. Musical operettas, cheerleading, twirling, and tumbling were all featured at the school.

A tribute by Kathy Steffens Nett:

To all of our teachers, cooks, custodians, coaches
Living and deceased,
who also served as principals
counselors, and mentors.
We thank them for not only teaching us
reading, writing, and arithmetic
But also for stretching our imaginations
and teaching us about
rhythm, notes and folk songs,
the moon and the stars,
Current events and geography, health and sex education
cleanliness and good nutrition.
We thank you too for teaching us good sportsmanship,
curtesy, compassion
self-confidence, courage and honesty.

It was a sad day for the Alamota School when the doors closed in May 1980. In forty-four years, 290 students attended the school.

Edward Habiger, whose six children attended Alamota, in a recent interview said, "When a school closes, the town dies." This is very apparent in Alamota, which was once a vibrant town with a bank, mercantile store-grocery, hotel, lumber yard, post office, creamery, feed store, grain elevator, train station, and the school. Now it doesn't even exist on most maps.

#105

Enterprise High School

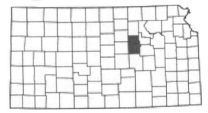

Mascot: Bulldogs

Colors: Red and White

Year Closed: 1962

Location: town of Enterprise, Dickinson County

Town History — Enterprise was established in 1870 along the Smokey Hill River. The founders selected the spot because of the small falls, known as Louden Falls, at that point in the river. In 1860, Christian Hoffman, a thirty-four-year old Swiss German with a wife and son, came to the county and settled twelve miles southwest of the falls. Drought and prairie fires caused him to travel to Atchison, Manhattan, and Junction City to find relief and aid for his struggling family. He passed by Louden Falls on these trips. While not large, his Swiss experience as a miller enabled him to appreciate the value of the falls as potential power for a mill. A sheriff's sale gave him the opportunity to purchase the 160 acres, including the waterfall, for $1,500 in 1868.

A dam was constructed and this first mill had the capacity to grind seventy-five barrels of flour every twenty-four hours. When the Union Pacific Railroad was extended from Junction City to Salina in 1867, it passed two miles north through Lamb's Point, or Detroit, and west for five more miles to reach Abilene. A spur, two-mile track was later added to Enterprise on the south.

The people who were attracted to this area were very thrifty. Most, like the Hoffman's, had been from the school of thrift and hard work in Germany and Switzerland. Their initiative brought them to immigrate to America. After several years, they acquired not only a knowledge of the English language, but the self-reliant spirit of frontier life. Settlers began taking up land in the immediate vicinity because of the proximity of the mill.

Education — From the *Enterprise Journal,* December 1899:

> The first school was opened in 1868 in the Dietrich Brothers slaughter house with Miss Hannah DeHaven as the teacher, but after a few months, a transfer of the property forced the school to move to the front room of Hoffman's log house. In 1870, School District #16 was organized and a school was built in the northeast corner of section 29. Here a Union Sunday School was held with G.R. Lamb as the superintendent.

In 1867 the first issue of the newspaper, *The Gazette,* revealed in the eight-page weekly what a powerful means the paper was in promoting community consciousness. Its enthusiastic description of the town would have made any citizen proud and eager to work for its growth and expansion. From a long article entitled "The City of Mills," it was written, "Enterprise is a booming town. We have large flourishing mills, the largest woolen factory in the state, and a saw mill while a paper mill is contemplated . . ."

The June 9, 1878, issue carried a column with a very vigorous argument that since the bonds were all paid and since there was taxable valuation in the amount of $45,186, Enterprise could easily build a $5,000 schoolhouse of four, good-sized rooms when Abilene had built a new $14,000 school house.

Hoffman's Legacy — Christian Hoffman's son, C.B. Hoffman, after spending one year at the German Methodist College in Warrenton, Missouri, returned home with a wife, Catherine America "Mecca" Hoffman. They had a new anti-religion and populist belief in the Anti-Monopoly Party. He was elected to the state legislature where he attacked the railroads over the issues of passes and freight rates. He published the *Anti Monopolist* and other newspapers and wrote numerous letters to periodicals. He was narrowly defeated in 1884 for the state senate as a Greenbacker-Independent, and again in 1889 and 1900 as a Fusionist. He was appointed to the board of regents of the agricultural college in Manhattan, later known as Kansas State University. Catherine, over the years, entertained in her home such well-known persons as Susan B. Anthony, Carrie Chapman Catt, Carrie Nation, Jane Addams, Elizabeth Cady Stanton, Mary Ellen Lease, Annie L. Diggs, and Edwin Markham.

Mecca Hoffman brought Carrie Nation to town for one of her famous and well documented raids on one of the saloons in Enterprise. Mecca was one of the leading crusaders for women's suffrage in the state. She and C.B. had as guests the famous (or infamous) Enos Mills, Elbert Hubbard, Hamlin Garland, Edwin Markham, Chancellor Snow, Senator Ingalls, Senator Capper, and Governors St. John, Glick, Humphrey, Allen, Leedy, Lewelling and Hoch.

A Normal Training College — C.B. Hoffman was the leader to establish Garfield Normal College in Enterprise. With Prof. J.M. Reid as president and seven teachers, the school opened in 1888. It was taken over by the United Brethren in January 1893 and 183 students were enrolled that year. It fell upon hard times in 1896 and the building reverted to ownership by the city of Enterprise. The next to run the college were the German Methodists. It was referred to as the Academy. The school was later sold to the Seventh Day Adventist Denomination and maintained in the community until the 1950s.

High School — It is in this little town that had such a vibrant and storied beginning that the first two-year high school class graduated in 1891. The first three-year high school class graduated in 1897, and the first four-year high school class graduated in 1907. Those interested in community improvement and education rallied under the leadership of the new high school principal, Prof. Yoder, to give Enterprise what she sadly needed, a modern high school building with a gymnasium and a beautiful, large auditorium for all community meetings. After a hard fight, the election was won by barely twenty-six votes. In his master's thesis on "Social Development of Enterprise Kansas," F.C. Havighurst wrote, "In 1917, four years after the election, I was told that the High School was built just so that Prof. Yoder could get a gymnasium for his basketball team and Mrs. C.B. Hoffman could have a meeting place for her clubs."

Among all of the unique activities in Enterprise, it was possibly the first town in the state to have a kindergarten. As early as 1884, Christian Hoffman had constructed a building for kindergarten which was conducted by Miss Mutzart until her marriage. She was a trained kindergarten teacher from Germany and, for a fee of fifty cents a month, taught German crocheting and fancy work as part of her curriculum. Miss Claudia Hare conducted a kindergarten in 1887, and in 1905 the annual meeting ordered the establishment of a permanent kindergarten.

Athletics — Enterprise had quite a baseball team in the years between 1910 and 1915. They were composed of crack ball players that had been recruited from the Hoffman mill. This ball team played many cities throughout the state and won just about every game. One of these players, Zach Wheat, went on and played for the Brooklyn Dodgers and was inducted into the Baseball Hall of Fame in 1959.

While baseball continued as the all-absorbing sport in Enterprise, it did not prevent the expansion and growth of other sports. The year 1907 brought a championship baseball team which defeated such towns as Newton, Wamego, and Emporia. When the team made a trip to Miltonvale (about sixty miles northwest), a special train of 304 fans accompanied it. That same year there was a tennis tournament, a military company, and basketball games at the Enterprise Academy. Football, basketball, and the baseball team played at the high school. There were track meets for the boys of all grades in the public schools.

Richard Taylor ('42) was editorialized as Mr. Kansas by the *Wichita Eagle* in a July 14, 1991 article:

> The good life in Kansas has no stronger, better, advocate than the Rev. Richard Taylor. That won't be changed with his retirement the other day from 43 years in various pulpits of the Kansas West Conference of the United Methodist Church.
>
> The Rev. Taylor's latest "pulpit" was the organization Kansans for Life at Its Best, which works for moderation in the lives of Kansans and against the slavery of alcohol and gambling addiction. Legislators became used to the sight of the tall, angular preacher sitting in the gallery or outside their offices, black hair combed straight back, dark eyes burning with the intensity of the man with a righteous cause.
>
> One word from his lips, however, would dispel all notion of severity, for Rev. Taylor has a sense of humor that God himself must enjoy. Though he was cruelly attacked at times, and though his own tongue could be sharp, Rev. Taylor always kept his sense of proportion and could laugh at himself. "Ole Taylor," some would call him, in jest, and he would chortle at the thought of connecting his name with that of a famous of old whiskey . . . Kansans wish him well, (in retirement) . . . and thank him for giving them more than four decades of "life at its best" in the Sunflower State.

Coach Loren Rock led the basketball and football teams for eleven years, from 1946 to 1958. In a tribute in the *Teller Times*, Reed Hoffman reported:

> "When the One Great Scorer comes to write against your name—he marks—not that you won or lost, but how you played the game." Grantland Rice.

> The boys are the honored guests tonight at the athletic banquet but Loren Rock, ending 11 successful years as coach of all sports at EHS will be the unsung hero. Loren is known throughout our area as a fine athlete, true sportsman, and a fine example to his players. Only a great attachment to our youth and this community could justify the financial sacrifice inherent in his years here. Coaches are hired as builders not only of "Character" but of "Victory". The record on both is outstanding. His basketball teams had a record of 184-87 and they competed with their ancient rivals Hope, Solomon, Assaria, Gypsum and Kipp. In nine years of 6-man football their record was 48-24.

The 1952-53 basketball team was 25-2, losing their final game 43-40 to the eventual state champions, Burns High School.

School Closing — With declining enrollment and after two bitter and close votes, the town voted to close the high school in 1962. There were 718 graduates from Enterprise High School (including the twenty from the two-year and forty-nine from the three-year high school). The last graduate was Miriam Rutz (alphabetically).

The most numerous surnames of the graduates were Hoffman-15, Jones-14, Gish-13, Smith-11, and Ehrsam-10.

#106

Assaria Rural High School

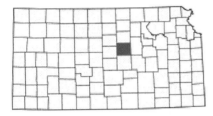

Mascot: Trojans

Colors: Red and White

Year Closed: 1967

Location: town of Assaria, south-central Saline County

Thirteen miles to the southwest of Assaria is the town of Lindsborg, which is a center of Swedish immigrants to Kansas in the 1870s and 1880s. Though Assaria was not as concentrated with Swedes as other areas, graduates from the high school were dominated with Swedish and Scandinavian surnames.

Education — The *Salina Evening Journal* reported the following on January 23, 1911:

A meeting of the teachers of Assaria and W.E. Conneley, county superintendent-elect, held at Assaria Friday night, the advisability of establishing a high school at Assaria was discussed. A program had been outlined, but because of the fact that several persons were unable to be there, it was not carried out. Another meeting will be held soon. According to the county superintendent an election will be held in the Assaria district next spring to determine whether or not a high school is to be established.

The *Live Wire-High* school paper, Vol. 1, No.1, November 1922, reported the following:

High school work was first begun in Assaria in 1910 under the supervision of the grammar school teacher. After a successful year, the patrons of District #36 authorized the school board to attempt to secure enough students to maintain a school.

The board hired an automobile and they went out to meet prospective students who stated their intentions of attending high school. After preparing three rooms in the second story of the school building and hiring S.E. Countryman as superintendent, regular high school work began. The district supported the high school for two years, but by the third year it received help from the Barnes High School tax. The first Assaria High School graduation class was in 1913 with three graduates.

"Form Literary Society" was the column heading in the *Salina Evening Journal* on October 12, 1914:

New feature of the Assaria High School work. A high school literary society was launched into existence last Friday afternoon when the high school pupils assembled to organize and elect officers. The purpose of this society are to give opportunity, outside of the regular class room work, for literary work and arouse an interest in debating and public speaking . . . a pie social will be given Friday evening at the city hall under the auspices of the high school. Women will bring pies.

The *Salina Daily Union* published this report on May 29, 1915:

Held Commencement
Miss Trulson Graduated From the Assaria High School. The high school commencement exercises were held last evening at the hall and there was an unusually large attendance. This year Assaria high school graduated one, Miss Florence Trulson ('15). There were two graduates last year, but this is the first year the school has run the full four year course. Prof. John A. Butler of Kansas University delivered the address. He took for his subject "Citizens of Tomorrow." The invocation was delivered by Rev. Semans, pastor of University Methodist church, Salina. Miss Trulson delivered a splendid oration . . .

District #36 land territory was too small to erect a suitable building. Hence, at the annual meeting of the district in April 1918, a motion was made to take advantage of the school laws of the state and erect a Rural High School building. The county superintendent decided on the rural high school district boundaries which included sixty-six sections, or sixty-six square miles. Before such a building could be erected, a vote needed to pass a bond by the patrons of the district.

The burden of this campaign was laid upon the shoulders of Rev. Cecil Semans. His work was never forgotten by those directly interested in the movement. For two weeks Rev. Semans untiringly canvassed those sixty-six

sections, and, when he presented his petition to the committee, he had more than enough qualified signers.

The *Salina Daily Union* wrote this report about Assaria's plan for a high school on Aug 31, 1918:

It has been a long time since the *Union* has been more pleased than when it heard that Assaria was going to build a new and modern high school building. Assaria has been inhabited by a progressive people but so many fine people have laid down since the war that it was refreshing to see these people determine to keep up their educational work.

The time has come for many high schools over the country. The big ones are all right for the cities and larger towns but every parent has the right to demand that his child be educated within the parental influence at least to the close of the high school . . .

The building of the high school started in May 1919. It was a decidedly modern and up-to-date structure. It was considered a model, as well as the best equipped high school building in the state. It was a three-story structure with twenty-seven rooms. On the first floor was the auditorium and gymnasium which had a seating capacity for over 600. In connection with the auditorium was a large stage, which was well equipped with scenery. To the east was the domestic science and art departments. To the west was the manual training shop.

Student Memories — The following is from a collection of memories from graduates of Assaria from as early as 1926 and continuing through the last graduating class in 1967. This memory book was written in 1986 for the centennial of the town. A few of these colorful stories are included to represent the era, the educational experiences, and the significance of teachers and community in educating their students:

Esther Hyrup ('24): we rode in a 'jump seat buggy' pulled by 2 horses or in a spring wagon that had sled runners that could be put on in the winter. In high school our buses were Model T Fords. Our ball games were with other high schools in the county, so we knew most of the players. We had no "snow days", we arranged to have places to stay in town, as school went on regardless of the weather. Uniforms . . . boys wore bib overalls and blue shirts. The girls wore middies and skirts.

Elvera Oline Olson ('26): the senior sneak day was a trip to Salina where we rented boats on the Smoky Hill River. The boys shook the boat, almost tipping the girls out. Such screaming!

Lucile Hanson Peterson ('26): the senior year was the best. We won the County basketball tournament and I was judged the No. 1 forward, was in the operetta, senior play and had some good times.

Veda May Young Pihl ('27): we had orchestra and band . . . I played slide trombone . . . we had glee club-I sang soprano. My favorite class was English. I took three years of Latin. If you want to learn English, then take Latin.

Laurina Peterson Redden ('29): some subjects in school were English, Algebra and penmanship . . . penmanship teacher, Earl Swedland . . . was left handed and I marveled at how well and beautifully he could write . . . after graduation I took a six weeks of training at Kansas Wesleyan where I earned my teaching certificate.

The Junior class of 1930 wrote in the yearbook a remarkably clever and well describe story of their class:

The task of writing an article worthy of the jolliest class of AHS is indeed outside human capabilities, considering the limit placed upon any individual by the few million words found in Webster's International. If we throw in some Greek, Hebrew, and Latin you will please pardon us, for it is merely our way of attempting to render a fitting tribute to afore said jolliest, jazziest, juberous, Juniors . . . we are composed of the lucky number, eighteen, as one with average intelligence could tell by counting, but there are always those who must be told before they believe . . . variety being recognized as the spice of life we have endeavored to follow the axiom generally and specifically . . . hence we range in weight from Herbert Almquist, 45 pounds to _____no fair to tell a class secret . . . in height we range from Edith Peterson who stretches to reach the top of the tape measure in her newest Parisian spike heels to Less King . . .

Isabelle Lindholm Becker ('32): I am 91 when writing this . . . I enjoyed all of the music . . . attempted playing an instrument in the band, but didn't do so well, so I went into plays and glee club and operettas which I enjoyed.

Berneta Nelson Forsberg ('34): we played "3 zone" basketball in 1931-34 with the two screw balls Henrietta Pearson and Almeda Peterson. I played forward. The two girls always had the rest of the team laughing nonstop. Then after our showers many of the girls stayed around waiting to get their hair set in pin curls by Hazel Ericson. I probably would have never learned to set my hair if it hadn't been for her.

Alice Ericson ('36): I played in the orchestra-violin and wasn't any good, but took a chair anyway. Mr. Kirk was the teacher. There were three of us that ran around together. Lynette Olson, Linnea Peterson, and I spent the nights at each other's houses and slept on the living room floor. Yes, we would call boys on the phone.

Ireta Young Swenson ('36): as a freshman I soon learned you could make a lot of mistakes and would get laughed at, and we girls were so timid. There were two senior boys-Claude Magnuson ('33) and Delton Carlson ('33) who we thought were "dream boats", and if they looked our way it was so thrilling. And you know how giggly girls are. A few of us would go out to the cars east of the building to eat our lunches. We got to playing penny ante. Well, that didn't last long-someone ratted on us and we were called into the principal's office. No more eating lunches in cars.

Dorothy Peterson Johnson ('39): we went to school in a Model A Ford and one morning the lug nut came loose and caused the rear left wheel to drop off and it went sailing past us. It climbed a telephone pole 15 feet and landed in the field. We retrieved it and used the lug nuts of the spare tire to get us to school. Our senior trip was to Wichita and the highlight was the Boeing air craft and creamery.

Vernon Swenson ('42): a day to remember. There were a lot of them but how about this one. One day in manual training class I told some classmates that I was quitting school. So sometime in the middle of the afternoon I picked up my books located them on my bike baskets and went home. The reception wasn't quite what I had hoped. No punishment, but just an affirmation that I would be going back the next day. Shortly after 4:00 PM the principal drove into the yard

and I went to the stairway landing and closed the door. Through the closed door I heard that I would be back in school tomorrow. Thanks to the principal and thanks to my parents, I was. How different, and not for the better, if I would not have. Thanks Assaria High School and all its supporting. I received a good education that helped me go ahead with the vocation of being a pastor and missionary in Africa. Life has been rich and Assaria has been part of it.

Frances Johnson Day ('44): I had an ear for music so I accompanied the glee clubs and mixed choirs a few times. My background in piano composed of 24 lessons when I was in the fourth grade . . . I would walk to Mrs. Lindberg's house after school . . . after each lesson, for which I would pay 25 cents, I would walk home another three miles. When I had progressed enough to use the pedal on the piano the lessons ended. We did not own a piano, only a pump organ. One of my teachers, Mr. Kirk, made a special trip to my parents' home, to tell them I had talent and should go on to Bethany college for a degree in music. Of course, there was no money for that . . . the summer between my junior and senior year I worked at the PX at Camp Phillips which helped me realize there was a war on. I became a pen pal to several GI's and sent them packages for Christmas. Later, some letters were returned marked "Killed in Action."

Glendon Anderson ('47): . . . In 1947, my senior year we were privileged to defeat Lindsborg in the regional basketball tournament which enabled us to participate in the state basketball tournament.

Audrey Johnson Miller ('51): Dorothy Barekman was our Latin teacher. She taught us Christmas carols in Latin. We went from class to class singing carols and they threw pennies at us.

Maxine Sellek Bilotti ('54): Assaria had some of the best teachers I have known. For a small school we were blessed. There was Josh-the typing and bookkeeping skills he gave me probably supported my early family . . . he could never get me through steno but I went from clerk to private secretary for a sales manager on what he taught me. And he was one of those teachers you could talk too . . . Jerry Andrews-he taught me to think . . . Miss Komarek-I have pictures of my four older daughters in Easter and Christmas outfits I made-Halloween costumes too . . . Miss Komarek also started my cooking skills-and I'm sure her "Joy of Cooking" rubbed off on me . . . Miss Morrison does anyone else remember the modern dance program . . . the impossible moves of the Angel Dance to "Ave Maria." How a small Kansas High school attracted that talent I'll never know . . . Mrs. Moling English teacher . . . my vocabulary and use of words she taught me . . . she gave me the love of literature . . . Mr. Bohing what a treasure . . . taught me to appreciate types of music . . . when our girls were in high school here in New Jersey we hosted two boys from England . . . they played in the "Stowemarket Brass Band." . . . they were amazed that this old lady picked up the trumpet and actually played a tune.

Mr. James Buxton came as the principal in 1961. He also taught algebra. He became a legend in Assaria and later at the Southeast Saline High School, retiring as the Superintendent. He was mentioned by many of his former students as someone who made a significant impact on their lives.

Douglas Forsberg ('61): I believe I was in the back of the room when Mr. Buxton scared me because he addressed me as Mr. Forsberg. I don't believe that anyone had ever called me that before . . . Mr. Buxton

also surprised a lot of us at the first school dance of that year. All of a sudden the lights dimmed to about the intensity of a smoke filled night club and it was the norm from then on to have the dance floor less brightly lit . . . Interesting that later as a school board member I was able to hire him as our district superintendent.

Judy Magnuson Lilly ('61): Speaking of teachers . . . Mr. Sloan who was our principal who wore undershirts to class. I can hardly believe that now. Maybe I dreamed it. What I am sure of it is that he used to come strutting into our algebra class every morning calling out "What do you wake up every morning saying?" We knew to shout back, "What you do to one side, you do to the other!"

Elaine Sellek Hunter ('62): Thinking back to math class, I still hear Mr. Buxton's voice saying, "In the equation, '$x=2$', how much is 'y', Miss Sellek?" Wasn't he a gem? One of the strongest assets was making class interesting. I loved it when he used the expression "Hold the phone!"

Shirley Sellek Herrick ('64): Jim Buxton was a great principal, motivator, and educator. He taught me in 4 years about people, life and living. He had what I call "presence," and he surely had eyes in the back of his head . . . He found in me potential I never knew I had. Lessons in life. Our senior trip . . . Chicago . . . Palmer House . . . served a glorified hamburger on a silver platter, with a silver lid no less.

Jill Magnuson Brax '65: . . . Being amazed at how some "unknown pranksters" repeatedly put Don Stone's little foreign car inside the swinging double doors of the old gym . . . Hearing the sound of the chalk on the black board as the following words were written-"President Kennedy is dead!" I feel so fortunate to have gone to a small high school in the middle of Kansas.

Athletics — Assaria dropped football as a sport for twenty-nine years due to a student dying on the football field. The baseball team was the state of Kansas, Class B Champion in 1960. The boys played baseball in the spring and fall. Baseball was dropped in the fall because there were no other schools playing the sport. Football was started again in the fall of 1958.

Assaria joined the McPherson County League even though they were in Saline County. The first year in the league, Assaria played at Windom which had not been beaten in three years. Windom had a beautiful field and even another practice field. Assaria won 7-6.

Notable Graduates — Josh Gottfried ('28) came back to Assaria to become a teacher and coach. A story of note was Mr. Gottfried as a driver's education teacher. He had taken a carload of students to Peabody for an event. It seemed that the car was running out of gas on the way home, and in an attempt to save gas, he would accelerate to eighty MPH, turn off the car ignition and coast down to about twenty MPH and then start the car again. The kids were amazed.

A notable graduate was Glendon Anderson ('47). He became the head basketball coach at Iowa State University at the age of twenty-nine. He had played in college at Colorado State. He was a two-time All American AAU player. He played at Assaria for Coach Josh Gottried and attributed much of his success to him.

Another graduate, Janie (Lilly) Miller ('56), graduated as a veterinarian from Kansas State University. She earned a Ph.D. from the University of Wisconsin. She discovered the virus that causes leukemia in cattle and developed the test to identify animals infected with the disease. The test greatly reduced the disease's threat to U.S. livestock production and exports and was adopted by the European Economic Community. Her distinguished research career was at the National Animal Disease Center in Ames, Iowa. She had numerous honors for distinguished contributions to science. She became the first recipient of a Lifetime Excellence in Research Award from the American Veterinary Medical Association.

School Closing — A total of 753 graduated from Assaria, from 1913 until the school closed in 1967. Among the most numerous surnames of the graduates were Johnson-46, Nelson-39, Olson-38, Peterson-36, Anderson-26, and Hanson-23. These six Swedish surnames made up over 26% of the total graduates from Assaria.

Assaria Rural High School

Saline County, KS

#107

Offerle High School

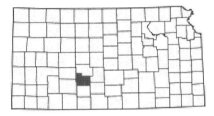

Mascot: Indians

Colors: Black and Gold

Year Closed: 1966

Location: town of Offerle, western edge of Edwards County

Town History — Offerle is on the main rail line of the Atchison, Topeka, and Santa Fe Railroad (today called the BSNF). It parallels US Highways 50-56. The name Offerle came from the Alsace-Lorraine region of Germany and the French border. German surnames were very prominent among the graduates of Offerle.

Education — The first grade school in Offerle was called Joint One, so named at a district meeting held in August, 1877. Ed Offerle was named director. Later the same year, he moved to California, and A.F. Teed was named director. Sixty-seven students were enrolled. The teacher's salary for the year was $249. Many of the children only went to school two or three months out of the year when there was no work at home to be done.

The school was a white wooden building. It faced south and was enclosed by a four-board fence with a flat-board across the top. A row of locust trees was planted inside the fence. The present locust trees (2018) on this spot are the result of the first trees planted 145 years ago.

Twenty years later, on April 14, 1898, District Joint One was disorganized by an act of the legislature. The school was then named Good Hope and later became District 43.

In 1913, a new two-room grade school was built. Mary Kent, Harry Brown's mother, taught at this school. The salary for a lady teacher was $10 a month.

In 1916, the first rural high school in the state of Kansas was built in Offerle. M.W. Oliphant was director and Harry Offerle was clerk. Pauline Parkhurst was the only teacher and her salary for the year was $120. Enrollment was fourteen pupils—nine girls and five boys. Civics, algebra, bookkeeping, and commercial languages were the subjects taught. The first class graduated in 1918 with Bernice Sams, Lucille Oliphant, Blanche Brumfield, and Edna Brecheisen graduating.

In 1920, two more rooms were added to the grade school, making four rooms total. In 1930, a gymnasium was built on the north side of the school and attached to the high school.

Athletics & Activities — There were always school plays, music, and football. Baseball was not included in the athletics program. The school rivals were primarily the schools of the 50-50 League of Spearville, Windt-horst, Hanston, Rozel, and Burdett.

The beautiful gymnasium with its hardwood beams, bleachers, and large court are still used today (2018) and are kept in immaculate condition. A grade school is still using the building and is part of the Kinsley School District.

Unification to Closing—In 1956 the new high school was built. This continued as District 43 until 1966 when it became unified with Kinsley and was changed to District 347. The last class from Offerle had five graduates with Kenneth Regnier the last to receive an Offerle diploma (alphabetically). During the forty-nine years as a high school, from 1918 until 1966, 353 received their diplomas from Offerle. The most numerous surnames of the graduates were Kurth-10, Hedges-10, and Offerle-9.

Offerle High School
Edwards County, KS

#108

Geneseo High School

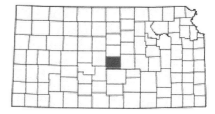

Mascot: Dragons

Color: Green and White

Year Closed: 1980

Location: town of Geneseo, northcentral Rice County

Educational History—The first school in Geneseo was a private one taught by Miss Inez Bell, a cousin of Clara Roper, in 1887. School was upstairs in the old opera house (located where the city hall is now, 2018). Desks were cracker boxes with two sides cut out and the pupils sat on the cold floor.

A private school was taught by Mrs. S.A. Critchfield in her own home. The next two years, school was in the

Methodist Episcopal Church. Mr. and Mrs. Sapp were the teachers with about fifty pupils.

In the fall of 1889, the first school building was built with Geneseo clay, and the brick was made in the Kanopolis kiln. The building had four rooms, two long halls, a basement for coal and a belfry with a school bell. Each room had a large stove for heat. An outside pump provided drinking water. The teachers did their own janitorial work. In 1890-91, the first course of study was developed for the high school by Superintendent S.E. Kirkpatrick. The first high school graduate was "Tillie" Critchfield in 1893 when there were six graduates (a two-year high school curriculum). That year $1,350 paid all teachers wages and $250 paid the coal bill. There were no athletics, no class organizations, and no special extraordinary gatherings.

In 1910, two rooms were added to the west side of the school. The lower one was the primary room. The upper one was a combined study hall and home economics department.

After considerable controversy in 1915, a gymnasium was built on the school grounds south of the school house. It was considered a great drawing card for the boys (at one time, there were no boys in the high school). From 1889-1910, the high school only had a two-year high school course. The four-year high school started in 1910, thus there were no graduates in 1911. The class of 1917 was the first to wear caps and gowns at graduation. In 1919, the high school had sixty-five students.

By 1925, the school building was in poor shape, so it was razed and the new building was put up. During 1925-26, children were attending school all over town in churches and the opera house. The new school was ready for graduation in May 1926. A new gymnasium, built north of the school building, was not added until 1956.

Strong in Music — Music was always an outstanding part of the Geneseo school system. Miss Slaybaugh was an exceptional teacher. She instilled the love of music in her students. Her deep commitment and guidance made a generation of pupils lifelong musical enthusiasts. Her reputation was as a believer that everyone had to be in the band. Morris Heitschmidt ('42) played the alto saxophone, played the piano for the grade school music classes, and sang into his nineties in the church choir, barber shoppers, and men's chorus in his community of McPherson.

Mr. Vernon Nicholson followed Miss Slaybaugh in the music department and reaped the benefits of great ground work that Miss Slaybaugh had laid. Morris's parents, Louis and Della Heitschmidt, owned and ran the hardware store, so after-school chores at the store did not allow him to play football. He was allowed to play basketball. Following graduation in 1942, Morris Heitschmidt immediately went into the Army and was sent to England for World War II.

Mr. Nicholson was also an influence on Helen Click Stockstill ('53). She played the French horn and in high school played the baritone. She sang in many solo contests and mixed choirs. She continued to sing all of her life in the chancel choir, directed the bell choir for twenty years, and was the church organist for eighteen years. She played the piano starting at the age of seven years and recalled her experiences with music:

> My music education was such a lifelong appreciation from my school training. We had a great marching band and played at parades and at the State Fair. My

exceptional education and loyalty to my school is a testament to my attending every year at the annual alumni banquets. I have not missed a single one-this year (2018) will be my 65th straight banquet.

Marilyn Siemsen '57 also had a fond memory of Mr. Vernon Nicholson:

I played the alto saxophone, and we marched so proudly at the State Fair in Hutchinson. He was a really good teacher.

Busing & Athletics

Busing & Athletics — There were no school buses in Geneseo until the later years. Helen Click Stockstill's mother always drove a car to away ball games. There were no girls sports, but Marilyn Siemsen Shuttleworth ('57) recalls going to away softball games and that Bushton had one very mean and aggressive pitcher. Little River was always the chief rival, though Chase was close behind.

Notable Graduates

Notable Graduates — James Sisson ('53) became an aeronautical engineer and scientist with NASA and helped as the designer of the "moon buggy." He studied under Dr. Von Braun at the University of Oklahoma.

Don Kratzer ('54) patented the "beach comber" and sold them all over the world. He was a field executive for John Deere with all of Arizona and southern Nevada as his territory. In that position, he kept getting the question if John Deere had a beach comber. He had no idea what this was, so he investigated the idea and the need. He shared the following story:

I was raised on the farm. I had built my first car when I was in the 6th grade. I learned from my father George Kratzer ('28) how to work with machinery and the inner working of machines. My dad was a charter member of the Flying Farmers and served as the Kansas President. Any successful farmer the 1940s through the 1970s had their own plane. I have been a pilot since 1958 and still have my license at the age of 83 (2018). I have always had an intrigue on how things work and continue to this day to tinker and enjoy the inner workings of machines.

Closing

Closing — By a vote of 4 to 3, Geneseo High School was closed in 1980. The school board of Unified District No. 444 met in Little River at the end of the school year. The future for the school had been in question for several years, with some talk of closing coming as early as the mid-1970s. At that time the board decided to give the school another year if enrollment reached fifty-five. "Operation Success" was launched and the goal met. Further slipping of enrollment, however, resulted in thirty-nine students in 1980. It was not the smallest school in the state but was among the smallest half-dozen.

The Lyons, Kansas newspaper published this article on March 1980:

Geneseo High School future has been in question for several years. The closing will leave only one high school in the district, the one at Little River that combines Little River and Windom and now has more than 100 students. Students will not automatically go to Little River but may choose from four High Schools of almost equal distance: Little River, Lyons, Bushton, and Ellsworth. The latter is slightly further than Geneseo, but mileage to the other three is almost the same. If a student would choose to go out of the district he or she would provide their own transportation. Geneseo citizens are not going to accept without challenging the school board decision last evening which would eliminate the Geneseo High School at the close of the year. Steve Prickett, president of the Citizen State Bank and father of two children, said Geneseo residents "definitely are going to make an effort to reverse the decision. Dean Gustus, owner of Gustus Manufacturing and former mayor, called the decision a shock and said, "We can't give up at this time."

Prickett said the first step in attempting to turn around the decision would be to check the legality of the board to act without a vote of the people. State law stipulated that under certain conditions the power to close a school goes from popular vote to a vote of the school board. Meetings of over 200 people were held on at least two occasions in March 1980. The vote was not to be overturned. The closing affected the jobs of the teaching staff of eight.

A total of 1,036 graduated from Geneseo High School from 1900-1980. The most numerous surnames of the graduates in those 81 years were Kratzer-20, Alexander-13, Holmes-11, Worl-11, Janssen-10, Janzen-9, Johnson-9, Ramsey-9, Rolfs-9, Splitter-9, Droegemeier-8, Handlin-8, Deardorf-7, Schmidt-7, Thompson-7, and six each for Gomez, Smith, White, and Willms. The last class in 1980 had nine graduates with Danny Taylor (alphabetically) the last to receive a diploma from Geneseo High School.

Geneseo High School
Rice County, KS

#109

Cullison High School

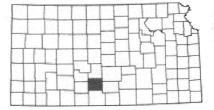

Mascot: Owls

Colors: Black and Yellow

Year Closed: 1967

Location: town of Cullison, west-central Pratt County

Town History—US Highway 54 and the Chicago, Rock Island, and Pacific Railroad parallel with each other and run through the town of Cullison. It is located ten miles southwest of the county seat, Pratt. When the railroads were built, it was necessary to have a depot and a source for water to fuel the steam engines about every ten miles. These strategically located depots were also used as shipping locations for grain, livestock, and general goods.

Education — The first school house was a small frame building standing one mile west and one-half mile south of the eventual school house in Cullison. In the fall of 1887, a vacant store building was rented on Main Street. A new brick building was completed in 1888 in the northeast portion of town. Seventy-five students were enrolled. The upper story served as a community hall for church services, entertainments, and social events. When the building was condemned in 1908, a two-room structure was built near the eventual high school lot. This structure soon became inadequate. A house was then purchased for the eighth grade and first year high school classes. Twelve freshmen began the year, but at the end of the year only six remained. This house proved unsatisfactory and a move was made to build a high school.

A new three-story high school building was built in 1916, and the first graduating class was in 1919 with six graduates. As the numbers of students increased and the curriculum grew, an addition was erected in 1928. In 1950, another addition was added to house the shop and music room. This left the bottom floor of the original building vacant and provided space for a bigger and more modern lunch room and recreation room.

Activities & Curriculum — In the fall of 1918 school started with a complete turnover in the teaching staff. Mr. A. Skidmore was the new principal, C.A. Schwab taught manual training, Miss Mildred Warner taught English and Latin, and Miss Helen Farnsworth taught music. YMCA and YWCA were both started this year as clubs in the school. The school started playing both boys and girls basketball this same year.

The annual yearbook in the spring of 1919 was named the *Sunflower*. Literary Societies were formed. The class motto was "Nec Pluribus Impar," which means "A Match for Many." The freshmen all took Latin and commented about the glorious time they spent translating it!

Music was one of the most popular and dominant programs in the school system. There were boys and girls glee clubs and an orchestra. A band that had less than two years of experience won the right to go to a national tournament in Colorado Springs in 1939.

Scholastically, the school excelled. Trophies show the winnings of county scholarship awards in 1925, 1926, 1927, and 1928. First place was won in state contests in 1930 and 1958. Debate and speech won high awards in the period from 1935 to 1950.

The play, *The Bond Between*, won a number one rating at the Skyline League One Act Play Festival in 1957. Several cases of the mumps prevented these thespians from competing at the district play contest.

The speech and drama club competed at the District Speech and Drama Festival in the spring of 1958. Tonya Henry ('58) got a number one rating for her humorous reading titled, "To Win or Not to Win." Jerrlea Johnson and Larry Holmes also received number one ratings. Tonya went on to state and received a number one rating. Jerrlea Johnson and Larry Holmes received number two ratings.

The 1957-58 Kayette's club had fifteen members. They sold Christmas cards, collected for March of Dimes, contributed to Meals for Millions and Care, directed Christmas assemblies, sponsored an all-school party, made Easter tray favors for the hospital, sent old nylon hose to Japan, cleaned lockers, polished trophies, stained and polished the piano, sponsored Class Night, hid Easter eggs for the lower grades, and all attended the union conference in Pretty Prairie. These service activities were representative of all the great opportunities that such a club provided.

Athletics

— A tornado in the summer of 1946 nearly destroyed the high school. All summer the repairs and reconstruction of the building took place.

The game of basketball was the dominant sport. The boys played in the Skyline League with rivals Coats, Sawyer, Byers, Isabel, Sun City, Nashville, Zenda, and Preston. First place trophies were won in 1955, 1960, and 1963 in the Skyline League. Cullison took first place in ten of the fifty-three years of its existence in the district elimination tournament.

The Class of 1955 took their senior sneak to Abilene and Wichita on February 1, 1955. The seven happy seniors sold magazine subscriptions, operated the concession stand at games, ran the pop and candy machines in the school, and put on a senior play titled *Papa Makes Good!* to help defray the cost of the trip. One month later, March 1955, the basketball team played in the state class BB basketball tournament.

The 1957 football team failed to win a game. They played in the Skyline League which by this year included Belpre, Wilmore, Mullinville, Haviland, Arlington, Bucklin, Friends, and Byers. The boys basketball team that year finished 9-10 with wins over Isabel, Greensburg, Sawyer, Friends, Wilmore, Bucklin, Sharon, and twice over Byers.

Closing

— In 1963 the Kansas legislature passed the School Unification Bill. This required each county to form a planning unit of consolidation, including establishing district boundaries. The plan was to be presented to the state superintendent of education for approval with plans to be voted on in a special election. These counties had until 1966 to have their unified districts consolidated.

Pratt County was the county seat at a central location and the largest city. They came up with an unusual plan. Skyline High School was built just two miles west of Pratt on forty acres of land that was purchased by eminent domain. The schools at Cullison, Coats, Byers, and Sawyer were closed and all unified into this new Skyline High School. This school, just two miles away from the Pratt High School was thought to be a useful location should the school ever fail and the buildings could be more useful for the county and the city of Pratt. Today (2018) there are 104 high school students enrolled at Skyline High School and 401 students enrolled at Pratt High School.

There were 523 graduates from Cullison High School in forty-nine years, 1919 through 1967. The most numerous surnames of the graduates were Greenstreet-14, Baker-13, Adams-11, Bryant-7, Miller-7, Smith-7, Toothaker-7, Hatfield-6, Jenkins-6, and Swonger-6. The last graduating class in 1967 had four graduates. The last to receive a diploma from Cullison High School was Janice Smith ('67) (alphabetically).

Acknowledgments

There were hundreds of phone calls, emails, and text messages shared with Kansans as well as out-of-state contributors. Kansas State Historical Society, county and community historical societies, town museums, city halls, school secretaries, and local cafes all answered my calls. The first contact led to another contact and direction to priceless information. Meetings were scheduled in coffee shops, truck stop cafes, libraries, schools, community centers, and museums all around the state.

I extend a special thank you to Hazel Hart. She diligently and patiently edited the copy for clearer understanding. She made suggestions for clarification and guided me in the restructuring of sentences that greatly improved the stories.

This is an attempt to thank all who answered the call and contributed to telling these stories of Kansas high schools and town histories. I hope that I have not missed anyone in the following list.

County	School	Name
Allen	LaHarpe	Linda Sweany
Anderson	Kincaid	Gary and Ann Donaldson, Tom Herynk, Irene Pinneo Louk, Gary Louck, Kristi Kenny—"The First 100 Years" 1995, by Irwin Albert
Atchison	Potter	Ramona Cummings, George Highfill, Ed Theis, Cheryl Adams Hefner
Barber	Sharon	Lennes Ranken, Martha McDaniel
Barton	Pawnee Rock	Dean Lakin, Roger Hanbardt
Brown	Robinson	Van Koelliker, Jim Koelliker, Dorothy BeDunnah
Bourbon	Fulton	Kathy Talbot, Virginia Durbin, *Ft. Scott Tribune Fulton Weekly Globe*, *The 1920 Osaga Historic Reflections of Bourbon County Kansas,* by Fred Campbell, Jr. & Don Miller
Butler	Towanda	Peggy Wendler, Frank Schomaker
Chase	Strong City	Emil and Jerri Mushrush, Peggy McGeorge
Chautauqua	Peru	*My Memories-My First 23 Years,* by Merle Palmer *Club 50,* by Steven Michael Farney, Vera Miller, Jim Rinck, Nancy McMullen, Chautauqua County Historical Society, Peru High School Summary by Virginia Carter Bean
Cherokee	McCune	Roger Parsons, Sharon Leonard
Cherokee	Weir	Lois Carlson
Cheyenne	Wheeler	Gary Cooper, Bob Stiell, Janet Carmen
Clark	Englewood	Harry Walker, Jim Gillespe, Kirby Pike, Jane Rankin-Record of The Englewood Schools
Clay	Longford	Wava Kramer
Cloud	Jamestown	Kathleen Anderson, Carol Glotzbach, Asa Grennan
Coffey	Gridley	Retha Steckles

County	Town	People / Sources
Comanche	Protection	Comanche County History by David Webb, Marge Sangster, Evelyn Hoch
Cowley	Cambridge	Armand Hillier, Sharon Stover, CHS Alumni Directory 1992
Crawford	Mulberry	Lee Ruth Massa, Kathleen Henegar
Decatur	Jennings	Lila Jennings, Kay Brown
Dickinson	Enterprise	Reed Hoffman
Dickinson	Talmage	Veryl Coup
Doniphan	White Cloud	Dick Tracy, Lois Elrod
Douglas	Lecompton	Paul Bahnmaier
Edwards	Offerle	Julie Ackerman
Elk	Howard	Marcia Taylor at Benson Museum
Ellis	Schoenchen	Lillian Leiker
Ellsworth	Kanopolis	April Miller
Finney	Pierceville	Pierceville Rural High School Alumni Association by Ruth Rundell Richards, Ida Bly Hall
Ford	Windthorst	Julie Ackermann
Franklin	Richmond	Pat Vining
Geary	Millford	Rosanne Ballou, Don Garrison, Geary County Historical Society
Gove	Gove	Franklin Powers, Bobby Randall
Graham	Bogue	Jane Noel Hansen, Thomas Thompson, Robert Thompson, Norma Switzer, Dianna Hart, Marllys Gustfason Yelton, Bluejay Yearbooks
Grant	Hickok	Carol Sterling
Gray	Ensign	Betty Herman, Jim Reinhart, Sarah McFarlane
Greeley	Horace	Nadine McVey: History of Greeley County
Greenwood	Severy	Marcia Moore
Hamilton	Coolidge	Lori Lennen, Mike Lennen, Gina Barrett, Jake Thornburgh, Karen Harper, Sally Smith, Ruth Schwertseder
Harper	Bluff City	Joan Wood, Jim Shellenhammer, Ben Horyna
Harvey	Walton	Dean Davis
Haskell	Santa Fe	Ann Martens, Haskell County Historical Society
Hodgeman	Hanston	John Ewy
Jackson	Delia	Laverne, Zlantik, Linda Smith, Anna Wilhelm, *Delia Centennial* 2006 by J.L. Zlantik
Jefferson	Winchester	Raymond Riley, *Winchester Herald* Papers by Bertha Lille Curry 1972
Jewell	Esbon	Jim Flavin, Esther Headrick, Glenna Fogo, Virginia Alexander, Roger Fedde
Johnson	Stillwell	Carol Armer, Karla Hollinghead, Elsa Almann
Kearney	Kendall	Julie McCombs, Kenny Wecker, Terry Maune Anna Graber, Kim Lohman Amy Hagerman
Kingman	Zenda	Jeanne Caywood Carson
Kiowa	Mullinville	*From Past to Present*, by

County	Town	Contributors
		Randall Gallion, Keith Chadd, and Mildred McFadden Douglas
Labette	Edna	Donna Vail, Joe Thompson, Jan Rhoades, Phil Blair
Lane	Alamota	Kathy Steffens-Nett, Sonya Reed
Leavenworth	Jarbalo	Ann Matthews, Virginia Seymour
Lincoln	Barnard	Scott Hart
Linn	LaCygnes	Judy Patterson, Ruth Reynolds
Logan	Russell Springs	Deb Mather, Frank Myers
Lyon	Americus	Betty Brown
Marion	Florence	Bob Harris, Michael Robinson
Marshall	Summerfield	Jackie Cameron
McPherson	Windom	Karen Ukens
Meade	Plains	Lana Miller, Wayne Powell, Lelia May George, K.E. Coats Plainshighschool.com
Miami	Bucyrus	Betty Binford, Joe Knight
Mitchell	Hunter	Terry Perry, Ann Perry, Mary Kralicek
Montgomery	Havana	Dale McBride, Ron Olyer, Beverly O'Conner
Morris	Dwight	Darrell Miller
Morton	Richfield	Phoebe Brummett, Barbara Vitt, Falcon Yearbook 2014
Nemeha	B&B	Arthena Massouth, Don Sailors, Shirley Sailors
Neosho	Stark	Jackie Smith, Wanita Cook, Roy Thornburg, Dennis Atwell
Ness	Utica	
Norton	Densmore	Beverly Boyd Lambert, Doyle Archer; *The Optimist,* by Rose French Gulick
Osage	Quenemo	Mike Ragen
Osborne	Alton	Deanna Roach, Karen Wallace
Ottawa	Delphos	Dana & Marcia Hauck
Pawnee	Rozel	Helen Thorne, Bill and Lois Price
Phillips	Prairie View	Dennis & Gloria Dewitt; *History of Phillips County*
Pottawatomie	Olsburg	Tami Howland
Pratt	Cullison	Mildred Eubanks
Rawlings	Herndon	Judy Ketterl
Rawlins	McDonald	Dennis Hubbard, Lyla Hubbard
Reno	Sylvia	Don Etchinson
Republic	Republic	Phyliss Hofts
Rice	Geneseo	Janet Splitter, Carolyn Katcher, Marilyn Siemsen, Morris Heitsschmidt, Hellen Stockstill
Riley	Randolph	Tami Howland
Rooks	Webster	Jean Grover Lindsey, Wayne Grover
Rooks	Woodston	*Woodston-The Story of a Kansas Town,* by Leo Oliva. Bob McCall
Rush	McCracken	Shirley Higgins
Russell	Waldo	Carolyn Schultz
Saline	Assaria	Judy Lilly
Shawnee	Berryton	Velma Howburt
Sedgwick	Mount Hope	Annette Gratton
Seward	Kismet	Lola McVey
Sherman	Esbon	Lloyd Holbrook, Eleanor Elliott, *Goodland News*

		Republic 1905, *Sherman County Herald* 1949	Wyandotte	Wilson	Woodson County Historical Society
Sheridan	Selden	Ellis Walker, William Thummel, Jan Rogers			Monte Gross
Sherman	Kanarado	Hazel Estes			Wyandotte County Historical Museum
Scott	Shallow Water	Dennis Siegrist, Scott Hissae, Kay Moeller			
Smith	Lebanon	Ava Mae Maydew, Gloria Snow			
Stafford	Hudson	Sally Bowers			
Stevens	Dermot	John Milburn, Phoebe Brummett			
Stanton	Manter	Katie Herrick, Stanton Historical Society			
Sumner	Geuda Springs	*Remembering Geuda Springs*, by Margaret Russell Stallard, Ronald Smith, Connie Shelton, Jane Moore			
Thomas	Gem	John Flannigan, Ray Imhoff			
Trego	Collyer	Larry Dienes, Gale Scanlon			
Wabancee	Paxico	Dan Wagner, The Pirate History of Paxico High School 1900-74			
Wallace	Wallace	Jean Pierce			
Washington	Morrowville	Norm Elliott, Dale Hiesterman			
Wichita	Marienthal	Jeff Ritter, Teri Ritter, Sandy Unruh, *History of Wichita County,* by the Wichita County Historical Society			
Wilson	Buffalo	Jackie Orrick, Joyce Gardner			
Woodson	Neosho Falls	Darrell Ellis, Ron Schaffer			

About the Author

James Kenyon was born and raised on a third generation family grain and livestock farm. He grew up caring for cattle, pigs, chickens, and horses near the small town of Bogue, Kansas, population 300. His roots make him a natural candidate for recording the histories of small-town schools and stories from the past decades of these communities. From his grandfather, John Gibbins, who was the superintendent of four high schools in Kansas and a college professor, to his three aunts and two sisters who were teachers, James was raised in a community that valued education. His mother, Anita Kenyon, was a school nurse for twenty years. James grew up in an era when the whole town was involved in raising a child. He was taught by aunts and neighbors throughout his school years. There were six students in his high school graduating class. He was taught trigonometry by Mrs. Fischels during her planning period and study hall, as she knew that he would need it for college.

James was a veterinarian for thirty-five years in a mixed animal practice in a beautiful Iowa college town. Through his mentoring, eighteen student workers went on to become veterinarians. He is a seven-time veterinarian for the Alaska Iditarod Dog Sled Race, was named Iowa Veterinarian of the Year, and was the state president of the Iowa Veterinary Medical Association, as well as the chairman of the Iowa Veterinary Medical Examining Board.

Today, James continues the family tradition of community involvement with twenty-four years of service on his local school board. This made him the fourth generation (spanning three different centuries) of his family to serve as a school board member. He credits the importance of team work and leadership learned in school as having guided him through his adult years.

His wife, an education doctorate, is a retired secondary level and college teacher. His oldest daughter is an elementary school counselor; her husband a judge. His second daughter is a veterinarian; her husband an architect and commercial real estate broker. His son and daughter-in-law are graphic designers.

James has five grandchildren.

www.jamesrkenyon.com

Index

Nothing feels better than home

While we at Meadowlark Books love to travel, we also cherish our home time. We are nourished by our open prairies, our enormous skies, community, family, and friends. We are rooted in this land and that is why Meadowlark Books publishes regional authors.

When you open one of our fiction books, you'll read delicious stories that are set in the Heartland. Settle in with a volume of poetry, and you'll remember just how much you love this place too - the landscape, its skies, the people.

Meadowlark Books publishes memoir, poetry, short stories, novels. Read stories that began in the Heartland, that were written here. Add to your Meadowlark Book collection now.

Specializing in Books by Authors from the Heartland Since 2014

Copies of this book may be ordered from the Meadowlark Bookstore online:

https://squareup.com/market/meadowlark-books/

or

Mail this form with check to:

Meadowlark Books

P.O. Box 333

Emporia, KS 66801

Phone: 620-794-9320

Email: info@meadowlark-books.com

*Please contact us for bulk orders

or discount pricing for resale.

Please send me _____ copies of *Golden Rule Days* @ 20.00/book = _____

Please send me _____ copies of *A Cow for College* @ $15.00/book = _____

Total Ordered = _____

Total Cost = $_____

Checks Payable to: *Meadowlark Books*

+ _____ ***$4.95 shipping****

Total Enclosed = $_____

Deliver to: _____ *(name)*

_____*(address)*

_____ *(city, state, zip)*

Phone: _____ **Email:** _____

Made in the USA
Lexington, KY
03 June 2019